> "America's leading source of self-help legal information." ★★★★
>
> —Yahoo!

LEGAL INFORMATION ONLINE ANYTIME

24 hours a day

www.nolo.com

AT THE NOLO.COM SELF-HELP LAW CENTER, YOU'LL FIND

- Nolo's comprehensive Legal Encyclopedia filled with plain-English information on a variety of legal topics
- Nolo's Law Dictionary—legal terms <u>without</u> the legalese
- Auntie Nolo—if you've got questions, Auntie's got answers
- The Law Store—over 250 self-help legal products including: Downloadable Software, Books, Form Kits and eGuides
- Legal and product updates
- Frequently Asked Questions
- NoloBriefs, our free monthly email newsletter
- Legal Research Center, for access to state and federal statutes
- Our ever-popular lawyer jokes

Quality LAW BOOKS & SOFTWARE FOR EVERYONE

Nolo's user-friendly products are consistently first-rate. Here's why:

- A dozen in-house legal editors, working with highly skilled authors, ensure that our products are accurate, up-to-date and easy to use
- We continually update every book and software program to keep up with changes in the law
- Our commitment to a more democratic legal system informs all of our work
- We appreciate & listen to your feedback. Please fill out and return the card at the back of this book.

OUR "NO-HASSLE" GUARANTEE

Return anything you buy directly from Nolo for any reason and we'll cheerfully refund your purchase price. No ifs, ands or buts.

Read This First

The information in this book is as up-to-date and accurate as we can make it. But it's important to realize that the law changes frequently, as do fees, forms and procedures. If you handle your own legal matters, it's up to you to be sure that all information you use—including the information in this book—is accurate. Here are some suggestions to help you:

First, make sure you've got the most recent edition of this book. To learn whether a later edition is available, check the edition number on the book's spine and then go to Nolo's online Law Store at www.nolo.com or call Nolo's Customer Service Department at 800-728-3555.

Next, even if you have a current edition, you need to be sure it's fully up to date. The law can change overnight. At *www.nolo.com*, we post notices of major legal and practical changes that affect the latest edition of a book. To check for updates, find your book in the Law Store on Nolo's website (you can use the "A to Z Product List" and click the book's title). If you see an "Updates" link on the left side of the page, click it. If you don't see a link, that means we haven't posted any updates. (But check back regularly.)

Finally, we believe accurate and current legal information should help you solve many of your own legal problems on a cost-efficient basis. But this text is not a substitute for personalized advice from a knowledgeable lawyer. If you want the help of a trained professional, consult an attorney licensed to practice in your state.

5th edition

The Employer's Legal Handbook

by Attorney Fred S. Steingold

Edited by Attorneys Amy DelPo & Lisa Guerin

FIFTH EDITION	NOVEMBER 2002
Editors	AMY DELPO
	LISA GUERIN
Legal Research	ELLA HIRST
Cover Design	KEN ARMISTEAD
	JUNE MIKI
Book Design	TERRI HEARSH
Indexer	NANCY MULVANY
Proofreading	ROBERT WELLS
Printing	CONSOLIDATED PRINTERS, INC.

Steingold, Fred.
    The Employer's legal handbook/by Fred S. Steingold.--5th ed.
        p. cm.
    Includes index.
    ISBN 0-87337-844-X
    1. Labor laws and legislation--United States--Popular works. I. Title.

KF3455.Z9 S74 2002
344.7301--dc21   2002029593

For information on bulk purchases or corporate premium sales, please contact the Special Sales Department. For academic sales or textbook adoptions, ask for Academic Sales. Call 800-955-4775 or write to Nolo, 950 Parker Street, Berkeley, CA 94710.

Acknowledgments

Several people generously contributed advice and information in the preparation of this book, including:

- James Bruno
- Fred Daily
- Tony Duerr
- Mark Hartley
- Joel Hearshen
- Jon Huegli
- Diane Hunter
- Nancy Keppelman
- Lonnie Loy
- Len Pytlak
- William Simmons, and
- Dave Tiedgen.

Special thanks to Barbara Kate Repa and Amy DelPo for their superb editorial guidance and to Jake Warner for his excellent additions to the manuscript.

Table of Contents

1 Hiring

A. Legal Guidelines for Hiring Employees 1/3

B. Job Descriptions 1/12

C. Job Advertisements 1/14

D. Job Applications 1/15

E. Interviews 1/20

F. Testing 1/22

G. Investigations 1/36

H. Making a Job Offer 1/50

I. Rejecting Applicants 1/50

J. Tax Compliance 1/52

K. Immigration Law Requirements 1/53

L. New Hire Reporting Form 1/53

2 Personnel Practices

A. Employee Files 2/2

B. Employee Handbooks 2/5

C. Employee Performance Reviews 2/16

D. Disciplining Employees 2/23

3 Wages and Hours

A. The Fair Labor Standards Act 3/3

B. Pay Requirements 3/9

C. Calculating Pay 3/20

D. Calculating Workhours 3/22

E. Keeping Records 3/29

F. Child Labor 3/29

G. Payroll Withholding 3/31

4 Employee Benefits

A. Healthcare Coverage 4/3

B. Retirement Plans 4/20

C. Other Employee Benefits 4/24

5 Taxes

A. Employer Identification Numbers 5/3

B. Federal Employment Taxes 5/6

C. Federal Self-Employment Taxes 5/8

D. Federal Tax Deductions for Salaries and Other Expenses 5/10

E. Independent Contractors 5/13

F. Statutory Employees 5/14

6 Family and Medical Leave

A. Who Is Covered 6/2

B. Reasons for Taking a Leave 6/2

C. Scheduling Leave 6/4

D. Temporary Transfer to Another Job 6/5

E. Substituting Paid Leave 6/6

F. Advance Notice of Leave 6/6

G. Certification 6/7

H. Health Benefits 6/9

I. Returning to Work 6/10

J. Related Laws 6/11

K. Enforcement 6/19

7 Health and Safety

A. The Occupational Safety and Health Act 7/3

B. Getting Help 7/8

C. State OSHA Laws 7/18

D. Hazardous Chemicals 7/21

E. Workers' Compensation 7/23

F. Disease Prevention 7/27

G. Tobacco Smoke 7/28

H. Drug and Alcohol Abuse 7/29

I. Repetitive Stress Disorder 7/32

8 Illegal Discrimination

A. Title VII of the Civil Rights Act 8/3

B. Sexual Harassment 8/8

C. Age 8/14

D. Pregnancy 8/16

E. Citizenship 8/16

F. Gay and Lesbian Workers 8/18

G. State and Local Laws 8/18

9 Workers With Disabilities

A. The Americans with Disabilities Act 9/3

B. Businesses That Are Covered 9/5

C. Who Is Protected 9/5

D. Exceptions to Coverage 9/10

E. Providing Reasonable Accommodations 9/11

F. Workers With Emotional or Mental Impairments 9/18

G. Financial Assistance 9/21

H. Health and Safety Standards 9/23

I. Medical Exams 9/25

J. Enforcement 9/25

10 Termination

A. Wrongful Discharge Cases 10/3

B. Guarding Against Legal Claims 10/7

C. Guidelines for Firing Employees 10/9

D. Investigating Complaints Against Workers 10/11

E. Alternatives to Firing 10/14

F. The Firing Process 10/14

G. Heading Off Trouble 10/18

H. Final Paychecks 10/20

I. Continuing Health Insurance 10/26

J. Unemployment Compensation 10/26

K. Protecting Your Business Information 10/29

L. Handling Postemployment Inquiries 10/31

11 Independent Contractors

A. Comparing Employees and Independent Contractors 11/2

B. The IRS Rules 11/6

C. Workers Automatically Classified As Employees 11/14

D. State Laws 11/15

E. The Risks of Misclassification 11/15

F. Hiring Independent Contractors 11/17

12 Unions

A. The National Labor Relations Act 12/2

B. Unionizing a Workplace 12/2

C. Employer Rights and Limitations 12/4

D. Employee Rights and Limitations 12/5

E. Making Unions Unnecessary 12/6

13 Lawyers and Legal Research

A. Getting Help From a Lawyer 13/2

B. Paying a Lawyer 13/6

C. Resolving Problems With Your Lawyer 13/8

D. Legal Research 13/9

Appendix

Resources

U.S. Department of Labor A/2

State Labor Departments A/2

State Agencies That Enforce Laws Prohibiting Discrimination in Employment A/7

Index

Chapter 1

Hiring

A. Legal Guidelines for Hiring Employees 1/3

    1. Avoiding Illegal Discrimination 1/3

    2. Respecting Applicants' Privacy Rights... 1/5

    3. Avoiding False Job Security Promises 1/6

    4. Preventing Negligent Hiring Claims 1/7

    5. Protecting Against Unfair Competition 1/9

    6. Hiring Young Workers 1/12

    7. Hiring Immigrants 1/12

B. Job Descriptions 1/12

    1. Necessary Elements 1/13

    2. Permitted Discrimination 1/13

C. Job Advertisements.. 1/14

D. Job Applications 1/15

    1. Avoiding Unlawful Questions 1/15

    2. The Legal Effect of Job Applications 1/19

E. Interviews 1/20

    1. Interviewing Protocol 1/20

    2. Legal Restrictions on Questions 1/21

F. Testing 1/22

    1. Skills Tests 1/22

    2. Aptitude and Psychological Tests 1/23

    3. Honesty Tests 1/24

4. Medical Tests 1/25

5. Drug Tests 1/26

G. Investigations 1/36

1. The Fair Credit Reporting Act 1/36

2. Information From Former Employers 1/38

3. School Transcripts 1/38

4. Credit History 1/39

5. Criminal History 1/39

6. Driving Records 1/50

H. Making a Job Offer 1/50

I. Rejecting Applicants 1/50

J. Tax Compliance 1/52

K. Immigration Law Requirements 1/53

L. New Hire Reporting Form 1/53

*M*any state and federal laws—as well as countless court decisions —set out legal protocol for every phase of the employment relationship, including the hiring process. If you've correctly sensed that many workers today are well in-formed about their legal rights and are willing to fight to enforce them, you may be concerned about making costly mistakes during hiring.

Fortunately, you can steer clear of most of the legal perils of hiring employees by understanding and following these sensible guidelines:

- avoid illegal discrimination
- respect the applicant's privacy rights
- don't imply job security—unless you mean it
- protect against unfair competition
- observe the legal rules for hiring young workers and immigrants, and

- follow federal and state rules for hiring independent contractors.

Section A of this chapter discusses these key principles—some of which apply throughout the employment relationship and are discussed elsewhere in this book as well.

Sections B through H of this chapter explain how to keep legal risks to a minimum as you write job descriptions, advertise for workers, design job applications, interview applicants, check into their backgrounds and offer them jobs.

Those hiring independent contractors should consult Chapter 11, where you'll find a detailed discussion of the legal and practical issues you'll have to consider.

A. Legal Guidelines for Hiring Employees

Most large companies maintain human resource departments and in-house lawyers to lead them through the intricacies of employment law. But if you run a small or mid-sized company, this is an unaffordable luxury. More likely, you keep a close eye on legal expenses and call a lawyer only when absolutely necessary.

The guidelines discussed here should reduce your need for outside legal help when hiring employees.

1. Avoiding Illegal Discrimination

Federal and state laws prohibit all but the smallest employers from discriminating against an employee or applicant because of race, color, gender, religious beliefs, national origin, disability or age (if the person is at least 40 years old). Also, many states and cities have laws prohibiting employment discrimination based on other criteria, such as marital status or sexual orientation.

These anti-discrimination laws—covered in depth in Chapters 8 and 9—apply to all stages of the employment process: preparing job descriptions, writing ads, conducting interviews, deciding whom to hire, setting salaries and job benefits, promoting employees and disciplining and firing them.

These laws only apply to employers who have more than a certain number of employees, different for each anti-discrimination law. And many state laws apply to smaller employers who are not covered by the federal laws. To find out whether your business must comply with these laws, see Chapters 8 and 9.

A particular form of discrimination becomes illegal when Congress, a state legislature or a city council decides that a characteristic—race, for example—bears no legitimate relationship to employment decisions. A law or ordinance is then passed prohibiting workplace discrimination based on that characteristic. Courts get involved, too, by interpreting and applying anti-discrimination laws and ordinances.

Obviously, as an employer, you need to know what types of discrimination are illegal. At the same time, however, anti-discrimination laws don't dictate whom you must hire. You can exercise a wide range of discretion based on business considerations. You remain free, for example, to hire, promote, discipline and fire employees and to set their salaries based on their skills, experience, performance and reliability—factors that are logically tied to a

valid business purpose. You only risk violating the law when you treat a person or a group differently for reasons that legislators and judges have decided don't serve a valid business purpose.

Some illegal practices are obvious—such as advertising a job for people ages 20 to 30 in violation of age discrimination laws, or paying lower wages to women than men for the same work in violation of equal pay laws.

Other types of discrimination are more subtle, but just as illegal. Employment practices that have a disproportionate and discriminatory impact on certain groups are also barred by anti-discrimination laws. For example, if your main means of seeking job candidates is through word of mouth and your workforce consists entirely of white men, the word-of-mouth recruitment can be illegal discrimination; it's likely that few people other than white men will hear about the job openings. The effect of the procedures is what counts.

To avoid violating anti-discrimination laws at the hiring stage:

- advertise job openings in diverse places so they come to the attention of diverse people
- determine which skills, education and other attributes are truly necessary to perform the job, so that you don't impose job requirements that unnecessarily exclude capable applicants, and
- avoid application forms and screening techniques that have an unfair impact on any group of applicants.

Running afoul of anti-discrimination laws can be both time-consuming and costly. An unhappy employee or applicant may sue your business. Federal and state agencies also may take legal action against it. And publicity about a violation of anti-discrimination laws can adversely affect your business reputation, driving down revenues. If word gets out that a company has discriminated against women employees, for example, women customers may avoid dealing with the company for years—even long after the discriminatory practices have been dropped.

2. Respecting Applicants' Privacy Rights

As an employer, you likely believe that the more information you have about job applicants, the better your hiring decisions will be. But there's a potential problem in mounting intensive background checks. Your attempt to assess an applicant by gathering information about the past can conflict with his or her right to privacy—and sometimes violate federal and state laws. (See Section G for guidelines on staying within the law when you gather transcripts, credit reports and other background information.)

In addition, laws and court rulings restrict your right to screen applicants through aptitude tests and drug tests. (See Section F.)

Another privacy concern, for which legal guidelines are less clear, is your ability to control what workers do outside of the workplace. Some states have granted a measure of legal protection for an employee's off-the-job conduct. Colorado, for example, has a statute prohibiting discharge based on lawful activity off the employer's premises.

But in other states, employers are free to reject a job applicant or fire an employee whose lifestyle or conduct away from work they find distasteful. Even in such states, however, caution is in order; to be on relatively safe legal ground, it's best to avoid rejecting or firing a worker for off-duty conduct or lifestyle unless you can tie the actions to actual or highly likely business losses. In Baltimore, for example, it was OK for a bus company to fire a driver who was publicly identified as the Grand Dragon of the Ku Klux Klan. The court considering the case found that there was a real threat of physical danger and a possibility of a boycott if the driver were retained.

If you base hiring decisions on applicants' off-duty conduct (assuming your state allows you to do so), make sure to apply your selection criteria evenhandedly. If, for example, you choose not to hire single parents, you must apply this standard to men and women alike or risk a discrimination lawsuit (see Chapter 8).

Some employers want to limit their employees to people who don't smoke, drink alcohol or use drugs—even off the job—to hold down healthcare costs or to keep a harmonious workforce. The emerging law is that you can't dictate such off-the-job behavior. (See Chapter 7, Section G, for more on smoking and Chapter 7, Section H, for more on drug testing.)

 **Will It Tell You What You Need to Know?**
It's often a waste of time and effort to acquire and review transcripts and credit reports —although occasionally they're useful. If you're

hiring a bookkeeper, for example, experience garnered on the job is much more important than the grades the applicant received in a community college bookkeeping program ten years ago. But if the applicant is fresh out of school and has never held a bookkeeping job, then a transcript may yield some insights. Similarly, if you're hiring a switchboard operator, information on a credit report would be irrelevant. But if you're filling a job for a bar manager who will be handling large cash receipts, you might want to see a credit report to learn if the applicant is in financial trouble.

3. Avoiding False Job Security Promises

Traditionally, employees have had no job security. Employment has been an at-will relationship. If there's no contract for a fixed term of employment, the employee works at the will of the employer and employee. The employer can fire the employee at any time— and the employee is free to quit at any time— for any reason or for no reason at all. That's still the basic law, although you can't fire someone for an illegal reason—because of the color of the employee's skin, for example, or because you prefer to put a younger person in the job.

The at-will relationship gives you maximum freedom to fire employees, but preserving your legal right to fire at will can be tricky. Courts in many states have held that if employers are not careful about what they tell the employee, what they write in employee handbooks and what they say in documents and letters, they may lose that right. For example:

- A law firm hired Joan as a receptionist and fired her eight months later. Joan sued the law firm. She claimed that when she was hired, she was assured that she would remain employed as long as she did a good job. The court held that such assurance was sufficient to create a contract that Joan would be fired only for a legitimate business reason. (*Hetes v. Schefman & Miller Law Office*, 393 N.W.2d 577 (1986).)

- A bingo hall hired Scott as a general manager and gave him an employee handbook. Later, Scott was fired without warning or suspension. He sued, claiming that the handbook stated that the employer could fire an employee only after warnings were given and disciplinary procedures were followed. The court ruled that the employer was required to follow the procedures set out in its own employee handbook and couldn't fire Scott at will. (*Lukoski v. Sandia Indian Management Co.*, 748 P.2d 507 (1988).)

During the hiring process, don't give assurances that you may not be able to honor and that may give an applicant a false sense of security. It can be difficult to restrain yourself when you're trying hard to entice an attractive candidate to join your workforce. You'll have a natural tendency to say positive things about your business, the candidate and the future employment relationship. But those upbeat statements can be turned against you if your promises don't come true or the employee is later fired.

Your best protection is to make sure your application forms, employee handbooks and offers of employment state that the job is at will—and to have the applicant acknowledge this in writing. Then you'll have an excellent chance of terminating the employment on your own terms, without legal repercussions. Be aware, however, that some judges approach the whole idea of at-will employment with a measure of hostility or skepticism. These judges may disregard even the most carefully worded at-will language if it seems to be contradicted by other oral or written statements you've made to the applicant or new employee.

Here's an example of language you may wish to include in your job application form:

At-Will Employment. I acknowledge that if hired, I will be an at-will employee. I will be subject to dismissal or discipline without notice or cause, at the discretion of the employer. I also understand that this means I am free to quit my employment at any time, for any reason, without notice. I understand that no representative of the company, other than the president, has authority to change the terms of an at-will employment and that any such change can occur only in a written employment contract.

JNO Initials

Another way to protect yourself is to make sure that you always have a good business-related reason for firing an employee. In legal parlance this is called firing "for cause." If you fire for cause, the firing will be lawful, even if a court later finds that the employee was not an at-will employee after all.

4. Preventing Negligent Hiring Claims

The main reason to investigate an applicant's background is to make sure the person will do a good job for you and fit in with your other employees. But sometimes there's an additional, equally powerful reason to make a thorough investigation. When you hire some-one for a position that may expose customers or others to danger, you must use special care in checking references and making other background checks.

Legally, you have a duty to protect your customers, clients, visitors and members of the general public from injury caused by employees whom you know, or should know, pose a risk of harm to others. In some states, you may also have a duty to protect other employees from an employee whom you know—or should know—is dangerous. If someone gets hurt or has property stolen or damaged by an employee whose background you didn't check carefully, you can be sued for negligent hiring.

Be especially vigilant when hiring mainte-nance workers and delivery drivers, whose jobs give them easy access to homes and apartments.

EXAMPLE: The Village Green, a 200-unit apartment complex, hires Elton as a maintenance worker and gives him a master key. Elton enters an apartment and sexually molests a four-year-old girl while the child's parents are running an errand. Had the company checked before hiring Elton, it would have discovered that Elton had just completed a prison term

Truth In Hiring

Statements you make while interviewing and making job offers may later be treated as binding contracts.

In a leading case, a New York law firm recruited a lawyer who was beginning to make a name for herself in environmental law. The carrot that was dangled in front of her was that she'd head an environmental law department that the firm was starting. She bit—but wound up being assigned to general litigation work instead.

Later, when she was fired as part of a cutback, she sued the firm, claiming she'd been damaged because the firm had thwarted her career objective of continuing to specialize in environmental law. The court of appeals held that her claim was valid. (*Stewart v. Jackson & Nash*, 976 F.2d 86 (2d Cir. 1992).)

The lesson of this and similar cases is that the type of work an employee does can be important. Employees often leave one employer to join another—or turn down opportunities—because a particular job seems to offer a greater chance for career advancement. To avoid claims that you misled an applicant about the nature of the work, stick to what you know the work will consist of rather than what you think the applicant may want to hear.

Similarly, if your company is considering staff reductions in the near future—because, for example, a major account is about to move out of the state—disclose this to applicants. Otherwise, you may find yourself on the defensive end of a lawsuit, especially if the employee left a secure job elsewhere to come work for you.

Consider, for example, the case of Andrew, who held a good job in New York City—a job that paid $120,000 a year. According to Andrew, executives of a Los Angeles company strongly urged him to take a job that they said would be secure and would involve significant pay increases. The executives portrayed the company as financially strong, with a profitable future. Brushing aside Andrew's request for a written employment contract, they told him, "Our word is our bond."

That was good enough for Andrew. He quit his New York job, bought a home in California, moved there with his wife and two children and began working for the L.A. company. Two years later, the company fired Andrew as part of a management reorganization. He sued, claiming that the company fraudulently induced him to give up his old job and move to California. He said that when the company executives induced him to change jobs, they falsely represented the company's financial condition—concealing the fact that the company's financial outlook was bleak and that the company was already planning to eliminate the job for which it was hiring him. The California Supreme Court held that Andrew could sue for both fraud and breach of contract. (*Lazar v. Superior Court (Rykoff-Sexton Inc.)*, 49 Cal. Rptr. 2d 377 (1996).)

for a sexual offense. The child's parents sue The Village Green for negligent hiring.

Doing a background check can be a delicate matter, because you are also legally required to respect the applicant's privacy. If you hire people for sensitive jobs, you must investigate their backgrounds as thoroughly as possible—without stepping over the line and violating their privacy rights. You can be faulted for not looking into an applicant's criminal convictions —but not for failing to learn about prior arrests that didn't result in convictions, since such arrest records are generally protected by privacy laws.

In doing background checks on applicants for sensitive jobs, check for felony convictions. Also, be diligent in contacting all previous employers. Keep a written record of your investigation efforts. Insist that the applicant explain any gaps in employment history. Consider turning over the pre-hire investigation to professionals who do this for a living. If you choose to follow this route—and can afford it—it can go a long way toward refuting later claims that you failed to use reasonable efforts to learn about the employee's history.

! Strict Rules May Apply to Background Checks. Any time you hire a business—such as a credit bureau or investigative agency—to gather information about applicants (or employees), you must follow the strict guidelines set forth in the Fair Credit Reporting Act or FCRA (15 U.S.C. § 1681 and following). This federal law requires you to, among other things, get the applicant's consent to the investigation and give the applicant a copy of the investigative report if you decide not to hire the applicant based on its contents. See Section G for more information on the FCRA.

5. Protecting Against Unfair Competition

Whenever you hire workers, you run the risk that they'll later start a competing business or go to work for a competitor. If so, they may use information or contacts they gained at your workplace to draw away business that otherwise would be yours.

Obviously, you need not be too concerned about the employee you hire to flip hamburgers or the clerk you hire to handle dry cleaning orders. But employees who have access to inside information about product pricing or business expansion plans, for example, may pose competitive risks. The same goes for employees who serve valuable and hard-won customers—such as a salesperson who handles a $200,000 account.

You can help protect your business from unfair competition by asking new hires to sign agreements not to take or disclose trade secrets and other confidential information. You can also ask selected employees to sign covenants not to compete with your business —although such covenants must be carefully written so that a former employee has a reasonable chance to earn a living.

 To learn more about noncompete and nondisclosure agreements—including how to create your own—see *How to Create a Noncompete Agreement,* by attorney Shannon Miehe (Nolo). To learn more about nondisclosure agreements, see *Nondisclosure Agreements: Protect Your Trade Secrets & More,* by attorneys Richard Stim and Stephen Fishman (Nolo).

a. Trade secrets

In hiring and working with employees, some business owners need to protect their unique assets from misuse. Some possibly protectible business assets may include, for example:

- a restaurant's recipes for a special salad dressing and muffin that draw people from miles around
- a heating and cooling company's list of 500 customers for whom it regularly provides maintenance, or
- a computer company's unique process for speedily assembling computer boards.

If they are treated as such, the recipes, the customer list and the assembly process are all trade secrets. Other examples are an unpatented invention, engineering techniques, cost data, a formula or a machine. To qualify for trade secret protection, your business information must meet two requirements.

First, you must show that you've taken steps to keep the information secret—for example, by:

- keeping it in a secure place such as a locked cabinet
- giving employees access to it on a need-to-know basis only
- informing employees that the information is proprietary, and
- requiring employees to acknowledge in writing that the information is a trade secret.

EXAMPLE: Sue works at Speedy Copy Shop. She has daily access to the list of larger accounts that are regularly billed more than $2,000 per month. Sue quits to open her own competing shop. Before she does, she copies the list of major accounts. One of her first steps in getting her new business going is to try to get their business away from her former employer. Speedy sues Sue for infringing on its trade secret. At trial, Speedy shows that it keeps the list in a secure place and permits access only to selected employees who need the information. In light of these precautions, the judge orders Sue not to contact the customers on the list and requires her to compensate Speedy for any profits she has already earned on those accounts.

Second, the information must not be freely available from other sources. If the recipe for a restaurant's award-winning custard tart can be found in a standard American cookbook or recreated by a competent chef, it isn't a trade secret. On the other hand, if the restaurant's chef found the recipe in a medieval French cookbook in a provincial museum, translated it and figured out how to adapt it to currently available ingredients, it probably would be considered obscure enough to receive trade secret protection—the recipe isn't readily available to other American restaurants.

In addition to the requirements that a trade secret must be guarded information that is somewhat obscure, judges sometimes look at how valuable the information is to you and your competitors and how much money and effort you spent in developing the trade secret.

For more information on the legal nuances of trade secrets, see *Trade Secrets,* by Roger M. Milgrim (Matthew Bender & Company), available at many law libraries.

b. Covenants not to compete

To prevent an employee from competing with you after leaving your workplace, consider having him or her sign a covenant not to compete (also called a noncompete agreement). In a typical covenant, the employee agrees not to become an owner or employee of a business that competes with yours for a specific time and in a specific location.

The best time to secure a covenant not to compete is when you hire an employee. An employee who is already on the payroll may be more reluctant to sign anything—and you'll have less leverage to negotiate the agreement.

Battles over the legality of these agreements must usually be resolved in court. Judges are reluctant to deprive people of their rights to earn a living, so the key to a legally enforceable covenant not to compete is to make its terms reasonable. In evaluating whether a covenant not to compete is reasonable, focus on three questions—each of which relates to the specific job and the specific employee.

- **Is there a legitimate business reason for restricting the future activities of the particular employee?** There probably is if you expect to spend significant time and money in training a high-level employee and plan to entrust him or her with

sensitive contacts on lucrative accounts. Such an employee could easily—and unfairly—hurt your business by competing with you. This would motivate a judge to find that you have a legitimate business reason for the covenant. On the other hand, if you require a new receptionist or typist to sign a similar covenant, a judge would probably find that you have no valid business purpose for restricting the employee's ability to work elsewhere.

- **Is the covenant reasonably limited in time?** A one-year limitation may be reasonable for a particular employee. A three-year limit might not be.

- **Is the covenant reasonably limited as to geographic scope?** A 50-mile limit may be reasonable for a particular employee. A limit spanning several states might not be deemed reasonable.

EXAMPLE: When Mary hires Sid to be the office manager for her profitable travel agency, she realizes that Sid will have access to major corporate accounts and daily contact with the corporate managers who make travel arrangements. Mary also knows that she'll spend considerable time in training Sid and invest more than $4,000 in specialized seminars that she will require Sid to attend. She asks Sid to sign a covenant not to compete in which Sid promises that while working for Mary and for two years afterwards, he won't work for or own a travel agency within 50 miles of Mary's agency. After six months, Sid quits and starts a competing agency one mile from Mary's. The judge enforces the covenant not to compete by forbidding Sid from operating his new business and by awarding damages to Mary.

⚠️ **Not All States Honor Noncompete Agreements.** Noncompete agreements can be difficult—or impossible—to enforce. In California, for example, courts virtually never enforce noncompete agreements against employees or ex-employees, due to a very restrictive statute. Other states enforce noncompetes only in limited circumstances. Even in the states where they are enforced, it's often hard to overcome a judge's reluctance to interfere with an employee's ability to earn a living. One way around this potential uphill battle is to ask employees to sign a nonsolicitation agreement and a nondisclosure agreement. Courts are much more willing to enforce these agreements. They can keep ex-employees from using your client or customer lists, luring employees to a competing business or stealing your trade secrets. If you can get all of these protections, you don't lose much by foregoing a noncompete agreement.

⚠️ If you base hiring decisions on applicants' off-duty conduct (assuming your state allows you to do so), make sure to apply your selection criteria evenhandedly. If, for example, you choose not to hire single parents, you must apply this standard to men and women alike or risk a discrimination lawsuit (see Chapter 8).

📖 To learn more about noncompete and nondisclosure agreements—including how to create your own—see *How to Create a Noncompete Agreement,* by attorney Shannon Miehe (Nolo).

6. Hiring Young Workers

Federal and state laws restrict your right to hire workers who are younger than 18 years old. These laws limit the type of work for which young people may be hired and the hours they may work. (See Chapter 3, Section F, for more information.)

7. Hiring Immigrants

Federal law prohibits hiring undocumented aliens. You and each new employee are required to complete INS Form I-9, Employment Eligibility Verification. (See Section K for details.)

B. Job Descriptions

Write a job description for each position you're seeking to fill. Listing the skills and attributes you're looking for in applicants will help make the hiring process more objective. It will also give you ready standards you can use to measure whether or not applicants are qualified—and which ones are most qualified. Current employees can often help you write job descriptions. They know how the business operates and the kind of skills that are needed.

In writing job descriptions, be careful not to violate the laws that prohibit discrimination in employment and that seek to assure employment opportunities for people with disabilities.

Basically, you can't discriminate against applicants on the basis of their race, skin color, gender, religious beliefs, national origin, disability or age (if the applicant is at least 40 years old). In addition, many states prohibit discrimination based on a variety of other characteristics, including marital status and sexual orientation. To learn about your state laws prohibiting discrimination in employment, see Chapter 8, Section G.

1. Necessary Elements

A well-drafted job description usually contains these components:

- **Qualifications, such as necessary skills, education, experience and licensure.** Be careful in setting requirements for education and experience. If set at an unnecessarily high level, your requirements may have the unintended effect of excluding a disproportionate number of women or applicants who are part of other groups protected by anti-discrimination laws.
- **Essential job functions.** The Americans with Disabilities Act (ADA) has forced employers to take a fresh look at job descriptions—and to decide what really is the core of each job. (For more on the ADA, see Chapter 9.) To help eliminate unfair discrimination against people with disabilities, the ADA seeks to make sure a person isn't excluded from a job simply because he or she can't perform some marginal duties listed in a job description. For example, suppose your job description for a file clerk includes answering the phone, but the basic functions of the job are to file and retrieve written materials. Other employees usually answer the phone. Someone whose hearing is

impaired may have trouble handling phone calls but be perfectly able to file and retrieve papers. Phone answering isn't an essential job function and shouldn't be listed as such.

- **Nonessential job functions.** You may wish to specify functions and duties that are desirable but not required for a particular job. That's OK—as long as the job description clearly states that these additional functions and duties are not job requirements. Suppose you're seeking a receptionist. If you never or seldom require the receptionist to type, typing isn't an essential function. Listing an unnecessary or marginal skill such as typing would unfairly disqualify a person with a paralyzed or missing left hand from the receptionist job. You could, however, mention typing as a desirable function if you made it clear that it's not required.

2. Permitted Discrimination

Anti-discrimination laws recognize that in certain very limited circumstances, an employer may have a legitimate reason to seek an employee of a particular gender, religion or ethnicity—even though such a preference would ordinarily be illegal. These are called bona fide occupational qualification (BFOQ) exceptions. Religion, sex or national origin can be a BFOQ only if it's a reasonably necessary qualification for the normal operation of a business or enterprise—and it almost never is. Race can never be a BFOQ.

Here are some guidelines.

background and acceptability to trading partners of customers. (*Avigliano v. Sumitomo Shoji of America, Inc.,* 638 F.2d 552 (2d Cir. 1981).) Aside from such a narrow situation, you can't use national origin as a BFOQ.

Gender. About the only time that gender can be a BFOQ is for jobs affecting personal privacy—for example, restroom attendants or security guards who are required to search employees—and acting and modeling work.

C. Job Advertisements

Even if you write a great job description, you could still get tripped up when summarizing the job in an advertisement. This can easily happen if you let someone write your ad who's not familiar with the legal guidelines. Nuances in an ad can be used as evidence of discrimination against applicants of a particular gender, age or other protected characteristic.

There are a number of semantical pitfalls to avoid in job ads.

Religion. Obviously, religion can be a job requirement where the job involves performing religious duties. The law recognizes, for example, that being Catholic is a valid qualification for performing the duties of a Catholic priest and being Jewish is a valid qualification for performing the duties of a rabbi. But beyond that, religion rarely can be a BFOQ. A court has allowed a Jesuit university to limit teaching jobs in its philosophy department to Jesuits. (*Pime v. Loyola University of Chicago,* 585 F. Supp. 435 (N.D. Ill., 1984).) But a school established under a will that required all teachers to be Protestant couldn't enforce that restriction as a job requirement; the school wasn't teaching religion. (*EEOC v. Kamehameha Schools/Bishop Estate,* 990 F.2d 458 (9th Cir. 1993).)

National origin. National origin can sometimes, but rarely, be a BFOQ. An American subsidiary of a Japanese company involved in international trade might be allowed to make Japanese nationality a job requirement because of the need for language proficiency, cultural

Don't Use	Use
Salesman	Salesperson
College Student	Part-time Worker
Handyman	General Repair Person
Gal Friday	Office Manager
Married Couple	Two-Person Job
Counter Girl	Retail Clerk
Waiter	Wait Staff
Young	Energetic

Requiring a high school or college degree may be discriminatory in some job categories.

You can avoid problems by stating that an applicant must have a "degree or equivalent experience."

The best way to write an ad that meets legal requirements is to keep it short and sweet: Stick to the skills needed and the basic responsibilities the job entails. Some examples:

"Fifty-unit apartment complex seeks experienced manager with general maintenance skills."

"Mid-sized manufacturing company has opening for accountant with tax experience to oversee interstate accounts."

"Cook trainee position available in new vegetarian restaurant. Flexible hours."

Help Wanted ads placed by federal contractors must state that all qualified applicants will receive consideration for employment without regard to race, color, religion, sex or national origin. Ads often express this with the phrase An Equal Opportunity Employer, or EOE.

Some employers who are not federal contractors also use this phrase in their ads; it's a good shorthand way to let potential employees know that you'll give them a fair shake, which can help you attract a more diverse group of applicants.

D. Job Applications

Develop a standard application form to make it easy to compare the experience and skills of applicants. Limit the form to job-related information that will help you decide who's the best person for the job. Questions like these are fairly standard:

- What is your name, address and phone number?
- Are you legally entitled to work in the United States?
- What position are you applying for?
- What other positions would you like to be considered for?
- Can you work overtime?
- If you are hired, when can you start work?
- What is your educational background—high school, college, graduate school and other (including school names, addresses, number of years attended, degree and major)?
- Describe your employment history—including name, address and phone number of each employer, supervisor's name, date of employment, job title and responsibilities and reason for leaving.
- Do you have any special training or achievements that are relevant to this position?

In designing a job application, keep two legal principles in mind:

- It's unlawful for you to seek certain information, as discussed in Section 1, below.
- You can use the application to inform the applicant about employment terms and to get the employee's permission to gather background information, as discussed in Section 2, below.

1. Avoiding Unlawful Questions

The chart below outlines the type of information that you can ask for in applications and during job interviews. Follow the chart to comply with federal laws. The chart may also be sufficient for complying with the laws of your state. To be sure, double-check with your state's fair employment office. (You can find a chart listing state fair employment laws and offices in Chapter 8.)

In addition to the areas covered in the chart, the Americans with Disabilities Act (ADA) prohibits any pre-employment questions about a disability. Before you make a job offer, you may ask questions about an applicant's ability to perform specific job functions. You may not, however, inquire about the nature or severity of a disability, ask about medical history or treatment or require any medical exam. These rules apply to application forms, job interviews and background or reference checks. (See Chapter 9 for more on the ADA.)

The Rules Change After You've Made a Job Offer. After you make a conditional job offer and before an applicant starts work, you're free to gather more details. At that point, you can require a medical exam or ask health-related questions—but only if you require this for all candidates who receive conditional offers in the same job category.

The U.S. Equal Employment Opportunity Commission (the government agency that enforces federal workplace discrimination laws) sets out the following examples of questions employers may not ask on application forms or in job interviews as prohibited by the ADA:

- Have you ever had or been treated for any of the following conditions or diseases? (Followed by a checklist of various conditions and diseases.)

- List any conditions or diseases for which you have been treated in the past three years.
- Have you ever been hospitalized? If so, for what condition?
- Have you ever been treated by a psychiatrist or psychologist? If so, for what condition?
- Have you ever been treated for any mental condition?
- Is there any health-related reason you may not be able to perform the job for which you are applying?
- Have you had a major illness in the last five years?
- How many days were you absent from work because of illness last year? (However, you may provide information on your attendance requirements and ask if the applicant will be able to meet those requirements.)
- Do you have any physical defects which preclude you from performing certain kinds of work?
- Do you have any disabilities or impairments which may affect your performance in the position you are applying for?

(However, it's OK to ask about the applicant's ability to perform specific job functions, with or without a reasonable accommodation—a concept covered in depth in Chapter 9.)
- Are you taking any prescribed drugs?
- Are you a drug addict or an alcoholic?
- Have you ever been treated for drug addiction or alcoholism?
- Have you ever filed for workers' compensation insurance?

Pre-Employment Inquires

Subject	Lawful Pre-employment Inquiries	Unlawful Pre-employment Inquiries
Name	Applicant's full name Have you ever worked for this company under a different name? Is any additional information relative to a different name necessary to check work record? If yes, explain.	Original name of an applicant whose name has been changed by court order or otherwise. Applicant's maiden name.
Address or Duration of Residence	How long have you been a resident of this state or city?	
Birthplace	None	Birthplace of applicant. Birthplace of applicant's parents, spouse or other close relatives. Requirements that applicant submit birth certificate, naturalization or baptismal record.
Age	Are you 18 years old or older? This question may be asked only for the purpose of determining whether applicants are of legal age for employment.	How old are you? What is your date of birth?
Religion or Creed	None	Inquiry into an applicant's religious denomination, religious affiliations, church, parish, pastor, or religious holidays observed.
Race or Color	None	Complexion or color of skin. Inquiry regarding applicant's race.
Photograph	None	Any requirement for a photograph prior to hire.
Height	None	Inquiry regarding applicant's height (unless you have a legitimate business reason).
Weight	None	Inquiry regarding applicant's weight (unless you have a legitimate business reason).
Marital Status	Is your spouse employed by this employer?	Requirement that an applicant provide any information regarding marital status or children. Are you single or married? Do you have any children? Is your spouse employed? What is your spouse's name?
Gender	None	Mr., Miss or Mrs. or an inquiry regarding gender. Inquiry as to ability or plans to reproduce or advocacy of any form of birth control. Requirement that women be given pelvic examinations.
Disability	These [provide applicant with list] are the essential functions of the job. How would you perform them?	Inquiries regarding an individual's physical or mental condition which are not directly related to the requirements of a specific job and which are used as a factor in making employment decisions in a way which is contrary to the provisions or purposes of the Civil Rights Act.

Pre-Employment Inquires (continued)		
Subject	**Lawful Pre-employment Inquiries**	**Unlawful Pre-employment Inquiries**
Citizenship	Are you legally authorized to work in the United States on a full-time basis?	Questions below are unlawful, but the applicant may be required to reveal some of this information as part of the federal I-9 process (see Section K): Of what country are you a citizen? Whether an applicant is naturalized or a native-born citizen; the date when the applicant acquired citizenship. Requirement that an applicant produce naturalization papers or first papers. Whether applicant's parents or spouse are naturalized or native-born citizens of the United States: the date when such parent or spouse acquired citizenship.
National Origin	Inquiry into language applicant speaks and writes fluently.	Inquiry into applicant's lineage; ancestry; national origin; descent; parentage, or nationality unless part of the federal 1-9 process in determining employment eligibility. Nationality of applicant's parents or spouse. Inquiry into how applicant acquired ability to read, write or speak a foreign language.
Education	Inquiry into the academic, vocational or professional education of an applicant and public and private schools attended.	
Experience	Inquiry into work experience. Inquiry into countries applicant has visited.	
Arrests	Have you ever been convicted of a crime? Are there any felony charges pending against you?	Inquiry regarding arrests which did not result in conviction. (Except for law enforcement agencies.)
Relatives	Names of applicant's relatives already employed by this company.	Address of any relative of applicant, other than address (within the United States) of applicant's father and mother, husband or wife and minor dependent children.
Notice in Case of Emergency	Name and address of person to be notified in case of accident or emergency.	Name and address of nearest relative to be notified in case of accident or emergency.
Organizations	Inquiry into the organizations of which an applicant is a member, excluding organizations the name or character of which indicates the race, color, religion, national origin or ancestry of its members.	List all clubs, societies and lodges to which the applicant belongs.

For additional information on hiring and the ADA, see the *Technical Assistance Manual on the Employment Provisions (Title I) of the Americans with Disabilities Act,* available from the Equal Employment Opportunities Commission, 1801 L Street, NW, Washington, DC 20507; phone: 202-663-4900. To be connected with the EEOC field office closest to you: 800-669-4000. You can also reach the agency through its website at www.eeoc.gov.

2. The Legal Effect of Job Applications

A well-written application form can help get the employment relationship off on a solid legal footing. Since it's filled out very early in the process, you can use the form to let the applicant know the basic terms and conditions of the job and the workplace. And, because the applicant signs the application, it can be a valuable piece of evidence if a question comes up later about what you actually promised about the job. (See Chapter 2.)

Section A3, above, suggests language to add to your job application form emphasizing your right to fire an employee at will—that is, without having to give any reason to justify the firing. Be aware, however, that putting this language in the application form won't by itself guarantee that a court will find an at-will employment relationship. As noted in Section A3, a judge may treat this at-will language as non-binding.

You can also use the job application to obtain the employee's consent to a background investigation and reference check. If the applicant consents to your investigation, he or she will have a tough time later claiming an invasion of privacy. And if you plan to hire another person or agency to conduct a background check, you may be legally required to get the applicant's consent first (see Section G).

Authorization. I authorize XYZ Company to obtain information about me from my previous employers, schools and credit sources. I authorize my previous employers, schools that I have attended and all credit sources to disclose to XYZ Company such information about me as XYZ Company may request.

 Initials

Impress on the applicant the need to be honest and accurate in completing the form. Lying or giving incomplete information on an application can be a good legal reason to fire an employee if the correct story later surfaces. So serious is application fraud—or resume fraud as it's sometimes called—that some courts have allowed employers to use it to justify a firing even though the employers didn't even know of the fraud when they let the employee go.

EXAMPLE: Dolores, age 42, applies for a job as a land surveyor with Progressive Engineering Consultants (PEC). In her application, Dolores states that she has a civil engineering degree from a prestigious college and is licensed by the state. The application form warns that false information will be a cause for immediate discharge. Relying on the application, PEC hires Dolores. Six months later, PEC becomes dissatisfied with Dolores's work and fires her, replacing her with a 30-year-old man. Dolores sues, claiming that the firm discriminated against her based on age and gender. PEC belatedly looks into her application statements and discovers that Dolores has neither the degree nor the license she said she had. Because of Dolores's lies, the judge dismisses the case without getting into the discrimination charges.

Including the following language in an application form can help you establish that you clearly told the applicant about the consequences of lying.

Accuracy. I verify that the statements I have made in this application are true and complete. I understand that if I am hired, any false or incomplete statements in this application will be grounds for immediate discharge.

JNO Initials

A few unscrupulous applicants have actually taken home an application form and asked other people to fill it out for them. This can increase the risk of the form being used as an exercise in creative and deceptive writing. To safeguard against such abuses, require applicants to complete the application form on your premises where you can keep an eye on them.

E. Interviews

Before you begin to interview applicants for a job opening, write down a set of questions focusing on the job duties and the applicant's skills and experience. Some examples:

"Tell me about your experience in running a mailroom."

"How much experience did you have in making cold calls on your last job?"

"Explain how you typically go about organizing your workday."

"Have any of your jobs required strong leadership skills?"

By writing down the questions and sticking to the same format in all interviews for the position, you reduce the risk that a rejected applicant will later complain about unequal treatment. It's also smart to summarize the applicant's answers for your files—but don't get so involved in documenting the interview that you forget to listen closely to the applicant. And don't be so locked in to your list of questions that you don't follow up on something significant that an applicant has said, or try to pin down an ambiguous or evasive response.

1. Interviewing Protocol

Get the interview started by giving the applicant some information about the job—the duties, hours, pay range, benefits and career opportunities. This will give the applicant a chance to get comfortable before you start in on the questions. Questions about the applicant's work history and experience that may be relevant to the job opening are always appropriate. But don't encourage the employee to divulge the trade secrets of a present or former employer—especially a competitor. That can lead to a lawsuit. And be cautious about an employee who volunteers such information or promises to bring secrets to the new position; such an employee will probably play fast and loose with your own company's secrets, given the chance.

Keep your antennae tuned carefully to the applicant who spouts a litany of complaints against former employers. If you hire that person, your business may well become the next object of the applicant's invective. And employees with a ton of gripes also tend to have an appetite for litigation. But watch your step if you learn that the applicant has sued a former employer for discrimination or filed a discrimination charge with the U.S. Equal Employment Opportunity Commission (EEOC). If you refuse to hire the applicant because of the prior proceedings, the EEOC may treat your refusal as a form of illegal retaliation, even though your business wasn't involved in the earlier problem. See Chapter 8, Section A, for more on retaliation claims.

Give applicants plenty of time to answer questions. Make sure they understand your questions; ask them to let you know if something is unclear. And ask them if they have any questions about your company or the job for which they're applying. Finally, let them know your time frame for getting back to them with a hiring decision so they won't bug you with premature phone calls.

 For additional suggestions on interviewing, see *267 Hire Tough Proven Interview*

Questions, by Mel Kleiman (HTG Press), and *The Manager's Book of Questions: 751 Great Interview Questions for Hiring the Best Person*, by John Kador (McGraw Hill).

2. Legal Restrictions on Questions

The Rules of Etiquette once dictated that you avoid discussing sex, religion or politics in a social setting. While that standard has been relaxed, it still applies to job interviews— along with similar cautions to avoid focusing on an applicant's age, ethnicity, birthplace or personal finances. In fact, such inquiries are not only bad manners; they're illegal, plain and simple.

During an interview, stay focused on job requirements and company policies. Suppose you're concerned that an applicant with young kids may spend too much time talking with them on the phone. You can't ask: "Do you have children?" or "Who watches the kids when you're at work?" But you can say to the applicant: "We don't allow personal phone calls during workhours. Do you have a problem with that?" The applicant then knows the ground rules and can let you know if a problem exists. Just be sure you apply your phone policy to all employees.

Review the legal restrictions on what you can and can't ask in a job application. (See Section D.) The same guidelines and restrictions apply to interviews. As with job applications, the focus of your interviews should be to find the best person for the job based on skill, experience, education and other qualifications needed to perform the job.

During an interview, you can ask about the applicant's ability to perform job tasks and about any needed accommodation. You'll be walking a fine line here, so take some time to avoid potential legal problems with disability laws. Remember to focus on the applicant's ability to do the job—not on the applicant's disability.

> **EXAMPLE:** Zack, who has only one arm, applies at ABC Industries for a job that requires driving. The interviewer avoids asking Zack if or how this disability would affect his driving. Instead, to comply with the law, the interviewer asks: "Do you have a valid driver's license?" "Can you drive on frequent long distance trips, with or without an accommodation?" The interviewer continues: "At least 80% of the time of this sales job must be spent on the road covering a three-state territory. What is your outside selling experience? What is your accident record?" All are permissible questions.

You can describe or demonstrate the specific job tasks, then ask whether the applicant can perform these tasks with or without an accommodation. If you're interviewing an applicant for a mailroom job, you can say: "The person in this job is responsible for receiving incoming mail and packages, sorting the mail and taking it in a cart to many offices in two buildings, one block apart. The mail clerk must also receive boxes of supplies weighing up to 50 pounds and place them on storage shelves six feet high. Can you perform these tasks with or without an accommodation?"

You can ask an applicant to describe or show how he or she will perform specific job functions—but only if you require this of everyone applying for a job in this category.

> **EXAMPLE:** PhoneSale, a telemarketing firm, requires all applicants to demonstrate selling ability by taking a simulated telephone sales test.

Be mindful that some applicants with disabilities will need accommodations to participate in the interview process. For example, you may need to provide an accessible location for an applicant in a wheelchair, a sign interpreter for a deaf person or a reader for a blind person. (See Chapter 9 for an extensive discussion of the disability law requirements.)

 You can find a number of articles about hiring and job interviews in the Employment Law Center of Nolo's website at www.nolo.com.

F. Testing

Pre-employment testing—which might include skills testing, aptitude testing, honesty testing, medical testing and drug testing—is most common in larger businesses. But no matter what size your business is, you should know the legal limits on your ability to test applicants.

1. Skills Tests

Most small businesses—especially new ones—operate on a slim profit margin. This means that your employees must be up to speed from day one. If you're hiring a typist, you may want to test the applicant for typing speed and accuracy. If you're hiring a person to be a clerk in your bookstore, you may want to test the applicant's knowledge of literature. If you're hiring a driver for a delivery van, a road test would be appropriate. As long as the skills you're testing for are genuinely related to the job duties, a skills test is generally legal.

To avoid discriminating against applicants protected by the Americans with Disabilities Act (ADA), be sure your tests measure the actual skills and abilities needed to do a job—for example, a typing test or a sales demonstration test. (For more on the ADA, see Chapter 9.)

Avoid tests that reflect impaired mental, sensory, manual or speaking skills unless those are job-related skills that the test is trying to measure. For example, written question-and-answer test for a job as a heavy equipment operator might screen out an applicant with dyslexia or other learning disability, even though the applicant has the necessary skills to operate heavy equipment.

2. Aptitude and Psychological Tests

Some employers use written tests—usually multiple choice tests—to get additional insight into applicants' abilities. Others attempt to probe the psyche of their applicants.

These tests are going out of fashion, and for good reason. A multiple choice aptitude test may discriminate illegally against minority applicants, because it really reflects test-taking ability rather than actual job skills. A personality test can be even riskier. Besides its potential for illegal discrimination, such a test may invade an applicant's privacy—by inquiring, for example, into religious beliefs or sexual practices. (See Section A2 for more on privacy concerns.)

If you do decide to use aptitude or personality tests, proceed cautiously. Make sure that the tests have been screened scientifically for validity and that they are correlated to job performance. Review them carefully for any questions that may intrude into the applicant's privacy.

Another concern for employers is the Americans with Disabilities Act (ADA), which lets you give a psychological test or exam to a job applicant—as long as the test or exam isn't medical. This can be tricky. A psychological test or exam is considered medical if it provides evidence that can help identify a mental disorder or impairment. A test or exam is permissible if it measures only such things as honesty, tastes and habits. But if it helps identify whether the applicant has excessive anxiety, depression or a compulsive disorder, it qualifies as a medical test and is illegal if given at the wrong time.

Be aware, too, that the ADA sets special requirements when you test people who have impaired sensory, speaking or manual skills. Sensory skills include the abilities to hear, to see and to process information. If the applicant wouldn't have to use the impaired skill on the job, you must design your tests so that he or she doesn't have to use the impaired skill to take the test.

EXAMPLE: Joe is applying for a position as a food handler which requires hardly any reading. Because of dyslexia, Joe has a very difficult time reading. He should be given an oral rather than a written aptitude test. By contrast, if you were interviewing Joe for a proofreader job—which clearly requires the ability to read without help—a written test would be appropriate and legal.

3. Honesty Tests

Lie detector or polygraph tests—rarely used by small businesses anyhow—are virtually outlawed by the federal Employee Polygraph Protection Act. With just a few exceptions, you can't require job applicants to take lie detector tests and you can't inquire about previous tests. The only private employers who can use lie detector tests to screen applicants are businesses that offer armored car, alarm and guard services or that manufacture, distribute or dispense pharmaceuticals—and even in those situations, there are restrictions on which applicants can be tested and how the tests must be administered.

About the only time a typical employer can use a lie detector test is to question an employee who is reasonably suspected of being involved in a workplace theft or embezzlement.

You must post a notice of the Employee Polygraph Protection Act where employees and job applicants can readily see it. For a poster containing the required notice, contact the local office of the Wage and Hour Division

---

Testing Run Amok

One large department store used a psychology test to screen applicants for security guard jobs. The test was based on the Minnesota Multiphasic Personality Inventory which has been used for decades and was widely accepted. Included in the test were hundreds of true or false questions, including:

- I feel sure there is only one true religion.
- My soul sometimes leaves my body.
- I believe in the second coming of Christ.
- I believe that there is a Devil and a Hell in afterlife.
- My sex life is satisfactory.
- I am very strongly attracted to members of my own sex.
- I have often wished I were a girl.
- I have never indulged in any unusual sex practices.
- I like to talk about sex.

A group of applicants in California sued the store, claiming that the test violated their rights to privacy and was discriminatory. The California Court of Appeals agreed, ruling that the questions were not job-related. The court held that the job applicants were entitled to a legal order prohibiting the store from using the test. (*Soroka v. Dayton Hudson Corp.*, 235 Cal. App. 3d 654 (1991).)

of the U.S. Department of Labor. (See Appendix for contact details.)

Some employers use written honesty tests to screen job applicants. Because these tests are often inaccurate and can invade an applicant's privacy or have a discriminatory impact, the legality of the tests is doubtful in most states. While honesty tests are not yet prohibited or restricted by federal law, Congress is considering possible legislation against them.

Limit honesty tests to situations in which you have a legitimate business reason to be concerned about workers' honesty—such as in hiring workers who will be handling large amounts of cash. Before using a test, ask to see scientific backup establishing the test's accuracy. And to protect yourself against charges of illegal discrimination, test all applicants for a particular job.

For detailed information on the Employment Polygraph Protection Act, including who the law covers, what the law requires and prohibits, tips for compliance and exceptions to the law, see *Federal Employment Laws: A Desk Reference*, by Amy DelPo and Lisa Guerin (Nolo).

4. Medical Tests

To avoid violating the Americans with Disabilities Act (ADA), don't ask the applicant about his or her medical history or conduct any medical exam before you make a job offer. You can, however, offer a job conditioned on the applicant passing a medical exam. If you do require such a post-offer exam, be sure you require exams for all entering employees who will be doing the same job.

EXAMPLE: Cornerstone Corporation has openings for construction crane operators. It offers Bill a job conditioned on a medical exam showing he doesn't have a medical condition, such as uncontrolled seizures, which may be risky to other workers. Because Cornerstone requires such exams for all the crane operators it hires, and because the exam screens out only those workers who would not be able to do the job safely, the exam is perfectly legal.

If you require medical exams only for people with known disabilities or those who you believe may have a disability, you'll violate the ADA. But the scope of medical exams needn't be identical for all employees. You can give follow-up tests or exams if further information is needed. Suppose, for example, that your restaurant requires a blood test for all prospective kitchen workers. If one person's test indicates a problem that may affect job performance or is a direct threat to health and safety, you can require further tests for that person.

After making a conditional job offer, you may require a full physical exam and you may ask questions that you couldn't ask at the pre-employment stage—for example, questions about previous illnesses, diseases or medications. You can probe to find out if the person has the physical or mental qualifications needed to perform the job—or to determine if a person can perform the job without posing a direct threat to the health or safety of others.

If you withdraw a conditional job offer based on results of an exam or inquiry, you must be able to show that:

- your reasons were job-related and consistent with business necessity, or the person was excluded to avoid a direct threat to health and safety, and
- no reasonable accommodation could be made or such an accommodation would cause undue hardship. (For more guidance, see Chapter 9, Section E.)

To avoid claims that you discriminated against a person with a disability, carefully document all medical inquiries and the responses to them. If you reject the prospective employee, be prepared to show how the medical facts relate to the person's ability to perform the job or reveal a direct threat to health and safety.

The U.S. Equal Employment Opportunity Commission, the enforcing agency of the ADA's employment provisions, has set out a number of examples of post-offer employment decisions that are likely to be permitted under the law.

- Hannah's workers' compensation history indicates she has filed several claims in recent years—all of which have been rejected. ABC Company has good reason to suspect that Hannah has submitted fraudulent claims. ABC withdraws its job offer. The withdrawal wouldn't violate the ADA because ABC's decision isn't based on a disability. But be careful. You could easily run afoul of state laws that specifically prohibit an employer from discriminating against employees or applicants because they've filed workers' compensation claims.

- Kendra's medical exam reveals an impairment that will require her to frequently be away from work for lengthy medical treatment. The job requires daily availability for the next three months. The company doesn't hire Kendra. This is permissible under the ADA because Kendra isn't available to perform the essential functions of the job, and no accommodation is possible.

5. Drug Tests

You have a legal right to insist on a drug-free workplace. The only problem is that testing to weed out drug users may conflict with workers' rights to privacy. The laws on drug testing vary widely from state to state and are changing quickly as legislators and judges struggle to strike a balance between workers' rights and the legitimate needs of businesses. (See chart, below.)

 Federal Contractors Must Comply With the Drug-Free Workplace Act. The law requires federal contractors and grantees to agree to maintain a drug-free workplace. If your business has a contract with the federal government for $100,000 or more (for something other than goods you're selling to the government), you need to notify employees that they're prohibited from unlawfully making, distributing, possessing or using controlled substances in your workplace. And you need to set up an awareness program that tells workers about the dangers of drug abuse while at work and lets them know about assistance programs that may be available.

Some state statutes allow you to test employees only in a narrow range of jobs, such as those concerned with safety. (See chart, below.) Fortunately, even restrictive states generally allow you much more leeway in screening job applicants than in testing employees who are already on board. If your state permits testing applicants or employees and you plan to do such testing, use the application form to let applicants know of this policy. State law may also require you to give applicants a written policy statement that's separate from the application. When applicants are told up front about drug testing, it's harder for them to later claim that they expected more privacy on drug testing results.

Because the laws of drug testing are in constant flux, consider talking to a lawyer before administering any tests.

Once an applicant becomes an employee, drug testing gets stickier. Testing is usually permitted when employees have been in an accident or you've seen them bring illegal drugs to work. Your legal right to test at random and without prior notice is unclear—and questionable.

In any drug testing, treat all individuals consistently, being careful not to single out any one group. And consult with competent drug testing experts to assure that your test procedures are as accurate as possible.

For help in developing a drug policy, contact the Center for Substance Abuse Prevention Workplace Helpline at 800-967-5752. You can also find lots of helpful information on their website at www.samhsa.gov/centers/csap/csap.html.

Recovering Addicts Are Protected from Discrimination. The Americans with Disabilities Act (ADA) prohibits you from discriminating against people because of past drug problems. This includes people who no longer use drugs illegally and those who are receiving treatment for drug addiction or who have been rehabilitated successfully.

Additional Laws May Apply. If the chart below indicates that your state has no statute, this means there is no law that specifically addresses the issue. However, there may be a state administrative regulation or local ordinance that does control. Call your state labor department for more information. (See the Appendix for contact details.)

State Drug and Alcohol Testing

Alabama

Ala. Code §§ 25-5-330 to 25-5-340

Employers affected: Employers who establish a drug-free workplace program to qualify for a workers' compensation rate discount.

Testing applicants: Must test upon conditional offer of employment. Must test all new hires. Job ads must include notice that drug and alcohol testing required.

Testing employees: Random testing permitted. Must test after an accident that results in lost work time. Must also test upon reasonable suspicion; reasons for suspicion must be documented and made available to employee upon request.

Employee rights: Employees have 5 days to contest or explain a positive test result. Employer must have an employee assistance program or maintain a resource file of outside programs.

Notice and policy requirements: All employees must have written notice of drug policy. Must give 60 days advance notice before implementing testing program. Policy must state consequences of refusing to take test or testing positive.

Drug-free workplace program: Yes.

Alaska

Alaska Stat. §§ 23.10.600 and following

Employers affected: Voluntary for employers with one or more full-time employees. (There is no state mandated drug and alcohol testing.)

Testing employees: Employer may test:
- for any job-related purpose
- to maintain productivity and safety
- as part of an accident investigation
- upon reasonable suspicion.

Employee rights: Employer must provide written test results within 5 working days. Employee has 10 working days to request opportunity to explain positive test results; employer must grant request within 72 hours or before taking any adverse employment action.

Notice and policy requirement: Before implementing a testing program employer must distribute a written drug policy to all employees and must give 30 days' advance notice. Policy must state consequences of a positive test or refusal to submit to testing.

Arizona

Ariz. Rev. Stat. § 23-493

Employers affected: Employers with one or more full-time employees.

Testing applicants: Employer must inform prospective hires that they will undergo drug testing as a condition of employment.

Testing employees: Employees are subject to random and scheduled tests:
- for any job-related purpose,
- to maintain productivity and safety,
- upon reasonable suspicion.

Employee rights: Policy must inform employees of their right to explain positive results.

Notice and policy requirement: Before conducting tests employer must give employees a copy of the written policy. Policy must state the consequences of a positive test or refusal to submit to testing.

Drug-free workplace program: Yes.

Arkansas

Ark. Code Ann. §§ 11-14-105 to 11-14-107

Employers affected: Employers who establish a drug-free workplace program to qualify for a workers' compensation rate discount.

Testing applicants: Must test upon conditional offer of employment. Job ads must include notice that drug and alcohol testing required.

Testing employees: Employer must test any employee
- on reasonable suspicion of drug use
- as part of a routine fitness-for-duty medical exam
- after an accident that results in injury
- as follow-up to a required rehabilitation program.

Employee rights: Employer may not refuse to hire applicant or take adverse personnel action against

State Drug and Alcohol Testing (continued)

an employee on the basis of a single positive test that has not been verified by a confirmation test. An applicant or employee has 5 days after receiving test results to contest or explain them.

Notice and policy requirements: Employer must give all employees a written statement of drug policy and must give 60 days' advance notice before implementing program.

Drug-free workplace program: Yes.

California

Cal. Lab. Code §§ 1025, 1026

Employers affected: No provisions for private employer testing. An employer with 25 or more employees must reasonably accommodate an employee who wants to enter a treatment program. Employer may fire or refuse to hire an employee whose drug or alcohol use interferes with job duties or workplace safety.

Connecticut

Conn. Gen. Stat. Ann. § 31-51t

Employers affected: Any individual, corporation, partnership or unincorporated association.

Testing applicants: Employer must inform job applicants in writing that drug testing is required as a condition of employment.

Testing employees: Employer may test:
- when there is reasonable suspicion that employee is under the influence of drugs or alcohol and job performance is or could be impaired
- when authorized by federal law
- when employee's position is dangerous or safety-sensitive
- as part of a voluntary employee assistance program.

Employee rights: Employer may not take any adverse personnel action on the basis of a single positive test that has not been verified by a confirmation test.

Florida

Fla. Stat. Ann. §§ 440.101 to 440.102

Employers affected: Employers who establish a drug-free workplace program to qualify for a workers' compensation rate discount.

Testing applicants: Must inform job applicants that drug and alcohol testing is required as a condition of employment.

Testing employees: Must test any employee:
- on reasonable suspicion of drug use
- as part of a routine fitness-for-duty medical exam
- as part of a required rehabilitation program.

Employee rights: Employees who voluntarily seek treatment for substance abuse cannot be fired, disciplined or discriminated against, unless they have tested positive or have been in treatment in the past. All employees have the right to explain positive results within 5 days. Employer may not take any adverse personnel action on the basis of an initial positive result that has not been verified by a confirmation test.

Notice and policy requirements: Prior to implementing testing, employer must give 60 days' advance notice and must give employees written copy of drug policy.

Drug-free workplace program: Yes.

Georgia

Ga. Code Ann. §§ 34-9-410 to 34-9-421

Employers affected: Employers who establish a drug-free workplace program to qualify for a workers' compensation rate discount.

Testing applicants: Applicants are required to submit to a substance abuse test after they have been offered employment.

Testing employees: Must test any employee:
- on reasonable suspicion of drug use
- as part of a routine fitness-for-duty medical exam
- as part of a required rehabilitation program.

Employee rights: Employees have 5 days to explain or contest a positive result. Employer must have an employee assistance program or maintain a resource file of outside programs.

State Drug and Alcohol Testing (continued)

Notice and policy requirements: Employer must give applicants and employees notice of testing; must give 60 days' notice before implementing program. All employees must receive a written policy statement; policy must state the consequences of refusing to submit to a drug test or of testing positive.

Drug-free workplace program: Yes.

Hawaii

Haw. Rev. Stat. § 329B-1

Testing applicants: Same conditions as current employees.

Testing employees: Employer may test employees only if these conditions are met:

- employer pays all costs including confirming test
- tests are performed by a licensed laboratory
- employee receives a list of the substances being tested for
- there is a form for disclosing medicines and legal drugs
- the results are kept confidential.

Idaho

Idaho Code §§ 72-1701 to 72-1706

Employers affected: Voluntary for all private employers.

Testing applicants: Employer may test as a condition of hiring.

Testing employees: May test as a condition of continued employment.

An employer who follows drug-free workplace guidelines may fire employees who refuse to submit to testing or who test positive for drugs or alcohol. Employees will be fired for misconduct and denied unemployment benefits.

Employee rights: An employee or applicant who receives notice of a positive test may request a retest within 7 working days. If the retest results are negative, the employer must pay for the cost; if they are positive, the employee must pay.

Drug-free workplace program: Yes (compliance is optional).

Illinois

775 Ill. Comp. Stat. § 5/2-104(C)(3)

Employers affected: Employers with 15 or more employees.

Testing employees: Employer may prohibit all employees from using or being under the influence of alcohol and illegal drugs. Employer may test employees who have been in rehabilitation. Employee may be held to the same standards as other employees, even if the unsatisfactory job performance or behavior is due to drug use or alcoholism.

Indiana

Ind. Code Ann. §§ 22-9-5-6(b), 22-9-5-24

Employers affected: Employers with 15 or more employees.

Testing employees: Employer may prohibit all employees from using or being under the influence of alcohol and illegal drugs. Employer may test employees who have been in rehabilitation. Employee may be held to the same standards as other employees, even if the unsatisfactory job performance or behavior is due to drug use or alcoholism.

Iowa

Iowa Code § 730.5

Employers affected: Employers with one or more full-time employees.

Testing applicants: Employer may test as a condition of hiring.

Testing employees: Employer may test employees:

- as a condition of continued employment
- upon reasonable suspicion
- during and after rehabilitation
- following an accident that caused a reportable injury or more than $1,000 property damage.

Employee rights: Employee has 7 days to request a retest. Employers with 50 or more employees must provide rehabilitation for any employee who has worked for at least one year and has not previously violated the substance abuse policy; no adverse action may be taken if employee successfully

State Drug and Alcohol Testing (continued)

completes rehabilitation. Employer must have an employee assistance program or maintain a resource file of outside programs.

Drug-free workplace program: Yes (compliance is optional).

Louisiana

La. Rev. Stat. Ann. §§ 49:1001 and following

Employers affected: Employers with one or more full-time employees. (Does not apply to oil drilling, exploration or production.)

Testing applicants: Employer may require all applicants to submit to drug and alcohol test. Employer does not have to confirm a positive result of a pre-employment drug screen, but must offer the applicant the opportunity to pay for a confirmation test and a review by a medical review officer.

Employee rights: Except for a pre-employment test, employer may not take adverse personnel action on the basis of an initial screen. Employees with confirmed positive results have 7 working days to request access to all records relating to the drug test. Employer may allow employee to undergo rehabilitation without termination of employment.

Maine

Me. Rev. Stat. Ann. tit. 26, §§ 681 to 690

Employers affected: Employers with one or more full-time employees. (Law does not require or encourage employers to conduct substance abuse testing.)

Testing applicants: Employer may require applicant to take a drug test only if offered employment or placed on an eligibility list.

Testing employees: Employer may test for probable cause, but may not base belief on a single accident; must document the facts and give employee a copy. May test when:

- there could be an unreasonable threat to the health and safety of coworkers or the public
- an employee returns to work following a positive test.

Employee rights: Employee who tests positive has 3 days to explain or contest results. Employee must be given an opportunity to participate in a rehabilitation program for up to 6 months; an employer with more than 20 full-time employees must pay for half of any out-of-pocket costs. After successfully completing the program, employee is entitled to return to previous job with full pay and benefits.

Notice and policy requirements: All employers must have a written policy approved by the state Department of Labor. Policy must be distributed to each employee at least 30 days before it takes effect. Any changes to policy require 60 days advance notice. An employer with more than 20 full-time employees must have an employee assistance program certified by the Office of Substance Abuse before implementing a testing program.

Maryland

Md. Code Ann., [Health-Gen.] § 17-214

Employers affected: Law applies to all employers.

Testing applicants: May use preliminary screening to test applicant. If initial result is positive, may make job offer conditional on confirmation test results.

Testing employees: Employer may require substance abuse testing for legitimate business purposes only.

Employee rights: The sample must be tested by a certified laboratory; at the time of testing employee may request laboratory's name and address. An employee who tests positive must be given:

- a copy of the test results
- a copy of the employer's written drug and alcohol policy
- written notice of any adverse action employer intends to take
- statement of employee's right to an independent confirmation test at own expense.

Minnesota

Minn. Stat. Ann. §§ 181.950 to 181.957

State Drug and Alcohol Testing (continued)

Employers affected: Employers with one or more full-time employees. (Employers are not required to test.)

Testing applicants: Employers may require applicants to submit to a drug or alcohol test only after they have been given a job offer and have seen a written notice of testing policy. May only test if required of all applicants for same position.

Testing employees: Employers may require drug or alcohol testing only according to a written testing policy. Testing may be done if there is a reasonable suspicion that employee:

- is under the influence of drugs or alcohol
- has violated drug and alcohol policy
- has been involved in an accident
- has sustained or caused another employee to sustain a personal injury. Random tests permitted only for employees in safety-sensitive positions. With 2 weeks' notice, employers may also test as part of an annual routine physical exam.

Employee rights: If test is positive, employee has 3 days to explain the results; employee must notify employer within 5 days of intention to obtain a re-test. Employer may not discharge employee for a first-time positive test without offering counseling or rehabilitation; employee who refuses or does not complete program successfully may be discharged.

Notice and policy requirements: Employees must be given a written notice of testing policy which includes consequences of refusing to take test or having a positive test result. Two weeks' notice required before testing as part of an annual routine physical exam.

Mississippi

Miss. Code Ann. §§ 71-7-1 and following; 71-3-205

Employers affected: Employers with one or more full-time employees. Employers who establish a drug-free workplace program to qualify for a workers' compensation rate discount must implement testing procedures.

Testing applicants: May test (must test, if drug-free workplace) all applicants as part of employment application process. Employer may request a signed statement that applicant has read and understands the drug and alcohol testing policy and/or notice.

Testing employees: May (must test, if drug-free workplace) require drug and alcohol testing of all employees:

- on reasonable suspicion
- as part of a routinely scheduled fitness for duty medical examination
- as a follow-up to a rehabilitation program
- who have tested positive within the previous 12 months.

Employee rights: Employer must inform an employee in writing within 5 working days of receipt of a positive confirmed test result; employee may request and receive a copy of the test result report. Employee has 10 working days after receiving notice to explain the positive test results. Private employer who elects to establish a drug-free workplace program must have an employee assistance program or maintain a resource file of outside programs.

Notice and policy requirements: 30 days before implementing testing program employer must give employees written notice of drug and alcohol policy which includes consequences

- of a positive confirmed result
- of refusing to take test
- of other violations of the policy.

Drug-free workplace program: Yes.

Montana

Mont. Code Ann. §§ 39-2-205 to 39-2-211

Employers affected: Employers with one or more employees.

Testing applicants: May test as a condition of hire.

Testing employees: Employees may be tested:

- on reasonable suspicion
- after involvement in an accident that causes personal injury or more than $1,500 property damage

State Drug and Alcohol Testing (continued)

- as a follow-up to a previous positive test
- as a follow-up to treatment or a rehabilitation program.

Employer may conduct random tests as long as there is an established date and all personnel are subject to testing.

Employer may require an employee who tests positive to undergo treatment as a condition of continued employment.

Employee rights: After a positive result, employee may request additional confirmation by an independent laboratory; if the results are negative, employer must pay the test costs.

Notice and policy requirements: Written policy must be available for review 60 days before testing.

Nebraska

Neb. Rev. Stat. §§ 48-1901 and following

Employers affected: Employers with 6 or more full-time and part-time employees.

Testing employees: Employer may require employees to submit to drug or alcohol testing and may discipline or discharge any employee who refuses.

Employee rights: Employer may not take adverse action on the basis of an initial positive result unless it is confirmed according to state and federal guidelines.

North Carolina

N.C. Gen. Stat. §§ 95-230 to 95-235

Employers affected: Law applies to all employers.

Testing employees: Employer must preserve samples for at least 90 days after confirmed test results are released.

Employee rights: Employee has right to retest a confirmed positive sample at own expense.

North Dakota

N.D. Cent. Code § 34-01-15

Employers affected: Any employer who requires a medical exam as a condition of hire or continued employment may include a drug or alcohol test.

Ohio

Ohio Admin. Code § 4123-17-58

Employers affected: Employers who establish a drug-free workplace program to qualify for a workers' compensation rate discount.

Testing applicants: Must test all applicants and new hires within at least 90 days of employment.

Testing employees: Must test employees:

- on reasonable suspicion
- following a return to work after a positive test
- after an accident which results in an injury requiring offsite medical attention or property damage over limit specified in drug and alcohol policy.

Employee rights: Employer must have an employee assistance plan. Employer must offer healthcare coverage which includes chemical dependency counseling and treatment.

Notice and policy requirements: Policy must state consequences for refusing to submit to testing or for violating guidelines. Policy must include a commitment to rehabilitation.

Drug-free workplace program: Yes.

Oklahoma

Okla. Stat. Ann. tit. 40, §§ 551 to 565

Employers affected: Employers with one or more employees. (Drug or alcohol testing not required or encouraged.)

Testing applicants: Employer may test applicants as a condition of employment; may refuse to hire applicant who refuses to undergo test or has a confirmed positive result.

Testing employees: Before requiring testing employer must provide an employee assistance program. Random testing is allowed. May test employees:

- on reasonable suspicion
- after an accident resulting in injury or property damage over $500
- as part of a routine fitness-for-duty examination
- or as follow-up to a rehabilitation program.

State Drug and Alcohol Testing (continued)

Employee rights: Employee has right to retest a positive result at own expense; if the confirmation test is negative employer must reimburse costs.

Notice and policy requirements: Before requiring testing employer must:
- adopt a written policy
- give a copy to each employee and to any applicant offered a job
- allow 30 days' notice.

Oregon

Or. Rev. Stat. §§ 659.225 to 659.227; 438.435

Employers affected: Law applies to all employers.

Testing applicants: Unless there is reasonable suspicion that an applicant is under the influence of alcohol, no employer may require a breathalyzer test as a condition of employment. Employer is not prohibited from conducting a test if applicant consents.

Testing employees: Unless there is reasonable suspicion that an employee is under the influence of alcohol, no employer may require a breathalyzer or blood alcohol test as a condition of continuing employment. Employer is not prohibited from conducting a test if employee consents.

Employee rights: No action may be taken based on the results of an on-site drug test without a confirming test performed according to state Health Division regulations. Upon written request test results will be reported to the employee.

Rhode Island

R.I. Gen. Laws §§ 28-6.5-1 to 28-6.5-2

Employers affected: Law applies to all employers.

Testing employees: May require employee to submit to a drug test only if there are reasonable grounds, based on specific observations, to believe employee is using controlled substances that are impairing job performance.

Employee rights: Employee who tests positive may have the sample retested at employer's expense and must be given opportunity to explain or refute

results. Employee may not be terminated on the basis of a positive result, but must be referred to a licensed substance abuse professional. After referral employer may require additional testing; may terminate employee if test results are positive.

South Carolina

S.C. Code Ann. §§ 41-1-15; 38-73-500

Employers affected: Employers who establish a drug-free workplace program to qualify for a workers' compensation rate discount.

Testing employees: Must conduct random testing among all employees. Must conduct a follow-up test within 30 minutes of the first test.

Employee rights: Employee must receive positive test results in writing within 24 hours.

Notice and policy requirements: Employer must notify all employees of the drug-free workplace program at the time it is established or at the time of hiring, whichever is earlier. Program must include a policy statement that balances respect for individuals with the need to maintain a safe, drug-free environment

Drug-free workplace program: Yes.

Tennessee

Tenn. Code Ann. §§ 50-9-101 and following

Employers affected: Employers who establish a drug-free workplace program to qualify for a workers' compensation rate discount.

Testing applicants: Must test applicants upon conditional offer of employment. Job ads must include notice that drug and alcohol testing required.

Testing employees: Employer must test upon reasonable suspicion; must document behavior on which the suspicion is based within 24 hours or before test results are released, whichever is earlier, and must give a copy to the employee upon request. Employer must test employees:
- who are in safety sensitive positions
- as part of a routine fitness-for-duty medical exam
- after an accident that results in injury

State Drug and Alcohol Testing (continued)

- as a follow-up to a required rehabilitation program.

Employee rights: Employee has the right to explain or contest a positive result within 5 days. Employee may not be fired, disciplined or discriminated against for voluntarily seeking treatment unless employee has previously tested positive or been in a rehabilitation program.

Notice and policy requirements: Before implementing testing program, employer must provide 60 days' notice and must give all employees a written drug and alcohol policy statement.

Drug-free workplace program: Yes.

Texas

Tex. Lab. Code Ann. §§ 411.091 to 411.093

Employers affected: Employers with 15 or more employees who have a workers' compensation insurance policy.

Notice and policy requirements: Must adopt a drug abuse policy and provide a written copy to employees.

Drug-free workplace program: Under current law the Workers' Compensation Commission is conducting a study about implementing a drug-free workplace requirement. Report due to the legislature in February 2003.

Utah

Utah Code Ann. §§ 34-38-1 to 34-38-15

Employers affected: Employers with one or more employees.

Testing applicants: Employer may test any applicant for drugs or alcohol as long as management also submits to periodic testing.

Testing employees: Employer may test employee for drugs or alcohol as long as management also submits to periodic testing. Employer may also require testing to:

- investigate an accident or theft
- maintain employee or public safety
- ensure productivity, quality or security.

Employee rights: Employer may suspend, discipline, discharge or require treatment on the basis of a confirmed positive test result.

Notice and policy requirements: Testing must be conducted according to a written policy that has been distributed to employees and is available for review by prospective employees.

Vermont

Vt. Stat. Ann. tit. 21, § 511

Employers affected: Employers with one or more employees.

Testing applicants: Employer may not test applicants for drugs or alcohol unless there is a conditional job offer, 10 days' advance notice and test is part of a comprehensive physical examination.

Testing employees: Random testing not permitted unless required by federal law. Employer may not require testing unless:

- there is probable cause to believe an employee is using or is under the influence
- employer has an employee assistance program which provides rehabilitation
- employee who tests positive and agrees to enter employee assistance program is not terminated.

Employee rights: Employer must provide an informal meeting for employee or applicant to explain a positive test result. Employee or applicant has right to an independent retest at own expense. Employee who successfully completes employee assistance program may not be terminated; may be suspended for up to 3 months to complete program. Employee who tests positive after completing treatment may be fired.

Current as of March 12, 2001

G. Investigations

Since some people give false or incomplete information in their job applications, it's a good idea to do some investigating to verify their application information. You might find out, for example, that an applicant doesn't have the work experience or occupational license that he or she claimed to have in a job application—or that the applicant didn't really leave the last job voluntarily. What's more, you might learn that the applicant has a history of violent behavior or even a criminal record that would disqualify him or her from a job that may put members of the public or other employees at risk.

Your need to investigate a job applicant is legitimate—but if you go overboard you may violate the job applicant's legal right to privacy. The best way to reduce the risk of an invasion of privacy claim is to:

- seek only the background information you really need to figure out whether the applicant is suited for the job, and
- inform the applicant, in the job application, that you will be requesting information from, for example, schools, credit reporting agencies, former employers and law enforcement agencies.

Ask the applicant to sign a consent form as part of the application process. The consent can either be a part of the application form itself or a separate document. The advantage of having the applicant sign a separate document is that you can easily photocopy it and send it to the people from whom you're seeking information. (See Section D2 for sample language.)

1. The Fair Credit Reporting Act

A federal law called the Fair Credit Reporting Act or FCRA (15 U.S.C. § 1681 and following) imposes strict rules on your ordering and use of "consumer reports" which includes background checks, credit reports and other information gathered on applicants for employment.

a. Which background checks are covered

The FCRA regulates your ordering and use of any report prepared by a consumer reporting agency (CRA)—any business that assembles such reports for other businesses. So if you order an applicant's credit payment record from a credit bureau, that clearly would be a consumer report covered by the FCRA. So would a report you order from a business about an applicant's driving record or criminal history (though ordering similar information from a governmental agency wouldn't be).

You may be thinking of hiring a CRA, such as a detective agency or professional investigator, to prepare an *investigative* consumer report based on interviews the CRA conducts with an applicant's or employee's friends, neighbors and associates. This would also constitute a consumer report—and would, therefore, be covered by the FCRA.

Checking an applicant's references may or may not come under the FCRA. If you or someone within your company does the checking, the FCRA doesn't apply—the statute doesn't cover any information you gather on your own. However, if you use an employment or reference-checking agency to do the job, you must comply with the FCRA.

b. Requirements for handling reports

Before you get a consumer report for employment purposes, you must notify the applicant or employee in writing and get that person's written permission to gather the information. And the agency you ask to prepare the report will require you to certify that you're complying with the federal law—and that you won't use the information in the report in violation of federal or state equal employment opportunity laws. These laws—discussed in Chapters 8 and 9—prohibit certain types of discrimination. Special rules apply if your business is in the trucking industry.

After you get the report, special rules apply if, based on the report, you're going to take *adverse action* against the applicant—in the hiring process, this is most likely to come up if you decide, based on the information on the report, not to hire the applicant.

Step 1: Before you take adverse action, you have to give the applicant or employee a *pre-adverse action disclosure.* You must include a copy of the consumer report and a copy of "A Summary of Your Rights Under the Fair Credit Reporting Act"—a publication prepared by the Federal Trade Commission (FTC). The business that prepared the consumer report will give you the Summary, or you can get a copy from the FTC's website at www.ftc.gov/os/statutes/2summary.htm.

Step 2: After you take an adverse action, you must notify the applicant or employee that you've taken the action. You can give notice orally, in writing, by email or by fax. Your *adverse action* notice must:

- give the name, address and phone number of the company (CRA) that supplied the report
- state that the CRA didn't make the decision to take adverse action and can't give specific reasons for it
- say that the applicant or employee has the right to dispute the accuracy or completeness of any information the CRA furnished, and
- say that the applicant or employee can get an additional free consumer report from the CRA upon request within 60 days.

c. Penalties for violating the FCRA

You face legal trouble if you don't get an applicant's or employee's permission before requesting a consumer report, or if you don't provide the required disclosures about adverse action. The applicant or employee may sue you for damages in federal court. If successful, the person may recover court costs and reasonable attorney fees. You can also be ordered to pay punitive damages—damages intended to punish you—for deliberate violations.

Also, federal and state agencies may sue you and obtain civil penalties.

For detailed information about the FCRA including who it covers, what it requires and prohibits and tips for compliance—see *Federal Employment Laws: A Desk Reference,* by Amy DelPo and Lisa Guerin (Nolo).

2. Information From Former Employers

Some job applicants exaggerate or even lie about their qualifications and experience. The best way to uncover this kind of puffery is to ask some former employers for the inside story.

Former employers are often reluctant to say anything negative for fear that if they speak frankly, they may be hit with a lawsuit for defamation. They're hesitant to do anything more than to verify that the former employee did in fact work there and to give the dates of employment. This reluctance can make it hard to get an accurate picture of an applicant's job history. As mentioned, it may be helpful to send the former employer a copy of the applicant's signed consent to a full disclosure of employment information. (See Chapter 10, Section L, for suggestions on giving references for former employees when you're the one being asked for information.)

In speaking with former employers, learn to read between the lines. If a former employer is neutral, offers only faint praise or over-praises a person for one aspect of a job only—"great with numbers" or "invariably on time"—there's a good chance some negative information is hiding in the wings. Ask former employers: "Would you hire this person back if you could?" The response may be telling. To help put the applicant in perspective, you might ask: "What are this person's greatest strengths—and greatest weaknesses?" Since no one is perfect, this may lead to a candid evaluation of the applicant.

If a reference isn't glowing and doesn't take in all aspects of the job, check several other references—and perhaps call back the applicant for a more directed interview.

For more details, see *Hiring, Staffing, Recruiting and Retention,* published by the Society for Human Resource Management. To order by phone, call the SHRM Bookstore at 703-548-3440. You can also order the book by mail by sending a check for $19.95 to the SHRM Bookstore, at P.O. Box 930132, Atlanta, GA 30201. You can also order the book online at www.shrmstore.shrm.org/shrm. If you are a SHRM member, the price is $16.95.

Reference Checks May Become More Informative. In response to the problem of unhelpful reference checks, many states have passed laws that allow employers to speak more frankly about their former employees.

Find out if your state has such a law. If so, don't assume that the former employers you call for reference checks know about it. Telling them about the protection they have under your state's law may allow you to get a fuller picture of a prospective employee. To find out about your state law, contact your state labor department. (See Appendix for contact details.)

3. School Transcripts

On-the-job experience generally is much more relevant to employment than an applicant's educational credentials. Still, you may have good reasons for requiring a high school diploma or college degree for some jobs. If so, you may want to see proof that the applicant really received the diploma or degree or took the courses claimed in the job application.

If you wish to see these records, ask the applicant to sign a written release acknowledging your right to obtain them. Federal law prohibits schools that receive federal funds from turning over the records without such a release—and many schools won't deliver records to anyone except a former student. This can, of course, complicate your verification, since it creates the possibility of forgery or tampering.

4. Credit History

Credit information usually isn't relevant to employment, but it might come into play if you hire someone who will handle money. Someone with large debts may be especially tempted to skim money from your business. And an applicant who can't keep his or her personal finances in order is probably not a good choice for a job managing your company's finances.

In most other situations, however, a credit check is an unnecessary intrusion into an applicant's private life. What's more, unless you have a good reason for doing a credit check for a particular job, you may run afoul of anti-discrimination laws. According to the EEOC, requiring an applicant to have good credit may subtly discriminate against some minority groups. State laws, too, may limit your use of credit information in deciding whether to hire someone.

Assuming that you have a good business reason to order a credit report on a job applicant, be sure to get the applicant's written permission first. This is required by the federal Fair Credit Reporting Act and may also be mandated by state law. (See Section G1, above.)

5. Criminal History

Asking an applicant about his or her arrest record or making a hiring decision based on that record can be a subtle form of discrimination that violates state and federal anti-discrimination laws. Many people are arrested and the charges are later dropped or found to be without merit. Asking about arrests can be particularly harmful to black applicants because blacks are arrested disproportionately to their population size. Very rarely is there a legitimate business reason to reject an applicant simply because of an arrest record.

Convictions are another matter. While it can be unlawful discrimination to automatically exclude every applicant who's ever had a conviction, anti-discrimination laws generally do allow you to inquire about an applicant's conviction record and to reject an applicant because of a conviction record that's job-related. If you're hiring a delivery truck driver, for example, it wouldn't violate the anti-discrimination laws to reject an applicant based on a conviction for drunk driving.

State laws may specifically prohibit you from asking about arrest records—and may go even farther in restricting your inquiries into an applicant's criminal history. (See the chart below.) In many states, for example, you can't ask an applicant about juvenile records. In some states, you can't ask about convictions for minor offenses or misdemeanors that go back more than five years if the applicant has had a clean slate since that time.

State Laws on Employee Arrest & Conviction Records

State	Rules for employers according to statutes	Rules for employers according to state agency guidelines
Alaska		Asking about arrest record is discriminatory; asking about convictions is permissible, but a conviction should not affect hiring unless it is directly related to job responsibilities.
Arizona Ariz. Rev. Stat. § 13-904		
California Cal. Lab. Code § 432.7	**May not ask** about: • arrest that did not lead to conviction • pretrial or post-trial diversion program. **May ask** about: • arrest if prospective employee is awaiting trial • conviction even if no sentence imposed.	
Colorado Colo. Rev. Stat. §§ 8-3-108; 24-72-308	**May not ask** about arrest for civil disobedience.	**May not ask** about arrests. **May ask** about convictions or court records if: • they are substantially related to applicant's ability to do job • every applicant is asked.
Connecticut Conn. Gen. Stat. Ann. §§ 31-51I; 46a-79	State policy encourages hiring qualified applicants including those with criminal records. May not disclose a job applicant's arrest record to an interviewer unless head of personnel.	
Delaware Del. Code Ann. tit. 11, § 4374(e)		
Georgia Ga. Code Ann. §§ 35-3-34; 42-8-63	Must supply an individual's fingerprints or signed consent to obtain a criminal record. If adverse employment decision is made on the basis of the record, must disclose to employee all information in the record and how it affected the decision.	
Hawaii Haw. Rev. Stat. §§ 378-2.5; 831-3.2	**May ask** about a conviction: • only if it has a rational relation to job • only after making a conditional offer of employment. May not examine any convictions over 10 years old.	**May ask** about convictions only if: • a conditional offer of employment is made • conviction occurred in the last 10 years • charges are related to the job.

Rights of employees and applicants	Special situations	State agency guidelines on the Web
		Alaska Department of Labor and Workforce Development. "Pre-employment questioning," in Alaska Employer Handbook, www.labor.state.ak.us/handbook/legal7.htm
May not be denied an occupational license solely on the basis of a felony or misdemeanor conviction, unless the offense has a reasonable relationship to the job.		
		Department of Fair Employment and Housing. "Pre-Employment Inquiry Guidelines" DFEH-161. www.dfeh.ca.gov/posters/postersEmp.asp
		Division of Civil Rights, Colorado Dept. of Regulatory Agencies. "Preventing Job Discrimination" www.dora.state.co.us/civil_rights/Publications/JobDiscrim2001.pdf
Do not have to disclose an arrest record that has been expunged.		
Probation for a first offense is not a conviction; may not be disqualified for employment once probation completed.		
If an arrest or conviction has been expunged, may state or testify that no record exists.		Hawaii Civil Rights Commission. "Guideline for Pre-Employment Inquiries" www.state.hi.us/hcrc/forms/pre-empinquire.pdf

State Laws on Employee Arrest & Conviction Records (continued)

State	Rules for employers according to statutes	Rules for employers according to state agency guidelines
Idaho		*May ask* for particulars of conviction records. Convictions should not be used to disqualify a candidate unless they are recent, repeated and related to job.
Illinois 775 Ill. Comp. Stat. § 5/2-103	*May not ask* about expunged or sealed records. *May not ask* about or use arrest record as a basis for discrimination in hiring or continued employment. Employer not prohibited from using other means to discover if person actually engaged in conduct.	
Iowa		*May not ask* about arrest records. *May ask about* conviction records only if related to job requirements. When asking should say that conviction record will not necessarily disqualify applicant.
Kansas Kan. Stat. Ann. §§ 12-4516; 21-4610; 22-4710	*May not ask* about or inspect criminal record unless employee signs release.	*May not ask* about arrests. *May ask* about conviction record only if substantially related to applicant's ability to perform job duties.
Maine Me. Rev. Stat. Ann. tit. 28-A, § 703-A		
Maryland Md. Code Ann., [Crim. Proc.] § 10-109	*May not ask* about any criminal charges that have been expunged. *May not* use employee's refusal to disclose information as basis for not hiring.	
Massachusetts Mass. Gen. Laws ch. 151B, § 4; ch. 276, § 100A (continued on next page)	*May not ask* about: • arrests which did not result in conviction • first-time convictions for drunkenness, simple assault, speeding, minor traffic violations or disturbing the peace • misdemeanor convictions 5 or more years old.	

Rights of employees and applicants	Special situations	State agency guidelines on the Web
		Idaho Human Rights Commission. "Pre-Employment Inquiries" www2.state.id.us/ihrc/preemp2.htm
		Iowa Civil Rights Commission. "Successfully Interviewing Job Applicants" www.state.ia.us/government/crc/successfullyinterviewingtitle.html
If an arrest, conviction or diversion record is expunged, employee does not have to disclose.	*May ask* about criminal records: • sensitive positions in state lottery, state gaming agency or pari-mutuel racing • brokers or investment advisors • commercial drivers.	Kansas Human Rights Commission. "Guidelines on Equal Employment Practices: Preventing Discrimination in Hiring" www.khrc.net/hiring.html
	Liquor retailers may not employ anyone convicted of selling liquor to minors or without a license within the past 2 years (first offense) or 5 years (second offense).	
Need not refer to or give any information about an expunged charge.		
If criminal record is sealed, may answer "no record" to any inquiry about past arrests or convictions.		

State Laws on Employee Arrest & Conviction Records (continued)		
State	**Rules for employers according to statutes**	**Rules for employers according to state agency guidelines**
Massachusetts (continued)	A job application question about prior arrests or convictions must also state that an applicant with a sealed record may answer "no record."	
Michigan Mich. Comp. Laws § 37.2205a	*May not ask* about misdemeanor charges that did not result in conviction.	*May ask* about: • criminal convictions • pending felony charges. *May not ask* about arrests which did not result in conviction.
Minnesota		Before making an adverse hiring decision based on a prior conviction, must consider how recent and job-related it is. It is advisable to tell applicants that these mitigating factors will be considered; failure to do so might be discriminatory.
Nevada Nev. Rev. Stat. Ann. § 179A.100	*May request* records of convictions or of current criminal charges, including parole or probation.	*May not ask* about arrests. *May ask* about: • felony convictions • recent misdemeanor convictions that resulted in imprisonment. Must include statement that a conviction will not necessarily disqualify applicant.
New Hampshire N.H. Rev. Stat. Ann. § 651:5 (X)(c)	*May ask about* previous criminal record only if question says, "that has not been annulled by a court."	
New Jersey N.J. Admin. Code tit. 13, §§ 59-1.2, 59-1.6	In order to determine work qualifications, employer *may obtain* all criminal record information including pending arrests and charges.	
New York N.Y. Correct. Law § 750; N.Y. Exec. Law § 296(16)	*It is unlawful* discrimination to ask about any arrests or charges that did not result in conviction, unless they are still pending. Employers with 10 or more employees may not deny employment based on a conviction unless: • it relates directly to the job • it would be an "unreasonable" risk to property or to public or individual safety.	*It is unlawful to ask* if applicant has ever been arrested. *It is lawful to ask* if applicant has ever been convicted of a crime.

Rights of employees and applicants	Special situations	State agency guidelines on the Web
	May ask about a felony charge before conviction or dismissal.	Michigan Civil Rights Commission. "Pre-Employment Inquiry Guide" www.mdcr.state.mi.us/mdcr/pamphlets/pamphlet_ pre_employment_inquriy_guide.shtml
		Minnesota Department of Human Rights. "Hiring, Job Interviews and the Minnesota Human Rights Act" www.humanrights.state.mn.us/site/docs/ employer_hiring.html
		Nevada Equal Rights Commission. "Pre-Employment Inquiry Guide" http:// detr.state.nv.us/nerc/nerc_preemp.htm
Anyone disqualified for employment based on criminal record must be given adequate notice and reasonable time to confirm or deny accuracy of information.		
Upon request must be given, within 30 days, a written statement of the reasons why employment was denied.		New York State Division of Human Rights. Rulings on Inquiries (Pre-employment) www.nysdhr.com/employment.html

State Laws on Employee Arrest & Conviction Records (continued)		
State	Rules for employers according to statutes	Rules for employers according to state agency guidelines
North Dakota N.D. Cent. Code § 12-60-16.6	May obtain criminal records of convictions or of charges occurring in the past year. Request must be in writing and contain two identifying items such as fingerprints, Social Security number, DOB or state ID number.	
Ohio Ohio Rev. Code Ann. §§ 2151.358(I), 2953.33	*May not ask* about: • juvenile records that have been sealed • any other sealed conviction unless it has a substantial and direct relation to the job.	
Oklahoma Okla. Stat. Ann. tit. 22, § 19(F)	*May not ask* about any criminal record that has been expunged.	
Oregon Or. Rev. Stat. §§ 181.555; 659.030	*May request* information on convictions and arrests less than one year old that have not been dismissed or resulted in acquittal. Must advise applicant or employee of request and tell State Police Department how the person was advised. May not discriminate against applicant or employee on the basis of an expunged juvenile record unless there is a "bona fide occupational qualification."	
Pennsylvania 18 Pa. Cons. Stat. Ann. § 9125	*May consider* felony and misdemeanor convictions only when they relate directly to person's suitability for the job.	Unless there is proof of business necessity, may not use arrest record to disqualify applicant. Inquiry into conviction must be substantially related to applicant's ability to perform major job duties. It is inadvisable to base rejection on convictions unless they are numerous, recent or job-related.
Rhode Island R.I. Gen. Laws §§ 12-1.3-4; 28-5-7(7)	*May not ask* about arrests. *May ask* about convictions.	

Rights of employees and applicants	Special situations	State agency guidelines on the Web
If record expunged, may state that no criminal action ever occurred. May not be denied employment for refusing to disclose sealed criminal record information.		
Before releasing criminal record information to employer, State Police Department must: • notify applicant or employee • provide copy of all information that will be sent to employer • advise applicant or employee of protections under federal civil rights law and of procedure for challenging information. May not release information until 14 days after notice sent.		
Must be informed in writing if refusal to hire is based on criminal record information.		Pennsylvania Human Relations Commission. "Pre-Employment Inquiries" www.phrc.state.pa.us/PA_Exec/PHRC/publications/literature/web_preempqs.htm
Do not have to disclose any conviction that has been expunged.		

State Laws on Employee Arrest & Conviction Records (continued)

State	Rules for employers according to statutes	Rules for employers according to state agency guidelines
South Dakota		*May not ask* about or check arrest, court or conviction records unless substantially related to job functions.
Texas Tex. Health & Safety Code Ann. § 765.001		
Utah Utah Admin. R. 606-2	*May not ask* about arrests. *May ask* about felony convictions; it is not advisable unless directly related to job.	
Virginia Va. Code Ann. § 19.2-392.4	*May not require* an applicant to disclose information about any criminal charge that has been expunged.	
Washington Wash. Rev. Code Ann. §§ 43.43.815; 9.94A.640		
Wisconsin Wis. Stat. Ann. § 111.31	It is a violation of state civil rights law to discriminate on the basis of a prior arrest or conviction record. *May not ask* about: • arrests unless charges are pending • convictions unless charges substantially relate to job.	

Rights of employees and applicants	Special situations	State agency guidelines on the Web
		South Dakota Division of Human Rights. "Pre-employment Inquiry Guide" www.state.sd.us/dcr/hr/preemplo.htm
	Criminal background check permitted for employment in a private "residential dwelling," which includes: condominium or apartment building, hotel, motel or bed and breakfast.	
		Rule R606-2. "Pre-Employment Inquiry Guide" www.rules.state.ut.us/publicat/code/r606/r606-002.htm
Need not refer to any expunged charges if asked about criminal record.		
Must be informed when employer receives a conviction record and must be given opportunity to examine the documents. If a conviction record has been cleared, may answer questions as though the conviction never occurred.	May request conviction records for positions that are bonded or that have access to: • confidential or proprietary business information • trade secrets • money or items of value.	
	May ask about criminal records for: • positions that require bonding • burglar alarm installers.	

Current as of June 2002

⚠️ **Expunging the Past.** Many states have laws that allow individuals to expunge, or seal, their criminal records. When a record is expunged, it is usually not available to anyone other than criminal justice agencies and the courts. If a criminal record has been expunged, a prospective employee is generally allowed to act as if the conviction never happened—in other words, the applicant is legally permitted to deny having a criminal record.

6. Driving Records

When a job requires the employee to drive, it's wise to check on an applicant's driving record. You usually can obtain driving records for a modest cost from the state authority that issues drivers' licenses.

H. Making a Job Offer

Be careful what you say orally and in writing when you make a job offer to any applicant. The positive statements you make to an applicant about long-term opportunities can come back to haunt you if you later fire the person. (See Section A3.) A judge or jury reviewing the firing may conclude that your glowing statements were actually a promise— a promise, perhaps, that the applicant's job would be secure for years or that he or she wouldn't be fired without good cause.

You can protect yourself from such misunderstandings by using an employment letter such as the one shown below.

I. Rejecting Applicants

It's courteous to let unsuccessful applicants know that you've hired someone else for the job. You don't, however, owe them an explanation about why they weren't hired. If pressed, simply tell them that the person you hired is, in your judgment, more appropriate for the job.

There's no ideal way to give someone the news that he or she didn't get the job. The least painful way—which also presents the fewest legal difficulties—is to send a short letter informing the rejected applicant of your decision. Send the letter as soon as you've decided whom you're going to hire or when you've narrowed the field down to a few candidates. There's no need to let applicants twist in the wind. Quickly sending your rejection letter will cut down on the number of post interview calls you get from unsuccessful applicants—calls that are uncomfortable for everyone.

Keep the letter simple and upbeat. And keep a copy in your files, along with the employment application and any information

Sample Employment Letter

June 10, 20XX

Dear Joe Nolo,

I am pleased to offer you a full-time position with our company as a tester beginning June 12. Your starting salary will be $1,000 per week.

When you applied, I gave you a copy of our employee handbook. The handbook sets out our current employment policies and describes your job benefits including medical coverage, paid vacation and sick leave. It also describes your responsibilities to the company. Each time the handbook is updated, you'll receive a revised copy.

The company's commitments to you and its other employees are stated in the handbook. The company has made no oral commitments to you. No one at the company is authorized to make oral commitments regarding employment—either now or in the future.

While I hope that everything works out here, you are an at-will employee. You have the right to terminate your employment at any time, for any reason, and so does the company.

If this offer of employment is acceptable to you, please sign a copy of this letter and return it to me within 10 days. I look forward to having you join our staff.

Sincerely,

Bob Bossman
Supervisor

I accept your offer of employment and acknowledge receiving a copy of your current employee handbook. I understand that my employment is at will and that either you or I can terminate my employment at any time, for any reason. No oral commitments have been made concerning my employment.

_____

Signature

_____

Date

you gathered during the screening process. Lawsuits by rejected applicants are rare, but you can't predict in advance which ones might take that step.

Sample Rejection Letter

June 10, 20XX

Dear Larry Leeds,

Thank you for taking the time to meet with me last Thursday to discuss the programmer position with our company. You were among many fine people who applied. I wanted to let you know that we selected another applicant for the position.

It was a pleasure meeting you and I wish you well in your job search.

Sincerely,

Bob Bossman
Bob Bossman
Supervisor

J. Tax Compliance

Before you hire employees, you must get an Employer Identification Number (EIN) from the IRS—although if you're a sole proprietor, you have the option of using your own Social Security number. To obtain an EIN, file Form SS-4, Application for Employer Identification Number. Some states have similar requirements. (See Chapter 5, Section A, for further information.)

When you hire an employee, have him or her complete Form W-4, the Employee's Withholding Allowance Certificate. This lets you know how many dependents or withholding allowances the employee is claiming and the employee's filing status—single, married or married but withholding at the higher single rate. Keep a signed Form W-4 on file for each employee. If an employee doesn't complete a Form W-4, you won't know how much income tax to withhold. In that case, you must withhold tax as if the employee were a single person claiming no withholding allowances.

You needn't send the signed Form W-4 to the IRS unless:

- an employee claims more than ten allowances, or
- the employee earns more than $200 per week and claims exemption from withholding.

You can find detailed information on your tax obligations as an employer in Chapter 5.

 The IRS has two free publications that may be useful in helping establish tax procedures for your business. *Circular E, Employers Tax Guide,* containing withholding tables, is updated periodically and mailed automatically to every business that has an Employer Identification Number.

IRS Publication 334, *Tax Guide for Small Business,* covers a wide range of tax issues. You can get it at your local IRS office or by calling 800-829-3676. You can also obtain IRS publications through the agency's website at www.irs.gov.

K. Immigration Law Requirements

Immigration laws, enforced by the Immigration and Naturalization Service (INS), prohibit employers from hiring aliens who don't have government authorization to work in the United States. There are specific procedures you must follow when hiring employees—even those who were born and raised in the town where your business is located.

You and the new employee must complete INS Form I-9, Employment Eligibility Verification. This one-page form is intended to ensure that the employee can legally work in the United States and has proof of his or her identity.

 For full details, see the free publication *Handbook for Employers: Instructions for Completing Form I-9,* available from the INS. Call the nearest regional office of the INS to obtain a copy. You can find a list of INS field offices at the agency's website at www.ins.usdoj.gov.

The employee completes Section 1 of the form, attesting that he or she is a citizen or national of the United States, a lawful permanent resident alien or an alien with work authorization. Only people in these three categories can lawfully work in the United States.

Section 2 of the form requires you to review documents—such as a passport or naturalization certificate—presented by the employee as proof of the employee's identity and employment eligibility.

You must indicate on Form I-9 which documents you've examined. It's your responsibility to decide whether the employee's documents appear valid. The INS advises that you must accept documents that reasonably appear to be genuine and to relate to the person presenting them. To do otherwise could be an unfair immigration-related employment practice and therefore illegal.

It's a good idea to keep photocopies of the employee's documents to prove that you reviewed these papers in case the INS questions your hiring practices in the future. Also, hang on to all Form I-9s for at least three years. If the employee stays with your company longer than that, keep the form for at least one year after he or she leaves. The INS has the right to see your I-9s. You can be fined up to $1,000 per employee if you can't produce them. (See Chapter 2, Section A, for information on where to keep I-9s.)

For more information on immigration law requirements, including detailed information on filling out Form 1-9, see *Federal Employment Laws: A Desk Reference,* by Amy DelPo and Lisa Guerin (Nolo).

L. New Hire Reporting Form

Federal law requires you to report certain identifying information about new employees and re-hired employees to a designated state agency. Under federal law, you have 20 days to provide this information, but some states require you to do it more quickly The information becomes part of the National Directory of New Hires. It's used primarily to locate parents so that child support orders can be enforced. Government agencies also use the data to prevent improper payment of workers' compensation, unemployment benefits or public assistance benefits.

Each state has its own form, but all require the following basic information:

- employee's name, address, Social Security number and date of hire, and
- employer's name, address and federal employer ID number.

Some states ask for additional information, such as your state unemployment compensation number, and the employee's driver's license number and date of birth, though providing this information may be optional.

Your state department of labor can tell you how to get the forms and where to send them. Or you can use a computer search engine such as Google to find out. Just type in *New Hire Reporting* and the name of your state. Most states provide the form online, and allow you to file it electronically.

Paperwork Checklist

Here's a list of documents and forms that you should consider each time you hire someone:

- ☐ **Employment Letter.** You can find an example of such a letter in Section H, above.

- ☐ **Employee Handbook.** If you have such a handbook and didn't give it to the employee during the application and interview stages, now is the time to do so. Get a written receipt and keep it in the employee's file. (For more on employee handbooks, see Chapter 2, Section B.)

- ☐ **Covenant Not to Compete.** This is useful if you have employees who could harm your business if they left to work for a competitor or started a business of their own in competition with yours. (For more information, see Section A5 of this chapter.)

- ☐ **Confidentiality Agreement.** Use such an agreement if you'll be disclosing trade secrets and other proprietary information to an employee.

- ☐ **INS Form I-9.** This form, required by the U.S. Immigration and Naturalization Service, is intended to help exclude undocumented aliens from the workforce. (See Section K of this chapter.)

- ☐ **IRS Form W-4.** Each employee must complete this form so you can properly determine the level of tax to withhold from every paycheck. (See Section J and Chapter 5, Sections B, C and D, for details.)

- ☐ **New Hire Reporting Form.** Within a short time after you hire someone—20 days or less, depending on your state's rules—you must file a New Hire Reporting Form with a designated state agency.

- ☐ **Employee Benefit Sign-Up.** If your business offers employee benefit programs such as health insurance or a 401(k) plan, you may have a sign-up procedure so employees can name their dependents and select options.

- ☐ **IRS Form SS-4** (new employers only). The IRS requires an Employer Identification Number for all employers except sole proprietorships. (See Chapter 5, Section A.) ■

Chapter 2

Personnel Practices

A. Employee Files 2/2

    1. Correcting Mistakes 2/3

    2. Confidentiality 2/3

    3. Medical Information 2/4

    4. Access by Employees 2/4

    5. Informing Employees 2/5

B. Employee Handbooks 2/5

    1. Advantages 2/5

    2. Contents 2/13

    3. Documenting Employee's Acceptance 2/16

C. Employee Performance Reviews 2/16

    1. Benefits of Evaluations 2/16

    2. The Evaluation Process 2/18

    3. Sample Employee Evaluation Form 2/19

D. Disciplining Employees 2/23

*Y*ou can avoid most legal problems in the workplace if you respect employees and treat them well. But no matter how caring you are, there will still be misunderstandings you'll be called upon to handle. Fortunately, the vast majority of job disputes can be resolved within the workplace if you listen patiently to what employees have to say and are prepared to make adjustments when legitimate complaints surface.

However, even though you treat workers fairly, there's always a chance that a dispute will get out of hand and an employee will sue your business for some perceived abuse of his or her rights. Or an unhappy employee may file a complaint with a government agency, alleging that you violated a statute or an administrative regulation. If that happens, you'll have to prove to a judge, jury, arbitrator or investigator that you met your legal obligations to the employee. That can be harder than you think. Key paperwork may have been lost—or never prepared in the first place. And witnesses may have forgotten what happened or have moved on to a new job, where you might have trouble finding them.

To maintain a solid legal footing, establish good written policies and then maintain a paper trail indicating how they are implemented. Written policies will help you if you have to defend yourself in a legal proceeding —and, equally important, can nip misunderstandings in the bud before they turn into pitched legal battles. They provide a cogent point of reference when you discuss problems with an employee, increasing the likelihood of reaching an amicable resolution.

The first step for most workplaces is to create an employee handbook that clearly explains company policies and employee rights and benefits. Follow up by keeping records of key employee contacts, including periodic evaluations of how employees are performing their jobs.

 Actions Speak Loudly, Too. You must start with sensible and fair policies and apply them with an even hand to all employees. A carefully developed paper trail is important, but if you've violated an employee's rights, the mere fact that you've created good paperwork won't shield you from the legal consequences.

For an in-depth discussion of employee problems and the personnel practices that you can use to deal with them, see *Dealing With Problem Employees: An Employer's Legal Guide*, by attorneys Amy DelPo and Lisa Guerin (Nolo).

A. Employee Files

Create a file for each employee in which you keep all job-related information, including:

- job description (see Chapter 1, Section B)
- job application (see Chapter 1, Section D)
- offer of employment (see Chapter 1, Section H)
- IRS Form W-4 (see Chapter 1, Section I)
- receipt for employee handbook (see Section B)
- periodic performance evaluations (see Section C)

- sign-up forms for employee benefits (see Chapter 4)
- complaints from customers and co-workers
- compliments from customers and co-workers
- awards or citations for excellent performance
- warnings and disciplinary actions, and
- notes on an employee's attendance or tardiness.

Employee files can be a two-edged sword. They can provide valuable documentation to support a firing, demotion or other action that's adverse to the employee—but the employee, in turn, can point to indiscreet entries and use them against you. It would be a mistake, for example, to include unsubstantiated criticism of an employee in the file or comments about the employee that are unrelated to job performance and qualifications.

Keep Immigration Forms in a Separate File. Although no law requires it, some employers prefer to place I-9 forms in a separate file. Government agencies are allowed to inspect all of your I-9 forms when they visit your workplace, and keeping the forms in a separate file protects your employees' privacy as to the rest of their personal documents. Also, federal law prohibits you from making employment decisions based on an individual's immigration status. Keeping employees' I-9 forms separate from their personnel files reduces the chance that managers and supervisors will learn an employee's immigration status and act on it. For more about I-9 forms, see Chapter 1, Section A7.

1. Correcting Mistakes

To err is human. To leave an error uncorrected is just plain dumb. It can lead people to conclude that you're callous or unfair or both—not a good impression to leave on those empowered to levy a damage award or penalties against you. And to knowingly keep false information on hand increases the risk of a lawsuit for defamation.

EXAMPLE: Joe doesn't show up for work for a week after his paid vacation has ended. You put a note in his file documenting this fact. Then you learn that on the last day of his vacation he was in a serious car accident and wound up in intensive care. Put these additional facts in Joe's file. If you don't, Joe will have good reason to be angry with you, and other people who later look at the file won't put much stock in anything else they find there.

2. Confidentiality

Keep employee files locked up. Make them available only to people in your company who have a legitimate business need to have access to the files—managers, for example, who must make decisions about promotions and discipline. Inform company personnel that the information in the files must remain confidential. While an employee or former employee may have a legal right to see his or her file (see Section 4), other people don't, unless they have a subpoena.

3. Medical Information

Special guidelines apply to medical information gathered in the workplace. The Americans with Disabilities Act (ADA) imposes very strict rules on how you must handle information obtained from post-offer medical examinations and inquiries. You must keep the information in medical files separate from nonmedical records, and you must store the medical files in a separate locked cabinet. To further guarantee the confidentiality of medical files, designate a specific person to have access to those files.

The ADA allows very limited disclosure of medical information. Under the ADA, you may:

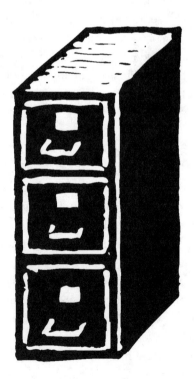

- inform supervisors about necessary restrictions on an employee's duties and about necessary accommodations
- inform first aid and safety workers about a disability that may require emergency treatment and about specific procedures that are needed if the workplace must be evacuated, and
- provide medical information required by government officials and by insurance companies that require a medical exam for health or life insurance.

Otherwise, don't disclose medical information about employees. Although the confidentiality provisions of the ADA protect only some disabled workers, the best policy is to treat all medical information about all employees as confidential. (For more on the ADA, see Chapter 9.)

4. Access by Employees

Many states have laws requiring employers to give employees—and former employees— access to their own personnel files. How much access varies from state to state. Typically, if your state allows employees to see their files, you can insist that you or another supervisor be present to make sure nothing is taken, added or changed. Some state laws allow employees to obtain copies of items in their files, but not necessarily all items. A state law, for example, may limit the employee to copies of documents that he or she has signed, such as a job application. If an employee is entitled to a copy of an item in the file or if you're inclined to let the employee have a copy of any document in the file, you—rather than the employee—should make the copy.

Usually, you won't have to let the employee see sensitive items such as information assembled for a criminal investigation, reference letters and information that might violate the privacy of other people. In a few states, employees may insert rebuttals if they disagree with information in their personnel files. And some states require employees to request to see their files in writing before employers have to grant access.

5. Informing Employees

Generally, the law doesn't require you to voluntarily tell employees what's in their employee files. You need only disclose information when an employee makes an appropriate request under an employee access law. (See Section 4 above.) About the only exception is the federal Fair Credit Reporting Act or FCRA (15 U.S.C. §§ 1681 and following), which requires you to tell employees if you're taking adverse action against them because of information in a consumer credit report. (See Chapter 1, Section G, for more information about your responsibilities under the FCRA.)

Still, it may be good practice to keep employees informed about what's going into their files. Otherwise, borderline employees may think they're doing fine and be justifiably surprised by a disciplinary action or firing. Admittedly, some employees can get demoralized if they're overwhelmed with negative information about their work, so some discretion is necessary in giving them feedback. But basically, letting employees know where they stand prevents surprises and can lead to improved performance. And if the employee doesn't shape up and winds up being fired, anyone reviewing the facts—a judge or jury, for example—will be more likely to side with you if you've given the employee fair warning about what was wrong.

B. Employee Handbooks

If you have more than one or two employees, consider creating an employee handbook that clearly explains your employment policies.

1. Advantages

An employee handbook can be of practical help in running your business. Once you give it to an employee, there can be no dispute over whether you gave the employee a list of paid days off or explained your vacation policies for new workers. It's all there in writing and everyone is getting the same information.

Beyond the practicalities, if your handbook is good, you get a bonus: a measure of legal protection if you're challenged by an employee in a court or administrative proceeding. A handbook that contains clear, reasonable policies—such as one stating that sexual harassment won't be tolerated in the workplace—is the critical beginning of your paper trail if problems develop later. It's an objective piece of evidence that shows you've adopted fair and uniform policies, and that you've informed your employees of exactly where they stand in their employment.

State Laws on Employee Access to Personal Records

State	Rules governing employee access to records	Access for employee's agent	Written request required
Alaska Alaska Stat. § 23.10.430	Employee may view and copy personnel files (applies to former employee as well).		
California Cal. Lab. Code §§ 432, 1198.5	Employee may inspect any records relating to performance or grievance. Employee may have copy of any document employee has signed.		
Connecticut Conn. Gen. Stat. Ann. §§ 31-128a, 31-128e	Employee may have access within a reasonable time after request. Employer must keep former employee files for at least one year after termination.		Yes.
Delaware Del. Code Ann. tit. 19, § 730	Unless there is reasonable cause, employer may limit access to once a year.	No access for employee's agent.	Yes. Employer may require employee to file a form and indicate either the reason for the review or what parts of the record employee wants to inspect.
Illinois 820 Ill. Comp. Stat. §§ 40/1 to 40/5	Employers with 5 or more employees must allow access twice a year at "reasonable" intervals within 7 working days after employee makes request (additional 7 days if employer cannot meet deadline).	Employee involved in a grievance may designate a representative of the union or collective bargaining unit or other agent to inspect records that may be relevant to resolving the grievance.	Yes. Employer may require use of a form.
Iowa Iowa Code § 91B.1	Employee may have access at time agreed upon by employer and employee.		
Maine Me. Rev. Stat. Ann. tit. 26, § 631	Within 10 days of submitting request, employee may view and copy personnel files (applies to former employee as well).	Within 10 days of submitting request, may view and copy personnel files.	Yes.

Conditions for viewing records	Copying records	Right to insert rebuttal
During regular business hours under "reasonable rules."	Employee pays (at employer's discretion).	
At "reasonable" times during employee's break or nonwork hours. If records are not kept on-site or employer does not make them available at the workplace, then employee must be allowed to inspect them at storage location without loss of pay.		
During regular business hours at or near worksite. Employer may require that files be viewed on the premises and in the presence of employer's designated official.		Yes.
During regular business hours. Employer may require that: • employees view files on own time • files be viewed on the premises • files be viewed in the presence of employer's designated official.	Employer not required to permit copying. Employee may take notes.	Yes.
During normal business hours at or near worksite or, at employer's discretion, during nonworking hours at a different location. Employer may require that files be viewed on the premises.	After reviewing files, employee may get a copy; employer may charge only actual cost of copies. If employee is unable to view files at worksite, employer, upon receipt of a written request, must mail employee a copy.	Yes.
Employer's representative may be present.	Employer may charge fee equivalent to commercial copying service.	
During normal business hours, where files are kept; employer has discretion to arrange a time and place more convenient for employee. If files are in electronic format, employer must provide equipment for viewing and copying.	Employee pays for copies.	

State Laws on Employee Access to Personal Records (continued)

State	Rules governing employee access to records	Access for employee's agent	Written request required
Massachusetts Mass. Gen. Laws ch. 149, § 52C	Employee must be given opportunity to review personnel files within 5 days of submitting request. (Law does not apply to tenured or tenure-track employees in private colleges and universities.) Employers with 20 or more employees must maintain personnel records for 3 years after termination.		Yes.
Michigan Mich. Comp. Laws § 423.501	Employee may have access at "reasonable" intervals, not more than twice a year.		Yes. Request must describe the record employee wants to review.
Minnesota Minn. Stat. Ann. §§ 181.960 to 181.964	Current employee: may review files within 7 days of request (14 if records kept out of state); employer not required to allow access more than once in 6 months. Former employee: may have access only once during the first year after termination (may request copy instead). Employer may not retaliate against employee who asserts rights under these laws.		Yes.
Nevada Nev. Rev. Stat. Ann. § 613.075	Employee who has worked at least 60 days must be given a "reasonable" opportunity to inspect records within 60 days of termination (applies to former employee as well).		
New Hampshire N.H. Rev. Stat. Ann. § 275:56	Employer must provide a "reasonable" opportunity to inspect records.		
Oregon Or. Rev. Stat. § 652.750	Employer must provide a "reasonable" opportunity to inspect records. Must keep records for 60 days after termination.		

Conditions for viewing records	Copying records	Right to insert rebuttal
At workplace during normal business hours.	Employee must be given a copy of record within 5 days of submitting a written request.	Yes.
During normal business hours at or near worksite. If this would require employee to take time off work, employer must provide another "reasonable" time and place for review.	After reviewing files, employee may get a copy; employer may charge only actual cost of duplication. If employee is unable to view files at worksite, employer, upon receipt of a written request, must mail employee a copy.	Yes. Statement may be no more than 5 pages.
Current employee: during employer's normal business hours at worksite or a nearby location; does not have to be during employee's working hours. Employer or employer's representative may be present. Former employee: may choose to request copy.	Employer provides copy free of charge. Current employee: must first review files then submit written request. Former employee: must submit written request; obtaining a copy satisfies access requirement.	Yes. Statement may be no more than 5 pages.
During normal business hours.	Employer may charge only actual cost of providing access and copies.	"Reasonable" written explanation; employer may specify length and format.
	Employer may charge a fee "reasonably" related to actual cost of supplying copies.	Yes.
At worksite or place of work assignment.	Employer provides certified copy to current or former employee (if request made within 60 days of termination) May charge only actual cost of duplication.	

State Laws on Employee Access to Personal Records (continued)

State	Rules governing employee access to records	Access for employee's agent	Written request required
Pennsylvania 43 Pa. Cons. Stat. Ann. §§ 1321 to 1322.1	Employer must permit employee to inspect records at "reasonable" times; unless there is reasonable cause, may limit access to once a year.	Employee must provide signed authorization designating agent; must be for a specific date and state the reason for inspection or the parts of the file agent authorized to review.	At employer's discretion. May require use of a form and a description of record employee wants to review.
Rhode Island R.I. Gen. Laws § 28-6.4-1	Employer must permit inspection when given at least 7 days advance notice (excluding weekends and holidays). May limit access to no more than 3 times a year.		Yes.
Washington Wash. Rev. Code Ann. § 49.12.240	Employee may have access at least once a year within a "reasonable" time after making a request.		
Wisconsin Wis. Stat. Ann. § 103.13	Employee may have access at least twice a year, within 7 working days after making request.	Employee involved in a grievance may designate a representative of the union or collective bargaining unit or other agent to inspect records that may be relevant to resolving the grievance.	At employer's discretion.

Conditions for viewing records	Copying records	Right to insert rebuttal
During normal business hours, where records are usually maintained, when there is enough time to complete review. Employer may require that • employee or agent view files on own time • files be viewed on the premises • files be viewed in the presence of employer's designated official.	Employer not obligated to permit copying. Employee may take notes.	Yes. Upon petition to the Bureau of Labor Standards.
At any "reasonable" time other than employee's work hours. Inspection must take place in presence of employer or employer's representative.	Employee may not make copies or remove files from place of inspection. Employer may charge a fee "reasonably" related to cost of supplying copies.	
		Yes. Employee may petition for annual review of all information in file. Former employee has rebuttal rights for 2 years after termination.
During normal working hours at a location reasonably near the employee's worksite. If this would require employee to take time off work, employer may provide another "reasonable" time and place for review that is more convenient for the employee.	Right of inspection includes right to make or receive copies. If employer provides copies, may charge only actual cost of reproduction.	Yes.

Current as of June 2002

A good handbook should tell your employees how to let you know if they feel unfairly treated or have a workplace problem. This gives you a chance to react before a small misunderstanding erupts into a full-blown legal dispute. As another benefit, a well-written handbook may reduce the anxiety that some employees feel about their jobs. Employees will know what the rules and procedures are and where they can turn if they need to discuss an issue.

Even a tiny business with only a handful of employees can benefit from an employee handbook—and you can produce one quickly and cheaply, using a self-help book or software program as a starting point. Modify the sample wording to fit your own needs. Then check with the state department of labor to make sure your handbook complies with the laws in your state. If you have specific legal questions, a brief consultation with a lawyer should be sufficient to clear them up. (See Chapter 13 for more on how to use a small business lawyer without breaking the bank.)

If yours is a very small business, keep your handbook short and sweet at the start. At that stage, it's easy to involve all employees in the writing process, so the handbook accurately covers their concerns. Then, as your business grows, the framework necessary for a more detailed version will be in place. Make sure to review your handbook and update it periodically, to reflect any changes in your policies.

Don't Increase Your Legal Exposure

Your handbook may be treated as a contract that can actually limit your right to fire employees. To avoid that result, state in the handbook that:

- employees do not have employment contracts unless they are in writing and signed by the company president, and
- your company reserves the right to terminate employees for reasons not stated in the handbook or for no reason at all.

Unfortunately, disclaimers in employee handbooks are not always enough to preserve an at-will relationship with employees. Courts these days tend to look at the handbook as a whole. They ask: "How would reasonable employees interpret the handbook? Would it be reasonable for employees to conclude that they have been given some rights?" If the answer to the second question is yes, some courts may find the employees do have legal rights to job security despite the disclaimer.

To prevent that result, look closely at each provision in your handbook from the point of view of employees. If employees are likely to conclude you're making binding commitments, fix the language so it's clear you're not.

Developing an Email Policy

If you provide employees with computers that allow for electronic mail or email communication, it's smart to develop a written policy so everyone knows the rules. For one thing, you may be assuming that you have the right to see all email messages sent on your equipment, while employees may be assuming they have a degree of privacy. For another thing, you may be assuming that employees are to use your email system only for company purposes, while employees may be assuming they can use it for unlimited personal purposes as well.

You're the sole judge of what to put into your email policy. The important thing is to make the rules clear so that employees can't create legal problems for you by claiming they were taken by surprise. Email, of course, is a relatively new means of communication, so the workplace norms are just starting to emerge. Here are some statements to consider when you develop an email policy:

- Our computers and email system are intended to facilitate business communications.
- Our management has access at all times to email communications sent or received on our computers and email system.
- All communications sent or received on our computers or email system are the property of our company.
- Employee privacy doesn't extend to such communications—whether intended for business or personal purposes.
- Employees must provide our management with all passwords and encryption keys.
- Employees may not use our computers or email system for commercial purposes unrelated to our company, or for sending offensive, harassing or defamatory messages.
- Employees who violate these policies may be subject to disciplinary action and may be discharged.

2. Contents

Here are topics to consider covering in an employee handbook.

Introduction. Begin the handbook by describing your company's history and business philosophy. This helps you set the tone— which can be friendly and welcoming if that's your style. Make it clear to employees from the start that the handbook doesn't cover every possible situation.

Hours. State the normal working hours and how overtime pay is authorized for those employees entitled to it. (See Chapter 3.)

Pay and salaries. Be clear on how pay and salaries are set and how they're raised. In very small businesses, this may be little more than a statement that levels of pay are established and adjusted by the company president taking into consideration past performance, cost of living changes and the ability of the business to pay. But if you do adopt a more formal procedure based on periodic performance reviews, explain how it works—and whether employees may be eligible for bonuses as well as salary increases.

Benefits. Benefits can be nearly as important as salary. Many larger businesses will have a separate publication covering this topic, but most savvy smaller businesses opt to cover it in their employee handbooks. Employee benefits typically include paid vacations, health benefits, sick pay and unpaid leaves for extended illness, pregnancy or family matters. (See Chapter 6 for information on the Family and Medical Leave Act.)

Since the law doesn't require you to provide paid sick days or vacation days, you're free to set the terms under which such benefits are granted—and an employee handbook is the ideal place to inform employees about the rules governing these benefits. Be clear on whether the employee can carry unused sick or vacation days into the next year and what happens to such benefits if an employee quits or gets fired. Finally, describe any 401(k) or retirement benefits you offer.

(See Chapter 4 for an extensive discussion of employee benefits.)

Drug and alcohol abuse. Most businesses have a policy prohibiting employees' use of alcohol or illegal drugs in the workplace. In addition, some businesses offer employees help in dealing with abuse of these substances—often through an employee assistance program in which the business pays for professional counseling. Spell out your policies.

Sexual harassment. Remind employees that sexual harassment is illegal and violates your

policies. (See Chapter 8, Section B, for more on sexual harassment.) Let them know that you won't tolerate unwelcome sexual comments or conduct and that you'll assist those who speak up about it in ending any harassment in the workplace. Finally, spell out your procedures for handling sexual harassment complaints. Specify how and to whom an employee can submit a complaint. Specify what you will do to investigate any complaints that you receive. Assure employees that you will handle every complaint as confidentially as possible.

Discrimination. Employees need to know that your business obeys all laws that prohibit discrimination, including discrimination based on race, color, religion, gender, national origin, age, pregnancy, citizenship or disability. State that you expect employees to conduct themselves in a non-discriminatory manner. (See Chapter 8 for more on illegal discrimination.)

Job attendance. Emphasize the importance of good attendance and showing up on time. Tell employees the types of absence that are excused—such as illness, and possibly a family member's death, for example. Also, if you believe it's likely to be a problem, clearly explain that piling up a load of unexcused absences or coming to work late too often can be a basis for disciplinary action or even firing.

Discipline. List the kinds of conduct that can get employees in trouble—for example, theft or violence. But again, let employees know this isn't an exclusive list and that you always reserve the right to decide to terminate an employee's employment. (See Section D.)

Grooming and Clothing Rules

If you have a reasonable business purpose for doing so, you can establish on-the-job standards for clothing and grooming as a condition of employment. There's nothing inherently illegal, for example, about requiring all employees to wear navy blue slacks during working hours.

Codes governing employees' appearance may be illegal, however, if they discriminate against a particular group of employees or potential employees. Stay away from imposing different rules on male and female employees. For example, if you have a retail store, you can't require female clerks to wear smocks while allowing male clerks to wear business attire. Courts do, however, allow some latitude in imposing different rules on men and women. For example, a court ruled that a company could lawfully allow women employees to wear jewelry while prohibiting men from doing so.

Several black men have won lawsuits against companies that refused to hire men with beards or that fired men who didn't comply with no-beard rules. Many black men find that if they shave their facial hair too closely, it will cause their whiskers to become ingrown and infected. A policy of banning beards might illegally discriminate against black men.

For the sake of creating a uniform company-wide appearance, you may provide workers with some or all of the clothing that they are required to wear on the job. You may even rent suits for your employees to assure that they will be similarly dressed.

Although generally legal, such policies can violate an employee's rights if the cost of the clothing is deducted from the employee's pay in violation of the Fair Labor Standards Act (FLSA). For example, it's illegal under the FLSA to deduct the cost of work-related clothing from an employee's pay so that his or her wages dip below the minimum wage standard. (For more on the FLSA, see Chapter 3.) And some states require employers to bear the costs of uniforms.

Employee safety. State that employee safety is a major concern of your business and that employees are expected to heed the posted safety rules and to call to your attention any potentially dangerous conditions.

Smoking. Most businesses need a written policy for on-the-job smoking. (See Chapter 7, Section G.) Because many cities and some states now prohibit or restrict workplace smoking, you need to check local ordinances to be sure that your policy is legal.

Complaints. Let employees know what procedures they can follow to resolve complaints. Having a written complaint procedure in your handbook can help shield your business from liability if an employee sues claiming illegal harassment or discrimination.

Workplace civility. State specifically that employees at all levels of the business are expected to treat each other with respect and that the success of the business depends on cooperation and teamwork among all employees.

3. Documenting Employee's Acceptance

Document that each employee received the handbook. This is also another good chance to reinforce to employees that the handbook isn't an employment contract, that it doesn't guarantee you'll continuously employ them and that you're not obligating your company to continue the current job benefits forever.

To do this, include with your handbook two copies of a statement such as the one below. Then ask each new employee to sign both copies to acknowledge that he or she has received the handbook and is familiar with its terms.

Keep one signed copy of the Employee Handbook Acknowledgment in the employee's personnel file maintained by your business. The employee can keep the other copy. Have each employee sign a similar receipt each time you distribute significant revisions or updates of your handbook.

C. Employee Performance Reviews

Most large companies review and evaluate their employees periodically. This is a sound management practice and one which even small companies should consider—especially for new employees.

1. Benefits of Evaluations

Evaluating employees periodically gives them a chance to improve if they're not performing well. If you later find it necessary to discipline or fire an employee, it won't come as a surprise to the employee.

By putting your evaluations in writing and saving them in the employee's file, you have a credible history of documented problems you can use if an employee claims that he or she was fired for an illegal reason. Legally, you don't have to have a good reason or any reason to fire an at-will employee, and you don't have to give notice in advance or afford the employee a chance to improve. (See Chapter 1, Section A3.) However, an employee who is fired may claim, for example, that the firing was based on illegal discrimination (see Chapter 8), so it's not wise to rely solely on your legal right to fire an employee.

You want to stand ready to rebut any possible claim that you fired an employee for an illegal reason such as discrimination based on race or sex. The best way to do this is to preserve, in written evaluations and other documents, the good reasons you relied on to fire the employee.

Sample Employee Handbook Acknowledgment

Welcome to XYZ Company. We hope that you will have a long and productive relationship with our company. To help with this, we are providing you with your own copy of our employee handbook. Please read this handbook carefully. The information in it will acquaint you with company policies and will answer many of your questions.

Please keep in mind that this handbook does not contain all of the information you will need as an employee. You will receive other information through written notices as well as orally. When the company changes a policy, it overrides the past policy.

This handbook is not an employment contract. Unless you have a written employment contract with XYZ Company signed by the president of the company, you legally are an at-will employee. This means you or the company may terminate our employment relationship at any time, with or without a reason.

In the future, your status as an at-will employee can only be changed through a written contract signed by both you and the president of XYZ Company. No oral statements, promises or contracts regarding the terms and conditions of your employment are valid.

Receipt and Acknowledgment

I have received a copy of XYZ Company's Employee Handbook. I have read the above information and I acknowledge that it is a correct statement of my employment status. I understand that this employee handbook is not a contract for employment and does not affect my employment status in any way.

_____
Signature

_____
Date

EXAMPLE: Charlotte works at the counter of Parts Plus, a retailer of auto parts. Parts Plus fires Charlotte after she's been there for 18 months. Charlotte sues, claiming that Parts Plus fired her in retaliation for complaining to a state agency about photos of nude women that were posted in the back room where she had to go to retrieve auto parts for customers. At trial, Parts Plus produces copies of written evaluations from Charlotte's file.

Eight months before the firing, Charlotte's supervisor had written: "You must become more familiar with our inventory of parts for imported cars. Also, you need to make fewer errors on the computer system."

Two months before the firing, the supervisor had written: "You're still having problems with imports. We will arrange for you to attend a computer training seminar at the community college at company expense, but you must improve your performance."

Company records separately show that Charlotte attended only one of the six training sessions and that two days before the firing, she mixed up orders for three good customers. The upshot: Because of its thorough documentation of Charlotte's ongoing problems, the judge dismisses Charlotte's case against Parts Plus.

Evaluations have two common purposes—to help employees improve their performances and to protect employers from false claims by former employees. To achieve both ends, thoroughly and objectively evaluate each employee at least twice a year—and more often if an employee is experiencing serious problems. Take the evaluation process seriously and do a careful, conscientious job. In some states, employees have successfully sued employers who used poor evaluation procedures for "negligent evaluation"—failing to review employees' work fully and honestly and to warn employees that they faced discipline or discharge if they failed to improve.

2. The Evaluation Process

To keep the evaluation process as consistent and objective as possible, devise an evaluation form that you can use with all employees in the same job category. (See Section C3, below, for a sample.) The form should focus on how well the employee has performed the various duties of the job.

Fill in the form before you meet with the employee, following these guidelines:

- Give a balanced picture of the employee's strengths and weaknesses.
- Use specific examples of where the employee has met, exceeded or fallen short of expectations.
- Let the employee know the areas in which he or she must improve. Set objective goals for the employee to meet.
- Where an employee's performance is substantially below par, set a date to meet again with the employee to review his or her progress.
- If the employee's failure to improve may lead to disciplinary measures or discharge, state this clearly in the evaluation.

Leave space on the form for the employee to comment on the evaluation and to acknowledge receiving a copy of it.

Once you've completed the written evaluation, meet with the employee to go over it. If you cringe at confronting an employee with criticism, try the sandwich approach: say something positive, something negative, then something positive.

Remember, too, that employees will find it easier to accept criticism—and try to improve their behavior—if you focus on workplace performance and not on the employee's personality. The overall tone of the evaluation should, of course, be as positive as possible; you want the employee to feel motivated rather than resentful.

Whatever your approach, you must tell it like it is. Should you later have legal trouble initiated by a fired employee, a judge or jury won't look at your evaluations in a vacuum. For example, they'll sense that something is wrong if you consistently rate a worker's performance as poor or mediocre—but continue to hand out generous raises or perhaps even promote the person. The logical conclusion: You didn't take seriously the criticisms in your evaluation report, so you shouldn't expect the employee to take them seriously, either.

Just as damaging is to give an employee glowing praise in report after report—perhaps to make the employee feel good—and then to fire the employee for a single infraction. That strikes most people as unfair. And unfair employers often lose court fights, especially in situations where a sympathetic employee appears to have been treated harshly.

If your system is working, employees with excellent evaluations should not need to be fired for poor performance. And employees with poor performance shouldn't be getting big raises.

Once Is Not Enough. Feedback should be an ongoing process. The written evaluation should be a culmination of the feedback you've given throughout the year. Your goal is to have no surprises about how an employee is doing. It's perfectly appropriate, too, to give an employee a written warning between evaluations if the employee is in jeopardy of being disciplined or fired. A copy, of course, should go in the employee's file.

Some employers encourage employees to give their own evaluation of how they're doing—and may also ask employees to rate their supervisors. You'll benefit by making the evaluation process a two-way street. Listen carefully to what the employees say. You'll likely learn a thing or two.

For an in-depth discussion of employee evaluations, including step-by-step instructions and sample forms, see *Dealing With Problem Employees: A Legal Guide,* by attorneys Amy DelPo and Lisa Guerin (Nolo).

3. Sample Employee Evaluation Form

The following form can be adapted to your needs—to meet your personal style, the setup of your workplace and the type of work you do.

2/20   THE EMPLOYER'S LEGAL HANDBOOK

CONFIDENTIAL
Employee Performance Evaluation

Employee name _____

Job title _____

Reviewer _____

Review date _____

JOB PERFORMANCE
(In responding, give specific examples of strengths and weaknesses as often as possible.)

General Quality of Work
(Focus on accuracy, attention to detail, originality, timeliness, organization, degree of supervision needed to accomplish tasks)

_____

_____

Dependability
(Focus on attendance, punctuality, attentiveness, ability to follow instructions, ability to meet deadlines)

_____

_____

Job Knowledge
(Focus on level of knowledge and skills required to master work required, willingness to take the initiative in tackling new tasks)

_____

_____

Personality
(Focus on cooperativeness, decision-making skills, ability to work for and with others, ability to handle confrontations)

_____

_____

Communication Skills
(Focus on ability to use language effectively, ability to express ideas clearly and grammatically, command of oral and written language, ability to explain concepts to others)

Management Ability
(Focus on ability to identify problems, ability to creatively solve problems, ability to plan, assign and schedule workload, ability to guide an individual or group to complete a task)

Other Job Requirements
(Focus on specific needs of business or needs for individual improvement: public contact, self-development, quality control, ability to stay within cost guidelines)

PERFORMANCE SUMMARY
What are the employee's outstanding and strongest points?

What are the employee's shortcomings and weaknesses?

Specific accomplishments and changes since last performance review.

GOALS FOR IMPROVEMENT
What can the employee do to be more effective or make needed improvements?

What additional training or equipment would be helpful?

In what ways could your job be changed to make better use of your skills and abilities?

_____

EMPLOYEE FEEDBACK
(To be completed by the employee.)
What are your most important accomplishments on the job over the past year?

_____

What are your weakest job performance areas, or those most in need of improvement?

_____

What steps could you take to improve?

_____

What can management do to support your efforts to improve?

_____

What are your supervisor's strengths and weaknesses in managing your work?

_____

Other work concerns you would like to discuss.

_____

_____

NEXT REVIEW
Date scheduled for next review _____
Particular areas targeted for improvement:

_____

_____

Employee Signature _____

Date _____

Supervisor's Signature _____

Date _____

D. Disciplining Employees

Periodic evaluations can work hand in hand with another management strategy—progressive discipline—to keep employees fairly informed of how they're doing and when their jobs are at risk.

Since losing a job can obviously be painful for an employee, some employers make it a practice to fire problem employees only after the workers have gone through a series of less drastic disciplinary moves. A system of progressive discipline may not be right for all businesses—particularly smaller ones. But if you do see fit to have such a policy in place, it can go a long way toward demonstrating your fairness if you eventually have to fire an employee and the employee sues you.

Among the steps you can build into your program are: verbal warnings, written warnings, counseling, probation, suspension and, finally, dismissal. A fired employee's potential wrongful termination claim will be weakened if you can show that the employee knew about the problems that eventually led to dismissal, but he or she muffed repeated opportunities to shape up.

If you follow this approach and generally practice a policy of progressive discipline, make it clear to employees that you reserve the right to fire employees at will—especially for serious infractions—and that your policy of progressive discipline is left to your discretion as an employer. (See below for an example of language to include in a disciplinary policy.)

Having a policy of progressive discipline can backfire if you create the impression that every employee transgression will be dealt with in that same way. A fired employee, for example, may claim that he or she had a right to be progressively disciplined before being fired.

Obviously, there are times when you may conclude that an employee's conduct is so offensive that decisive action—including immediate discharge—is warranted. To keep an enlightened management policy from turning into a fixed employee right, make it clear that you have the option to dispense with progressive discipline, depending on the situation. (See the sample policy below for guidance.)

 For an in-depth discussion of progressive discipline, including step-by-step instructions and a sample written policy, see *Dealing With Problem Employees: A Legal Guide,* by attorneys Amy DelPo and Lisa Guerin (Nolo).

The Right to Have a Co-Worker Present. All employees have the right to have a co-worker present with them at investigatory interviews or meetings that the employee believes will result in disciplinary action from their employer. This right is called a Weingarten right after a U.S. Supreme Court decision. (To read that decision—*NLRB v. J. Weingarten*, 420 U.S. 251 (1975)—go to Nolo's Legal Research Center at www.nolo.com.) That decision only gave the right to employees who were members of a union. In 2000, however, that right was expanded to non-union employees as well.

Although no court has held that employers have an affirmative duty to inform employees of this right, it's prudent to do so—and to allow the employee to have a witness by his or her side in disciplinary meetings.

Sample Written Progressive Discipline Policy

The following is a sample written progressive discipline policy that you can include in your handbook. But remember, if you do include it in your handbook, you have to follow it.

Any employee conduct that, in the opinion of XYZ Company, interferes with or adversely affects our business is sufficient grounds for disciplinary action. This action can range from oral warnings to immediate discharge. Depending on the conduct, it is our general policy to take disciplinary steps in the following order:

- verbal warnings
- written warnings
- suspension, and
- termination.

To decide on the appropriate action, we may consider: the seriousness of your conduct, your employment record, your ability to correct the conduct, actions we have taken for similar conduct by other employees, how your action affects customers and other circumstances.

Some conduct may result in immediate dismissal. Here are examples:

- acting violently or threatening to do so
- theft of company property
- excessive tardiness or absenteeism
- arguing or fighting with customers or co-workers
- using or possessing alcohol or illegal drugs at work
- coming to work under the influence of alcohol or illegal drugs
- failing to carry out reasonable job assignments
- making false statements in a job application
- violating company rules and regulations, and
- unlawful discrimination or harassment.

These are only examples. You may terminate your employment at any time; the company reserves the same right.

Chapter 3

Wages and Hours

A. The Fair Labor Standards Act 3/3

    1. Covered Businesses 3/3

    2. Exempt Employees 3/5

B. Pay Requirements 3/9

    1. Minimum Wage 3/9

    2. Equal Pay for Equal Work 3/15

    3. Paying Overtime 3/16

    4. Compensatory Time 3/19

C. Calculating Pay 3/20

    1. Forms of Pay 3/21

    2. Time Off 3/22

D. Calculating Workhours 3/22

    1. Travel Time 3/22

    2. On-Call Periods 3/23

    3. Sleep Time 3/23

    4. Lectures, Meetings and Training Seminars 3/24

    5. Meal and Rest Breaks 3/24

E. Keeping Records 3/29

F. Child Labor 3/29

    1. Agricultural Jobs 3/30

    2. Nonagricultural Jobs 3/31

G. Payroll Withholding 3/31

    1. Meals, Housing and Transportation 3/31

    2. Debts Owed to an Employer... 3/32

    3. Debts and Wage Garnishments 3/32

    4. Child Support 3/33

    5. Back Taxes 3/33

A slew of statutes—federal and state —regulate workplace wages and hours, imposing strict requirements on employers. These laws require, for example, that you:

- pay an employee at least the minimum hourly wage unless he or she is exempt from wage-and-hour statutes (see Sections B1 and A2)
- pay a premium rate for overtime work (see Section B3)
- pay for all the time an employee works (see Section D)
- pay men and women equally for doing the same work (see Section B2)
- follow special rules if you employ young workers (see Section F), and
- observe legal limits on payroll deductions (see Section G).

For the most part, complying with wage-and-hour laws is simple and routine: You calculate wages using easy-to-understand formulas, and you retain time and payment records for employees. There are, however, some legal subtleties that can affect your ability to carry out your aims. So in addition to discussing the wage-and-hour basics, this chapter covers potential problem areas.

Check State Laws, Too. This chapter focuses primarily on the federal wage-and-hour laws. Always keep in mind that you may also be covered by a state law, which may be more stringent than the federal law. In that case, you must comply with the more stringent state law requirements. For details, consult your state labor department. (See the Appendix for contact information.)

A. The Fair Labor Standards Act

The main federal law affecting workers' pay is the Fair Labor Standards Act or FLSA (29 U.S.C. §§ 201 and following) which Congress passed in 1938. We explain that law below. Don't forget, however, that your state may also have a wage and hour law that you have to follow. Contact your state labor department for more information (see Appendix for contact details).

1. Covered Businesses

Your business is covered by the FLSA if you have $500,000 or more in total annual sales. If your business earns less than $500,000 in sales, individual employees may come under the FLSA if their work involves interstate commerce. This includes almost every employee, because courts have interpreted the term "interstate commerce" broadly. An employee of a smaller business is covered by the FLSA if, for example, he or she:

- sends mail to or receives mail from other states
- makes phone calls to or receives them from other states
- keeps records of interstate transactions
- handles goods moving in interstate commerce
- crosses state lines as part of the job, or
- does clerical, custodial or maintenance work for a business that is engaged in interstate commerce or makes goods in interstate commerce.

It's possible—but highly unlikely—that your business will fall within a handful of specific exemptions to the FLSA. For example, most small farms are exempt. For specific details on what businesses are exempt, check with the nearest office of the U.S. Labor Department's Wage and Hour Division. (See the Appendix for contact details.)

 If you want to research the exemptions to FLSA coverage, you'll find most of them in 29 U.S.C. § 213. Look in an annotated edition of the United States Code, which is what your local library is most likely to have. You can also access it through Nolo's Legal Research Center at www.nolo.com. The annotated edition contains summaries of court decisions that will help you

understand the courts' rulings about this complex law. In addition, see Title 29 of the Code of Federal Regulations, which goes into great detail on virtually every aspect of the FLSA—but be forewarned that the details can be mind-numbing to the point of incomprehensibility. Fortunately, the Department of Labor operates an excellent, user-friendly website at www.dol.gov. There, you can find easy-to-understand articles and guidelines about various federal labor laws that you must follow, including wage-and-hour laws.

For detailed information on the FLSA, see *Federal Employment Laws: A Desk Reference*, by Amy DelPo & Lisa Guerin (Nolo).

Independent Contractors Aren't Covered

The FLSA covers only employees—not independent contractors. Whether a worker is an employee for purposes of the FLSA generally depends on the economic realities and not on the IRS definition of an independent contractor. Your state's definition of independent contractor also does not apply.

To determine whether a worker has sufficient economic independence to qualify as an independent contractor under the FLSA, consider the following questions:

- Do you have the right to control the work? The more right of control you have, the more the worker looks like an employee.
- Does the worker have an opportunity for profit and loss? If the worker bears the economic risk of doing business, then that's a factor in favor of independent contractor status.

- Does the worker have any investment in equipment and facilities? The greater the investment, the more it appears that the worker is an independent contractor.
- Do the worker's services require special skills? The more specialized the skills, the more likely it is that the worker is an independent contractor.
- How permanent is the relationship between you and the worker? If it's pretty permanent, that's a factor in favor of employee status.
- Are the worker's services an integral part of your business? If so, it's more likely that the worker is an employee.

(See Chapter 11 for a detailed discussion of independent contractors.)

2. Exempt Employees

Even though your business is covered by the FLSA, some employees may be exempt from that law's minimum wage and overtime pay requirements. This is a complex area of law and a source of many misunderstandings. (See Section B3 for employees who are exempt only from overtime provisions.)

Most employees who are exempt from the minimum wage and overtime pay requirements fall into one of five categories:

- executive employees
- administrative employees
- professional employees
- outside salespeople, and
- people in certain computer-related occupations.

There are a few miscellaneous categories of workers who are exempt as well.

a. Executive, administrative and professional employees

Generally, these are employees who are paid a minimum weekly salary as specified by law and who spend at least 80% of the workday performing duties that require a measure of discretion and independent judgment. Beyond that, each category of worker has special qualifiers.

An executive, for example, is someone who manages two or more employees within a business or a department, and who can hire, fire and promote employees. An administrative employee performs specialized or technical work related to management or general business operations. A professional employee performs original and creative work or work requiring advanced knowledge normally acquired through specialized study.

There's a long test and a short test for each category. If an employee meets the short test, he or she is exempt and need not meet the long test.

Workers who earn at least $250 per week (a category that likely includes virtually all exempt workers) must meet the requirements of a "short test"—so named to distinguish it from the "long test" that applies to workers who earn less than $250 per week. The long test for each exemption is harder to satisfy— we give both tests below.

Administrative employees. Regardless which test applies, an administrative employee must either (1) regularly and directly assist the owner of a business or another executive or administrative employee, (2) perform specialized or technical work under only general supervision, or (3) perform special assignments under only general supervision. In addition, the employee must meet one of these tests, depending on the employee's salary:

Short test (for workers who earn at least $250 per week in salary):

1. the employee's primary duty must be either
   a. performing either office or non-manual work directly related to management policies or the general business operations of the employer or its customers, or
   b. duties relating to administration of a school system or educational institution, in work directly related to academic training or instruction, and

2. the employee's primary duties include work requiring the exercise of discretion and independent judgment.

Long test (for employees who earn between $155 and $250 per week in salary):

1. the employee must meet the first requirement of the short test, and
2. the employee must customarily and regularly exercise discretion and independent judgment (this requires more independence than the second requirement of the short test, above), and
3. the employee may not spend more than 20% of working hours (or 40%, for retail or service workers) on activities that are not closely related to the first two requirements of the test.

Executive employees. *Short test* (for employees who earn at least $250 per week in salary):

1. the employee's primary duty is managing an enterprise or one of its subdivisions, and
2. the employee regularly and customarily directs the work of two or more employees within that enterprise or subdivision.

Long test (for employees who earn between $155 and $250 per week in salary):

1. the employee meets both requirements of the short test
2. the employee has hiring and firing authority, or the employee's recommendations on hiring and firing are given particular weight
3. the employee customarily and regularly exercises discretion, and
4. the employee spends no more than 20% of work hours (or 40%, for retail or service employees) on activities that

are not directly and closely related to the factors listed above.

Professional employees. *Short test* (for employees who earn at least $250 per week in salary):

1. the employee's work requires advanced knowledge and education
2. the employee's work requires invention, imagination or talent in a recognized artistic field, or
3. the employee works as a teacher.

Long test (for employees who earn between $170 and $250 per week in salary):

1. the employee meets the above requirements of the short test
2. the employee's work is predominantly intellectual and varied in character (rather than routine mental or manual work), the accomplishment of which cannot be standardized as to time
3. the employee's work requires the consistent exercise of discretion and judgment, and
4. the employee spends no more than 20% of work time on activities that are not an essential part, or necessarily incidental to, the work described above.

The fine points of these exemptions are explained in a free booklet titled *Regulations Part 541: Defining the Terms—Executive, Administrative, Professional and Outside Sales.* It's available from the nearest office of the Wage and Hour Division of the U.S. Department of Labor. For a list of Wage and Hour Division offices by state, consult the Department of Labor's website at www.dol.gov/dol/esa/public/contacts/whd/america2.htm. You can also contact the Department of Labor by phone at 202-693-6450.

The long test requirement that executives and administrators spend at least 80% of the workday in certain activities is reduced to 60% for employees of retail and service establishments. Further, the percentage test doesn't apply at all to an executive who's in charge of an independent business establishment or branch or who owns at least a 20% interest in the business.

Job titles alone don't determine whether someone is an exempt executive, administrative or professional employee. The actual work the employee performs is what counts. Still, it's possible to make some generalizations about who's exempt and who isn't.

Typical Exempt Jobs
Department Head	Personnel Director
Financial Expert	Executive Assistant
Physician	Lawyer
Credit Manager	Safety Director
Account Executive	Tax Specialist

Typical Nonexempt Jobs
Clerk	Bank Teller
Receptionist	Newspaper Reporter
Secretary	Bookkeeper
Inspector	Trainee

Mislabeling Can Be Dangerous. Some employers try to avoid the minimum wage and overtime requirements by labeling all entry level employees Assistant Managers—then requiring them to work well past the 40-hour workweek with no further compensation. The Department of Labor is well aware of such abuses. Employers who mislabel employees to circumvent the law are playing a dangerous game and may wind up paying stiff penalties.

Docking Pay Can Cost You

An employee must be paid a salary to fall under the executive, administrative or professional exemption. The FLSA treats an employee as salaried only if his or her pay isn't reduced because of variations in the quality or quantity of work performed.

If you dock an employee's salary for personal absences of less than a day at a time, the employee may legally be deemed to be an hourly employee—and no longer exempt from the minimum wage and premium overtime requirements. For example, if a salaried employee misses a few hours of work to take care of personal business, don't reduce his or her salary to make up for that time. If you reduce the employee's salary on an hourly basis, the Department of Labor may conclude that employee is really an hourly worker and not eligible for the overtime exemption.

The reasoning is that salaried workers often put in many hours of overtime without getting paid for it, so it's unfair to reduce their pay if they miss a few hours now or then.

Also, don't deduct for absences caused by jury duty, appearances in court as a witness or temporary military leave. For example, if an exempt employee misses two or three days for jury duty but works the rest of the week, you should pay the full salary for that week.

b. Outside salespeople

An outside salesperson is exempt from FLSA coverage if he or she:

- regularly works away from your place of business while making sales or taking orders, and
- spends no more than 20% of worktime doing work other than selling for your business.

Typically, an exempt salesperson will be paid primarily through commissions and will require little or no direct supervision in doing the job.

c. Computer specialists

This exemption applies to computer system analysts, programmers and software engineers who are paid at least $27.63 an hour.

An employee will likely be exempt from the wage-and-hour laws if his or her primary duties consist of such things as determining functional specifications for hardware and software, designing computer systems to meet user specifications and creating or modifying computer programs.

d. Miscellaneous workers

Several other types of workers are exempt from the minimum wage and overtime pay provisions of the FLSA. The most common include:

- employees of seasonal amusement or recreational businesses
- employees of local newspapers having a circulation of less than 4,000

- newspaper delivery workers
- switchboard operators employed by phone companies that have no more than 750 stations, and
- workers on small farms.

The Consequences of Bending the Rules

The Wage and Hour Division of the U.S. Department of Labor enforces the wage-and-hour requirements of the FLSA. Almost always, it is tipped off to investigate a business by an unhappy employee who has complained.

In theory, you can be fined up to $10,000 for violating the FLSA—and even spend time in jail for a second offense, if it's willful. But fines and jail time are used in only the most blatant cases.

More typically, you'll be required to pay the employee all unpaid wages including overtime pay, and you may be slapped with a modest fine or penalty. The real cost comes in the time and expense of being involved in enforcement proceedings—not to mention the damage to workers' morale and the animosity that can be created in the workplace, particularly if several employees claim their rights were violated.

It's illegal to fire or discriminate against an employee for filing a complaint or participating in a legal proceeding under the FLSA. And many states have similar laws prohibiting such retaliation.

e. Apprentices

An apprentice is a worker who's at least 16 years old and who has signed an agreement with you to learn a skilled trade. Apprentices are exempt from the minimum wage and overtime requirements of the FLSA (see Section B1 for apprentice wage requirements). But beware that your state may have a law limiting the number of hours you can hire someone to work as an apprentice. State law may also require you to pay the apprentice a certain percentage of the minimum wage. Check with your state labor department for more information. (See the Appendix for contact details.)

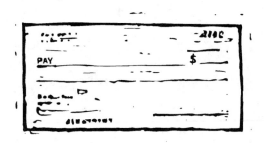

B. Pay Requirements

The FLSA and many state laws set a minimum wage and require premium pay for overtime work. In addition, the FLSA requires that men and women receive equal pay for equal work.

1. Minimum Wage

If your business is covered by the FLSA, you must pay all covered employees at least the minimum wage—currently $5.15 an hour. Federal law allows you to pay a training wage

of $4.25 an hour to employees under 20 years of age during their first 90 days on the job. You're not allowed to fire employees just so you can replace them with young workers and pay them the lower training wage.

The law in your state may set a minimum wage higher than the federal rate. If so, you must pay your workers the higher state rate. In the few states that have a lower minimum, the federal rate controls. Check with your state department of labor for increases that may not be reflected in the chart below. (See the Appendix for contact details.) You can also check the Updates section on Nolo's website at www.nolo.com.

Under the FLSA, you must pay an apprentice a progressively increasing wage that averages at least 50% of the journeyman's rate over the period of the apprenticeship. However, state law may require you to pay apprentices more.

Note that this chart also includes information on state tip credits—rules that may allow you to pay tipped employees less than the minimum wage, as long as they make a certain amount in tips. Tip credits are explained in Section C1.

Additional Laws May Apply. If the chart below indicates that your state has no statute, this means there is no law that specifically addresses the issue. However, there may be a state administrative regulation or local ordinance that does control. For example, an increasing number of cities are enacting so-called living wage ordinances that set a higher hourly wage rate than does the federal law. Call your state labor department for more information. (See the Appendix for contact details.)

State Minimum Wage Laws

"Maximum Tip Credit" means the maximum amount of actual tips that an employer can credit against the employee's hourly wage rate. That is, the employer can subtract the tip credit from the minimum wage, and only pay the employee the difference. Where the tip credit is a percentage, it means that up to that percent of the basic minimum hourly rate may be deducted as a tip credit for tipped employees. In no case may the total amount of employee's wages plus tips equal less than the basic minimum wage rate. If an employee's tips exceed the maximum tip credit, the employee gets to keep the extra amount.

"Minimum Cash Wage" is what the employer must actually pay a tipped employee per hour. It's equal to the regular minimum wage less the tip credit.

Jurisdiction	Citation & Notes	Basic Minimum Hourly Rate (*=Tied to Federal rate)	Maximum Tip Credit (tips only, not food and lodging unless specified)	Minimum Cash Wage for Tipped Employee	Definition of Tipped Employee by Minimum Tips Received (monthly unless otherwise specified)
United States	29 U.S.C. § 206	$5.15	$3.02	$2.13	More than $30
Alabama	No minimum wage law				
Alaska	Alaska Stat. § 23.10.065; 8 AAC 15.120	$5.65* $0.50 above FLSA rate	$0	$5.65	N/A
Arizona	No minimum wage law				
Arkansas	Ark. Code Ann. § 11-4-210 4 or more employees	$5.15	50%	$2.575	Not specified
California	8 Cal. Admin. Code § 11000	$6.75	$0	$6.75	
Colorado	Colo. Rev. Stat. § 8-6-109 Minimum wage applies to these industries: retail and service, commercial support service, food and beverage and health and medical.	$5.15	$3.02	$2.13	More than $30
Connecticut	Conn. Gen. Stat. Ann. § 31-58(j)	$6.70 or 0.5% above FLSA minimum if higher	Generally, $0.35	$6.35	Not specified
	Hotel, restaurant		29.3%	$4.74	At least $10 weekly for full-time employees or $2.00 daily for part-time
	Bartenders		8.2%	$6.15	Not specified
	Beauty shop		none	$6.70	Not specified

State Minimum Wage Laws (continued)

Jurisdiction	Citation & Notes	Basic Minimum Hourly Rate (*=Tied to Federal rate)	Maximum Tip Credit (tips only, not food and lodging unless specified)	Minimum Cash Wage for Tipped Employee	Definition of Tipped Employee by Minimum Tips Received (monthly unless otherwise specified)
Delaware	Del. Code Ann. tit. 19, § 902(a)	$6.15 or FLSA rate if higher	$3.92	$2.23	More than $30
District of Columbia	D.C. Code Ann. § 32-1003(1)	$6.15* $1 above FLSA rate	55%	$2.77	Not specified
Florida	No minimum wage law				
Georgia	Ga. Code Ann. § 34-4-3(a) 6 employees or more and sales of more than $40K per year.	$5.15	Minimum wage does not apply to those who receive tips.	N/A	
Hawaii	Haw. Rev. Stat. § 387-1 to 2	$5.75	$0.25	$5.50	More than $20, and employee's cash wage plus tips must be at least $.50 higher than the minimum wage
		$6.25 as of 2003	$0.25	$6.50	More than $20, and employee's cash wage plus tips must be at least $.50 higher than the minimum wage
Idaho	Idaho Code § 44-1502 For employees under 20 years old, $4.25 for first consecutive 90 days.	$5.15	35%	$3.35	More than $30
Illinois	820 Ill. Comp. Stat. § 105/4 4 or more employees	$5.15*	$2.06	$3.09	$20
Indiana	Ind. Code Ann. § 22-2-2-4 2 or more employees Under the age of 20, minimum wage is $4.25 for first consecutive 90 days.	$5.15	$3.02	$2.13	Not specified
Iowa	Iowa Code § 91D.1	$5.15* (doesn't apply to first 90 calendar days of employment)	40%	$3.09	More than $30

State Minimum Wage Laws (continued)					
Jurisdiction	**Citation & Notes**	**Basic Minimum Hourly Rate** (*=Tied to Federal rate)	**Maximum Tip Credit** (tips only, not food and lodging unless specified)	**Minimum Cash Wage for Tipped Employee**	**Definition of Tipped Employee by Minimum Tips Received** (monthly unless otherwise specified)
Kansas	Kan. Stat. Ann. § 44-1203 Employers not covered by the FLSA	$2.65	40%	$1.59	Not specified
Kentucky	Ky. Rev. Stat. Ann. § 337.275	$5.15*	$3.02	$2.13	More than $30
Louisiana	No minimum wage law				
Maine	Me. Rev. Stat. Ann. tit. 26, § 664	$5.75 or FLSA rate if higher	50%	$2.88	More than $20
		$6.25 in 2003 or FLSA rate if higher	50%	$3.13	More than $20
Maryland	Md. Code Ann., [Lab. & Empl.] § 3-413	$5.15*	$2.77	$2.38	More than $30
Massachusetts	Mass. Gen. Laws ch. 151, § 1	$6.75 or $0.10 above FLSA rate if higher	$4.12	$2.63	More than $20
Michigan	Mich. Comp. Laws § 408.384 2 or more employees Excludes all employers subject to FLSA, unless state minimum wage is higher than federal.	$5.15	$2.50	$2.65	Not specified
Minnesota	Minn. Stat. Ann. § 177.24 Large employer (enterprise with annual receipts of $500,000 or more)	$5.15	None	$5.15	
	Small employer (enterprise with annual receipts of less than $500,000)	$4.90	None	$4.90	
Mississippi	No minimum wage law				
Missouri	Mo. Rev. Stat. § 290.502	$5.15*	Up to 50%	$2.575	
Montana (continued on next page)	Mont. Code Ann. § 39-3-404 Businesses with gross annual sales of more than $110,000	$5.15*	None	$5.15*	

State Minimum Wage Laws (continued)

Jurisdiction	Citation & Notes	Basic Minimum Hourly Rate (*=Tied to Federal rate)	Maximum Tip Credit (tips only, not food and lodging unless specified)	Minimum Cash Wage for Tipped Employee	Definition of Tipped Employee by Minimum Tips Received (monthly unless otherwise specified)
Montana (continued)	Mont. Code Ann. § 39-3-409 Businesses with gross annual sales of $110,000 or less	$4.00	None	$4.00	
Nebraska	Neb. Rev. Stat. § 48-1203 4 or more employees	$5.15	$3.02	$2.13	Not specified
Nevada	Nev. Rev. Stat. Ann. § 608.250	$5.15*	None	$5.15	
New Hampshire	N.H. Rev. Stat. Ann. § 279:21	$5.15*	$2.57	$2.38	More than $20
New Jersey	N.J. Stat. Ann. §§ 34:11-56a4; 34:11-57 Rules may vary depending on occupation.	$5.15*	$2.13	$3.02	Not specified
New Mexico	N.M. Stat. Ann. § 50-4-22	$4.25.	$2.125	$2.125	More than $30
New York	N.Y. Lab. Law § 652	$5.15*	Tip credit varies from $.80 to $2.05, depending on occupation.		Not specified
North Carolina	N.C. Gen. Stat. § 95-25.3	$5.15*	$3.02	$2.13	More than $20
North Dakota	N.D. Cent. Code § 34-06-03	$5.15	33%	$3.45	More than $30
Ohio	Ohio Rev. Code Ann. § 4111.02 Employers with gross annual sales over $500K	$4.25 $2.80	50%	$2.125	More than $30
	Employers with gross annual sales from $150K to $500K	$3.35	50%		More than $30
	Employers with gross annual sales less than $150K	$2.80	50%		More than $30
Oklahoma (continued on next page)	Okla. Stat. Ann. tit. 40, § 197.2 10 or more full time employees OR gross annual sales more than $100K	$5.15*	50% For tips, food and lodging combined.	$2.58	Not specified

			State Minimum Wage Laws (continued)		
Jurisdiction	Citation & Notes	Basic Minimum Hourly Rate (*=Tied to Federal rate)	Maximum Tip Credit (tips only, not food and lodging unless specified)	Minimum Cash Wage for Tipped Employee	Definition of Tipped Employee by Minimum Tips Received (monthly unless otherwise specified)
Oklahoma (continued)	All other employers who are not subject to the FLSA	$2.00			Not specified
Oregon	Or. Rev. Stat. § 653.025	$6.50	None	$6.50	
Pennsylvania	43 Pa. Cons. Stat. Ann. § 333.104	$5.15*	$2.32	$2.83	More than $30
Rhode Island	R.I. Gen. Laws § 28-12-3	$6.15	$3.26	$2.89	Not specified
South Carolina	No minimum wage law				
South Dakota	S.D. Codified Laws Ann. § 60-11-3 to 3.1	$5.15	$3.02	$2.13	More than $35
Tennessee	No minimum wage law				
Texas	Tex. Lab. Code Ann. § 62.051 Employers not covered by FLSA	$5.15*	$3.02	$2.13	More than $20
Utah	Utah Code Ann. § 34-40-103 Those not covered by the FLSA	$5.15*	$3.02	$2.13	More than $30
Vermont	Vt. Stat. Ann. tit. 21, § 384(a) 2 or more employees	$6.25 or FLSA rate if higher	45%	$3.44	More than $30
Virginia	Va. Code Ann. § 40.1-28.10 4 or more employees	5.15*	Actual amount received		Not specified
Washington	Wash. Rev. Code Ann. § 49.46.020 Adjusted annually for inflation	$6.90 in 2002	None	$6.90	
West Virginia	W.Va. Code § 21-5C-2a 6 or more employees at one location Only employers who are not covered by the FLSA	$5.15	20%	$4.12	Not specified
Wisconsin	Wis. Stat. Ann. § 104.02	$5.15	$2.42	$2.33	Not specified
Wyoming	Wyo. Stat. § 27-4-202	$5.15	$3.02	$2.13	More than $30

Current as of May 2002

Poster Requirements

Federal law requires you to display the Federal Minimum Wage poster prominently in the workplace. It's available at the nearest office of the U.S. Department of Labor's Wage and Hour Division. You can also download this poster from the Department of Labor's website at www.dol.gov. Your state labor department may also be able to provide this poster as well as any poster that may be required by state law. (See the Appendix for contact details.)

2. Equal Pay for Equal Work

You must provide equal pay and benefits to men and women who do the same work or work that requires equal skill, effort and responsibility. This is required by the Equal Pay Act—an amendment to the FLSA (29 U.S.C. § 206). Many states have a similar law mandating equal pay between men and women. Job titles aren't decisive in assessing whether two jobs are equal; the work duties are what count. The Equal Pay Act makes it unlawful, for example, for the owner of a hotel to pay its janitors (primarily men) at a different pay rate than its housekeepers (primarily women) if both are doing essentially the same work.

The Equal Pay Act is enforced by the U.S. Equal Employment Opportunities Commission or EEOC. (See Chapter 8, Section A, for a discussion of EEOC enforcement procedures.) If your state has an equal pay law, it will be enforced by your state labor department. (See Appendix for contact details.)

a. Employees covered

The Equal Pay Act applies to all employees covered by the minimum wage and overtime pay provisions of the FLSA. (See Sections A1 and A2.) In addition, the Equal Pay Act applies to executive, administrative and professional employees—even though these employees are exempt from the minimum wage and overtime provisions.

The Equal Pay Act doesn't prohibit pay differences based on:

- a seniority system
- a merit system
- a system that pays a worker based on the quantity or quality of what he or she produces, or
- any factor other than the worker's gender—starting salaries, for example, that are based on a worker's experience level.

EXAMPLE: The Ace Tool and Die Company was founded in 1960. The company initially hired 50 male tool and die makers. Many of those men are still working there. Since 1980, the company has expanded and hired 50 more tool and die makers, half of them male and half female. All of the tool and die makers at Ace are doing equal work, but because the company awards raises systematically based on the length of a worker's employment there, many of the older male workers earn substantially more per hour than their female co-workers who are doing equal work. The pay system at Ace Tool and Die doesn't violate the Equal Pay Act because the pay differences between genders are based on a bona fide seniority system.

b. Determining job equality

Jobs don't have to be identical for the courts to consider them equal. In general, two jobs are equal for the purposes of the Equal Pay Act when both require the same levels of skill, effort and responsibility—and are performed under similar conditions.

There's room for interpretation, but if there are only small differences in the jobs, they should be regarded as equal.

> **EXAMPLE:** At a ceramics company, the major difference between the jobs performed by women and men is a weight-lifting restriction—men are required to lift heavier items than women. The women and men are performing equal work because heavy lifting is only a small part of the job. (*Schultz v. Saxonburg Ceramics Inc.*, 314 F. Supp. 1139 (W.D. Pa., 1970).)

For detailed information on the Equal Pay Act, see *Federal Employment Laws: A Desk Reference*, by Amy DelPo & Lisa Guerin (Nolo).

3. Paying Overtime

The FLSA requires you to pay nonexempt workers at least one and one-half times their regular rates of pay for all hours worked in excess of 40 in one week. In 1938, when the FLSA was enacted, the nation was just recovering from the Depression. Congress believed that imposing an overtime penalty on employers would induce shorter working hours and help the nation solve its economic problems by spreading work around. The premium overtime rule may have outlived its original purpose—but the law is still on the books, creating headaches for employers.

The FLSA doesn't require you to pay an employee at an overtime rate simply because he or she worked more than eight hours in one day. Generally, the FLSA mandates that you calculate and pay overtime by the week. The workweek may begin on any day of the week and any hour that you, the employer, establish. Generally, in applying the minimum wage and overtime pay rules, each workweek stands alone; you can't average two or more workweeks. And you can't manipulate the start of the workweek merely to avoid paying overtime.

State Law May Be More Stringent. Your state may have a different rule on overtime pay than the FLSA. Alaska and California, for example, require employers to pay overtime to employees who work more than eight hours in a day. Remember, when there is a conflict between state and federal law, you must comply with the more stringent requirement. To find out the details of your state law, consult your state labor department. (See the Appendix for contact information.)

 For a full description of federal overtime rules, see the publication *Overtime Compensation under the Fair Labor Standards Act,* available at no charge at the nearest office of the U.S. Department of Labor's Wage and Hour Division. (See the Appendix for contact details.)

a. Exempt employees

The employees described in Section A2 are exempt from the overtime pay requirements of the FLSA. In addition, a number of other employees are exempt.

Transportation workers. Taxicab drivers are exempt from the overtime pay requirements of the FLSA. Drivers and other employees of trucking companies are not covered by the FLSA but are subject to the Interstate Commerce Act, which is administered by the Department of Transportation.

Certain commissioned employees of retail or service establishments. An employee of a retail or service establishment will be exempt from the overtime pay requirements of the FLSA if:

- the employee's regular rate of pay is more than one and one-half times the minimum wage, and
- more than half the employee's pay comes from commissions.

Vehicle salespeople and mechanics. The FLSA exempts from its overtime pay requirements employees who sell cars, trucks, trailers, farm implements, boats or aircraft. Also exempt

are parts clerks and mechanics who service cars, trucks or farm implements, if they're working for a nonmanufacturing business that sells these items.

Newspeople. Announcers, news editors and chief engineers of certain small radio and TV stations are exempt from the overtime pay requirements.

Employees of motion picture theaters. Employees of movie theaters need not be paid for overtime work at the premium rate.

Farmworkers. Farmworkers need not be paid for overtime work at the premium rate.

b. Partially exempt employees

Special overtime rules apply to some employees.

Employees of hospitals and residential care facilities. Those who have agreements for a 14-day work period must receive overtime premium pay for all hours over eight hours a day or 80 hours in the 14-day work period—whichever amounts to more.

Training time. Employees who lack a high school diploma or who haven't finished eighth grade can be required to spend up to ten hours a week in reading and basic skills programs. These employees must receive their regular wages for time spent in training, but these hours don't count toward the 40-hour-per-week threshold for overtime.

c. Computing overtime pay

The U.S. Department of Labor's Wage and Hours Division offers these guidelines on how to compute overtime pay:

Hourly rate. If an employee works more than 40 hours during a week, you must pay at least one and one-half times the regular hourly rate for each hour over 40.

> **EXAMPLE:** An employee whose regular rate is $6 an hour works 44 hours in a workweek. You must pay the employee at least $9 for each hour over 40. Pay for the week would be $240 ($6 x 40 hours) for the first 40 hours, plus $36 for the four hours of overtime—a total of $276.

Piece rate. To obtain the regular pay rate for an employee who is paid on a piecework basis, divide the total weekly earnings by the total number of hours worked that week. You must pay the employee the full piecework earnings, plus an additional one-half times this regular rate for each hour over 40 that he or she works.

> **EXAMPLE:** An employee paid on a piecework basis works 45 hours in a week and earns $315. The regular rate of pay for that week is $315 divided by 45, or $7 an hour. In addition to the straight time pay, you must pay the employee $3.50 (half the regular rate) for each hour over 40, or $17.50.

Another way to pay pieceworkers for overtime is to pay one and one-half times the piece rate for each piece produced during the overtime hours. However, you and the employee must agree to this payment arrangement in advance. The piece rate you pay for the first 40 hours must always be enough to give the employee at least the minimum wage for each hour of the regular work week.

Salary. To obtain the regular rate of pay for an employee paid a salary for a regular or specified number of hours a week, divide the salary by the number of hours for which the salary is intended as compensation. You and the employee may have agreed to a salary that meets the minimum wage requirement that you pay for whatever number of hours are worked each week. Here, to obtain the regular rate, divide the salary by the number of hours worked. Both the regular rate and the overtime rate will vary, depending on how many hours are worked each week.

> **EXAMPLE:** You've agreed to pay an employee a salary of $300 a week. If the employee works 50 hours, the regular rate is $6 ($300 divided by 50 hours). So in addition to the salary, you must pay $3 (half the regular rate) for each of the ten overtime hours—a total of $330 for the week. If the employee works 60 hours, the regular rate will be $5 ($300 divided by 60 hours). In that case, you'll owe an additional $2.50 for each of the 20 overtime hours—a total of $350 for the week.

In no case can the regular rate be less than the minimum wage required by the FLSA.

If a salary isn't paid weekly, you must determine the weekly pay to compute the regular rate and overtime. If, for example, the salary is paid twice a month, multiply by 24 and then divide by 52 weeks to get the weekly equivalent.

Attitudes on Overtime Are Changing

In the recent past, most workers loved overtime work. It represented an opportunity to get ahead financially—maybe a chance to buy a boat or start a college fund for the kids.

Many workers still feel that way, but others don't feel driven to amass as much money as possible from their work. Those who aren't thrilled by overtime work may have family responsibilities or may simply place a high value on their private time.

The law allows you to schedule overtime for workers, but it may be a more sound management practice to give them some choice in the matter. Otherwise, the workers who don't relish overtime work may feel abused and will drag down morale in the workplace. If you anticipate that you'll be requiring overtime work for certain positions, put that fact in the job description so workers are aware of that likelihood right from the start. Applicants who abhor overtime work can decide to seek work elsewhere.

4. Compensatory Time

The practice of granting hour-for-hour compensatory time—for example, giving a worker six hours time off one week as compensation for six hours of overtime worked the previous week—isn't usually allowed for private sector employees covered by the FLSA. The rule is different for public employees. Employers and employees are often puzzled when they learn that comp time isn't permitted in the private sector, because it seems like a sensible and mutually beneficial way to handle overtime in many situations.

You do, however, have a few options for avoiding premium overtime pay by giving a worker time off instead of money. One way is to rearrange an employee's work schedule during a workweek.

> **EXAMPLE:** Susan, a paralegal at the law firm of Smith and Jones, normally works an eight-hour day, Monday through Friday. One week, Susan and the lawyers need to meet a deadline on a brief due in the court of appeals. So that week, Susan works ten hours a day, Monday through Thursday. The law firm gives Susan Friday off and pays her for a 40-hour week at her regular rate of pay. This is legal because Susan hasn't worked any overtime as defined by the FLSA; only the hours over 40 hours a week count as overtime hours.

If an employee works more than 40 hours in one week, it's sometimes possible to reduce the worker's hours in another week so that the amount of the employee's paycheck remains constant. This is legal if:

- the time off is given within the same pay period as the overtime work, and
- the employee is given an hour and one-half of time off for each hour of overtime worked.

> **EXAMPLE:** Frames and Things, a shop that specializes in framing paintings, employs Jared and pays him $560 at the close of each two-week pay period. Because a

week-long street art fair is expected to generate a great demand for framing services, the shop's owner wants Jared to work longer hours that week. However, the owner doesn't want to increase Jared's paycheck. She asks Jared to work 50 hours during art fair week and gives him 15 hours off the next week. Since Jared is paid every two weeks, Frames and Things may properly reduce Jared's hours the second week to keep his paycheck at the $560 level.

State regulations may further restrict the use of comp time. For example, some states require employers to pay overtime when an employee works more than eight hours in a day. In those states, the strategies discussed above won't work. Contact your state's labor department for more information. (See the Appendix for contact details.)

⚠ **Private Deals Can Be Risky.** It's unlikely that a federal or state labor investigator will look into your comp time arrangements unless an employee files a complaint. Knowing this, you may be tempted to work out comp time deals with employees to meet your needs and theirs. This can be dangerous. You never know when a friendly, loyal employee may turn sour and look for some legal technicalities to use against you.

💡 **Relief May Be on the Way.** Because employers and employees alike feel that the current rules on comp time are too rigid, Congress is working on changes. One plan being considered would allow you to offer employees a choice between receiving overtime pay or one and one-half hours of comp time for each hour of overtime worked.

State Pay Interval Laws

In addition to the wage-and-hour laws that many states have adopted (such as minimum wage laws shown in the chart in Section B1), some states have pay interval laws specifying how often employees must be paid. The FLSA requires only that the pay period be one month or less. State laws often require shorter pay periods—such as every two weeks. If you have a question about pay periods, call your state's labor department. (See the Appendix for contact details.)

C. Calculating Pay

The FLSA doesn't mandate any specific system of paying employees. You can pay them based on time at work, piece rates or some other measure. But in all cases, an employee's pay divided by the hours worked during the pay period must equal or exceed the minimum wage.

EXAMPLE: Sam, a clerk-typist for Dr. Martinez, works part-time. Dr. Martinez pays Sam $7 an hour for each hour that he works.

EXAMPLE: Emily is a parts department employee at Import Autos Inc., a car dealership. Import Autos pays Emily $250 a week for 40 hours of work. Even though Emily's wages are based on a week of work, her hourly rate is $6.25 per hour ($250 divided by 40).

EXAMPLE: Arturo, a roofing worker, is employed by Home Contractors Ltd. Home Contractors pays Arturo $3 for each bundle of shingles he installs. He never installs less than 100 bundles in any 40-hour week. His pay rate is $7.50 per hour (100 bundles x $3 each, divided by 40).

1. Forms of Pay

Under the FLSA, you must pay employees in cash or something that can be readily converted into cash—a check, for example, or other legal forms of compensation (such as food and lodging). Coupons, tokens or "scrip" that can only be spent at your store do not count as wages. And if you grant discounts to employees, you can't count these discounts toward the minimum wage requirement.

a. Tips

When an employee routinely earns at least $30 a month in tips, the federal law allows you to pay the employee as little as $2.13 an hour, as long as that amount plus the tips the employee actually earns bring the employee's hourly earnings to the current minimum wage

level. If it doesn't, you must pay the employee enough so that the hourly rate plus tips equals at least the minimum wage.

EXAMPLE: Alphonse is a waiter at Chez Nous, where he averages $10 an hour in tips. Chez Nous need only pay Alphonse $2.13 an hour because when his tips are added to that hourly rate, his total pay exceeds the minimum wage rate.

Many states have their own tip credit requirements. See the chart in Section B1 for details.

b. Commissions

Commissions that you pay people for sales may take the place of wages for purposes of the FLSA. However, if the commissions divided by hours worked don't equal the minimum wage, you must make up the difference.

EXAMPLE: Julia is a salesperson at Electronics Plus. She's paid a percentage of the dollar volume of the sales she completes. During one slow week, she averaged only $2 in commissions per hour. Under the FLSA, Electronics Plus must pay Julia an additional $3.15 for each hour she worked through the first 40 hours of that week; that will bring her total pay up to the minimum wage level of $5.15 an hour.

2. Time Off

The FLSA doesn't require you to pay employees for time off, such as vacation, holidays or sick days. It may be standard practice for you to pay employees for such time spent away from work, but the FLSA only covers payment for time on the job.

Some state laws require paid time off for jury duty and voting. In addition, laws in some states require you to give employees time off for National Guard or other military duty—and a set time off to attend a child's school conferences. Most state laws provide that you can't fire or discriminate against an employee for taking such time off. Contact your state labor department for more information (see Appendix for contact details).

Don't Ignore Your Promises or Practices. If you promise paid vacations, holidays or sick days in an employee handbook or other written policy, or if you customarily grant such paid time off, you may be legally bound to give those benefits to all employees, regardless of whether your state law requires it.

D. Calculating Workhours

The Portal-to-Portal Pay Act (29 U.S.C. § 251), requires you to pay non-exempt employees for any of their time that you control and that benefits you. In general, time on the job doesn't include the time employees spend washing up or changing clothes before or after work, nor does it include meal periods when employees are free from all work duties.

It's OK to round off records of worktime to the nearest five-minute mark on the clock—but not if it results in paying workers for less time than they actually worked. In other words, you can only round up.

1. Travel Time

You needn't pay employees for the time they spend commuting between their homes and the normal job site; that's not considered on-the-job time. But you do have to pay for commuting time which is actually part of the job.

If you run a plumbing repair service, for example, and require workers to stop by your shop to pick up orders, tools and supplies before going out on calls, their workday begins when they check in at your shop.

Otherwise, just about the only situation in which you must pay workers for commuting time is when they're required to go back and forth from the normal worksite at odd hours in emergency situations.

EXAMPLE: Neil normally works 9 to 5 as a computer technician at Arbor City Computer and is paid hourly. One day, about two hours after Neil gets home, his supervisor calls him to say that some computer equipment is malfunctioning and preventing the late shift of employees from doing their work—and asks him to go back to the office immediately to help correct the problem. It takes him half an hour to get there, two hours to fix the problem and half an hour to drive home again. Arbor City must pay Neil for three extra hours—two workhours plus the extra hour of commuting time required by the company's emergency.

2. On-Call Periods

You must count as payable time any periods when employees are not actually working, but are required to stay on your premises while waiting for a work assignment. If you require employees to be on call but you don't make them stay on your premises, then these two rules generally apply.

- You don't count as payable time the on-call time that employees can control and use for their own enjoyment or benefit.
- You do count as payable time the on-call time over which employees have little or no control and which they can't use for their own enjoyment or benefit.

EXAMPLE: Medi-Transit operates a non-emergency ambulance service that transports patients from hospitals to nursing homes. The company hires Ryan to drive an ambulance from 8 to 5, Monday through Friday, and also requires him to carry a beeper one night a week so he can handle an occasional assignment after normal working hours. Since Ryan is free to pursue personal and social activities during nonworking hours, Medi-Transit doesn't have to pay him for his on-call time.

Unless there's an employment contract that states otherwise, you can generally pay a different hourly rate for on-call time than you do for regular worktime. But keep in mind that you must pay employees at least the minimum wage for each hour worked.

3. Sleep Time

If you require an employee to be on duty at the worksite for less than 24 hours at a time, you generally must count as payable any time during which the employee is allowed to sleep in a shift of duty.

Similarly, if you require an employee to be at work for 24 hours or more, you also generally must count sleep time as payable worktime. But there's a way around this: You and the employee may agree to exclude up to eight hours per day from payable time as sleep and meal periods. However, if conditions are such that the employee can't get at least five hours of sleep during the eight-hour sleep-and-eat period, or if the employee ends up working during that period, then those eight hours revert to being payable time.

4. Lectures, Meetings and Training Seminars

Generally, if you want a nonexempt employee to attend a lecture, meeting or training seminar, you'll have to pay for that employee's time—including travel time if the meeting is away from the worksite.

About the only situation in which you don't have to pay for the employee's time is if:

- the employee attends the event outside of his or her regular working hours
- attendance is voluntary
- the instruction session isn't directly related to the employee's job, and

- the employee doesn't perform any productive work during the instruction session.

5. Meal and Rest Breaks

Under the FLSA, you don't have to pay a covered employee for time spent on an actual meal period. But the key is that the employee must be completely relieved from work during that period so that he or she can enjoy a regularly scheduled meal. If, for example, you require an employee to remain at his or her desk during the meal period or to keep an eye on machinery, you must pay for the meal time.

Similarly, you don't have to pay for rest periods or coffee breaks if the employee is truly free from job duties. If an employee must listen for the phone or watch for merchandise deliveries during the break, it's not free time and you must pay for it.

Many states have laws requiring employers to provide meal and rest breaks and specifying minimum times that must be allowed. (See the chart below.) In some states, these breaks must be paid. If your state requires more than the FLSA, then you must follow the stricter state law requirement.

⚠️ **It's Better Not to Quibble.** Most employees today expect to get one or two paid breaks during an eight-hour shift. Such breaks may help employees work more efficiently, since they'll return to the job refreshed. It can put a damper on employee morale if you try to avoid paying for that time.

State Meal and Rest Breaks

California

Cal. Lab. Code § 512

Applies to: Employers in most industries.

Exceptions: Excludes professional actors, sheep-herders under Agricultural Occupations Order and personal attendants under Household Occupations Order.

Meal break does not apply to motion picture, agricultural & household occupations.

Meal Break: 30 minutes, after 5 hours, except when workday will be completed in 6 hours or less and there is mutual employer/employee consent to waive meal period.

On-duty meal period counted as time worked and permitted only when nature of work prevents relief from all duties and there is written agreement between parties.

Rest Break: Paid 10-minute rest period for each 4 hours worked or major fraction thereof; as practicable, in middle of each work period. Not required for employees whose total daily work time is less than $3^1/_2$ hours.

• • •

Applies to: Broadcasting industry and motion picture industry.

Meal Break: $^1/_2$ hour, to not more than 1 hour, after 6 hours, with subsequent meal periods required 6 hours after termination of preceding meal period. On-duty meal period counted as time worked and permitted only when nature of work prevents relief from all duties and there is written agreement between parties.

Colorado

Wage Order # 22

Applies to: Retail trade, food and beverage, public housekeeping, medical profession, beauty service, laundry and dry cleaning and janitorial service industries.

Exceptions: Excludes certain occupations, such as teacher, nurse and other medical professionals.

Meal Break: 30 minutes after 5 hours of work. On-duty meal period permitted when nature of work prevents relief from all duties; such meal period must be paid.

Rest Break: Paid 10-minute rest period for each 4-hour work period or major fraction thereof; as practicable, in middle of each work period.

Connecticut

Conn. Gen. Stat. Ann. § 31-51ii

Applies to: All employers, except as noted.

Exceptions: Does not apply to employers who provide 30 or more minutes of paid or meal periods within each $7^1/_2$ hour work period.

Does not apply if collective bargaining agreement in effect on 7/1/90 or written agreement between employer and employee provides for different breaks.

Labor Commissioner is directed to exempt by regulation any employer on a finding that compliance would be adverse to public safety, or that duties of a position can be performed only by one employee, or in continuous operations under specified conditions, or that employer employs less than 5 employees on a shift at a single place of business provided the exemption applies only to employees on such shift.

Meal Break: 30 minutes after first 2 hours and before last 2 hours for employees who work $7^1/_2$ consecutive hours or more.

Delaware

Del. Code Ann. tit. 19, § 707

Applies to: All employers, except as noted.

Exceptions: Excludes teachers and workplaces covered by a collective bargaining agreement or other written employer/employee agreement providing otherwise.

State Meal and Rest Breaks (continued)

Exemptions may also be granted where compliance would adversely affect public safety; only one employee may perform the duties of a position; an employer has fewer than five employees on a shift at a single place of business; or where the continuous nature of an employer's operations requires employees to respond to urgent or unusual conditions at all times and the employees are compensated for their meal break periods.

Meal Break: 30 minutes after first 2 hours and before the last 2 hours, for employees who work 7½ consecutive hours or more.

Illinois

820 Ill. Comp. Stat. § 140/3

Applies to: All employers.

Exceptions: Employees whose meal periods are established by collective bargaining agreement.

Employees who monitor individuals with developmental disabilities or mental illness, or both, and who are required to be on-call during an entire 8-hour work period; these employees must be allowed to eat a meal while working.

Meal Break: 20 minutes, after 5 hours, for employees who work 7½ continuous hours or more.

Kentucky

Ky. Rev. Stat. Ann. §§ 337.355, 337.365

Applies to: All employers, except as noted.

Exceptions: Excludes employers subject to Federal Railway Labor Act.

Meal Break: Reasonable off-duty period (ordinarily 30 minutes but a shorter period may be permitted under special conditions) between 3rd and 5th hour of work. Coffee breaks and snack time may not be included in meal period.

Employee may be entitled to different meal period, pursuant to collective bargaining agreement or mutual agreement between employer and employee.

Rest Break: Paid 10-minute rest period for each 4-hour work period.

Rest period must be in addition to regularly scheduled meal period.

Maine

Me. Rev. Stat. Ann. tit. 26, § 601

Applies to: Places of employment where 3 or more employees are on duty at one time and the nature of their work allows them to take frequent breaks during the workday.

Exceptions: General rule not applicable if collective bargaining or other written employer-employee agreement provides otherwise.

Meal Break: 30 minutes after 6 consecutive hours of work, except in cases of emergency.

Massachusetts

Mass. Gen. Laws ch. 149, § 100

Applies to: All employers, except as noted.

Exceptions: Excludes iron works, glass works, paper mills, letterpress establishments, print works and bleaching or dyeing works.

Meal Break: 30 minutes, if work is for more than 6 hours.

Minnesota

Minn. Stat. Ann. §§ 177.253, 177.254

Applies to: All employers.

Exceptions: Excludes certain agricultural and seasonal employees.

Different rest and meal breaks are permitted pursuant to a collective bargaining agreement.

Meal Break: Sufficient unpaid time for employees who work 8 consecutive hours or more.

Rest Break: Paid adequate rest period within each 4 consecutive hours of work, to utilize nearest convenient restroom.

State Meal and Rest Breaks (continued)

Nebraska

Neb. Rev. Stat. § 48-212

Applies to: Assembly plant, workshop or mechanical establishment, unless establishment operates three 8-hour shifts daily.

Meal Break: 30 minutes off premises, between 12 noon and 1 p.m. or at other suitable lunch time.

Nevada

Nev. Rev. Stat. Ann. § 608.019

Applies to: Employers of two or more employees.

Exceptions: Employees covered by collective bargaining agreement.

Meal Break: 30 minutes, if work is for 8 continuous hours.

Rest Break: Paid 10-minute rest period for each 4 hours worked or major fraction thereof; as practicable, in middle of each work period. Not required for employees whose total daily work time is less than 3$^1/_2$ hours.

New Hampshire

N.H. Rev. Stat. Ann. § 275:30-a

Applies to: All employers.

Meal Break: 30 minutes after 5 consecutive hours, unless the employer allows the employee to eat while working and it is feasible for the employee to do so.

New York

N.Y. Lab. Law § 162

Applies to: Factories.

Meal Break: 1 hour noonday period.

Labor Commissioner may give written permission for shorter meal period.

. . .

Applies to: All other establishments and occupations covered by the Labor Law.

Meal Break: 30 minute noonday period for employees who work shifts of more than 6 hours that extend over the noonday meal period.

45 minutes for employees who workshifts of more than 6 hours, if their shift starts between 1 p.m. and 6 a.m.

Labor Commissioner may give written permission for shorter meal period.

. . .

Applies to: All industries and occupations.

Meal Break: An additional 20 minutes between 5 p.m. and 7 p.m. for those employed on a shift starting before 11 a.m. and continuing after 7 p.m.

Labor Commissioner may give written permission for shorter meal period.

. . .

Applies to: All industries and occupations.

Meal Break: 1 hour in factories, 30 minutes in other establishments, midway in shift, for those employed more than a 6-hour period starting between 1 p.m. and 6 a.m.

Labor Commissioner may give written permission for shorter meal period.

North Dakota

N.D. Admin. Code § 46-02-07-02

Applies to: Applicable when two or more employees are on duty.

Exceptions: Collective bargaining agreement takes precedence over meal period requirement.

Meal Break: 30-minutes, if employee desires, on each shift exceeding 5 hours.

Employees who are completely relieved of their duties but required to remain on site do not have to be paid.

Oregon

Or. Admin. R. § 839-020-0050

Applies to: All employers except as noted.

Exceptions: Agricultural employees.

State Meal and Rest Breaks (continued)

Employees covered by a collective bargaining agreement.

Meal Break: 30-minute break for each work period of 6 to 8 hours, between 2nd and 5th hour for work period of 7 hours or less and between 3rd and 6th hour for work period over 7 hours; or at least 20-minute paid break, where employer can show that such a paid meal period is industry practice or custom; or, where employer can show that nature of work prevents relief from all duty, an eating period with pay while on duty for each period of 6 to 8 hours.

Rest Break: Paid 15-minute rest period for every 4-hour segment or major portion thereof in one work period; as feasible, approximately in middle of each segment of work period.

Rest period must be in addition to usual meal period and taken separately; not to be added to usual meal period or deducted from beginning or end of work period to reduce overall length of total work period.

Rest period is not required for employees age 18 or older who work alone in a retail or service establishment serving the general public and who work less than 5 hours in a period of 16 continuous hours, as long as employee has opportunity to use rest room.

Rhode Island

R.I. Gen. Laws § 28-3-14

Applies to: Factory, workshop and mechanical or mercantile establishments.

Exceptions: Certain nighttime switchboard operators.

Meal Break: 20 minutes after 6 hours of work.

Employees are not entitled to a break if their shift lasts for 6½ hours or less and ends by 1 p.m.; or if their shift lasts for 7½ hours or less and ends by 2 p.m., as long as employee has opportunity to eat during employment.

Tennessee

Tenn. Code Ann. §§ 50-2-103(d), 50-1-305

Applies to: All employers.

Meal Break: 30 minutes for employees scheduled to work 6 consecutive hours or more.

Also must provide break for mothers to express breast milk for infants.

Vermont

Vt. Stat. Ann. tit. 21, § 304

Applies to: All employers.

Meal Break: Employees must be afforded a reasonable opportunity to eat and use toilet facilities during work periods.

Washington

Wash. Admin. Code § 296-126-092

Applies to: All employers except as noted.

Exceptions: Excludes newspaper vendor or carrier, domestic or casual labor around private residence, sheltered workshop and agricultural labor.

Meal Break: 30-minute break, if work period is more than 5 consecutive hours, to be given not less than 2 hours nor more than 5 hours from beginning of shift. Employees who work 3 or more hours longer than regular workday are entitled to an additional ½ hour, before or during overtime.

Rest Break: Paid 10-minute rest period for each 4-hour work period, scheduled as near as possible to midpoint of each work period. Employee may not be required to work more than 3 hours without a rest period.

Scheduled rest periods not required where nature of work allows employee to take intermittent rest periods equivalent to required standard.

Although agricultural workers are excluded from the general rest requirement, a separate regulation requires a paid 10-minute rest period in each 4-hour period of agricultural work.

State Meal and Rest Breaks (continued)	
West Virginia *W.Va. Code § 21-3-10a* **Applies to:** All employers. **Meal Break:** 20-minute break for each 6 consecutive hours worked, where employees are not allowed to take breaks as needed and/or permitted to eat lunch while working. **Rest Break:** Rest breaks of 20 minutes or less must be counted as paid work time.	**Wisconsin** *Wis. Admin. Code § DWD 274.02* **Applies to:** All employers. **Meal Break:** 30 minutes close to usual meal time or near middle of shift is recommended but not required. Shifts of more than six hours without a meal break should be avoided. Current as of May 2002

E. Keeping Records

The FLSA requires you to keep records of wages and hours. If an employee is subject to both minimum wage and overtime provisions, you must keep records for that employee showing:

- the employee's name, address, occupation and gender
- the employee's birthdate if he or she is younger than 19 years old
- the hour and day when each workweek began
- the total hours worked each workday and each workweek
- total daily or weekly earnings
- regular hourly pay rate for any week when overtime was worked
- total overtime pay for the workweek
- deductions from or additions to wages
- total wages paid each pay period, and
- date of payment and pay period covered.

Different records are required for exempt employees, and you must keep special information for employees to whom you extend lodging or other facilities. You must retain most records for all current employees and for at least three years after an employee stops working for your company.

Your state may impose different or additional requirements. Contact your state labor department for details (see Appendix for contact information).

 For details on your recordkeeping duties, get the publication *Records to be Kept by Employers under the FLSA*. It's available at the nearest office of the U.S. Labor Department's Wage and Hour Division. (See the Appendix for contact details.)

F. Child Labor

The FLSA has special rules for younger workers. Those rules are designed to discourage young people from dropping out of school too soon and to protect them from dangerous work such as mining, demolition and wrecking, logging and roofing. Check with the local wage-and-hour office of the U.S. Department of Labor for a current list of jobs that are considered to be hazardous to young people. (See the Appendix for contact details.)

State laws may impose additional restrictions on hiring young workers. The rules are different for youngsters in agricultural and non-agricultural jobs.

1. Agricultural Jobs

The FLSA defines agriculture to include:

- cultivating and tilling the soil
- dairying
- producing, cultivating, growing and harvesting any agricultural or horticultural commodities
- raising livestock, bees, fur-bearing animals or poultry, or
- any practices performed by a farmer on a farm as part of farming—for example, forestry, lumbering and preparing items for market.

In agricultural work, the following rules apply:

- You may hire a worker who is 16 years or older for any work, whether hazardous or not, for unlimited hours.
- You may hire a worker who is 14 or 15 years old for any nonhazardous agricultural work outside of school hours.
- You may hire a worker who is 12 or 13 years old for any nonhazardous agricultural work outside of school hours if the child's parents work on the same farm or if you have their written consent.
- You may hire a worker who is under 12 years old for nonhazardous work on a farm outside of school hours if the farm isn't covered by minimum wage requirements—but you need the written consent of the child's parents.
- You may hire a worker who is ten or 11 years old if you've been granted a waiver by the U.S. Department of Labor to employ the youngster as a hand harvest laborer for no more than eight weeks in any calendar year.

If you own or operate a farm, you can hire your own children to do any kind of work on the farm, regardless of their ages.

Occupations Hazardous to Young Workers

The U.S. Department of Labor has identified several agricultural occupations that are deemed hazardous for children age 15 and under, including:

- operating a tractor that has more than 20 horsepower
- working in a yard, pen or stall occupied by a bull, a stud horse maintained for breeding purposes or a sow with suckling pigs
- felling timber with a diameter of more than six inches
- working from a ladder or scaffold at a height of more than 20 feet, and
- handling or using blast agents.

For a complete list of hazardous agricultural occupations, contact the nearest office of the U.S. Department of Labor (see the Appendix for contact details) or check the Department's website at www.dol.gov.

2. Nonagricultural Jobs

The FLSA sets out a number of restrictions on young workers hired to do nonagricultural jobs.

- You may hire a worker who is 18 years or older for any job, hazardous or not, for unlimited hours.
- You may hire a worker who is 16 or 17 years old for any nonhazardous job, for unlimited hours.
- You may hire a worker who is 14 or 15 years old outside school hours in various nonmanufacturing, non-mining, nonhazardous jobs, but some restrictions apply. The employee can't work more than three hours on a school day, 18 hours in a school week, eight hours on a non-school day or 40 hours in a non-school week. Also, work can't begin before 7 a.m. or end after 7 p.m., except from June 1 through Labor Day, when evening hours are extended to 9 p.m.

Fourteen years old is the minimum age for most work, but there are a few jobs that workers younger than 14 can perform, including:

- delivering newspapers
- performing in radio, TV, movie or theatrical productions
- working in a nonfarm business solely owned by their parents—if it's not a manufacturing or hazardous job
- gathering evergreens, and
- making evergreen wreaths.

G. Payroll Withholding

Federal law requires you to withhold income taxes and Social Security and Medicare contributions from employees' paychecks. States and municipalities that have income taxes also require withholding—usually under a system that parallels the federal procedures. (See Chapter 5, Section B, for more about federal payroll taxes.)

Under federal law, you may also deduct the cost of meals, housing and transportation, loans, debts owed to you, child support and alimony, payroll savings and insurance premiums. There are exceptions to these rules, and limits on how much you can withhold or deduct.

State Rules May Differ. Your state may prohibit some deductions that would be allowed under federal law. In this situation you must follow your state's law. Before you take any deductions, contact your state labor department to learn your state's rules (see Appendix for contact information).

1. Meals, Housing and Transportation

Under federal law, you may legally deduct from an employee's paycheck the reasonable cost or fair value of meals, housing, fuel and transportation to and from work even if these deductions reduce the worker's pay to less than minimum wage. But you must show that you customarily paid these expenses and that:

- they were for the employee's benefit

- you told the employee in advance about the deductions from a paycheck, and
- the employee voluntarily accepted the meals and other accommodations against minimum wage.

2. Debts Owed to an Employer

If you lend money or extend credit to an employee, federal law allows you to withhold money from his or her pay to satisfy that debt. However, it's illegal to make such a deduction if it would drop the employee's pay below the minimum wage.

> **EXAMPLE:** Roadmaster Auto Parts Store hires Bruce at $6.15 an hour to make deliveries. One morning, the battery in Bruce's car dies. Roadmaster allows him to replace the battery with a new one from the store's stock—and Bruce agrees that Roadmaster can deduct the price, $80, from his paycheck. Under the FLSA, Roadmaster can legally deduct no more than $40 per week (40 hours x $1) from Bruce's gross pay to cover the battery. To deduct more would drop Bruce's pay rate of $6.15 per hour to below the required minimum of $5.15.

3. Debts and Wage Garnishments

You may be sent an order from a judge requiring your business to withhold money from an employee's paycheck to satisfy a debt the employee owes to someone else. This order is part of a legal process called wage attachment or wage garnishment. Usually, a judge will issue such an order only after a judgment has been signed stating that the employee actually owes the money—but such a judgment may not be necessary for garnishments based on an employee's failure to pay student loans, child support, alimony or taxes.

If you receive a garnishment order, read it carefully—it will specify deadlines you must meet for processing the order. You may have to pay a penalty if you don't comply with the terms and timetables of the garnishment. Procedures vary from state to state, but most likely you'll be required to file a form with the court disclosing how much you owe to the employee for wages. Then you'll be required to send a portion of those wages to the court or, perhaps, to the creditor or creditor's lawyer.

A federal law, the Consumer Credit Protection Act (15 U.S.C. § 1673), prohibits a judgment creditor from taking more than 25% of an employee's net earnings through a wage garnishment. A few states offer greater protection to the employee. In Delaware, for example, a judgment creditor can't take more than 15% of an employee's wages. Usually the papers you receive as part of the garnishment order will explain how much of the employee's earnings you should deduct and where to send the money.

The Consumer Credit Protection Act also prohibits you from firing an employee because of a garnishment order to satisfy a single debt. But if two judgment creditors garnish an employee's wages or one judgment creditor garnishes an employee's wages to pay two different judgments, you're free to fire that employee. Again, some state laws place stricter limits on your right to fire an employee because of garnishments. In Washington, for example, you can't fire a worker for judgments owed unless his or her wages are garnished by three different creditors or to satisfy three different garnishments within a year. In Connecticut, you can't fire a worker unless you've had to deal with more than seven creditors or judgments in a single year.

Although statutes limit your right to fire employees because of garnishments, you can still fire such employees for a legitimate business reason—or for any reason, if the employee works at will—as long as you can establish that the firing wasn't based on the garnishments.

4. Child Support

The federal Family Support Act of 1988 (102 U.S.C. § 2343) requires that new or modified child support orders include an automatic wage withholding order. If you receive a copy of such an order, you must withhold a portion of the employee's pay and send it on to the parent who has custody of the child.

You can't discipline, fire or refuse to hire someone just because his or her pay is subject to a child support wage withholding order.

5. Back Taxes

If an employee owes taxes to the federal government and doesn't pay, the IRS can grab most—but not all—of the employee's wages. The amount the employee gets to keep is determined by the number of his or her dependents and the size of the standard deduction to which the employee is entitled.

If you receive a wage levy notice from the IRS, don't ignore it. If you go ahead and pay the employee in full, you'll be liable to the IRS for whatever amount you wrongly pay.

Most state and some municipal taxing authorities have similar power to seize a portion of an employee's wages. Contact your state tax board for more information. ■

Chapter 4

Employee Benefits

A. Healthcare Coverage 4/3

   1. Types of Coverage 4/3

   2. Making the Best Choice 4/3

   3. Coverage Limitations 4/4

   4. Continuing Coverage for Former Employees 4/5

   5. Reducing Costs 4/19

   6. Medical Savings Accounts 4/19

B. Retirement Plans 4/20

   1. Defined Benefit Plans 4/20

   2. Defined Contribution Plans 4/20

   3. 401(k) Plans 4/21

   4. Meeting IRS and ERISA Requirements 4/22

C. Other Employee Benefits 4/24

   1. Life Insurance 4/24

   2. Disability Insurance 4/25

   3. Educational Assistance Programs 4/25

   4. Dependent Care Assistance 4/26

   5. Adoption Assistance Programs 4/26

*E*mployee benefits are such a common part of the workplace terrain today that many assume these benefits are required by law. But generally, the decision about whether or not to provide such benefits is up to you.

Even though providing benefits is largely optional, enlightened employers generally do offer some type of benefit package. Offering benefits can reflect your commitment to keeping a satisfied workforce and help you remain competitive in attracting competent workers.

Federal tax laws allow an employer to deduct the cost of many employee benefits as a business expense, which greatly reduces the financial burden of providing these benefits. Benefits that qualify for favorable tax treatment include health and dental coverage, term life insurance, disability insurance, approved pension plans, educational assistance programs and dependent care assistance. But if a benefit plan is rigged to favor the owners of a business or employees who receive the highest compensation, the plan may not qualify for a tax deduction.

If you opt to provide healthcare coverage or pension plans, federal and state laws may impose requirements on these plans. (See Sections A and B.)

Employees Can Help You Plan

In putting together a benefit program, consider taking a survey of employees or setting up an employee committee to recommend the benefits they'd most like to have. Then, after exploring the options and deciding on the benefits you'll offer, communicate that decision—and your reasons for the choice—to the employees.

Perhaps some employee suggestions will be too expensive or even impossible to adopt. You may want to reconsider others in the future. Whatever the situation, when employees go to the trouble of making suggestions, make sure to let them know that you gave their ideas serious consideration.

A. Healthcare Coverage

Healthcare coverage is the benefit most employees covet. Medical treatment is expensive today, and it's difficult for an individual to find affordable coverage. Of course, employees enjoy the greatest benefits if the employer foots the entire bill. But even if an employer doesn't pay the cost of coverage—or pays just a part of it—the employee benefits by being able to participate at relatively low group rates.

Providing healthcare coverage is optional for employers. Hawaii is the sole exception. Its Prepaid Healthcare Act (§ 393-1 and following of the Hawaii Statutes) requires employers to provide coverage to every employee who earns a monthly wage of at least 86.67 times that state's minimum wage—$5.75 an hour, increasing to $6.25 on January 1, 2003.

1. Types of Coverage

Traditionally, employers who provide healthcare coverage do so through an indemnity or reimbursement plan which pays the doctor or hospital directly, or reimburses the employee for medical expenses he or she has already paid. Blue Cross/Blue Shield is a traditional type of plan.

While traditional coverage allowing employees to seek out their preferred medical provider is still widely used, a growing number of employers today provide coverage through the alternatives of a health maintenance organization (HMO) or a preferred provider organization (PPO).

An HMO is a group of hospitals and doctors who provide specified medical services to employees for a fixed monthly fee. Within the HMO service area, covered employees must use the HMO hospitals and doctors unless it's an emergency or they receive permission to go elsewhere.

A PPO is a network of hospitals and doctors who agree to provide medical care for specified fees. Often the network is put together by an insurance company that also administers the program. Employees usually can choose between using the network's hospitals and doctors or going elsewhere (although an employee may have to pay a higher fee to use doctors or facilities outside of the plan).

2. Making the Best Choice

If you choose to provide health insurance coverage to employees, explore all the alternatives: group health insurance policies, HMOs and PPOs. Until you compare, you won't know which arrangement will be least costly to your business and your employees.

Under some plans, employees pay for a portion of their medical expenses—usually called copayments. The theory is that employees will seek only essential treatment if they're paying some of the cost.

Your business must decide who will pay the monthly, quarterly or semi-annual premium for healthcare coverage. Among the choices for who pays the tab:

- Your business can pick up the full amount.
- You can split the cost of premiums with the employee—perhaps paying 80% and having the employee pick up the other 20% through a paycheck deduction.

- You can pay for the employee's coverage in full, but require the employee to pay the extra cost of covering his or her dependents.
- You can require the employee to pay the entire charge—although the employee won't perceive that as much of a benefit, the group plan will undoubtedly be cheaper than individual coverage.

Another way to shift some costs to your employees is through a deductible plan, which requires employees to pay a specified amount of medical bills each year—$500, for example—before the plan's coverage kicks in.

Consider Flexible Coverage Arrangements. Depending on where your business is located and how many employees you have, you may be able to offer your employees several different choices of coverage. For example, some employers opt to pay 100% of coverage under an HMO. If the HMO doesn't require all employees to join, some employers allow employees who opt out to buy their own coverage. Then the employers reimburse them at the HMO rate. Depending on the required copayments, deductibles and other plan features, employees who select a different plan may pay a bit more or less than the HMO rate.

You should decide, too, whether to cover employees who work part-time. You might, for example, provide full benefits for those who work 30 hours or more per week, and prorated benefits for those who work at least 20 hours but less than 30. Such an approach may help you qualify for cheaper group rates.

Children May Have Rights, Too. If you have a group healthcare plan, a child of a divorced employee may have a right to coverage—even if the child doesn't live with the employee or isn't a financial dependent of the employee. An employee's child will be covered if a domestic relations settlement agreement or a court order requires such healthcare coverage. If you receive a copy of such a settlement agreement or court order and are unsure about what to do, check with the plan administrator or an employee benefits lawyer.

3. Coverage Limitations

The Americans with Disabilities Act (ADA) is designed to eliminate workplace discrimination against people with disabilities. (See Chapter 9.) The ADA doesn't require you to offer healthcare benefits to employees, but it does require you to give people with disabilities the same healthcare benefits you offer to others. If your business is covered by the ADA, you may not deny insurance coverage or limit benefits based on a worker's disability.

Your plan probably violates the ADA if it excludes specific disabilities, such as deafness, AIDS or schizophrenia. Similarly, it's illegal to exclude groups of disabilities—for example, cancers, muscular dystrophy and kidney diseases—or to exclude all conditions that substantially limit a major life activity.

Many states also have laws prohibiting discrimination in healthcare benefits. These laws may apply to your business even if it's too small to be covered by the ADA.

a. Preexisting conditions

There are legal limits on your ability to offer a healthcare plan that doesn't cover preexisting conditions. A healthcare plan will violate the ADA if it excludes specific preexisting conditions, such as blood disorders. In EEOC parlance, such exclusions are "disability based" and therefore not permissible.

The Health Insurance Portability and Accountability Act (Public Law 104-191)—in effect since mid-1997—further limits your right to exclude preexisting conditions in any healthcare plan that you provide to employees. That law provides that any exclusion for a preexisting condition:

- must relate to a condition for which the employee received medical advice or treatment during the six months before the employee's enrollment date
- cannot last for more than 12 months— 18 months for late enrollees—after the employee's enrollment date, and
- cannot include pregnancy.

State laws may also regulate your ability to offer a plan with preexisting condition exclusions.

For publications explaining the complexities of the healthcare portability law, call the federal Department of Labor's publication hotline at: 800-998-7542. Or check its website: www.dol.gov/dol/pwba.

b. Treatment restrictions

A plan that doesn't cover experimental drugs or treatment or that excludes elective surgery doesn't violate the ADA. Similarly, it's not a violation to put a monetary cap on certain types of treatment—for example, to limit payments for X-rays or blood transfusions— even though such a cap may adversely affect people with certain disabilities.

Discrimination in Group Health Plans

Under federal law, a group health plan can't discriminate in eligibility for coverage or premiums based on an employee's:

- health status
- medical condition
- claims experience
- medical history
- genetic information
- evidence of insurability, or
- disability.

This list applies to the employee's dependents as well.

But the law doesn't require a group plan to cover any given procedure—and a group plan may limit the level of benefits it provides, as long as the plan doesn't discriminate among similarly situated employees.

4. Continuing Coverage for Former Employees

A federal law called the Consolidated Omnibus Budget Reconciliation Act or COBRA (29 U.S.C. §1162) applies to your business if you have 20 or more employees and you offer a group healthcare plan. If your business is too small to be covered by COBRA, you might still have to comply with a similar state law. (See the chart below.) If COBRA applies to your business, you must offer employees and former employees the option of continuing their healthcare coverage if their coverage is lost or reduced because:

- their employment has been terminated for any reason—except gross misconduct
- their hours have been reduced, or
- they've become eligible for Medicare.

Members of the employee's family must also be given the opportunity to continue their coverage. The chart below depicts the circumstances—called qualifying events—that trigger an employer's obligation to allow continuing healthcare coverage under a group plan. COBRA gives rights to different people, depending on the qualifying event.

How long the benefits must be continued is determined by the qualifying event and by whether the covered employee is disabled.

The employee must pay the cost of continuing coverage under COBRA, including both your share and the employee's share of the premiums. You can charge 102% of the premium cost—using the extra 2% to cover administrative costs. The cost to the employee or the employee's family for continuing coverage must be similar to the cost of covering people still on your payroll.

COBRA covers HMO and PPO plans in addition to traditional group insurance plans. COBRA also covers all other types of medical benefits, including dental and vision care and plans under which an employer reimburses employees for medical expenses.

Continuing Coverage for Former Employees

Qualifying Event	People Entitled to Continue Coverage	How Long
The employee quits or retires	Employee, spouse, dependents	18 months; 29 months for disabled worker
You fire or lay off the employee for reasons other than gross misconduct	Employee, spouse, dependents	18 months; 29 months for disabled worker
You reduce the employee's hours so he or she loses coverage	Employee, spouse, dependents	18 months; 29 months for disabled worker
The employee dies	Surviving spouse, dependents	36 months
The employee divorces or becomes legally separated	Former spouse, dependents	36 months
The employee goes on Medicare	Spouse, dependents	36 months
A dependent loses coverage through marriage or age	Dependent	36 months

If your business is covered by COBRA and has a group healthcare plan, the plan administrator—the person who handles the plan's paperwork—must give employees and their spouses a written explanation of their COBRA rights when they first become eligible to participate in the plan. A single notice can be sent to an employee and spouse if they live at the same address. Otherwise, the spouse is entitled to a separate notice.

Help Is Available. Small businesses usually find it convenient to let the insurance company serve as the plan administrator and coordinate COBRA notices. The insurance company can provide even more help and information, including a clear explanation of how the plan meets the requirements of COBRA and similar state laws. Any reputable company should be able to provide clear, concise explanatory materials that you can hand out to your employees and, if asked, may send representatives to conduct training seminars and answer employee questions.

When a qualifying event occurs that gives an employee or family member the right to continue coverage, you must notify the plan administrator within 30 days. The plan administrator then has 14 days to notify the beneficiaries of their rights under COBRA. These beneficiaries have 60 days following the notice to let you know if they want to continue their coverage. If so, the employee or eligible family member sends you the premium each month and you send it on to the insurance company. If the beneficiaries don't

send the payment when due—or within the grace period—you can cut off coverage.

A number of states also have laws giving former employees the right to continue group healthcare insurance coverage after leaving a job. Depending on the state where you do business, state law may give employees more rights, provide for longer continued coverage or apply to smaller employers. (See the chart below.)

State Health Insurance Laws

Alabama

Ala. Code § 27-55-3

No general continuation laws, but subjects of domestic abuse, who have lost coverage under abuser's plan and who do not qualify for COBRA, may have 18 months coverage (applies to all employers).

Arkansas

Ark. Code Ann. § 23-86-114

Employers affected: All employers who offer group health insurance.

Eligible employees: Employees continuously insured for previous 3 months.

Qualifying event: Termination of employment; death of employee; change in marital status.

Length of coverage for employee: 120 days.

Length of coverage for dependents: 120 days.

Time employee has to apply: 10 days.

Special benefits: Excludes: dental care; prescription drugs; vision services.

California

Cal. Health & Safety Code §§ 1373.6, 1373.621; Cal. Ins. Code § 10128.50

Employers affected: Employers with 2 to 19 employees.

Eligible employees: Employees continuously insured for previous 3 months.

Qualifying event: Termination of employment; reduction in hours.

Length of coverage for employee: 18 months. (29 months if disabled at termination or during first 60 days of continuation coverage.)

Length of coverage for dependents: 18 months. (29 months if disabled at termination or during first 60 days of continuation coverage; 36 months upon death of employee, divorce or legal separation, loss of dependent status, employee's eligibility for Medicare.)

Time employer has to notify employee of continuation rights: 15 days.

Time employee has to apply: 31 days after group plan ends; 30 days after COBRA or Cal-COBRA ends.

Special benefits: Includes vision and dental benefits (if the employer offers them).

Special situations: Employee who is 60 or older and has worked for employer for previous 5 years may continue benefits for self and spouse beyond COBRA or Cal-COBRA limits.

Colorado

Colo. Rev. Stat. § 10-16-108

Employers affected: All employers who offer group health insurance.

Eligible employees: Employees continuously insured for previous 3 months. (If eligible due to reduction in hours, must have been continuously insured for previous 6 months.)

Qualifying event: Termination of employment; reduction in hours; death of employee; change in marital status.

Length of coverage for employee: 18 months.

Length of coverage for dependents: 18 months.

Time employer has to notify employee of continuation rights: Within 10 days of termination.

Time employee has to apply: 31 days after termination.

Special benefits: Excludes: specific diseases; accidental injuries.

Connecticut

Conn. Gen. Stat. Ann. § 38a-538; § 31-51o

Employers affected: All employers who offer group health insurance.

Eligible employees: Employees continuously insured for previous 3 months.

Qualifying event: Layoff; reduction in hours; termination of employment; death of employee; change in marital status.

State Health Insurance Laws (continued)

Length of coverage for employee: 18 months.

Length of coverage for dependents: 18 months. (36 months upon death of employee or divorce.)

Time employer has to notify employee of continuation rights: 14 days.

Time employee has to apply: 60 days.

Special benefits: Excludes: specific diseases; accidental injuries.

Special situations: Facility closes or relocates: employer must pay for insurance for employee and dependents for 120 days or until employee is eligible for other group coverage, whichever comes first. (Employee entitled to regular continuation coverage at the end of 120 days.)

District of Columbia

D.C. Code Ann. § 32-731

Employers affected: Employers with fewer than 20 employees.

Eligible employees: All insured employees are eligible.

Qualifying event: Any reason employee or dependent becomes ineligible for coverage.

Length of coverage for employee: 3 months.

Length of coverage for dependents: 3 months.

Time employer has to notify employee of continuation rights: Within 15 days of termination of coverage.

Time employee has to apply: 45 days after termination of coverage.

Special benefits: Excludes: dental or vision only insurance.

Florida

Fla. Stat. Ann. § 627.6692

Employers affected: Employers with fewer than 20 employees.

Eligible employees: Full-time (25 hours/week) employees covered by employer's health insurance plan.

Qualifying event: Layoff; reduction in hours; termination of employment; death of employee; change in marital status.

Length of coverage for employee: 18 months.

Length of coverage for dependents: 18 months.

Time employer has to notify employee of continuation rights: Carrier notifies employee within 14 days of learning of qualifying event (employee is responsible for notifying carrier).

Time employee has to apply: 30 days from receipt of carrier's notice.

Georgia

Ga. Code Ann. §§ 33-24-21.1 to 33-24-21.2

Employers affected: All employers who offer group health insurance.

Eligible employees: Employees continuously insured for previous 6 months.

Qualifying event: Termination of employment (except for cause).

Length of coverage for employee: 3 months plus any part of the month remaining at termination.

Length of coverage for dependents: 3 months plus any part of the month remaining at termination.

Special situations: Employee, spouse or former spouse, who is 60 or older and who has been covered for previous 6 months may continue coverage until eligible for Medicare. (Applies to companies with more than 20 employers; does not apply when employee quits for reasons other than health.)

Illinois

215 Ill. Comp. Stat. §§ 5/367e, 5/367.2

Employers affected: All employers who offer group health insurance.

Eligible employees: Employees continuously insured for previous 3 months.

Qualifying event: Termination of employment.

State Health Insurance Laws (continued)

Length of coverage for employee: 9 months.

Length of coverage for dependents: 9 months.

Time employee has to apply: 10 days after termination or receiving notice from employer, whichever is later, but not more than 60 days from termination.

Special benefits: Excludes: dental care; prescription drugs; vision services; disability income; specified diseases.

Special situations: Upon death or divorce, 2 years coverage for spouse under 55; until eligible for Medicare or other group coverage for spouse over 55.

Indiana

Ind. Code Ann. § 27-8-15-31.1

Employers affected: Employers with 2 to 50 employees.

Eligible employees: Employed by same employer for at least one year and continuously insured for previous 90 days.

Qualifying event: Termination of employment; reduction in hours; dissolution of marriage; loss of dependent status.

Length of coverage for employee: 12 months.

Length of coverage for dependents: 12 months.

Time employer has to notify employee of continuation rights: 10 days after employee becomes eligible for continuation coverage.

Time employee has to apply: 30 days after becoming eligible for continuation coverage.

Iowa

Iowa Code §§ 509B.3 to 509B.5

Employers affected: All employers who offer group health insurance.

Eligible employees: Employees continuously insured for previous 3 months.

Qualifying event: Any reason employee or dependent becomes ineligible for coverage.

Length of coverage for employee: 9 months.

Length of coverage for dependents: 9 months.

Time employer has to notify employee of continuation rights: 10 days after termination of coverage.

Time employee has to apply: 10 days after termination of coverage or receiving notice from employer, whichever is later, but no more than 31 days from termination of coverage.

Special benefits: Excludes: dental care; prescription drugs; vision services.

Kansas

Kan. Stat. Ann. § 40-2209(i)

Employers affected: All employers who offer group health insurance.

Eligible employees: Employees continuously insured for previous 3 months.

Qualifying event: Any reason employee or dependent becomes ineligible for coverage.

Length of coverage for employee: 6 months.

Length of coverage for dependents: 6 months.

Time employee has to apply: 31 days from termination.

Kentucky

Ky. Rev. Stat. Ann. § 304.18-110

Employers affected: All employers who offer group health insurance.

Eligible employees: Employees continuously insured for previous 3 months.

Qualifying event: Any reason employee or dependent becomes ineligible for coverage.

Length of coverage for employee: 18 months.

Length of coverage for dependents: 18 months.

Time employer has to notify employee of continuation rights: Employer must notify insurer as soon as employee's coverage ends; insurer then notifies employee.

State Health Insurance Laws (continued)

Time employee has to apply: 31 days from receipt of notice.

Special benefits: Excludes: specific diseases; accidental injury.

Louisiana

La. Rev. Stat. Ann. §§ 22:215.7, 22:215.13

Employers affected: All employers who offer group health insurance.

Eligible employees: Employees continuously insured for previous 3 months.

Qualifying event: Termination of employment.

Length of coverage for employee: 12 months.

Length of coverage for dependents: 12 months.

Time employee has to apply: Must apply and submit payment before group coverage ends.

Special benefits: Excludes: dental care; vision care; specific diseases; accidental injury.

Special situations: Surviving spouse who is 50 or older may have coverage until remarriage or eligibility for Medicare or other insurance.

Maine

Me. Rev. Stat. Ann. tit. 24-A, § 2809-A

Employers affected: All employers who offer group health insurance.

Eligible employees: Employees continuously insured for previous 3 months.

Qualifying event: Termination of employment.

Length of coverage for employee: One year (either group or individual coverage at discretion of insurer).

Length of coverage for dependents: One year upon death of insured, if original plan provided for coverage (either group or individual coverage at discretion of insurer).

Time employee has to apply: 90 days from termination of group coverage.

Special situations: Temporary layoff or work-related injury or disease: Employee and dependents entitled to one year group or individual continuation coverage. (Must have been continuously insured for previous 6 months; must apply within 31 days.)

Maryland

Md. Code Ann., [Ins.] §§ 15-402 to 15-409

Employers affected: All employers who offer group health insurance.

Eligible employees: Employees continuously insured for previous 3 months.

Qualifying event: Involuntary termination of employment; death of employee; change in marital status.

Length of coverage for employee: 18 months.

Length of coverage for dependents: 18 months upon death of employee; upon change in marital status, 18 months or until spouse remarries or becomes eligible for other coverage.

Time employer has to notify employee of continuation rights: Must notify insurer within 14 days of receiving employee's request.

Time employee has to apply: 45 days from termination of coverage. Employee begins application process by requesting an election of continuation notification form from employer.

Massachusetts

Mass. Gen. Laws ch. 175, § 110G; ch. 176J, § 9

Employers affected: All employers who offer group health insurance; special rules for employers with Small Group Health Insurance (2 to 19 employees).

Eligible employees: All insured employees are eligible.

Qualifying event: Involuntary layoff; death of insured employee. For Small Group Health Insurance employer add: reduction in hours; divorce or legal separation; loss of dependent status; employee's eligibility for Medicare; employer's bankruptcy.

Length of coverage for employee: 39 weeks (but may not exceed time covered under original coverage).

State Health Insurance Laws (continued)

Small Group Health Insurance employer: 18 months. (29 months if disabled.)

Length of coverage for dependents: 39 weeks. (Divorced or separated spouse entitled to benefits only if included in judgment decree.)

Small Group Health Insurance employer: 18 months upon termination or reduction in hours; 29 months if disabled; 36 months on divorce, death of employee, employee's eligibility for Medicare, employer's bankruptcy.

Time employer has to notify employee of continuation rights: When employee becomes eligible for continuation benefits.

Time employee has to apply: 30 days. Small Group Health Insurance employer, 60 days.

Special situations: Termination due to plant closing: 90 days coverage for employee and dependents, at the same payment terms as before closing.

Minnesota

Minn. Stat. Ann. § 62A.17

Employers affected: All employers who offer group health insurance.

Eligible employees: All insured employees are eligible.

Qualifying event: Termination of employment; reduction in hours.

Length of coverage for employee: 18 months.

Length of coverage for dependents: 18 months.

Time employer has to notify employee of continuation rights: Within 10 days of termination of coverage.

Time employee has to apply: 60 days from termination of coverage or receipt of notice, whichever is later.

Mississippi

Miss. Code Ann. § 83-9-51

Employers affected: All employers who offer group health insurance.

Eligible employees: Employees continuously insured for previous 3 months.

Qualifying event: Termination of employment; divorce, employee's death; employee's eligibility for Medicare; loss of dependent status.

Length of coverage for employee: 12 months.

Length of coverage for dependents: 12 months.

Time employee has to apply: Must apply and submit payment before group coverage ends.

Special benefits: Excludes: dental and vision care; any benefits other than hospital, surgical or major medical.

Missouri

Mo. Rev. Stat. § 376.428

Employers affected: All employers who offer group health insurance.

Eligible employees: Employees continuously insured for previous 3 months.

Qualifying event: Termination of employment.

Length of coverage for employee: 9 months.

Length of coverage for dependents: 9 months.

Time employer has to notify employee of continuation rights: No later than date group coverage would end.

Time employee has to apply: 31 days from date group coverage would end.

Special benefits: Excludes: dental and vision care; any benefits other than hospital, surgical or major medical.

Must include: maternity benefits if they were provided under group policy.

Montana

Mont. Code Ann. § 33-22-508

Employers affected: All employers who offer group health insurance.

Eligible employees: Employees continuously insured for previous 3 months.

State Health Insurance Laws (continued)

Qualifying event: Termination of employment; employer going out of business.

Length of coverage for employee: No time limit specified.

Length of coverage for dependents: No time limit specified.

Time employee has to apply: 31 days from date group coverage would end.

Special situations: Reduction in hours: one year's coverage (if employer consents).

Nebraska

Neb. Rev. Stat. §§ 44-1640, 44-7406

Employers affected: Employers not subject to federal COBRA laws.

Eligible employees: All insured employees are eligible.

Qualifying event: Involuntary termination of employment (layoff due to labor dispute not considered involuntary).

Length of coverage for employee: 6 months.

Length of coverage for dependents: One year upon death of insured employee.

Time employer has to notify employee of continuation rights: Within 10 days of termination of employment must send notice by certified mail.

Time employee has to apply: 10 days from receipt of notice.

Special situations: Subjects of domestic abuse, who have lost coverage under abuser's plan and who do not qualify for COBRA, may have 18 months coverage (applies to all employers).

Nevada

Nev. Rev. Stat. Ann. §§ 689B.245 to 689B.246; 689B.0345

Employers affected: Employers with less than 20 employees.

Eligible employees: Employees continuously insured for previous 12 months.

Qualifying event: Involuntary termination of employment; involuntary reduction in hours; death of employee; divorce or legal separation; loss of dependent status; employee's eligibility for Medicare.

Length of coverage for employee: 18 months.

Length of coverage for dependents: 36 months.

Time employer has to notify employee of continuation rights: 14 days after receiving notice of employee's eligibility.

Time employee has to apply: Must notify employer within 60 days of becoming eligible for continuation coverage; must apply within 60 days after receiving employer's notice.

Special situations: Leave without pay due to disability: 12 months for employee and dependents (applies to all employers).

New Hampshire

N.H. Rev. Stat. Ann. § 415:18(VII)

Employers affected: Employers with 2 to 19 employees.

Eligible employees: All insured employees are eligible.

Qualifying event: Any reason employee or dependent becomes ineligible for coverage.

Length of coverage for employee: 18 months. (29 months if disabled at termination or during first 60 days of continuation coverage.)

Length of coverage for dependents: 18 months. (29 months if disabled at termination or during first 60 days of continuation coverage; 36 months upon death of employee, divorce or legal separation, loss of dependent status, employee's eligibility for Medicare.)

Time employer has to notify employee of continuation rights: Within 15 days of termination of coverage.

State Health Insurance Laws (continued)

Time employee has to apply: Within 31 days of termination of coverage.

Special benefits: Includes dental insurance.

Special situations: Layoff or termination due to strike: 6 months coverage with option to extend for an additional 12 months. Surviving, divorced or legally separated spouse who is 55 or older: may continue benefits until eligible for Medicare or other employer-based group insurance.

New Jersey

N.J. Stat. Ann. §§ 17B:27-30, 17B:27-51.12, 17B:27A-27

Employers affected: Employers with 2 to 50 employees.

Eligible employees: Employed full time (25 or more hours).

Qualifying event: Termination of employment; reduction in hours

Length of coverage for employee: 12 months.

Length of coverage for dependents: 180 days upon death of employee (applies to all employers).

Time employer has to notify employee of continuation rights: At time of qualifying event employer or carrier notifies employee.

Time employee has to apply: Within 30 days of qualifying event.

Special benefits: Coverage must be identical to that offered to current employees.

Special situations: Total disability: Employee who has been insured for previous 3 months and dependents entitled to continuation coverage that includes all benefits offered by group policy (applies to all employers).

New Mexico

N.M. Stat. Ann. § 59A-18-16

Employers affected: All employers who offer group health insurance.

Eligible employees: All insured employees are eligible.

Qualifying event: Termination of employment.

Length of coverage for employee: 6 months.

Length of coverage for dependents: May convert to individual policy upon death of employee, divorce or legal separation

Time employer has to notify employee of continuation rights: Must give written notice at time of termination.

Time employee has to apply: 30 days after receiving notice.

New York

N.Y. Ins. Law §§ 3221(f), 3221(m)

Employers affected: All employers who offer group health insurance.

Eligible employees: All insured employees are eligible.

Qualifying event: Termination of employment; death of employee; divorce or legal separation; loss of dependent status; employee's eligibility for Medicare.

Length of coverage for employee: 18 months. (29 months if disabled at termination or during first 60 days of continuation coverage.)

Length of coverage for dependents: 18 months. (29 months if disabled at termination or during first 60 days of continuation coverage; 36 months upon death of employee, divorce or legal separation, loss of dependent status, employee's eligibility for Medicare.)

Time employee has to apply: 60 days after termination or receipt of notice, whichever is later.

Special situations: Employee who has been insured for previous 3 months and dependents. May convert to an individual plan instead of group continuation (must apply within 45 days of termination).

State Health Insurance Laws (continued)

Employee who is 60 or older and has been continuously insured for at least 2 years is entitled to a converted policy with set maximum premium limits.

North Carolina

N.C. Gen. Stat. § 58-53-25

Employers affected: All employers who offer group health insurance.

Eligible employees: Employees continuously insured for previous 3 months.

Qualifying event: Termination of employment.

Length of coverage for employee: 18 months.

Length of coverage for dependents: 18 months.

Time employer has to notify employee of continuation rights: Employer has option of notifying employee as part of the exit process.

Time employee has to apply: 60 days.

Special benefits: Excludes: dental care; prescription drugs; vision care; any benefits other than hospital, surgical or major medical.

North Dakota

N.D. Cent. Code § 26.1-36-23

Employers affected: All employers who offer group health insurance.

Eligible employees: Employees continuously insured for previous 3 months.

Qualifying event: Termination of employment.

Length of coverage for employee: 39 weeks

Length of coverage for dependents: 39 weeks. 36 months if required by divorce or annulment decree.

Time employee has to apply: Within 10 days of termination or of receiving notice, whichever is later, but no more than 31 days from termination.

Special benefits: Excludes: dental care; prescription drugs; vision care; any benefits other than hospital, surgical or major medical.

Ohio

Ohio Rev. Code Ann. §§ 3923.38; 1751.53

Employers affected: All employers who offer group health insurance.

Eligible employees: Employees continuously insured for previous 3 months who are entitled to unemployment benefits.

Qualifying event: Involuntary termination of employment.

Length of coverage for employee: 6 months.

Length of coverage for dependents: 6 months.

Time employer has to notify employee of continuation rights: At termination of employment.

Time employee has to apply: Whichever is earlier: 31 days after termination; 10 days after termination if employer gave notice prior to termination; 10 days after employer gives notice.

Special benefits: Excludes: dental care; prescription drugs; vision care; any benefits other than hospital, surgical or major medical.

Oklahoma

Okla. Stat. Ann. tit. 36, § 4509

Employers affected: All employers who offer group health insurance.

Eligible employees: Insured for at least 6 months. (All other employees and their dependents entitled to 30 days continuation coverage.)

Qualifying event: Any reason coverage terminates.

Length of coverage for employee: 3 months for basic coverage, 6 months for major medical.

Length of coverage for dependents: 3 months for basic coverage, 6 months for major medical.

Special benefits: Includes maternity care.

Oregon

Or. Rev. Stat. §§ 743.600 to 743.610

Employers affected: Employers not subject to federal COBRA laws.

State Health Insurance Laws (continued)

Eligible employees: Employees continuously insured for previous 3 months.

Qualifying event: Termination of employment.

Length of coverage for employee: 6 months.

Length of coverage for dependents: 6 months.

Time employee has to apply: 10 days after termination or receiving notice, whichever is later, but not more than 31 days.

Special benefits: Excludes: dental care; prescription drugs; vision care; any benefits other than hospital, surgical or major medical.

Special situations: Surviving, divorced or legally separated spouse who is 55 or older and dependent children entitled to continuation benefits until spouse remarries or is eligible for other coverage. Must include dental, vision or prescription drug benefits if they were offered in original plan (applies to employers with 20 or more employees).

Pennsylvania

40 Pa. Cons. Stat. Ann. § 756.2

No laws for continuation insurance. Employees who have been continuously insured for the previous 3 months may convert to an individual policy.

Rhode Island

R.I. Gen. Laws § 27-19.1-1

Employers affected: All employers who offer group health insurance.

Eligible employees: All insured employees are eligible.

Qualifying event: Involuntary termination of employment; death of employee; permanent reduction in workforce; employer's going out of business.

Length of coverage for employee: 18 months (but not longer than continuous employment).

Length of coverage for dependents: 18 months (but not longer than continuous employment).

Time employer has to notify employee of continuation rights: Employers must post a conspicuous notice of employee continuation rights.

Time employee has to apply: 30 days from termination of coverage.

South Carolina

S.C. Code Ann. § 38-71-770

Employers affected: All employers who offer group health insurance.

Eligible employees: Employees continuously insured for previous 6 months.

Qualifying event: Any reason employee or dependent becomes ineligible for coverage.

Length of coverage for employee: 6 months (in addition to part of month remaining at termination).

Length of coverage for dependents: 6 months (in addition to part of month remaining at termination).

Time employer has to notify employee of continuation rights: At time of termination must clearly and meaningfully advise employee of continuation rights.

Special benefits: Excludes: accidental injury; specific diseases.

South Dakota

S.D. Codified Laws Ann. §§ 58-18-7.5, 58-18-7.12; 58-18C-1

Employers affected: All employers who offer group health insurance.

Eligible employees: Employees continuously insured for previous 6 months.

Qualifying event: Termination of employment; death of employee; divorce or legal separation; loss of dependent status; employee's eligibility for Medicare.

Length of coverage for employee: 18 months. (29 months if disabled at termination or during first 60 days of continuation coverage.)

State Health Insurance Laws (continued)

Length of coverage for dependents: 18 months. (29 months if disabled at termination or during first 60 days of continuation coverage; 36 months upon death of employee, divorce or legal separation, loss of dependent status, employee's eligibility for Medicare.)

Special situations: Employer goes out of business: 12 months coverage for all employees. Employer must notify employees within 10 days of termination of benefits; employees must apply within 60 days of receipt of notice or within 90 days of termination of benefits if no notice given.

Tennessee

Tenn. Code Ann. § 56-7-2312

Employers affected: All employers who offer group health insurance.

Eligible employees: Employees continuously insured for previous 3 months.

Qualifying event: Termination of employment; death of employee; change in marital status.

Length of coverage for employee: 3 months (in addition to part of month remaining at termination).

Length of coverage for dependents: 3 months (in addition to part of month remaining at termination); 15 months upon death of employee or divorce.

Special situations: Employee or dependent who is pregnant at time of termination entitled to continuation benefits for 6 months following the end of pregnancy.

Texas

Tex. Ins. Code Ann. §§ 3.51-6(d)(3), 3.51-8

Employers affected: All employers who offer group health insurance.

Eligible employees: Employees continuously insured for previous 3 months.

Qualifying event: Termination of employment (except for cause); employee leaves for health reasons.

Length of coverage for employee: 6 months.

Length of coverage for dependents: 6 months.

Time employee has to apply: 31 days from termination of coverage or receiving notice from employer, whichever is later.

Special situations: Layoff due to strike: employee entitled to continuation benefits for duration of strike, but no longer than 6 months.

Utah

Utah Code Ann. §§ 31A-22-703, 31A-22-714

Employers affected: All employers who offer group health insurance.

Eligible employees: Employees continuously insured for previous 6 months.

Qualifying event: Termination of employment.

Length of coverage for employee: 6 months.

Length of coverage for dependents: 6 months.

Time employer has to notify employee of continuation rights: In writing within 30 days of termination of coverage.

Time employee has to apply: Within 30 days of receiving notice.

Special benefits: Excludes: accidental injury; catastrophic benefits; dental care; specific diseases.

Vermont

Vt. Stat. Ann. tit. 8, § 4090a

Employers affected: All employers who offer group health insurance.

Eligible employees: Employees continuously insured for previous 3 months.

Qualifying event: Termination of employment; death of employee.

Length of coverage for employee: 6 months.

Length of coverage for dependents: 6 months.

Time employee has to apply: 30 days from termination of employment.

State Health Insurance Laws (continued)

Virginia

Va. Code Ann. §§ 38.2-3541; 38.2-3416

Employers affected: All employers who offer group health insurance.

Eligible employees: Employees continuously insured for previous 3 months.

Qualifying event: Any reason employee or dependent becomes ineligible for coverage.

Length of coverage for employee: 90 days.

Length of coverage for dependents: 90 days.

Time employee has to apply: Must pay 3 months' premium before termination.

Special situations: Employee may convert to an individual policy instead of group continuation coverage (must apply within 31 days of termination).

Washington

Wash. Rev. Code Ann. § 48.21.250

Employers affected: Optional for all employers who offer group health insurance (except during strike).

Eligible employees: All insured employees are eligible.

Qualifying event: Any reason employee or dependent becomes ineligible for coverage.

Length of coverage for employee: Term and rate of coverage agreed upon by employer and employee.

Length of coverage for dependents: Term and rate of coverage agreed upon by employer and employee.

Special situations: Layoff or termination due to strike: 6 months coverage (mandatory for all employers). In other situations: if continuation benefits are not offered, employee may convert to an individual policy (must apply within 31 days of termination of group coverage).

West Virginia

W.Va. Code §§ 33-16-2, 33-16-3(e)

Employers affected: Employers providing insurance for at least 10 employees.

Eligible employees: All insured employees are eligible.

Qualifying event: Involuntary layoff.

Length of coverage for employee: 18 months.

Wisconsin

Wis. Stat. Ann. § 632.897

Employers affected: All employers who offer group health insurance.

Eligible employees: Employees continuously insured for previous 3 months.

Qualifying event: Any reason employee or dependent becomes ineligible for coverage.

Length of coverage for employee: 18 months (or longer at insurer's option).

Length of coverage for dependents: 18 months (or longer at insurer's option).

Time employer has to notify employee of continuation rights: 5 days from termination of coverage.

Time employee has to apply: 30 days after receiving notice.

Wyoming

Wyo. Stat. § 26-19-113

Employers affected: Employers not subject to federal COBRA laws.

Eligible employees: Employees continuously insured for previous 3 months.

Qualifying event: Termination of employment.

Length of coverage for employee: 12 months.

Length of coverage for dependents: 12 months.

Time employee has to apply: 31 days from termination of coverage.

Special benefits: If dental, vision care or any benefits other than hospital, surgical or major medical were included in the group policy, they may be continued at employee or dependent's request.

5. Reducing Costs

Small businesses often feel overwhelmed by the spiraling costs of providing healthcare benefits to employees. But there are some steps you can take that may help hold down costs, mostly by eliminating unnecessary medical expenses.

Look for a healthcare plan that practices managed care—requiring participants to get a second opinion before they have surgery or requiring pre-approval by the insurance company for expensive diagnostic procedures.

Requiring employees to pay a part of the monthly coverage fee as well as a portion of each medical bill may encourage employees to be judicious in seeking treatment.

Look into offering coverage through a Health Maintenance Organization (HMO) or Preferred Provider Organization (PPO) instead of traditional insurance or reimbursement coverage. But be sure to shop around make sure that the overall cost of a PPO or HMO plan really is lower than traditional coverage.

Money put into preventive care is well spent. You can, for example, call in experts to teach employees the benefits of a healthy diet, exercise and preventive care. Beyond that, you can set a good example by making low-fat food available in your lunchroom and installing exercise equipment in an unused area of the workplace. Consider paying for seminars to help employees quit smoking. And encourage periodic physical checkups—perhaps by offering to pay part of the usual deductible payment

6. Medical Savings Accounts

If you have 50 or fewer employees, you can offer your employees the option of opening a medical savings account (MSA), also called an Archer MSA in recognition of Rep. Bill Archer, R-Texas. An Archer MSA is a tax-exempt trust or custodial account in which an employee can save money for future medical expenses. The employee then uses the account in conjunction with a high deductible health plan to meet his or her healthcare needs.

This type of account offers employees several benefits, including:

- The money in the MSA grows tax-free.
- Employees can claim a tax deduction for the contributions that they make to their MSAs.
- The contributions remain in the employee's MSA until the employee uses them.

The MSA program is currently set to expire on December 31, 2003. Unless Congress acts to change the law, no new MSAs may be established after this date.

Coverage for Pregnant Women and Older Workers

Federal law imposes some special insurance requirements for pregnant women and older workers.

Women. You must treat women affected by pregnancy and related conditions the same as other employees based on their ability or inability to work. For example, if a woman can't work because she's pregnant, you must provide her with the same health-care coverage as you generally provide to employees who become ill or have a disability. (See Chapter 8, Section D, for more on the Pregnancy Discrimination Act.) The Family and Medical Leave Act allows workers to take up to 12 weeks a year of unpaid leave connected with childbirth, adoption and foster placement. (See Chapter 6.)

Older Workers. You must offer workers age 40 and older the same healthcare coverage you offer to younger workers—and, if your plan requires that all your workers be covered, you can't make older workers pay more to join. But if the insurance isn't mandatory, older workers can be charged more, so long as actuarial charts show their healthcare costs are higher.

B. Retirement Plans

Retirement plans provide income to older people when they're no longer part of the workforce. If the plans you offer meet certain IRS guidelines, your contribution to the benefits qualifies as a business expense and is deduct-ible from your company's gross income. We look at a few of your options below. If you are interested in providing retirement benefits to your employees, talk to a benefits specialist to find a plan that will work for you.

1. Defined Benefit Plans

In a defined benefit plan, you promise to pay an employee a fixed amount of money, usually in monthly increments, after he or she retires. You may base the payments on a formula that combines the number of years the employee has worked and the amount of his or her earnings. You may also choose some other method of setting the timing and amount, such as a fixed monthly sum not tied to length of service or earnings.

To fund a defined benefit plan, employers typically invest money in stocks, bonds and mutual funds that are expected to grow over the years. You must contribute enough to the plan to pay the promised benefit. Otherwise, you'll have to make up the difference if the plan's investments go bad.

To help protect employees if a business lacks the funds to pay that difference, employers who offer defined benefit plans must generally contribute to the Pension Benefit Guaranty Corporation. For details, visit the agency's website at www.pbgc.gov.

2. Defined Contribution Plans

In a defined contribution plan, you set up an account for the employee and contribute to it. At retirement, the employee gets whatever is in the account. You don't promise that the employee will receive a specific amount of income after retirement.

You may structure the defined contribution plan as a money purchase pension plan, in which case you'll promise to contribute a specific amount per employee each year, such as five cents for each hour worked. Or you may structure it as a profit sharing plan in which you have the discretion to decide each year how much to contribute, with your contributions allocated to the employees' accounts in a specified way—usually in proportion to their pay. In either case, the size of the pension checks an employee receives each month after retirement will vary according to the interest rate paid on the employee's pension account and other economic factors.

3. 401(k) Plans

A 401(k) plan consists of a retirement account for each employee who participates. An employer can choose whether or not to make contributions and how extensive those contributions will be. You might, for example, choose to contribute only if company profits reach a certain level or to match contributions of only the lower-paid employees. The total amount you can contribute annually to all of an employee's defined contribution plans—including a 401(k)—is $40,000 or an amount equal to the employee's compensation, whichever is less.

Even if you don't contribute to the 401(k) plan, it still constitutes a valuable benefit to employees because it helps them save for retirement with tax-deferred dollars. If you set up an employee-funded 401(k) plan, employees can defer the income tax on the money they stash away, which allows their investments to grow faster.

A typical plan, administered by a major mutual fund company, calls for regular payroll deductions from an employee's earnings, in an amount specified by the employee. The IRS limits on the employee's contributions are as follows:

Year	Contribution Limit
2002	$11,000
2003	$12,000
2004	$13,000
2005	$14,000
2006	$15,000

After 2006, these limits will be increased in $500 increments to reflect inflation.

Employees who are 50 or older can also make annual "catch-up" contributions as follows:

Year	Catch-Up Contribution Limit
2002	$1,000
2003	$2,000
2004	$3,000
2005	$4,000
2006	$5,000

The employee gets to allocate his or her account among several different mutual funds —and to change the mix from time to time. The funds on the menu run the gamut from conservative to aggressive, so the employee can choose the level of risk with which he or she feels most comfortable. Be aware, however, that it may cost you a few thousand dollars to set up a 401(k) plan for your business—and there may be ongoing expenses for plan administration. (See Section 4b, below.)

⚠ Special Protection for Older Employees. The Older Workers' Benefits Protection Act, an amendment to the Federal Age Discrimination in Employment Act (29 U.S.C. § 621), generally prohibits you from providing reduced benefits to older people in your retirement plan. But the Act does allow for some lesser coverage for certain benefits, such as health and disability insurance, if you can show there's a rational

cost reason for doing it. For more information on benefit rules for older workers, see *Federal Employment Laws: A Desk Reference,* by Amy DelPo & Lisa Guerin (Nolo)—it includes a chapter explaining the requirements of the Older Workers' Benefits Protection Act.

4. Meeting IRS and ERISA Requirements

When maintaining a retirement plan for your employees, you must comply with two sets of laws: the Internal Revenue Code, which sets out the tax law requirements for your plan, and the Employee Retirement Income Security Act, or ERISA (29 U.S.C. § 1001 and following), which sets out the administrative requirements for your plan.

a. Tax law requirements

While you don't have to include all workers in your retirement plan, there are complicated laws that govern whom you can include, whom you can exclude and for what reasons. In addition, you can't structure the plan to benefit only the top executives or to otherwise discriminate against lower-paid workers.

A retirement plan that passes muster with the IRS is called a qualified plan—meaning your contribution qualifies as a tax-deductible business expense. Your contributions won't be taxed as income to employees until they actually receive the benefit.

For a helpful introduction to these requirements, see IRS Publication 535, *Business Expenses,* available at no charge from the nearest IRS office or on the IRS website at www.irs.gov.

Getting Help With the Technicalities

The usual and safest way to make sure your pension plan meets ERISA and tax law requirements is to seek assistance from a qualified expert—perhaps a lawyer or CPA experienced in pension plan matters. But that may be expensive, especially for a smaller business.

As an alternative, try contacting a few insurance companies and other groups that handle 401(k) and other benefit plans. They'll provide much information at no cost and will crunch numbers for you so you'll know the best way to structure the plan so that most employees can participate.

In addition to resolving technical problems, benefit providers may offer seminars to help your employees make sound investment choices.

---

b. Administration requirements

Under ERISA, you'll need to appoint a plan administrator—someone who is responsible for following through on the law's paperwork requirements. This can be a person in your business or an outsider who's associated with the retirement plan. If you have a relatively small business, it may be simpler and cheaper to have an outsider—such as a worker at a bank or mutual fund company—act as plan administrator. It's difficult to develop enough expertise within your business to meet all the legal requirements that affect retirement plans.

The ERISA requirements are heavy on paperwork. There are a number of documents your plan administrator must give to participating employees.

Summary plan description. This is a booklet that describes how your plan operates. Your plan administrator must give employees the summary plan description within 90 days after they begin participating in the plan. Employees are also entitled to plan updates. The description must include the formula for determining an employee's benefits or the contributions that you'll make to the plan. It must also explain any formula for vesting—the point at which the employee's right to retirement benefits becomes locked in and can't be taken away.

Summary annual report. This is a yearly accounting of the plan's financial condition and operations.

Survivor coverage data. This is a statement of how much the plan will pay to the surviving spouse of an employee if the employee dies.

In addition, each year the plan administrator must give participants a detailed, individual statement of the benefits they've earned. And you must annually file with the IRS a Form 5500, which includes a census of employees and participants and is accompanied by summary financial reports.

Get Help If You Can. ERISA is an extremely complicated law that can trip up even the most well-intentioned and savvy employer. Unless you have a large company with an experienced benefits administrator, you'd be wise to hire a professional to help you meet the law's requirements. Often, whatever company administers your plan for you will also take care of ERISA. Talk to your plan administrator to be sure.

c. Plan termination requirements

If you decide to terminate a defined benefit plan—one which promises specific benefits—you must notify covered employees of the approaching termination at least 60 days before the plan ends.

If you decide to reduce the rate of benefit accruals or terminate either a defined benefit plan or a money purchase plan, you must notify covered employees a reasonable period of time before the amendment takes effect.

⚠ Former Spouses' Retirement Benefit Rights. In many divorces, an employee's retirement benefits are divided as part of the property settlement. The spouse of an employee may acquire rights under what ERISA calls a qualified domestic relations order (QDRO). When that happens, your company has ERISA obligations to the employee's spouse similar to your obligations to the employee. These include reviewing the court order to see if it meets the requirements for a QDRO, paying out money to the spouse as required by the order and giving the spouse plan information if benefits aren't paid to the spouse immediately.

Who's In—And Who's Out

You don't have a completely free hand in deciding who to include in a retirement plan. In general, ERISA requires you to include everyone who:

- is 21 years old or older, and
- has worked for your business for a year—1,000 or more hours in the last 12 months.

You can require employees to be with your company for two years before they will be eligible to participate in the plan. But if you do, you must also provide that an employee's rights become fully vested as soon as he or she begins participating in the plan.

C. Other Employee Benefits

Here's a rundown of several other benefit programs that the IRS recognizes as tax-deductible business expenses.

1. Life Insurance

One of the least expensive benefits you can offer to employees is group term life insurance. This is life insurance that pays off only if the employee dies during the policy term—usually five, ten or 20 years. You can deduct the premiums you pay for up to $50,000 of group term life insurance for each employee. And employees don't pay tax on the premiums you pay.

If your business doesn't have at least ten full-time employees, you'll need to meet some special requirements to qualify for this tax treatment. For example, you'll have to provide life insurance for *all* full-time employees, and you can't require physical exams for the coverage. However many employees you have, you can't weight your group-term plan in favor of highly paid employees.

Some employers pay for the first $10,000 or so of term life coverage, giving the employee the option of buying additional coverage under the same group plan. This allows employers to offer a growing benefit without having to put out a growing outlay of cash.

In selecting a group insurance policy, look for one that allows a terminated employee to switch to an individual policy without having to prove that he or she is still insurable. Of course, after such a conversion, a former employee becomes responsible for paying the premiums.

2. Disability Insurance

Consider offering disability insurance to help employees offset income lost if they suffer a serious injury or illness. You can probably find a group policy under which you pay part of the premium and the employee pays part. Some plans give employees the option of continuing their coverage after they leave your business. They then become responsible for the entire premium.

Your business can take a tax deduction for the premiums it pays, but if an employee receives payments under the insurance policy, the employee will owe income tax on those payments. If the employer and employee each pay part of the premium, the employee

will owe income tax on part of the payments received.

3. Educational Assistance Programs

You may want to pay all or part of the cost of schooling that employees pursue outside working hours. You can set up a written plan with guidelines for the type of continuing education your business will finance, how much you're willing to spend and the point at which you'll reimburse an employee for tuition.

Under such a plan, you can deduct as a business expense up to $5,250 per year for the educational costs you pay for an employee— and these costs are not included in the employee's taxable income.

A few restrictions apply.

- The education assistance program can't favor highly paid employees or their spouses or dependents.

- No more than 5% of the program's payments during a year can be used to benefit a business's shareholders or owners—or their spouses or dependents.
- You can't offer employees a choice between receiving the educational assistance or other payment that's includable in the employees' gross income.
- Assistance can't be used for courses involving sports, games or hobbies.

4. Dependent Care Assistance

The tax laws let your business deduct expenses you pay for assistance to employees who must care for their dependents—a major concern today as more workers have to take care of young children, aging parents or both.

Your payments qualify for the tax deduction if they enable an employee to care for:

- a dependent age 12 or younger for whom the employee can claim a personal exemption
- a dependent who's physically or mentally incapable of taking care of himself or herself, or
- the employee's spouse, if the spouse can't take care of himself or herself.

The amounts you deduct can be for bills you pay or money you reimburse to an employee for:

- at-home child care
- in-home care for elderly or disabled adults who live with the employee
- care at a licensed nursery school or kindergarten, or
- care at a dependent care center that provides day care for more than six people.

You can also provide dependent care assistance at your own on-site facility.

Dependent care payments up to $5,000 a year ($2,500 for a married employee filing a separate return) are tax-free to the employee; as noted, your business can deduct these payments as a business expense. For employees with lower household incomes, there's a dependent care tax credit that will be more valuable to them than any dependent care assistance provided by an employer, even though the care the employer provides won't be included in the employee's income for tax purposes. If you offer a dependent care plan, let employees know about tax credit alternatives so they can choose the best option.

5. Adoption Assistance Programs

You can assist employees with adoption expenses—up to $10,000 for the adoption of an eligible child. You'll need to write up an adoption assistance plan and make sure it meets requirements similar to the ones that apply to educational assistance programs. (See Section C3.)

With such a plan in place, you can deduct your payments for adoption expenses as a business expense. If an employee's tax return shows adjusted gross income of $150,000 or less, the employee can exclude the amounts you pay for adoption expenses. For those who make more than $150,000, the exclusion is phased out.

These numbers will increase from time to time for cost-of-living adjustments.

Cafeteria Plans

Under a cafeteria plan, an employee gets to choose from a menu of benefits such as:

- health insurance
- dental coverage
- vision care
- disability insurance
- group term life insurance
- group legal services
- additional contribution to a 401(k) plan
- additional paid vacation days, and
- cash.

Typically, the employer provides a monthly allowance to be allocated by the employee. If an employee selects benefits that exceed the allowance, the employee pays the additional amount through payroll deductions. If an employee doesn't use the full allowance, the leftover amount is added to his or her paycheck.

These plans are attractive because they allow employees to tailor their benefits to their particular needs, while giving the employer some control over benefit costs.

Chapter 5

Taxes

A. Employer Identification Numbers 5/3

    1. How to Apply 5/3

    2. When to Get a New Number 5/4

B. Federal Employment Taxes 5/6

    1. Federal Income Tax Withholding (FIT) 5/6

    2. Social Security Taxes (FICA) 5/6

    3. Federal Unemployment Taxes (FUTA) 5/7

    4. Periodic Deposits 5/7

C. Federal Self-Employment Taxes 5/8

D. Federal Tax Deductions for Salaries and Other Expenses 5/10

    1. Salaries 5/10

    2. Vacation Pay 5/10

    3. Bonuses and Gifts 5/10

    4. Meals and Lodging 5/11

    5. Fringe Benefits 5/13

E. Independent Contractors 5/13

F. Statutory Employees 5/14

*A*s an employer, one of your roles is that of tax collector. The government treats you as an unpaid revenue agent whose job it is to withhold income taxes and Social Security and Medicare taxes from employees' paychecks and pay over those amounts to the IRS. In addition, Uncle Sam requires you to match employees' Social Security and Medicare taxes and to pay a federal unemployment tax based on your payroll. And Uncle's nieces and nephews in state government also look to you to help rake in their dough.

You must also account to every employee for the taxes you've withheld and the amounts being sent to the government.

Whether you personally handle employee tax matters or turn them over to someone else—a bookkeeper or an accountant—you must understand at least the fundamentals of the system. If you handle taxes incorrectly, you can be hit with interest and penalties. And you may even be held personally liable if your business fails to transmit employee withholdings to the government. The IRS doggedly pursues its targets, so you don't want to get caught in its clutches.

This chapter will help you acquire a good working knowledge of how the tax laws affect you as an employer and how the pieces of the tax system fit together.

Determine how involved you want to be in handling employee taxes and whether there are tasks you want to delegate to others.

If you want to do it yourself, the IRS puts out some excellent publications to guide you through the process. Relevant IRS publications are noted throughout this chapter. You can get them at your local IRS office, by calling the IRS at 800-829-3676 or by visiting the agency's website at www.irs.gov.

A part-time bookkeeper can help compile organized, detailed business records without demanding too much of your time. An accountant can help you set up a plan for your bookkeeper to follow and periodically monitor it to ensure that you meet all tax obligations.

A word of caution about one other possible source of assistance: IRS employees. Most of them are hardworking and well-meaning, but their training and supervision are often inadequate. Unfortunately, it's common to receive bad advice in answer to your questions. And if the advice proves to be so inaccurate that it causes you to be assessed interest and penalties, the fact that you got it from an IRS employee won't get you off the hook. In short, it's often cheaper to rely on the advice of an experienced small business accountant than to rely on a free oral opinion from the IRS.

Beware of the State

This chapter focuses on federal tax law. In addition to being scrupulously mindful of federal payroll taxes, find out whether your state and municipality impose payroll taxes. For example, if your state or city has an income tax, you may be required to withhold taxes from employees' pay much like the federal system—but some states and cities follow different procedures. Contact your state and city treasurers for detailed information.

A. Employer Identification Numbers

When you start your business, get an Employer Identification Number (EIN) from the IRS. You must do this regardless of whether your business is a sole proprietorship, a partnership, an S corporation, a regular corporation—sometimes called a C corporation—or a limited liability company (LLC). Technically, if you're a sole proprietor and have no employees, you can use your personal Social Security number instead of an EIN. But even in that situation, it's a good business practice to get an EIN to differentiate cleanly between your personal and business finances.

1. How to Apply

To get an EIN, file Form SS-4, Application for Employer Identification Number. The instructions tell you where to send the completed form. A completed sample form is shown below.

The form isn't difficult to fill out if you follow the IRS instructions. Here are a few pointers.

Space 1. Insert your official corporate name if you're a corporation. If you're a partnership, use the partnership name shown in your partnership agreement. If you're a sole proprietor, insert your full name.

Space 11. Here you're asked to state the closing month of your business accounting year. Your answer, however, isn't binding. You make your binding election of a fiscal

year-end on the first federal income tax return that you file for the business.

Sole proprietors, partnerships, S corporations and personal service corporations are generally required to use a calendar year—that is, a year ending December 31—for tax purposes. Personal service corporations have two basic characteristics:

- the professional employees of the corporation own the stock, and
- the corporation performs its services in the fields of health, law, engineering, architecture, accounting, actuarial science, performing arts or consulting.

To use a tax year other than a calendar year, an S corporation must demonstrate to the IRS that it has a substantial business reason to do so, such as the seasonal nature of the business. Basically, the IRS wants to make sure that permitting you to claim a tax year other than the calendar year won't substantially distort your income.

 See IRS Publication 589, *Tax Information on S Corporations,* and IRS Publication 538, *Business Purpose Tax Year,* for details.

A regular corporation that's not a personal service corporation has more freedom in choosing a fiscal year. Most small businesses find that where there's a choice, the calendar year is the most convenient way to proceed. Sometimes, however, there are tax planning reasons for a business owner to choose a different tax year for the business.

An accountant or other experienced tax advisor can help you decide whether or not you and your corporation can realize a tax advantage by using a fiscal year instead of a calendar year.

Space 12. The IRS will send you computer-generated payroll tax forms based on your answer to this question.

Space 13. These numbers can be estimated.

Space 16a. This question refers to the business, not the owner. Normally, a partnership or corporation has only one Employer Identification Number (EIN). A sole proprietor may have several businesses, each with a separate number.

You'll need your EIN before you file a tax return or make a tax deposit. In some cases, a bank will require you to have an EIN before you open a business account.

There are three ways to obtain the number.

- **By mail.** If you have enough lead time, you can mail Form SS-4 to the IRS and wait for the number to be mailed to you. This will take about four weeks.

- **By telephone.** To get a Form SS-4 processed more quickly, use the TELE-TIN system operated by the IRS. Complete the form and, before you mail it, phone in the information to the IRS at the telephone number given for your region, as listed in the form's instruction sheet. An IRS employee will assign you an EIN, which you'll then write in the upper right corner of the form before sending it to the IRS.

- **By fax.** You can fax your IRS Form SS-4. To obtain the fax number, ask at the IRS office where you pick up your Form SS-4. You'll get your EIN in a day or two. This is slower than the telephone method, but it avoids the frustration of repeated calling if the TELE-TIN voice line is tied up.

Use your EIN on all business tax returns, checks and other documents you send to the IRS. Your state tax authority may also require your EIN on state tax forms.

2. When to Get a New Number

If your S corporation chooses to change to a regular corporation—or your regular corporation chooses to change to an S corporation—it doesn't need a new EIN; the one you already have is still sufficient. However, you'll need to get a new EIN if any of these changes occur in your business:

- You incorporate your sole proprietorship or partnership.
- Your sole proprietorship takes in partners and begins operating as a partnership.
- Your partnership is taken over by one of the partners and begins operating as a sole proprietorship.
- Your corporation changes to a partnership or to a sole proprietorship.
- You purchase or inherit an existing business that you'll operate as a sole proprietorship.
- You represent an estate that operates a business after the owner's death.
- You terminate an old partnership and begin a new one.

Form **SS-4**

(Rev. December 2001)
Department of the Treasury
Internal Revenue Service

Application for Employer Identification Number

(For use by employers, corporations, partnerships, trusts, estates, churches, government agencies, Indian tribal entities, certain individuals, and others.)

▶ See separate instructions for each line. ▶ Keep a copy for your records.

EIN

OMB No. 1545-0003

Type or print clearly.

1 Legal name of entity (or individual) for whom the EIN is being requested
Ted Anderson

2 Trade name of business (if different from name on line 1)
The Poster Warehouse

3 Executor, trustee, "care of" name

4a Mailing address (room, apt., suite no. and street, or P.O. box)
555 Main Street

5a Street address (if different) (Do not enter a P.O. box.)

4b City, state, and ZIP code
Ann Arbor, MI 48104

5b City, state, and ZIP code

6 County and state where principal business is located
Washtenaw

7a Name of principal officer, general partner, grantor, owner, or trustor
Ted Anderson

7b SSN, ITIN, or EIN

8a Type of entity (check only one box)

☒ Sole proprietor (SSN) 555 55 5555
☐ Partnership
☐ Corporation (enter form number to be filed) ▶
☐ Personal service corp.
☐ Church or church-controlled organization
☐ Other nonprofit organization (specify) ▶
☐ Other (specify) ▶

☐ Estate (SSN of decedent)
☐ Plan administrator (SSN)
☐ Trust (SSN of grantor)
☐ National Guard   ☐ State/local government
☐ Farmers' cooperative   ☐ Federal government/military
☐ REMIC   ☐ Indian tribal governments/enterprises
Group Exemption Number (GEN) ▶

8b If a corporation, name the state or foreign country (if applicable) where incorporated

State

Foreign country

9 **Reason for applying** (check only one box)
☒ Started new business (specify type) ▶
Consulting
☐ Hired employees (Check the box and see line 12.)
☐ Compliance with IRS withholding regulations
☐ Other (specify) ▶

☐ Banking purpose (specify purpose) ▶
☐ Changed type of organization (specify new type) ▶
☐ Purchased going business
☐ Created a trust (specify type) ▶
☐ Created a pension plan (specify type) ▶

10 Date business started or acquired (month, day, year)
August 1, 20XX

11 Closing month of accounting year
December 1, 20XX

12 First date wages or annuities were paid or will be paid (month, day, year). **Note:** *If applicant is a withholding agent, enter date income will first be paid to nonresident alien. (month, day, year)* . . . . ▶ September 1, 20XX

13 Highest number of employees expected in the next 12 months. **Note:** *If the applicant does not expect to have any employees during the period, enter "-0-."* . . . . ▶

Agricultural	Household	Other
1	0	0

14 Check **one** box that best describes the principal activity of your business.
☐ Construction   ☐ Rental & leasing   ☐ Transportation & warehousing   ☐ Health care & social assistance   ☐ Wholesale-agent/broker
☐ Real estate   ☐ Manufacturing   ☐ Finance & insurance   ☐ Accommodation & food service   ☐ Wholesale-other   ☐ Retail
☒ Other (specify) Consulting

15 Indicate principal line of merchandise sold; specific construction work done; products produced; or services provided.
Consulting

16a Has the applicant ever applied for an employer identification number for this or any other business? . . . . ☐ Yes ☒ No
Note: *If "Yes," please complete lines 16b and 16c.*

16b If you checked "Yes" on line 16a, give applicant's legal name and trade name shown on prior application if different from line 1 or 2 above.
Legal name ▶   Trade name ▶

16c Approximate date when, and city and state where, the application was filed. Enter previous employer identification number if known.
Approximate date when filed (mo., day, year)   City and state where filed   Previous EIN

Third Party Designee	Complete this section **only** if you want to authorize the named individual to receive the entity's EIN and answer questions about the completion of this form.	
	Designee's name	Designee's telephone number (include area code) ( )
	Address and ZIP code	Designee's fax number (include area code) ( )

Under penalties of perjury, I declare that I have examined this application, and to the best of my knowledge and belief, it is true, correct, and complete.

Name and title (type or print clearly) ▶ Ted Anderson, Owner

Applicant's telephone number (include area code)
(313) 555-5555

Signature ▶ *Ted Anderson*   Date ▶ 7/14/XX

Applicant's fax number (include area code)
( )

For Privacy Act and Paperwork Reduction Act Notice, see separate instructions.   Cat. No. 16055N   Form **SS-4** (Rev. 12-2001)

B. Federal Employment Taxes

There are several types of employment-related taxes the federal government exacts from businesses.

 These taxes are all explained clearly and in great detail in *Circular E, Employer's Tax Guide,* published by the IRS. Updated whenever the tax rates change, *Circular E* is available at all IRS offices and is mailed automatically to all businesses with an EIN.

1. Federal Income Tax Withholding (FIT)

You must withhold income taxes from employees' paychecks based on:

- the employee's filing status (single, married or married but withholding at the higher single rate)
- the number of dependents (withholding allowances) declared by the employee, and
- the size of the employee's salary.

Each employee should give you a signed Form W-4 stating the withholding allowance. Save these forms. You needn't send them to the IRS unless the employee:

- claims more than ten allowances, or
- claims to be exempt from withholding and normally earns more than $200 a week.

Use the tables in *Circular E* to figure out how much income tax to withhold.

 IRS Publication 334, *Tax Guide for Small Business*, and if you're just getting started, IRS Publication 583, *Taxpayers Starting a Business*, are well worth reading. These publications are free from your local IRS office or can be obtained by calling the main IRS number: 800-829-3676. You can also obtain them at the IRS website at www.irs.gov.

Working for Yourself: Laws & Taxes for Independent Contractors, Freelancers & Consultants, by Stephen Fishman (Nolo), is a comprehensive guide for those starting their own businesses. It includes detailed information on taxes.

Small-Time Operator, by Bernard Kamoroff (Bell Springs Publishing), is a modestly priced and clearly written book that covers not only taxes but also many other practical aspects of doing business, including bookkeeping.

U.S. Master Tax Guide, (Commerce Clearing House), is updated annually and available in law libraries, business school libraries and the reference departments of major public libraries. It features in-depth explanations of tax complexities.

The Kiplinger Tax Letter, published by the Kiplinger Washington Editors, is a bi-weekly newsletter. It's pricy but does keep you up to date on what's happening in the tax field. The breezy—some would say breathless—style is fun to read. To subscribe, call 800-544-0155.

Also, you can buy software that handles payroll, including tax computations. Look into QuickPay, OneWrite and Peachtree.

2. Social Security Taxes (FICA)

You must withhold the employee's share of the Social Security tax and Medicare tax from the employee's pay. And you must also pay the employer's share.

The amounts to be withheld are listed in the most current edition of *Circular E*. For 2002, for example, the employer and the employee are each required to pay 7.65% on the first $84,900 of the employee's annual wages; the 7.65% figure is the sum of the 6.2% Social Security tax and the 1.45% Medicare tax. There is no Social Security tax on the portion of the employee's annual wages that exceed $84,900—only the Medicare tax; the employer and the employee each pay the 1.45% Medicare tax on the excess amount. The rates and the cut-off point for the Social Security tax change annually.

Withholding From an Owner's Paycheck

If you own most or all of the stock of a regular corporation, chances are you probably pay yourself a salary—which means that you're an employee as well as an owner. Similarly, if you're an owner and officer of an S corporation and perform substantial services for the company, you're considered an employee for tax purposes.

With either type of corporation, if you receive compensation for your services, you must complete and submit a Form W-4 to the corporation just like any other employee, and the corporation must withhold income, Social Security and Medicare taxes from your paychecks.

3. Federal Unemployment Taxes (FUTA)

Finally, you must report and pay the federal unemployment tax (FUTA). The employer is responsible for paying this tax; it's not withheld from the employee's pay. The FUTA rate through 2007 is 6.2% of the first $7,000 of the employee's wages for the year. Employers are given a credit for participating in state unemployment programs. The credit reduces the FUTA rate to 0.8% for most employers—which translates into $56 for an employee earning $7,000 or more per year. Use Form 940 or 940EZ to report federal unemployment tax. Sole proprietorships and partnerships don't pay the FUTA on the owners' compensation.

4. Periodic Deposits

You must periodically deposit the withheld income tax and the employer's and employee's shares of Social Security taxes at an authorized financial institution—usually a bank. The IRS sends you coupons to use in making these deposits. It also provides instructions on how often you're required to deposit these funds, which depends on the size of your payroll and amounts due; a typical small business makes monthly deposits.

Deposit Taxes on Time. Be sure to withhold taxes as required by the tax laws—and to deposit those taxes on time. There are substantial penalties if you don't. And if you're an owner of a small business and personally involved in its management, you can be held personally liable for these taxes and the additional penalties, even if the business has the funds to pay them. The IRS has discretion to go after whomever it chooses. If your business suddenly runs into financial trouble, put the withheld taxes at the top of the list for payment. If that means not paying suppliers and others, so be it. The debts of the other creditors can be wiped out in bankruptcy if the business continues to go downhill. Not so with the withheld taxes. You can remain personally liable for these amounts even if the business goes through bankruptcy.

Get a copy of IRS Publication 509, *Tax Calendars,* to see when to file returns and make tax payments. It's available from your local IRS office or can be obtained by calling the main IRS number: 800-829-3676, or by going to the IRS website at www.irs.gov. The publication is updated annually.

C. Federal Self-Employment Taxes

The self-employment tax applies to income you receive from actively working in your business—but not as an employee of that business. Technically, it's not an employment tax, but a first cousin to that tax—so closely related that you should be aware of it to fully understand employment taxes.

Payroll Taxes Made Easy

If you're overwhelmed by the requirements for calculating payroll taxes and the fine points of when and where to pay them, you can pay a bank or payroll service to do the work for you. A reputable payroll tax outfit that offers a tax notification service will calculate the correct amount due, produce the checks to pay the employees and the taxes and notify you when the taxes are due.

One big advantage of a payroll service over a bank is that a bank will withhold the amount of the tax from your account when the payroll is done, even though the tax isn't due yet. That means the bank, not you, gets the use of the money in the interim. If your payroll service offers tax notification, it will prepare the checks and tell you when they must be deposited. Depending on how often you must make payments, that can give you the use of the money for an extra month or more.

At the end of each quarter, the payroll service will produce your quarterly payroll tax returns and tell you how to file them. At the end of the year, the service will also prepare W-2 forms and federal and state transmittal forms.

Payroll services can be cost-effective for even very small businesses. But when you look for one, it pays to shop around. Avoid services that charge setup fees—basically, a fee for putting your information into its computer—or extra fees to prepare W-2 forms or quarterly and annual tax returns.

If you're a sole proprietor or a partner, you must pay the federal self-employment tax in addition to regular income tax. The self-employment tax is equal to the employer's and employee's portion of the Social Security and Medicare taxes that you and your employer would pay on your compensation if you received it as an employee.

Compute this tax each year on Schedule SE, then attach it to your personal Form 1040. Add the self-employment tax to the income tax that you owe. In 2002, for example, the self-employment tax is set at 15.3% on earnings up to $84,900 and 2.9% on earnings over $84,900.

If you have income from another job that's subject to withholding—common for people just getting started in business—the income from your other job will reduce the tax base for your self-employment tax.

EXAMPLE: Morton works ¾ time as a chemistry instructor at a local college, where he receives an annual salary of $50,000. He also does consulting, as a sole proprietor, for several chemical companies and earns an additional $40,000 a year after expenses. The $50,000 salary at the college—which is subject to withholding by the employer—is used to reduce the $84,900 cap on income that's subject to the 15.3% self-employment tax. So Morton computes the tax at the rate of 15.3% on $34,900 of his consulting business income ($84,900 less $50,000 = $34,900). On the remaining portion—$5,100 ($40,000 less $34,900 = $5,100)—he computes the tax at the rate of 2.9%.

Computing Your Estimated Taxes

Many taxpayers receive income from sources other than paychecks—for example, from investments and royalties. These taxpayers often owe surprising amounts in income taxes on April 15. Sometimes, that's because they had no employer to withhold income tax during the year. Other times, it's because even though there was an employer, the amounts withheld were insufficient to cover the taxpayer's non-employment income.

As you may know, the IRS doesn't want you to wait until April 15 to pay. Instead, the IRS requires you to pay your taxes in advance in quarterly installments if not enough is being withheld from your salary. These installments are known as estimated taxes. If you don't pay sufficient taxes in advance, you face the burden of paying interest and penalties.

In figuring out what your tax bill will be and whether you need to pay any quarterly installments of estimated taxes, don't overlook the self-employment tax that is added to your regular income tax on your Form 1040 as part of your tax obligation. Make sure your quarterly installments are large enough to cover your self-employment tax as well as your usual income tax.

For more on this subject, see IRS Publication 505, *Tax Withholding and Estimated Tax,* available at the nearest IRS office or from the IRS website at www.irs.gov.

D. Federal Tax Deductions for Salaries and Other Expenses

A number of employee-related expenses can be deducted from business income in computing your federal income tax.

1. Salaries

You can deduct from gross income the salaries, wages and other forms of compensation that you give to employees for their services, as long as the payments are reasonable. Fortunately, you have broad discretion to decide what's reasonable. Short of a scam—such as paying a huge salary to a spouse or relative who does little or no work—the IRS will almost always accept your notion of what pay is reasonable.

If your business is on the cash method of accounting, you deduct the payments that were actually made during the tax year. For employers using an accrual method of accounting, the rule is different and more complicated. The salaries are deductible for the tax year in which you established your obligation to make the payments, even if you deferred payment to a later time.

2. Vacation Pay

You can also deduct vacation pay from business income in determining the base for your federal income tax.

If you're on a cash basis accounting method, you deduct vacation pay as wages when you pay the employee.

If you use an accrual method, you can deduct vacation pay in the year it's earned only if you pay it by the close of your tax year or within two and a half months after the close. If you pay later than this, you deduct it in the year you actually pay it.

3. Bonuses and Gifts

Many businesses give bonuses to employees to reward them for a job well done or because the company has had a profitable year. You can take a tax deduction for bonuses you pay to employees if they're intended as additional payment for services and not as gifts; most bonuses qualify for deduction. The bonuses are subject to payroll tax withholding.

Cash and Accrual Methods: Defined

Most small businesses and many mid-sized businesses use the cash method of accounting. With the cash method, you include in your gross income all the cash, checks and other payments you receive during the tax year. Usually, you deduct expenses in the tax year in which you pay them.

There are, however, a few exceptions. Some business costs, such as the purchase of a building, must be spread over a number of years; this is known as capitalization. And if you prepay expenses, you can only deduct them for the year to which they apply. If, for example, you pay a two-year premium on a liability insurance policy, you can only deduct half one year and must wait until the next year to deduct the other half.

With the accrual method, income is included in gross income when you earn it even though you don't get paid until the next tax year. Suppose you're in the business of selling television sets and you do your taxes on a calendar year basis. On December 28, you sell a TV set. In January, you bill the customer and in February, you receive payment. The income was earned on December 28, so it's included with the gross income for that year rather than the next. Similarly, you deduct or capitalize expenses when you become liable for them, whether or not you pay them in the same year.

The accrual method is more complicated than the cash method and can lead to more mistakes. Before choosing the accrual method, get professional advice to make sure that it is best for your business and meets IRS guidelines.

If your business distributes cash or gift certificates that can be converted to cash, the value of these gifts is considered additional wages or salary regardless of the amount—and is subject to employment taxes and withholding rules.

Noncash gifts are also generally treated as income to the employee, but not those that are clearly of an advertising nature, such as pens embossed with your company name that cost $4 or less. Other noncash gifts to employees may also be excluded from the employee's income if they are of nominal value.

> **EXAMPLE:** To promote employee goodwill, Pebblestone Partnership distributes turkeys, hams and other merchandise of nominal value at holidays. The partnership also gives each employee a check for $200. The value of the turkeys, hams and other merchandise isn't salaries or wages, but the partnership can deduct the cost of these items as a business expense. The checks can also be deducted, but must be treated as income to the employees subject to withholding.

4. Meals and Lodging

You can deduct at least some of the cost of meals and lodging you provide to employees if these expenses are a reasonable part of doing business. In some cases, the value of the meals or lodging you furnish must be reported as part of the employees' income for tax purposes.

a. Meals

Normally, you can deduct as a business expense only 50% of the cost of providing meals to employees. You can, however, deduct the full cost if:

- you operate a restaurant or catering service and furnish the meals to employees at the worksite
- you furnish the meals as part of a recreational or social activity, such as a company picnic, or
- the value of the meals is included in employees' income. Meals must be included in an employee's income unless the meals are furnished on your premises and for your convenience, or consist of food that qualifies as a minimal fringe benefit—coffee, doughnuts or soft drinks, for example, or the occasional meal you provide to enable an employee to work overtime.

EXAMPLE: Carol is a waitress at Sunshine Cafe. The restaurant provides two meals at no charge during her 7 a.m. to 4 p.m. workday. Sunshine Cafe encourages—but doesn't require—Carol to eat breakfast there before starting work. She must eat lunch there. Since Carol works during the normal breakfast and lunch periods, the value of her breakfast and lunch are not treated as income to her. If Sunshine Cafe allows Carol to have free meals there on her days off, the value of those meals would be included as income to Carol.

EXAMPLE: Frank is a clerk at Omni Department Store, working 9 a.m. to 5 p.m. Omni gives Frank his lunch without charge at a lunch buffet it maintains at the store. This helps Omni limit Frank's lunch break to 30 minutes—a benefit to Omni since its busiest time is during the normal lunch period. If Frank left the store to have lunch, he'd be away much longer than 30 minutes. The value of these meals is not income to Frank.

In addition to the above situations, you can deduct the full cost of the meals you serve on your premises to all employees—as long as more than one-half of them receive this benefit as a convenience to your business. In the example above, suppose that Omni Department Store were to provide the lunch buffet to 30 of the store's 50 employees as a convenience to the store. Omni could deduct the cost of providing the food to the other 20 employees as well.

b. Lodging

You can deduct as a business expense the cost of furnishing lodging to employees if it's a reasonable part of doing business. Generally, you must include the value of lodging as part of the employees' income. The value can be excluded, however, if you furnish the lodging on your business premises for your convenience and require the employee to live there to perform the job.

EXAMPLE: Felice is a swimming pool attendant at The Highlands, a resort complex that's 15 miles from town. The Highlands gives Felice the choice of living at the resort free of charge. If Felice chooses to live at The Highlands, the resort must include the value of the lodging in her income. It is not necessary for Felice to live at the resort to properly perform her job duties. It's merely a matter of convenience.

5. Fringe Benefits

Your business may be able to deduct as a business expense a number of employee fringe benefits, including:

- health and dental insurance
- medical reimbursement plans for items not covered by health insurance
- group term life insurance—limits apply, based on the policy value
- educational assistance programs
- adoption assistance programs
- moving expenses
- qualified employee benefit plans, including profit-sharing plans, stock bonus plans and money purchase pension plans, and
- cafeteria plans that allow employees to choose among two or more benefits consisting of cash and qualified benefits.

(See Chapter 4 for a detailed discussion of employee benefits.)

Be aware that there are restrictions—some of them complex—on deducting these benefits and that deductions may be available to some forms of business and not others. Not only are employee benefits tax deductible by your business, but they also are not taxed to the employee.

But while these benefits sound attractive, there are two serious drawbacks. First, many small businesses—particularly those just starting out—won't have the funds to finance them. Second, the IRS has stringent rules to discourage top-heavy plans—those designed to benefit primarily the owners and highly paid employees of a business. If your plan doesn't meet these guidelines, your business won't be able to deduct the cost.

E. Independent Contractors

Some people you hire will be independent contractors rather than employees. (The differences between these two categories are explained in detail in Chapter 11.) If you do hire someone who meets the IRS tests for an independent contractor, you don't have to withhold income taxes or Social Security taxes from that person's pay, nor are you required to make an employer's contribution to the worker's Social Security fund.

If, however, you pay an independent contractor $600 or more during a calendar year, you must report this to the IRS on Form 1099-MISC.

EXAMPLE: Marilyn, a computer consultant, works out of her home. She's listed in the

Yellow Pages of the telephone book and offers her services to many different businesses during the course of a year. In January, Flowers Unlimited hires Marilyn to install a new computer it has purchased and pays her $350 for this work. Two months later, Flowers Unlimited has Marilyn add a second computer and install a local area network, paying her $500. Toward the end of the year, Flowers Unlimited asks Marilyn to design special software to track inventory and sales; she's paid $2,000 for this assignment. Flowers Unlimited doesn't withhold income taxes or make Social Security payments. Because Marilyn is an independent contractor, and because Flowers Unlimited paid her more than $600 during the year, the business sends the IRS and Marilyn a Form 1099-MISC showing it paid Marilyn $2,850 during the year.

Ask all independent contractors you hire to complete Form W-9, giving their Social Security numbers or their Employer Identification Numbers. You'll need this information when you report the payments you made. Because some independent contractors have tried to foil the IRS's attempts to track income, the government has enacted regulations to protect the integrity of the system. If an independent contractor doesn't give you an identification number—Social Security or Employer Identification Number—or if the IRS says you were given a wrong number, you may have to withhold 31% of the independent contractor's pay to assure that taxes aren't evaded.

Be Sure Workers Are Properly Classified. The IRS believes it has lost large amounts of tax revenues because many employers and workers have improperly agreed to classify the workers as independent contractors rather than employees. In many of these cases, the employer hasn't withheld taxes—and the worker has neglected to report the income and pay tax on it.

Given that background, the IRS feels its tax collection record is better when workers are classified as employees rather than as independent contractors. For that reason, it enforces strict tests for determining who is and who isn't an independent contractor—and if you misclassify someone who should have been called an employee, you may be heavily penalized. (To avoid costly problems, see Chapter 11 for a fuller explanation of the IRS criteria.)

F. Statutory Employees

Statutory employees are a kind of legal hybrid. They tend to be people you might ordinarily think of as independent contractors rather than employees, but they are employees because the laws says they are. For statutory employees, your responsibilities for withholding taxes are less extensive than your responsibilities for other employees. You don't withhold income taxes from their pay, but you must withhold Social Security and Medicare taxes and you must make the matching employer's contribution.

The following are statutory employees:

Delivery people. A driver who either distributes meat products, vegetable or fruit products, bakery products or beverages other than milk, or who picks up or delivers laundry or dry cleaning, if the driver is your agent or is paid on commission.

Insurance salespeople. A full-time life insurance salesperson.

Home workers. A person who works at home on materials that you supply and that must be returned to you or someone you name, if you also furnish specifications for how the work is to be done.

Traveling salespeople. A full-time traveling salesperson, who's not an agent or commission driver, who works on your behalf and turns in orders to you from wholesalers, retailers, contractors, hotels, restaurants or other similar businesses. The goods sold must be merchandise for resale or supplies used in the buyer's business operation.

There's another twist in the statutory employee story: Not every person who falls into one of the above four categories is treated as a statutory employee. A statutory employee must meet three additional conditions.

- There must be a service contract stating or implying that the person must personally perform the services.
- Someone other than the worker must have invested substantially in the facilities used to perform the services—except for a car or truck.
- The worker must perform the services on a continuing basis.

If these conditions all apply, then you become responsible for withholding the worker's share of Social Security and Medicare taxes and paying the employer's share.

One more wrinkle: You need only pay federal unemployment tax (FUTA) on statutory employees who are delivery people or traveling salespeople.

 For more information on statutory employees, see IRS Publication 15-A, *Employer's Supplemental Tax Guide.* ∎

Chapter 6

Family and Medical Leave

A. Who Is Covered 6/2

B. Reasons for Taking a Leave 6/2

    1. Birth, Adoption or Foster Care 6/3

    2. Family Health Problems 6/3

    3. Employee's Health Problems 6/4

C. Scheduling Leave 6/4

D. Temporary Transfer to Another Job 6/5

E. Substituting Paid Leave 6/6

F. Advance Notice of Leave 6/6

G. Certification 6/7

    1. Requesting Clarification 6/7

    2. Second and Third Opinions 6/8

    3. Recertification 6/9

H. Health Benefits 6/9

I. Returning to Work 6/10

    1. Job Protection 6/10

    2. Exemption for Highly Paid Employees 6/10

    3. Fitness to Work 6/11

J. Related Laws 6/11

    1. State Laws 6/11

    2. Americans with Disabilities Act 6/18

K. Enforcement 6/19

*I*t's often been difficult for a working individual to deal with family obligations such as caring for a seriously ill child or parent, or attending to the special needs of a newborn infant or newly adopted child. And some employees who have taken time off work to recover from their own serious illnesses have worried about being demoted or fired.

To help employees balance the demands of the workplace with personal and family needs, Congress enacted the Family and Medical Leave Act or FMLA (29 U.S.C. § 2601 and following). Under the FMLA, if your business has 50 or more employees, it may be required to give an employee up to 12 weeks of unpaid leave for certain family and medical reasons. And the law requires you to return the employee to the same or a similar position when the leave is over—except when it would be prohibitively expensive for a business to take back a highly paid employee.

Your state might have its own family leave law. To find out more about state law requirements, see Section J.

A. Who Is Covered

The FMLA covers your business if you have 50 or more employees who work within a 75-mile radius. The count, for FMLA purposes, includes all employees on your payroll—part-time, full-time and those already on leave.

An employee in a covered business is eligible for FMLA leave only if he or she has worked for you:

- for at least 12 months (these months do not have to be consecutive), and
- for at least 1,250 hours during the 12 months before the leave.

Informing Employees

If your business is subject to the FMLA, you must display in the workplace a poster titled "Your Rights Under the Family and Medical Leave Act of 1993." It's available at the nearest office of the U.S. Department of Labor's Wage and Hour Division. Your state labor department may also be able to provide this poster, as well as posters describing workplace rights and responsibilities under state law. (See the Appendix for contact details.)

You must also inform employees about their rights to FMLA leave in your employee handbook, if you have one. Otherwise, you must give employees written guidance when they request FMLA leave. The easiest way to do this is to give them a copy of the booklet *Compliance Guide to the Family and Medical Leave Act*. It's free at the nearest office of the U.S. Department of Labor's Wage and Hour Division. (See Appendix for contact details.)

B. Reasons for Taking a Leave

If your business is covered, you must grant unpaid leave to an eligible employee to attend to a child, to care for a parent or spouse or to recover from a serious illness. Generally, the employee is entitled to a total of 12 work-weeks of leave during any 12-month period.

1. Birth, Adoption or Foster Care

An eligible employee may take a total of 12 workweeks of unpaid leave because of the birth of a child or because a child has been placed with the employee for adoption or foster care. Under the FMLA, foster care is defined as 24-hour care for a child away from his or her parents or guardians—and it must be based on a court order or an agreement approved by a state agency.

The period for taking leave based on birth, adoption or child care expires one year after the child is born or placed. Men as well as women are eligible for this leave. An expect-ant mother may begin FMLA leave before the birth of the child for prenatal care or if her condition makes her unable to work. You can require medical documentation of the need for prenatal care or inability to work before you grant a prebirth leave.

Similarly, FMLA leave can begin before actual placement or adoption of a child if an absence from work is necessary. Such an absence may be necessary, for example, if an employee must attend counseling sessions, appear in court, consult with a lawyer or doctor representing the birth parent or submit to a physical exam.

Special Rules for Spouses. If a husband and wife both work for your company, you can limit the total number of workweeks taken by both spouses to care for a child to 12 during any 12-month period. Interestingly, if the child's parents are not married to one another, each parent is entitled to the full allotment of 12 workweeks of leave.

2. Family Health Problems

An eligible employee may take a total of 12 workweeks of unpaid leave during any 12-month period to care for a spouse, son, daughter or parent who has a serious health condition.

The FMLA rules for determining who has a serious health condition are complicated. Generally, however, an injury or illness may qualify as a serious health condition if it involves inpatient care—an overnight stay in a hospital or other medical care facility. The person who has been hospitalized is considered to have a serious health condition for as long as he or she can't work, attend school or perform other normal life activities.

In addition, an injury or illness may qualify as a serious health condition if the patient requires continuing treatment and cannot perform normal activities for more than three consecutive days. A person who needs con-tinuing treatment for pregnancy or prenatal care, a chronic health condition or a long-term or permanent health condition may also be deemed to have a serious health condition.

Family Ties

The FMLA defines family relationships in both expected and unexpected ways.

A spouse is an employee's husband or wife as recognized under state law, which may include common law spouses in the minority of states that recognize common law marriage. Same-sex partners don't qualify as spouses.

An employee's parent can be a biological parent or a person who took the place of a parent when the employee was a child—someone, for example, who took care of and financially supported the child. However, in-laws aren't considered parents under the FMLA.

An employee's son or daughter can be a biological, adopted or foster child, a step-child or a legal ward. It can also be a child whom the employee cares for and financially supports. The child must be under age 18—or, if age 18 or older, he or she must be incapable of caring for himself or herself because of a mental or physical disability.

3. Employee's Health Problems

An eligible employee may take a total of 12 workweeks of unpaid leave during any 12-month period for a serious health condition that makes the employee unable to perform his or her job. (For more on serious health conditions, see Section B2, above.)

C. Scheduling Leave

You and an employee can agree to flexible work scheduling for the leave time to which employees are entitled under the FLMA.

The leave may be intermittent rather than consecutive if you agree to make it so.

> **EXAMPLE:** Bill, an employee of Rendex Corporation, normally works Monday through Friday. Bill's wife has given birth to a son. Rendex and Bill agree that he'll use his leave rights in two-day segments by working Monday through Wednesday and staying home on Thursday and Friday.

You and an employee may also agree that the leave will be taken through reducing the weekly workhours.

> **EXAMPLE:** Carla, an employee of Cormark Company, has adopted a daughter. Cormark and Carla agree that she'll exercise her leave rights by temporarily working from 1:00 to 5:00 p.m. rather than her normal 8 a.m. to 5 p.m. schedule.

> **EXAMPLE:** Tim works for Enterprise Associates. His father has a serious health condition requiring radiation treatments each week at a university medical center 100 miles away. Tim needs to drive his dad to treatment every Friday. Enterprise Associates must allow Tim to use unpaid leave time to take Fridays off work.

Creative Solutions for Hard Problems

Family and medical leave laws address only a small part of the issues facing employers and employees in balancing the competing demands of the family and the workplace. To ensure a happy and productive workforce, you may need to work with employees to come up with creative solutions. Consider this list of possibilities from Renee Magid, founder and president of the consulting firm Initiatives Inc.:

- flexible career paths
- flexible worktimes for full-time employees
- permanent part-time employment, with benefits
- job sharing
- work-at-home options
- cafeteria-style benefit plans
- education and support programs
- financial assistance with child care, and
- direct child care.

For more information, contact Initiatives Inc., 400 Commerce Drive, Suite A, Ft. Washington, PA 19034; 215-628-8438.

D. Temporary Transfer to Another Job

If it is disruptive to your business to allow a particular employee to have a flexible or reduced work schedule, check to see whether there's another job open that will accommodate the employee's request with less disruption. If so, you can transfer the employee temporarily to the other job. The alternative job must have equivalent pay and benefits. The duties, however, needn't be equivalent.

EXAMPLE: Hilda works for Project Systems Inc. as a manager of ten employees. She is suffering from a major depressive episode which will require psychotherapy three times a week for six months. Project Systems must grant Hilda's request for a reduced leave schedule to permit her to get the necessary treatment. The company also transfers Hilda temporarily to a research position in which her absences will be less disruptive to the company.

Workplace Politics: A Delicate Business

When you temporarily transfer an employee, other employees—especially those who have been eyeing the open job—may feel resentful. This is a delicate situation and you may be inclined to reduce tensions by informing the other employees about the medical reasons behind the transfer. Restrain yourself. Unless you have the transferred employee's permission to disclose the reasons for the transfer, you must respect that person's privacy.

E. Substituting Paid Leave

You're not required to pay for FMLA leave, but if you offer paid time off—vacation, personal, family or sick leave—as a job benefit, you or the employee can substitute paid leave for unpaid FMLA leave in most situations.

Accrued paid vacation or personal leave. You or the employee can substitute accrued paid vacation or personal leave for unpaid FMLA leave whether based on birth, childcare, foster placement, caring for an ill family member or attending to the employee's own medical needs.

Accrued paid family leave. You can substitute accrued paid leave for unpaid FMLA leave based on birth, adoption, foster placement or caring for an ill family member. An employee can require such a substitution only for reasons permitted by your company's leave plan.

> **EXAMPLE:** Lou works for Star Baking Company. Star's leave plan allows paid family leave for an employee to care for a child, but not a parent. Lou needs to care for his mother. He can't require Star to substitute paid family leave for unpaid FMLA leave.

Accrued paid medical or sick leave. You can substitute paid medical or sick leave for unpaid FMLA leave based on the employee caring for an ill family member or the employee's own serious health condition. An employee can only require a substitution if the reasons for the leave are normally covered by your company's leave plan. For example, an employee can't require you to substitute paid leave to care for a seriously ill family member unless your plan specifies that leave can be used for this purpose. And an employee doesn't have the right to substitute paid medical or sick leave for a serious health condition that's not covered by your leave plan. In such a case, the employee is restricted to the unpaid leave available under the FMLA.

How Much Time Off Is Owed. If an employee uses paid leave under circumstances that don't qualify as FMLA leave, the leave won't count against the 12 weeks of FMLA leave to which the employee is entitled. For example, if an employee uses paid sick leave for a condition which isn't a serious health condition as defined in the FMLA, the time off doesn't count against the 12 weeks of unpaid FMLA leave to which he or she may later be entitled.

F. Advance Notice of Leave

Often, an employee can foresee the need for an unpaid leave. For example, most employees know well in advance when a baby will be born, and they usually have ample knowledge of when a placement will occur for adoption or foster care. Similarly, an employee often is aware early on of planned medical treatment for a serious health condition of the employee or of a family member. You can require, in these situations, that an employee notify you at least 30 days before the unpaid leave is to begin.

But such advance notice isn't always possible—and the FMLA takes this into account. For example, if a child is born prematurely or an adoption or placement goes through unexpectedly, the employee can give you a shorter notice; the test is what is practical. Typically, the employee should at least notify you orally within one or two business days of learning of the need for leave.

Similarly, where there's a medical emergency involving the employee or a member of the employee's family, it usually won't be practical for the employee to give you any advance notice of the need for unpaid leave. In such cases, advance notice isn't required. Where the need for FMLA leave isn't foreseeable, the employee or a family member can notify you either in person or by phone, fax or email of the circumstances requiring the leave.

If an employee's leave is based on a serious health condition that requires planned medical treatment, you can require the employee to make a reasonable effort to schedule the treatment so that it won't unduly disrupt your business.

G. Certification

Theoretically, an employee could abuse the system by falsely claiming that he, she or a family member has a serious health condition. The FMLA recognizes this and allows you to require proof—a certificate from the patient's doctor stating:

- the date when the serious health condition started
- the length of time the condition is likely to last
- diagnosis of the condition
- treatment prescribed, and

- whether inpatient treatment is required.

You're free to decide when to ask for a certificate and when not to—but it's best to follow a uniform policy, rather than being selective. Otherwise, someone who's required to provide a certificate may claim you're discriminating against them. You may have trouble justifying why a particular employee was singled out.

Since most people are honest, the simplest and legally safest policy is an honor system in which you accept employees' statements at face value.

1. Requesting Clarification

Depending on the reason for FMLA leave, you can require that additional information be included on the certificate.

a. Employee's own condition

If the employee seeks medical leave because of his or her own serious health condition, you can require that the certificate state that the employee can't perform work of any kind, or that the employee can't perform the essential functions of the job. Give the employee or the doctor a list of the job's essential functions.

b. Family member's condition

If the employee seeks leave to care for a family member, you can require that the certificate state that the patient needs help in meeting basic medical, hygiene, nutritional, safety or transportation needs—or that the employee's presence would be beneficial or desirable. The employee must indicate on the certificate what care he or she will provide and how long that care is likely to be required.

c. Intermittent leave or reduced leave schedule

If the employee seeks to take intermittent leave or asks for a shortened work schedule, you can require that the certificate state the medical need for or desirability of such leave and how long the situation requiring leave is expected to last.

Certification Made Easy

The U.S. Department of Labor has developed Form WH-380, *Certification of Physician or Practitioner*, for doctors to use in certifying medical conditions under the FMLA. While this form is optional, using it is probably the best way to assure that you and the doctor comply with FMLA regulations.

Most doctors will have copies of the form, but to make sure the process goes smoothly, have a supply on hand for employees to take to their doctors. The forms are available at the nearest office of the U.S. Department of Labor's Wage and Hour Division. (See the Appendix for contact details.)

2. Second and Third Opinions

If an employee submits a complete certificate signed by the doctor, you can't ask the doctor for more information to verify it. You can, however, require the employee to get an opinion from a second doctor. This can be someone you designate or approve—but it can't be someone you regularly employ, such as a company doctor. And you, rather than the employee, must pay for the second opinion.

Weigh the Odds of Asking for More. Just because the FMLA allows you to get a second opinion doesn't mean it's a smart thing to do. Often it's not. Think long and hard before getting adversarial with employees over health determinations. If you make an employee jump through hoops to qualify for an unpaid absence, you'll probably wind up with a resentful employee who will never again give you his or her full effort and loyalty. And the fallout from being unnecessarily suspicious about one employee can easily infect the entire workplace.

If you wind up with conflicting opinions, you can require a third opinion from another doctor—one approved by both you and the employee. This third opinion is binding on both of you.

Healthcare Providers: What's in a Name?

Generally, a doctor of medicine or osteopathy will sign the employee's medical certificate or render the second or third opinion. But technically, under the FMLA and its regulations, such certificates can be signed by a healthcare provider—a term that includes not only MDs and DOs, but others such as podiatrists, dentists, clinical psychologists, optometrists and chiropractors.

In addition, nurse practitioners and nurse-midwives who diagnose and treat certain conditions, especially at health maintenance organizations and in rural areas where other healthcare providers may not be available, are included as healthcare providers, as are Christian Science practitioners.

---

3. Recertification

You can ask an employee to give you a re-certification of a medical condition to support a leave request. You can request a recertification at reasonable intervals—generally not more often than every 30 days. The intervals can be shorter, however, if:

- the employee requests an extension of leave
- circumstances have changed significantly —for example, the duration or nature of the illness becomes different than anticipated, or
- you receive information casting doubt on the continuing validity of the certification.

H. Health Benefits

If you have a group health plan for employees, you must maintain coverage for employees who are on FMLA leave. You must keep the coverage at the same level the employees would have if they worked continuously.

In some cases, however, you can require an employee to repay the premiums you paid for this continuing coverage. Generally, you can demand reimbursement if the employee doesn't come back to work after the leave period expires. But you can't demand reimbursement if the employee doesn't return to work because:

- the employee or a family member has suffered continuation, recurrence or onset of a serious health condition—the kind of thing that would have justified taking the unpaid leave in the first place, or
- there are other circumstances beyond the control of the employee. Examples

of this include: an employee's spouse is unexpectedly transferred to a job location more than 75 miles from the employee's worksite, a person other than an immediate family member has a serious health condition and the employee is needed to provide care or the employee is laid off while on leave.

The FMLA regulations give two examples of situations within the employee's control: an employee desires to remain with a parent in a distant city even though the parent no longer requires the employee's care; a mother decides not to return to work to stay home with a newborn child. In such cases, the employee must repay the health insurance premiums you paid for coverage during his or her leave.

 Don't Retaliate Against Employees for Exercising Leave Rights. The FMLA prohibits you from firing or otherwise retaliating against an employee who has asked for leave or taken leave under the statute. Retaliation can take many forms. It can be blatant (such as transferring the employee to a job that pays less or carries less status) or more subtle (such as assigning the employee less desirable tasks). Any type of retaliation puts you at risk of a lawsuit or governmental action to enforce the FMLA.

I.   Returning to Work

The FMLA normally gives employees the right to return to their jobs when their leave has been completed.

1. Job Protection

When an eligible employee returns from taking a leave, your company must restore the employee to the job that he or she held when the leave began or to a similar job—one with equivalent pay, benefits and other terms of employment. However, an employee has no greater right to reinstatement or other benefits than if he or she had been continuously employed during the FMLA leave period.

> **EXAMPLE:** Anton takes ten weeks of unpaid family leave from his job as a production worker at Smokestack Industries, Inc. While he's away, Smokestack eliminates the night shift on which Anton was working and lays off all employees working on that shift. Smokestack would have laid off Anton had he been working instead of taking leave. Smokestack doesn't have to re-employ Anton.

2. Exemption for Highly Paid Employees

Recognizing that it's difficult for many businesses to carry on in the absence of the customary executives and decision makers, the FMLA lets you decline to take back some highly paid employees after their leave. The exemption applies only if:

- the employee is among the highest paid 10% of the salaried people you employ within 75 miles of the place where the employee works, and

- taking back the employee will cause "substantial and grievous economic injury" to your business.

Unfortunately, the FMLA regulations don't precisely set the level of economic hardship or injury that excuses you from taking back an employee. Future regulations may provide more guidance. For now, though, it's clear that minor inconveniences and costs are not enough to justify cutting off a key employee who's taken a leave. On the other hand, you don't have to show that taking back the employee would threaten the existence of your business.

One test is whether it's feasible to temporarily replace or do without the employee on FMLA leave—or whether you must hire a permanent replacement. If the employee on leave is your company's $75,000 a year sales manager, you may find that no competent people are willing to take over the job on a short-term basis. And since you need a sales manager, you have no real choice but to hire a permanent replacement. Reinstating the employee on leave to an equivalent job may be much too costly for your business—particularly if you must create a new job to do this. In such a situation, you'd likely be excused from taking back the employee after the leave.

As soon as you determine that substantial economic harm will result if you take back a key employee who has sought a leave under the FMLA, notify him or her in writing. In a letter, explain that your decision is based on your wish to prevent major injury to the business. If the employee then starts or continues the leave, you'll be protected by the FMLA.

Note that if an employee doesn't return to work after you notify him or her that you intend not to hire him or her back, you must still maintain the employee's health benefits for the full leave period and you can't recover the cost of health insurance premiums. (See Section H, above.)

3. Fitness to Work

If an employee has taken a leave because of a serious health condition, the FMLA lets you require a medical certification that he or she is able to resume work. You can only impose this requirement if it's part of a policy you uniformly apply to employees returning from medical leave.

There may be a state law, local ordinance or union contract that governs the terms under which employees who have taken medical leave can return to work. The FMLA doesn't supersede these other legal controls. You must also comply with the Americans with Disabilities Act (ADA) rule that any physical required of an employee returning to work must be job-related. (For more on the ADA, see Chapter 9 and Section J2, below.)

J. Related Laws

You must comply with other laws that affect an employee's right to take a leave.

1. State Laws

The vast majority of states have laws guaranteeing some form of family or medical leave. (See the chart below.) The FMLA doesn't cancel out state law provisions that provide greater family or medical leave rights or apply to smaller employers than the FMLA does. Leaves granted under a state leave law and the FMLA usually run simultaneously and are not added together.

> **EXAMPLE:** State law where Tess works entitles her to 16 weeks of leave over two years. Tess takes her 16 weeks of state-permitted leave in one year. This also exhausts her 12 weeks of FMLA

leave for that year—she can't take 16 weeks plus 12 weeks.

Additional Laws May Apply. If the chart below indicates that your state has no statute, this means there is no law that specifically addresses the issue or offers greater protections than the FMLA. However, there may be a state administrative regulation or local ordinance that does control. Call your state labor department for more information. (See the Appendix for contact details.)

"Small Necessities" Laws May Be the Next Big Thing

In what may be the start of a trend, several states have enacted "small necessities" laws to help employees balance their work, personal and family responsibilities. These laws recognize that employees sometimes need to be away for short periods during a workday. Employees, for example, may need to take off briefly to attend a parent-teacher conference or other important school activity, or they may need to take a child or elderly parent to a doctor's appointment.

Details of these laws vary from state to state, though school-related matters are most often recognized as a valid reason to take some hours of leave time. The California law, for example, applies if you employ 25 or more people at one location. If so, you can't fire or discriminate against an employee for taking up to eight hours of leave time a month (maximum of 40 hours a year) to participate in activities at a child's

or grandchild's school or daycare facility. The employee must give you reasonable notice, and can use existing vacation, personal leave or comp time for this purpose—and, in some cases, unpaid leave may be available.

You can find information about your state's law in the chart "State Family and Medical Leave Laws"—contact your state labor department to find out more about your obligations. If your business is covered by both the FMLA and state law, you'll need to comply with both. Typically, there's not much overlap between the FMLA and the state small necessities law, so the time off allowed for small necessities will be in addition to time off under the FMLA.

If your state doesn't have a small necessities law, consider including a policy in your employee handbook for dealing with such leave. (See Chapter 2, Section B, for more on employee handbooks.)

State Family and Medical Leave Laws			
State *Citations* Main Differences From FMLA	**Employers Covered**	**Eligible Employees**	**Type and Amount of Leave** for various kinds of family & medical leave
California *Cal. Gov't. Code § 12945;* *Cal. Lab. Code § 230 and* *following* Pregnancy-related disability leave extended to employers and employees not covered by FMLA.	5 or more employees —must offer pregnancy leave 25 or more employees—must offer domestic violence leave and school activity leave	All	**Pregnancy:** up to 4 months for disability related to pregnancy **Domestic violence issues:** Reasonable time for issues dealing with domestic violence, including health, counseling and safety measures 40 hours per year for **School activities**
Colorado *Colo. Rev. Stat. § 19-5-211*	All employers who offer leave for birth of a child	Adoptive parents	**Adoption:** Must allow same leave as for childbirth
Connecticut *Conn. Gen. Stat. Ann.* *§§ 31-51kk and following;* *§ 46a-51(10);* *§ 46a-60(7)* Includes parents-in-law under parent definition. Covers employees who've worked less than 1,250 hours. Allows more than 12 weeks leave in a particular year.	75 employees for FML 3 employees for maternity disability	1 year and at least 1,000 hours for employer in past 12 months	16 weeks per any 24-month period for: **Childbirth** **Adoption** **Sickness of "family member"** **AND** 16 hours of unpaid leave during any 24-month period for **Own serious health condition** "Reasonable" amount for **Pregnancy/Maternity**
District of Columbia *D.C. Code Ann. §§ 32-501* *and following; 32-1202* Definition of family member includes persons sharing employee's residence and with whom employee has a committed relationship. Allows more than 12 weeks leave in a particular year.	At least 20 employees	Worked at company for at least one year, and who has worked at least 1,000 hours during the previous 12-month period	16 weeks of unpaid leave during any 24-month period for **Childbirth** **Adoption** **Pregnancy/Maternity** **Sickness of "family member"** 24 hours per year for **School activities**

State Family and Medical Leave Laws (continued)

State *Citations* Main Differences From FMLA	Employers Covered	Eligible Employees	Type and Amount of Leave for various kinds of family & medical leave
Hawaii *Haw. Rev. Stat. §§ 398-1 and following; 378-1* Covers employees who have worked less than FMLA requires. Family members include parents-in-law, stepparents, grandparents, grandparents-in-law. Leave to care for ill family member does not include employee's own serious health condition.	100 employees or more for FML leave All employers for pregnancy leave	6 months of service for FML benefits No minimum for pregnancy leave	4 weeks per calendar year for **Childbirth** **Adoption** **Sickness of "family member"** "Reasonable period" for **Pregnancy/ Maternity** (required by statute and case law)
Illinois *820 Ill. Comp. Stat. § 147/15*	All	6 months, at least half-time	8 hours per year for **School activities**
Iowa *Iowa Code § 216.6*	4 or more employees	All	Up to 8 weeks for **Disability due to pregnancy**
Kentucky *Ky. Rev. Stat. Ann. § 337.015* Age of child.	All	Adoptive parents No hour requirements	Up to 6 weeks for **Adoption** of a child under 7 years old
Louisiana *La. Rev. Stat. Ann. §§ 23:341-342; 23:1015 and following; 40:1299.124* Extends pregnancy leave to employers with less than 50 employees, and those who have worked less than 1,250 hours.	At least 25 employees in the state for pregnancy/ maternity All employers for school activities 20 or more workers for bone marrow provisions	Any employee for school activities or pregnancy Those who work 20 or more hours per week for bone marrow donor	A "reasonable period of time" not to exceed four months, if necessary for: **Pregnancy** 16 hours per year for **School activities** 40 hours of paid leave to **Donate bone marrow**
Maine *Me. Rev. Stat. Ann. tit. 26, § 843 and following* Covers employers in the 15-49 employee range. Age of adopted child.	At least 15 workers in Maine	At least one year of service	10 weeks in any two-year period for **Childbirth** **Adoption** (age 16 or younger) **Sickness of family member**

State Family and Medical Leave Laws (continued)			
State *Citations* Main Differences From FMLA	**Employers Covered**	**Eligible Employees**	**Type and Amount of Leave** for various kinds of family & medical leave
Massachusetts *Mass. Gen. Laws ch.* *149, §§ 52D; 105A and* *following;* *Ch. 151B, § 1* Extends maternity leave requirement to employers of 6 to 49 employees. Adds "small necessities" leave to employees covered by FMLA.	At least 6 employees for maternity leave All employers for school activities	For childbirth and adoption leave: Full-time female employees who have completed probationary period or 3 months of service if no set probationary period For other leave, all employees covered by the FMLA	8 weeks for: **Childbirth** **Adoption** (for child under 18, or under 23 if disabled) 24 hours per year, total for **School activities** or Events directly related to **medical or dental care of a minor child or elderly relative**
Minnesota *Minn. Stat. Ann.* *§ 181.940 and following* Extends maternity leave requirement to employers of 21 to 49 employees.	21 or more workers for maternity leave All employers for school activities At least 20 employees for bone marrow donation	At least one year, at least half-time for maternity leave At least one year for school activities At least 20 hours per week for bone marrow donation	6 weeks for **Childbirth** **Adoption** Can use own accrued sick leave for **Care of sick or injured child** 16 hours in 12-month period for **School activities** (includes activities related to child care, preschool, or special education) Up to 40 hours paid leave per year for **Bone marrow donation**
Montana *Mont. Code Ann.* *§ 49-2-310 & 311* Extends pregnancy leave mandate to employers of less than 50 employees and covers workers who have not worked 1,250 hours.	All employers	All	"Reasonable period of time" for **Childbirth** **Pregnancy**
Nebraska *Neb. Rev. Stat. § 48-234*	Employers that allow workers to take leave for the birth of a child	Adoptive parents	**Adoption:** Same amount of leave as is afforded biological parents for the birth of a child, to adopt a child under the age of 9 or a special needs child under the age of 19

State Family and Medical Leave Laws (continued)

State *Citations* Main Differences From FMLA	Employers Covered	Eligible Employees	Type and Amount of Leave for various kinds of family & medical leave
Nevada *Nev. Rev. Stat. Ann.* *§ 392.920*	All	Parent, guardian or custodian of a child	**School activities:** Employers may not fire or threaten to fire a parent, guardian or custodian for attending a school conference or responding to a child's emergency
New Jersey *N.J. Stat. Ann.* *§ 34:11B-1 to B-16* Family member includes parents-in-law	At least 50 employees		12 weeks of unpaid leave in any 24-month period for **Childbirth** **Adoption** **Sickness of family member**
New Hampshire *N.H. Rev. Stat. § 354-A:7*	At least 6 employees	All	Leave for temporary disability due to **Pregnancy/Childbirth**
New York *N.Y. Lab. Law §§ 201-c;* *202-a*	Employers that allow workers to take leave for the birth of a child for adoption At least 20 employees for bone marrow donation	Adoptive parents of preschool age children and disabled children under 18 At least 20 hours of work per week for bone marrow donation	**Adoption:** Same amount of leave as is afforded biological parents for the birth of a child Up to 24 hours of leave for **Bone marrow donation**
North Carolina *N.C. Gen. Stat. § 95-28.3*	All employers	Parents and guardians of children in school	4 hours of leave per year to participate in child's **School activities**
Oregon *Or. Rev. Stat. §§ 659A.150-* *186; 69A.312* Extends FMLA-style benefits to employers of 24 to 49 employees and covers workers who have worked less than 1,250 hours.	At least 25 workers for FML leave All employers for bone marrow donation	At least 180 days, at least 25 hours per week, for FML leave At least 20 hours per week for bone marrow donation	12 weeks per year for **Pregnancy/Maternity** **Childbirth** **Adoption** **Sickness of family member** **Own serious health condition** **EXCEPT** (1) employee may take 12 weeks for pregnancy plus 12 weeks for maternity, sickness of family member or own serious health condition (2) employee may take 12 weeks for maternity or adoption plus 12 weeks to care for sick child Up to 40 hours or amount of accrued paid leave (whichever is less) for **Bone marrow donation**

State Family and Medical Leave Laws (continued)

State *Citations* Main Differences From FMLA	Employers Covered	Eligible Employees	Type and Amount of Leave for various kinds of family & medical leave
Rhode Island *R.I. Gen. Laws* *§ 28-48-2 and 3* No allowance for intermittent leave; parents-in-law included in family definition.	Employers with 50 or more employees	Those who have worked 30 or more hours per week for employer for at least 12 consecutive months	Up to 13 weeks in any two calendar years for **Childbirth** **Adoption** **Sickness of family member**
South Carolina *S.C. Code Ann.* *§ 44-43-80*	At least 20 workers at one site	At least 20 hours per week	**Bone marrow donation:** cannot retaliate against workers who use up to 40 hours to donate bone marrow
Tennessee *Tenn. Code Ann.* *§ 4-21-408* Maternity leave only	Employers of 100 or more	All female employees who have worked 12 consecutive months	**Pregnancy/Maternity disability:** Up to 4 months leave with 3 months advance notice, unless a medical emergency requires the leave to begin sooner
Vermont *Vt. Stat. Ann. tit. 21,* *§§ 471 and following* Family member includes parent-in-law; stepchild. Serious health condition is more narrowly defined than under FMLA.	Employers of 10 or more workers must provide parental leave; employers of 15 or more workers must provide family leave	At least one year, at least 30 hours per week	12 weeks per year **Childbirth** **Adoption** (age 16 or under) **Sickness of family member** Up to 4 hours of unpaid leave in a 30-day period (but not more than 24 hours per year) To participate in child's **School activities** or To **Take a family member to a medical or professional appointment** or To respond to a **Family member's medical emergency**
Washington *Wash. Rev. Code Ann.* *§§ 49.12.350 and 360*	At least 100 employees	At least one year, at least 35 hours per week	**Adoption:** must provide the same leave as childbirth to adoptive parents and stepparents of children under the age of six **Sickness of family member:** can use accrued sick leave to care for sick child
Wisconsin *Wis. Stat. Ann. § 103.10* Extends FMLA-type benefits to persons not meeting the 1,250 hours requirement	At least 50 employees	Worked at company for at least one year, and has worked at least 1,000 hours during the previous 12-month period	8 weeks total per year: 6 weeks for **Childbirth** **Adoption** **PLUS** 2 weeks for **Sickness of family member** **PLUS** 2 weeks for **Own serious health condition**

2. Americans with Disabilities Act

An employee who becomes disabled has rights under the Americans with Disabilities Act (ADA) as well as the FMLA. (See Chapter 9.) It requires special attention to coordinate your responsibilities under these two laws.

The FMLA entitles an employee to a reduced work schedule until 12 weeks of leave are used, with health benefits maintained during this period. At the end of the FMLA leave, you must reinstate the employee to the same or an equivalent position.

If the employee can't perform the equivalent job because of a disability and he or she has used up his or her FMLA leave, the ADA may permit or require you to place the employee in a part-time job, with only the benefits provided to part-time employees. In some cases, you may have to let an employee take unpaid leave beyond the 12 weeks allowed by the FMLA. Under the ADA, such additional leave may be required as a reasonable accommodation to a disabled employee if the additional leave wouldn't impose an undue hardship on your business.

Here are two other variations:

- The ADA may require you to offer an employee a job with a reasonable accommodation. If the FMLA entitles an employee to unpaid leave, you can't avoid granting the leave by requiring the employee to take an accommodation instead.

- If you require certification that an employee is fit to return to work as permitted by the FMLA under a uniform policy imposed by your business, you must also comply with the ADA requirement that the certification be related to the job.

The relationship between the FMLA and the ADA is extremely complicated. For an in-depth analysis of these overlapping statutes, go to www.eeoc.gov, and look for the fact sheet called *The Family and Medical Leave Act, the Americans with Disabilities Act, and Title VII of the Civil Rights Act of 1964*. It explains how these laws fit together.

K. Enforcement

An employee who believes his or her rights have been violated may file a complaint against your business with the U.S. Secretary of Labor or your state labor department, or may file a private lawsuit. If a violation is proven, you may have to pay the employee wages, employment benefits or other compensation, depending on the nature of the violation. If no such loss has occurred—for example, you unlawfully denied FMLA leave —you may have to reimburse the employee for the cost of providing care for a child or ill family member, up to a sum equal to 12 weeks of wages. You may also be ordered to reinstate or promote the employee, to pay penalties and interest and to pay reasonable fees for the employee's lawyer and expert witnesses.

A number of government publications offer guidance on the emerging legal requirements for family and medical leave.

Compliance Guide to the Family and Medical Leave Act is free at the nearest office of the U.S. Department of Labor's Wage and Hour Division. (See the Appendix for contact details.)

For more depth, get *Federal Regulations Part 825, The Family and Medical Leave Act of 1993*, also free from the Department of Labor. You can access the regulations through the Department of Labor's website at www.dol.gov. To find the regulation, click on the "Laws and Regs" button on the home page. That will lead you to a list of regulations. The family leave regulation is 29 Code of Federal Regulations, Part 825. ■

Chapter 7

Health and Safety

A. The Occupational Safety and Health Act 7/3

    1. Who Is Covered 7/4

    2. Safety Standards 7/4

    3. Posting, Reporting and Recordkeeping 7/4

    4. Training 7/5

    5. Inspections 7/6

    6. Penalties for Violations 7/7

    7. Workers' Rights 7/8

B. Getting Help 7/8

    1. Worksite Consultations 7/9

    2. Safety Codes 7/16

C. State OSHA Laws 7/18

D. Hazardous Chemicals 7/21

E. Workers' Compensation 7/23

    1. Coverage Requirements 7/23

    2. Arranging for Coverage 7/24

    3. Controlling Costs 7/25

    4. Injuries and Illnesses Covered 7/26

    5. Benefits Paid 7/26

    6. Independent Contractors 7/27

F. Disease Prevention 7/27

G. Tobacco Smoke 7/28

H. Drug and Alcohol Abuse 7/29

    1. Illegal Drug Use 7/30

    2. Alcoholism 7/31

I. Repetitive Stress Disorder 7/32

*A*s an employer, there are many good reasons—in addition to your humane instincts—for creating a safe and healthy workplace. Obviously, healthy workers will be happier and more productive. There will be fewer disruptions of work schedules due to absenteeism. And health insurance costs may be reduced. An incidental benefit may be an improvement in worker efficiency; workers generally are more efficient in a safer workplace. Then there are the more obvious obligations: federal and state laws and an increasing number of local ordinances require you to take steps to make the workplace safe and healthy.

Workers today are well informed about the link between workplace conditions and health problems. Most know, for example, that secondhand smoke can cause or aggravate respiratory and heart problems, and that repetitive motions can lead to carpal tunnel syndrome. And an increasing number of workers will not hesitate to press legal claims against employers who fail to rectify unsafe or unhealthy conditions.

In addition to health and safety statutes, state law requires your business to provide workers' compensation coverage to pay for medical bills and partial wage loss when an employee is injured in the workplace. By reducing on-the-job injuries and eliminating the workplace causes of disease, you can lower the cost of workers' compensation coverage. (See Section E.)

Get Employees Involved. In meeting your legal responsibilities for keeping the workplace safe and healthy, don't overlook an obvious resource: the workers. Involve them in identifying safety and health problems and suggesting ways to solve such problems. Organizing a safety committee made up of equal numbers of employees and managers is a good starting point. Consider holding company safety seminars at which you encourage employee suggestions. If workers can voice their safety concerns to you and to other workers who are able to initiate changes, there's less chance that they'll jump the gun and go straight to government authorities to report a complaint. Having such a safety committee can also earn you a break on workers' compensation insurance premiums.

A. The Occupational Safety and Health Act

In 1970, Congress passed the Occupational Safety and Health Act or OSHA (29 U.S.C. §§ 651 to 678)—a comprehensive law designed to reduce workplace hazards and to improve health and safety programs for workers. It broadly requires employers to provide a workplace free of physical dangers and to meet specific health and safety standards. Employers must also provide safety training to employees, inform them about hazardous chemicals, notify government administrators about serious workplace accidents and keep detailed safety records.

Although there can be heavy penalties for not complying with OSHA, such penalties are usually reserved for extreme cases in which workplace conditions are highly dangerous and the employer has ignored warnings about them. If your workplace is inspected—an unlikely event for a typical small business—OSHA will work with you to eliminate hazards.

⚠ **Don't Forget State Law!** In addition to federal law, you must comply with state law. To learn more about state health and safety laws, see Section C.

1. Who Is Covered

Generally, you must comply with the Act if your business affects interstate commerce. The legal definition of interstate commerce is so broad that almost all businesses are covered. But Congress did make some very limited exceptions. OSHA won't apply to your workplace if:

- you're self-employed and have no employees
- your business is a farm that employs only your immediate family members, or
- you're in a business such as mining, which is already regulated by other federal safety laws.

2. Safety Standards

OSHA sets a general standard for all covered businesses. As an employer, you must provide a place of employment that's "free from recognized hazards that are causing or are likely to cause death or serious physical harm to employees." Recognized hazards are not clearly defined, which can make it difficult for you to know how to comply with the law. The broad language covers an almost impossibly large range of potential harm—from

sharp objects that might cause cuts to radiation exposure.

But there's more. In the Act, Congress created the Occupational Safety and Health Administration—also called OSHA—as a unit of the U.S. Department of Labor. And Congress authorized this agency to set additional workplace standards, which it has done in great profusion. The specific standards cover a wide range of workplace concerns, including:

- exposure to hazardous chemicals
- first aid and medical treatment
- noise levels
- protective gear—goggles, respirators, gloves, work shoes, ear protectors
- fire protection
- worker training, and
- workplace temperatures and ventilation.

3. Posting, Reporting and Recordkeeping

You must post a notice called "Job Safety and Health Protection," which is available from the nearest OSHA office. If your business is located in a state that has its own approved OSHA program, you may have to post a state form instead of the national version. Check with your state OSHA office to find out. (See the listing in Section C for contact details.)

You must notify OSHA within eight hours after learning that an employee has died from a job-related accident or that three or more employees have been hospitalized because of a workplace accident. Call or visit an OSHA office to report the location and time of the incident, the number of fatalities or hospitalized employees, the name and phone number of a contact person and a brief description of the incident. Expect a follow-up investigation.

Unless your business is exempt from OSHA recordkeeping requirements (see below), you must maintain several types of records.

Injury and illness log. You must keep a log (OSHA Form 200) of all workplace injuries and illnesses, except minor injuries requiring only first aid. Throughout February, you must post the log for the previous year.

Medical records. You must keep up-to-date medical records and records of employee exposure to hazardous substances or harmful physical agents.

Training records. You must keep records of your safety training sessions and make them available for review by employees.

Retention. You must maintain required records for specified periods of time—sometimes as long as 30 years.

 For more information on OSHA's provisions, requirements and enforcement procedures, see *Federal Employment Laws: A Desk Reference,* by Amy DelPo & Lisa Guerin (Nolo).

Exemption From Recordkeeping

The OSHA requirements for recordkeeping apply only to businesses with ten or more employees—although state OSHA regulations may impose recordkeeping requirements on smaller businesses. In addition, the following businesses are exempt from recordkeeping:

- retail trade—except for businesses selling general merchandise, building materials and garden supplies
- real estate, insurance and financial businesses, and
- service businesses—except for hotels and other lodging places, repair facilities, amusement and recreation facilities and health services.

4. Training

OSHA considers safety training to be part of your general duty to provide a safe workplace, but individual OSHA rules also impose more specific training requirements, depending on what your business does and what hazards might be present in your workplace. These rules are too extensive to summarize here, but following some commonsense guidelines will help you get started. For example, make sure that all employees know about the materials and equipment with which they'll be working, the known hazards in your business and how you're controlling those hazards. Pay special attention to the use of chemicals, making sure to train employees in:

- methods of detecting the release of a hazardous chemical in the work area—for example, monitoring devices or appearance or odor of chemicals when being released
- physical and health hazards of the chemicals
- measures employees can take to protect themselves from the hazards—safe work practices, emergency procedures and protective equipment, and
- details of your labeling system and worksite locations where employees can find chemical safety data. (See Section D.)

Don't let an employee start a job until he or she has received instructions in how to do it safely. The exact training you offer will, of course, vary according to the nature of the business. It may be helpful to call in an OSHA consultant to recommend specific training for your workplace.

Don't overlook the need to train existing employees who are moving into new jobs or are starting to use new equipment. And all employees need refresher instruction from time to time, since it's human nature to become complacent and forget the safety rules.

You must maintain records of your safety training efforts and be prepared to show these records to OSHA inspectors.

5. Inspections

OSHA inspectors can inspect your workplace at any time without advance notice or authorization by a court. Based on what they find there, they can issue citations and impose penalties. However, inspectors are unlikely to make random inspections unless you're in a particularly hazardous business, such as construction. There aren't enough inspectors to go around; OSHA must use its resources prudently.

If you have a workplace with ten or fewer employees and you're in an industry that has a low injury rate, you're exempt from random inspections by federal OSHA officials. State safety and health laws, however, may empower local inspectors to randomly inspect smaller businesses. But if yours is a small insurance agency, retail store, computer repair shop or similar low-injury business, your chances of receiving a random inspection are remote.

Most small businesses are inspected only if:

- an employee has complained to OSHA
- a worker has died from a job-related injury, or
- three or more employees have been hospitalized because of a workplace condition. Of course, you're required to report such fatalities and hospitalizations to OSHA. (See Section A3.)

Even though you may be at low risk of inspection, you're not free to ignore safety and health concerns. You're legally required

to take the initiative in identifying and eliminating safety and health problems that can
affect employees.

⚠ Inspectors Can Obtain Search Warrants.
OSHA officials can't inspect your place
without your consent. If you refuse an inspector
entry, he or she must obtain a search warrant
from a judge before coming into your workplace. But by insisting on a search warrant, you
practically assure that when the inspector returns,
he or she will go through your place with a fine-
tooth comb. Cooperation rather than resistance
is usually the wiser course of action. However,
if you're nervous about what an inspection may
disclose, ask the inspector for an extension of
time and seek advice immediately from a lawyer.

A typical inspection follows a set pattern.

The opening conference. The inspector meets
with you and a representative selected by
your employees. All of you discuss procedures
for the inspection. The inspector reviews
your records on health and safety problems
as well as any steps you've taken to monitor
workplace conditions like noise, ventilation
and hazardous chemicals.

The walkaround. The inspector observes
the working conditions, looking for signs of
health and safety hazards. Are all required
signs and notices posted? Are there strong
odors in the air? Eye irritants? Dust or fumes?
How about noise and temperature levels? Are
there signs of spilled or leaking chemicals?
These and other problems are noted. The
inspector may make measurements of noise
levels and take samples of dust and air to be
analyzed.

Review of safety and health programs. The
inspector checks to make sure that you have
qualified people and the right equipment to
monitor levels of hazardous materials—and
also looks at whether your employees are
taking part in training programs on workplace hazards and emergency procedures.

The closing conference. The inspector
discusses the safety hazards that have been
found and ways to correct the problems.
You're given a specific deadline by which you
must make the corrections. The inspector
documents all violations of OSHA standards
and, if a violation is more than a minor one,
issues a citation. If you receive an OSHA
citation, you must post it near where the
violations occurred. This allows employees to
get involved in any further enforcement
actions by OSHA.

6. Penalties for Violations

Penalties ordered by OSHA depend on the
seriousness of the violation. For willful or
repeated violations, your company may have
to pay thousands of dollars in penalties. And
if a worker has died because you violated
OSHA standards, you could even be sent to
prison. For less serious violations—problems
that are unlikely to cause serious harm or
death—the penalty may be up to $1,000. In
assessing penalties, OSHA looks at several
factors, including:

- the seriousness of the hazard
- your history of violations
- whether you've made a good faith effort
  to comply with OSHA standards, and
- the size of your business.

You can challenge an OSHA citation through an appeal process. If the citation is issued by the federal OSHA, you have 15 days to file a notice of contest with the agency. If a state OSHA issues citations in your state, check with that agency to confirm the filing deadline. It makes sense to consult a lawyer before embarking on an appeal.

After the notice of contest is filed, an administrative law judge will conduct a hearing, giving you and others concerned a chance to present evidence. If you disagree with the decision of the administrative law judge, there's an additional appeal process within OSHA. Ultimately, you can appeal to a court if you can't reach an acceptable resolution within OSHA. Fortunately, most OSHA disputes are resolved through voluntary settlements.

7. Workers' Rights

Workers have two basic rights under OSHA—rights that make good common sense.

First, workers have a right to complain to OSHA about safety or health conditions without being penalized for doing so. Firing or discriminating against employees who have made such complaints is a violation of OSHA provisions.

Second, in some situations, workers have a right to refuse to work if they think the workplace is unsafe. The legal test is this: Does the worker have a reasonable and good faith belief that there's an immediate risk of serious injury or death? If so, the worker can walk off the job and refuse to work until you've corrected the problem or you've determined, after an investigation, that there's

no imminent danger. While you investigate or correct the problem, you can place the worker temporarily in another job at equal pay. It's usually unwise to react by demoting or firing the complaining employee—that can be another violation of OSHA if the complaint is determined to be well founded.

EXAMPLE: Mildred runs a local delivery service. One afternoon, Arlene, one of the drivers, hears that the brakes locked that morning on one of the business vans. She refuses to drive that van until the brakes are checked out by a qualified mechanic. Mildred, believing that the brake problem was caused by careless driving, orders Arlene to use the van. When Arlene says no, Mildred fires her. Arlene sues. Even though the brakes are later found to be adequate, Arlene wins because the court determines that, based on the information she had, Arlene had a reasonable and good faith belief that she'd be exposed to an immediate risk of serious injury or death if she used the truck. Mildred is ordered to reinstate Arlene and to pay her for the time she missed since being fired.

B. Getting Help

Your eyes will probably glaze over at the thought of poring over pages of federal regulations on health and safety in the workplace. Fortunately, there are easier ways to learn what you must do to comply with OSHA requirements—and doing your homework will cost you little or nothing.

1. Worksite Consultations

Each state has an agency (funded mostly by the federal office of OSHA) that offers free, on-site consultations. (See the listing below.)

As in a formal OSHA inspection, you and the consultant will tour the workplace together. The consultant will point out safety and health risks and then, at a closing conference, give you practical advice on how to eliminate hazards. He or she won't issue citations or propose penalties, however. Nor will the consultant provide information about your workplace to the OSHA inspection staff, except in extreme circumstances.

Although OSHA encourages employees to participate in the consultant's walk-through, you're free to exclude employees from the consultation process—unless a union contract gives employee representatives the right to take part.

Opening the Door to Enforcement Action. If the consultant finds a "serious condition"—one from which it's reasonably predictable that death or serious harm could result—he or she will work with you to control or eliminate the hazard within a time period that you jointly determine. If the consultant isn't satisfied with your progress, he or she may report you to an OSHA official. According to OSHA, consultants rarely find conditions which require them to report a business.

Sources for OSHA Consultations

Alabama

Safe State Program
University of Alabama
432 Martha Parham West
Post Office Box 870388
Tuscaloosa, AL 35487
205-348-3033
http://deip.ccs.ua.edu/safe_state_osha.htm

Alaska

Consultation Section
ADOL/AKOSH
3301 Eagle Street
Post Office Box 107022
Anchorage, AK 99510
Juneau 907-465-4855
Anchorage 907-269-4955
www.labor.state.ak.us/lss/oshhome.htm

Arizona

Consultation and Training
Industrial Commission of Arizona
Division of Occupational Safety and Health
800 West Washington
Phoenix, AZ 85007-9070
602-542-5795
www.ica.state.az.us/ADOSH/oshatop.htm

Arkansas

OSHA Consultation
Arkansas Department of Labor/AOSH
10421 West Markham
Little Rock, AR 72205
501-682-4521
www.ark.org/labor/divisions/aosh_p1.html

Sources for OSHA Consultations (continued)

California

CAL/OSHA Consultation Service
2424 Arden Way, Suite 410
Sacramento, CA 95825
916-263-0704
800-963-9424
www.dir.ca.gov/DOSH/consultation.html

Colorado

Occupational Safety & Health Section
Colorado State University
115 Environmental Health Building
Fort Collins, CO 80523
970-491-6151
www.bernardino.colostate.edu/enhealth/
  7c1.html

Connecticut

Division of Occupational Safety & Health
Connecticut Department of Labor/CONN-
  OSHA
38 Wolcott Hill Road
Wethersfield, CT 06109
860-566-4550
www.ctdol.state.ct.us/osha/consulti.htm

Delaware

Occupational Safety and Health
Division of Industrial Affairs
Delaware Department of Labor
4425 Market Street
Wilmington, DE 19802
302-761-8200
www.delawareworks.com/divisions/
  industaffairs/occu.safety.htm

District of Columbia

Office of Occupational Safety and Health
Department of Employment Services
609 H Street, NE
Washington, DC 20002
202-576-6339
http://does.dc.gov/services/wkr_osh.shtm

Florida

University of South Florida
Safety Florida Consultation Program
4003 East Fowler Avenue
Tampa, FL 33617
813 974-9972
www.safetyflorida.usf.edu

Georgia

OSHA 21 Safety Consultation Program
Georgia Institute of Technology
O'Keefe Building, Room 025
Atlanta, GA 30332-0837
404-894-8276
www.gri.gatech.edu/safety.htm

Hawaii

Consultation and Training Branch
Department of Labor and Industrial Relations
830 Punchbowl Street
Honolulu, HI 96813
808-586-9100
www.state.hi.us/dlir/hiosh/consult.htm

Idaho

Safety & Health Consultation Program
Boise State University
Environmental Health and Safety Department

Sources for OSHA Consultations (continued)

1113 Denver Avenue
Boise, ID 83725
www2.boisestate.edu/ehs/Consultation.htm

Illinois
Illinois Onsite Consultation Program
Industrial Services Division
Department of Commerce and Community
  Affairs
State of Illinois Center
100 West Randolph Street
Suite 3-400
Chicago, IL 60601
312-814-2337
800-972-4216
www.commerce.state.il.us/workforce/OSHA/
  OSHA_home.htm

Indiana
Department of Labor
Bureau of Safety, Education and Training
402 West Washington Street, Room W195
Indianapolis, IN 46204-2287
317-232-2688
www.in.gov/labor/buset

Iowa
IOSH Consultation and Education
Iowa Bureau of Labor
1000 East Grand
Des Moines, IA 50319
515-281-7629
www.state.ia.us/iwd/labor/iosh/consultation/
  index.htm

Kansas
Industrial Safety and Health
Kansas Department of Human Resources
512 South West 6th Street
Topeka, KS 66603-3150
785-296-2251

Kentucky
Division of Education & Training
Kentucky Labor Cabinet
1047 U.S. Highway 127, South
Frankfort, KY 40601
502-564-3070
www.kylabor.net/kyosh/oshcons.htm

Louisiana
OSHA-C Consultation
Louisiana Department of Labor
Office of Workers Compensation
1001 North 23rd Street, Room 230
Post Office Box 94040
Baton Rouge, LA 70804-9094
225-342-5665
800-201-2495

Maine
SafetyWorks
Bureau of Labor Standards
Workplace Safety and Health Division
45 State House Station
Augusta, ME 04333-0045
207-624-6400
877-723-3345
www.state.me.us/labor/consult.htm

Sources for OSHA Consultations (continued)

Maryland

MOSH Consultation Services
312 Marshall Avenue, Room 600
Laurel, MD 20707
410-880-6131
301-483-8635
www.dllr.state.md.us/labor/volc.html

Massachusetts

Division of Occupational Safety
Dept. of Workforce Development
1001 Watertown Street
West Newton, MA 02165
617-727-3982
www.state.ma.us/dos/consult/consult.htm

Michigan

Consultation Education & Training Division
Department of Consumer and Industry
  Services
Bureau of Safety & Regulation
7150 Harris Drive
Lansing, MI 48909
517-322-1809
www.cis.state.mi.us/bsr/divisions/cet/
  cet_ser.htm

Minnesota

Workplace Safety Consultation
Department of Labor and Industry
443 Lafayette Road N.
St. Paul, MN 55155-4311
651-284-5060
800-657-3776
www.doli.state.mn.us/wsc.html

Mississippi

Center for Safety and Health
Mississippi State University
106 Crosspark Drive, Suite C
Pearl, MS 39208
601-939-2047
www.msstate.edu/dept/csh

Missouri

On-Site Safety and Health Consultation Service
Department of Labor and Industrial Relations
3315 West Truman Boulevard
Jefferson City, MO 65109
573-751-3403
800-475-2130
www.dolir.state.mo.us/ls/onsite/index.html

Montana

Safety and Health Bureau
Department of Labor & Industry
Post Office Box 1728
1805 Prospect Avenue
Helena, MT 59624
406-444-6401
http://erd.dli.state.mt.us/Safety/SBhome.htm

Nebraska

OSHA Consultation Program
Labor and Safety Standards
Nebraska Department of Labor
Post Office Box 95024
301 Centennial Mall, South
Lincoln, NE 68509-5024
402-471-4717
www.dol.state.ne.us/nwd

Sources for OSHA Consultations (continued)

Nevada
Safety Consultation & Training Section
Division of Industrial Relations
1301 Green Valley Parkway
Suite 200
Henderson, NV 89014
702-486-9159
http://4safenv.state.nv.us

New Hampshire
Department of Health & Human Services
6 Hazen Drive
Concord, NH 03301-6527
603-271-2024
www.dhhs.state.nh.us/CommPublicHealth/
  oshcs.nsf/vMain?Openview

New Jersey
On-Site Consultation Program
Division of Public Safety & Occupational
  Safety & Health
New Jersey Department of Labor
John Fitch Plaza
Post Office Box 110
Trenton, NJ 08625
609-984-0785
www.state.nj.us/labor/wps/psosh/onsite/
  onsite.htm

New Mexico
Occupational Health & Safety Bureau
New Mexico Environment Department
Environmental Protection Division
525 Camino de los Marquez
Suite 3

Post Office Box 26110
Sante Fe, NM 87502
505-827-4230
www.nmenv.state.nm.us/NMED/
  env_prot.html

New York
Division of Safety and Health
Department of Labor
State Office Campus
Building 12
Room 158
Albany, NY 12240
www.labor.state.ny.us/business_ny/
  employer_responsibilities/safety_health.html

North Carolina
Bureau of Consultative Services
North Carolina Department of Labor
Occupational Safety and Health Division
4 West Edenton Street
Raleigh, NC 27601
919-807-2899
www.dol.state.nc.us/osha/consult/consult.htm

North Dakota
Occupational Safety and Health Consultation
  Program
North Dakota Department of Health
1200 Missouri Ave., Box 5520
Bismarck, ND 58506
701-328-5188
http://ndsafety.net

Sources for OSHA Consultations (continued)

Ohio

OSHA On-Site Consultation Services
Ohio Department of Commerce
50 West Broad Street, 29th Floor
Columbus, OH 43215
614-644-2631
800-282-1425
www.com.state.oh.us/ODOC/laws/
  default.htm

Oklahoma

OSHA Consultation Division
Oklahoma Department of Labor
4001 North Lincoln Boulevard
Oklahoma City, OK 73105-5212
405-528-1500
888-269-5353
www.state.ok.us/~okdol/osha/index.htm

Oregon

Oregon OSHA
Department of Consumer & Business Services
350 Winter Street, NE, Room 430
Salem, OR 97310
503-378-3272
www.orosha.org

Pennsylvania

PA/OSHA Consultation Program
Indiana University of Pennsylvania
Walsh Hall, Room 210
302 East Walk
Indiana, PA 15705-1087
724-357-2396
800-382-1241
www.hhs.iup.edu/sa/OSHA/index.htm

Rhode Island

Division of Occupational Health & Radiation
  Control
Rhode Island Department of Health
3 Capitol Hill, Room 206
Providence, RI 02908
401-277-2438
www.state.ri.us/dohrad.htm

South Carolina

Office of OSHA Voluntary Programs
Department of Labor, Licensing & Regulations
110 Centerview Drive
Columbia, SC 29210
803-734-9599
www.llr.state.sc.us/ovp.asp

South Dakota

Engineering Extension
South Dakota State University
Box 510, West Hall
907 Harvey Dunn Street
Brookings, SD 57007
605-688-4101
www3.sdstate.edu/Academics/CollegeOf
  Engineering/EngineeringResourceCenter/
  EngineeringExtension

Tennessee

TOSHA Consultative Services
Tennessee Department of Labor
Safety, Health and Standards Division
710 James Robertson Parkway, 3rd Floor
Nashville, TN 37243-0659
615-325-9901
www.state.tn.us/labor-wfd/toshcons.html

Sources for OSHA Consultations (continued)

Texas
Occupational Safety and Health Consultation
Workers' Compensation Commission
4501 Springdale
Suite A
Austin, TX 78723
512-804-4640
800-687-7080
http://twcc.state.tx.us/services/oshcon.html

Utah
Job Safety and Health Consultation Services
 Program
Utah Labor Commission
160 East 300 South
Salt Lake City, UT 84114-6650
801-530-6855
http://worksafe.laborcommission.utah.gov

Vermont
Division of Occupational Safety & Health
Vermont Department of Labor & Industry
National Life Building, Drawer 20
Montpelier, VT 05620-3401
802-828-2765
www.state.vt.us/labind/vosha.htm

Virginia
On-Site Consultation Services
Virginia Department of Labor & Industry
13 South Thirteenth Street
Richmond, VA 23219
804-786-8707
www.dli.state.va.us/programs/
 consultation.htm

Washington
WISHA Services
Washington Department of Labor & Industries
Division of Industrial Safety & Health
Post Office Box 44851
Olympia, WA 98504
360-902-5638
800-423-7233
www.lni.wa.gov/wisha

West Virginia
Safety & Health Consultation
Division of Labor
State Capitol Complex Bldg. 6, Room B-749
1800 East Washington Street
Charleston, WV 25305
304-558-7890
www.state.wv.us/labor/employer

Wisconsin
OSHA Consultation
Department of Health and Family Services
Division of Public Health
1 West Wilson Street
Madison, WI 53703
608-266-0417
www.dhfs.state.wi.us/dph_boh/osha_cons/
 index.htm

Wyoming
Wyoming Workers' Safety / OSHA
Department of Employment
122 West 25th, Herschler Bldg., 2 East
Cheyenne, WY 82002
307-777-7786
http://wydoe.state.wy.us/employer.asp

2. Safety Codes

Written safety codes are a good way to let employees know that you take safety seriously. Since each workplace is different, you'll have to make sure that your safety code is tailored to the specific needs of your business.

OSHA has suggested a safety code that you may find useful as a starting point—but you'll undoubtedly need to make changes to make it fit.

 For additional help with OSHA rules and regulations, see the *OSHA Handbook for Small Business*—OSHA Publication 2209—available from the U.S. Government Printing Office, Washington, DC 20402, 202-783-3238. It contains self-inspection checklists covering such topics as fire protection, personal protective equipment and clothing, walkways, floor and wall openings, stairs and stairways, elevated surfaces, exit doors, hand tools and equipment. These checklists can help you and employees identify potential problems.

You can also find lots of helpful materials on OSHA's website at www.osha.gov.

If you want to order the full text of the OSHA regulations, these materials are available from the U.S. Government Printing Office at a small cost, or can be found in the Code of Federal Regulations at most law libraries. There are four separate sets of standards:

General Industry—29 Code of Federal Regulations 1910

Construction—29 Code of Federal Regulations 1926

Maritime Employment—29 Code of Federal Regulations 1915–1919

Agriculture—29 Code of Federal Regulations 1904.

Safety Code of ABC, Inc.

1. All employees of this company must follow these safe practice rules and report all unsafe conditions or practices to a supervisor.

2. Supervisors will require employees to comply with all safety rules.

3. All employees periodically will be given instruction on workplace safety and health.

4. Anyone under the influence of alcohol or drugs will not be allowed on the job while in that condition.

5. No one will be permitted or required to work while his or her ability or alertness is impaired by fatigue or illness.

6. Employees must make sure that all guards and other protective devices are in place, and must wear protective equipment and clothing in specified work areas.

7. Horseplay, scuffling and other acts which may endanger employees are prohibited.

8. Work should be planned to prevent injuries when working with equipment and handling heavy materials. Back injuries are the most frequent and often the most persistent and painful type of workplace injury.

9. Workers must not handle or tamper with electrical equipment, machinery or air or water lines unless they have received instructions from their supervisors.

10. Report injuries promptly to a supervisor. A first aid kit is located at _____ _____ .

    Emergency phone numbers are located at _____ .

Adapted from: *OSHA Handbook for Small Business*

C. State OSHA Laws

If a state has a health and safety law that meets or exceeds federal OSHA standards, the state can take over enforcement of the standards from federal administrators. This means that all inspections and enforcement actions will be handled by your state OSHA rather than its federal counterpart.

So far, 23 states have been approved for such enforcement regarding private employers. They include: Alaska, Arizona, California, Hawaii, Indiana, Iowa, Kentucky, Maryland, Michigan, Minnesota, Nevada, New Mexico, North Carolina, Oregon, South Carolina, Tennessee, Utah, Vermont, Virginia, Washington and Wyoming. (See the contact details below.)

New York and Connecticut also have OSHA-type laws, but they only apply to government employees. Other states are considering passing OSHA laws—and some of the above states are considering amending coverage and content of existing laws.

If your business is located in a state that has an OSHA law, contact your state agency for a copy of the safety and health standards that are relevant to your business. State standards may be more strict than federal standards, and the requirements for posting notices may be different.

State OSHA Offices

Alaska Department of Labor and Workforce Development
1111 West 8th Street, Room 304
Post Office Box 21149
Juneau, AK 99802-1149
907-465-4855
www.labor.state.ak.us/lss/oshhome.htm

ADOSH, Industrial Commission of Arizona
800 West Washington
Phoenix, AZ 85007-2922
602-542-5795
www.ica.state.az.us/ADOSH/oshatop.htm

Cal-OSHA, California Department of Industrial Relations
455 Golden Gate Avenue, 10th Floor
San Francisco, CA 94102
415-703-5050
www.dir.ca.gov/occupational_safety.html

Public sector only
Conn-OSHA, Connecticut Department of Labor
38 Wolcott Hill Road
Wethersfield, CT 06109
860-566-4550
www.ctdol.state.ct.us/osha/osha.htm

HIOSH, Hawaii Department of Labor and Industrial Relations
830 Punchbowl Street, Room 423
Honolulu, HI 96813
808-586-9116
www.state.hi.us/dlir/hiosh

State OSHA Offices (continued)

IOSHA, Indiana Department of Labor
Indiana Government Center—South
402 West Washington Street, Room W195
Indianapolis, IN 46204
317-232-2655
www.in.gov/labor/iosha

IOSH, Iowa Division of Labor Services
1000 East Grand Avenue
Des Moines, IA 50319-0209
515-281-3606
www.state.ia.us/iwd/labor/index.html

KYOSH, Kentucky Labor Cabinet
1047 U.S. Highway 127 South
Frankfort, KY 40601
502-564-3070
www.kylabor.net/kyosh/index.htm

MOSH, Maryland Division of Labor and Industry
Department of Labor, Licensing and
  Regulation
1100 North Eutaw Street, Room 613
Baltimore, MD 21201-2206
410-767-2115
www.dllr.state.md.us/labor/mosh.html

MIOSHA, Bureau of Safety & Regulation
Michigan Department of Consumer & Industry
  Services
Post Office Box 30643
7150 Harris Drive
Lansing, MI 48909-8143
517-322-1814
www.cis.state.mi.us/bsr

MNOSHA, Minnesota Department of Labor and Industry
443 Lafayette Road North
St. Paul, MN 55155-4307
651-284-5050
www.doli.state.mn.us/mnosha.html

OSHES, Nevada Division of Industrial Relations
1301 N. Green Valley Parkway, Suite 200
Henderson, NV 89074
702-486-9044
http://dirweb.state.nv.us/oshes.htm

Public sector only
PEOSH, New Jersey Department of Labor
John Fitch Plaza—Labor Building
Market and Warren Streets
Post Office Box 110
Trenton, NJ 0826-0010
609-292-3923

New Mexico Environment Department
Environmental Protection Division
Occupational Health and Safety Bureau
Post Office Box 26110
525 Camino de los Marquez, Suite 3
Santa Fe, NM 87502
505-827-4230
www.nmenv.state.nm.us/NMED/
  env_prot.html

Public sector only
New York Department of Labor
W. Averell Harriman State Office Building-12,
  Room 500

State OSHA Offices (continued)

Albany, NY 12240
518-457-9000
www.labor.state.ny.us/working_ny/
worker_rights/safety_health.html

North Carolina Department of Labor
4 West Edenton Street
Raleigh, NC 27601-1092
919-807-2860
www.dol.state.nc.us/osha/osh.htm

OR-OSHA, Oregon Occupational Safety and Health Division
Department of Consumer & Business Services
350 Winter Street, NE, Room 430
Salem, OR 97310
503-378-3272
www.cbs.state.or.us/external/osha

South Carolina Department of Labor, Licensing and Regulation
3600 Forest Drive
Post Office Box 11329
Columbia, SC 29204
803-734-9644
www.llr.state.sc.us/osha.asp

TOSHA, Tennessee Department of Labor & Workforce Development
710 James Robertson Parkway
Nashville, TN 37243-0659
615-741-2582
www.state.tn.us/labor-wfd/mainsafety.html

UOSH, Utah Labor Commission
160 East 300 South, 3rd Floor
Post Office Box 146650

Salt Lake City, UT 84114-6650
801-530-6901
www.labor.state.ut.us/Utah_Occupational
Safety_Hea/utah_occupational_safety_hea.html

VOSHA, Vermont Department of Labor & Industry
National Life Building, Drawer 20
Montpelier, VT 05620-3401
802-828-2765
www.state.vt.us/labind/vosha.htm

VOSH, Virginia Department of Labor & Industry
Powers-Taylor Building
13 South Thirteenth Street
Richmond, VA 23219
804-371-2327
www.dli.state.va.us/programs/safety.htm

WISHA, Washington Department of Labor & Industries
Post Office Box 44001
Olympia, WA 98504-4001
7273 Linderson Way SW
Tumwater, WA 98501-5414
360-902-5799
www.lni.wa.gov/wisha

Wyoming Department of Employment
Workers' Safety / OSHA
Herschler Bldg., 2nd Floor East
122 West 25th Street
Cheyenne, WY 82002
307-777-7786
http://wydoe.state.wy.us

D. Hazardous Chemicals

The OSHA rules include a section called the Hazard Communication Standard. Many people call this the right-to-know law. Basically, the standard requires you to give information to your employees about the hazardous chemicals they handle.

Many states also have right-to-know laws, including those shown on the chart below.

These informational requirements vary somewhat from state to state. If your business handles any chemicals, be sure to get a copy of your state's rules. Because most of the state laws are similar to the federal right-to-know rules, this discussion will focus on the federal law. If your state has standards that are more stringent than the federal ones, there are still some unresolved questions about whether you need only comply with the federal standards. Until this legal issue is clearly resolved, it's wisest to follow the stricter standards.

To understand the right-to-know laws—state or federal—you must first become familiar with the Material Safety Data Sheets (MSDS) supplied by manufacturers of all hazardous chemicals. They contain a wealth of information, including:

- the physical hazards of the chemical, such as flammability and explosiveness
- health hazards—the symptoms of exposure and the medical conditions that can be made worse by exposure
- how the chemical enters the body and the limits of safe exposure
- whether the chemical is known to cause cancer

- how to safely handle the chemical
- recommended protection methods including protective clothing and equipment, and
- first aid and emergency procedures should a chemical be mishandled.

Obviously, if an employee is working with hazardous chemicals, this is essential information. That's why the law requires you to keep the MSDS for each hazardous chemical and make it accessible to employees. You must also keep a list of all the hazardous chemicals used in your business and label all containers. And you're required to train employees in the safe use of hazardous chemicals.

EXAMPLE: Ace Water Treatment Corporation sells water treatment systems to rural homeowners whose water comes from underground wells. Ace issues demonstration kits to its sales staff so they can demonstrate to potential customers the extent of impurities in the homeowner's water supply. In one test, the salesperson adds a few drops of potassium hydroxide to a sample of the customer's water so that certain impurities will collect at the bottom of the test tube. Potassium hydroxide is a hazardous chemical sometimes known as lye.

Right to Know Laws (Hazardous Chemicals)

Alabama	Ala. Code § 22-33-1
Alaska	Alaska Stat. § 18.60.067
Arizona	Ariz. Rev. Stat. § 23-410; Ariz. Rev. Stat. § 23-427
California	Cal. Lab. Code §§ 6360, 6398, 6401.7
Connecticut	Conn. Gen. Stat. Ann. § 31-369
Delaware	Del. Code Ann. tit. 16, § 2406; Del. Code Ann. tit. 16, § 2415
District of Columbia	D.C. Code Ann. § 32-1101
Florida	Fla. Stat. Ann. § 442.115
Hawaii	Haw. Rev. Stat. § 396-6
Illinois	820 Ill. Comp. Stat. § 255/1
Indiana	821 Ind. Code Ann. § 22-8-1.1-1
Iowa	Iowa Code § 89B.8
Maine	Me. Rev. Stat. Ann. tit. 26, § 1709; tit. 22, § 1471-M
Maryland	Md. Code Ann., [Lab. & Empl.] §§ 5-401, 5-408
Massachusetts	Mass. Gen. Laws ch. 111F, § 15
Michigan	Mich. Comp. Laws §§ 408.1014a, 408.1014j
Minnesota	Minn. Stat. Ann. § 182.653
Montana	Mont. Code Ann. §§ 50-78-101, 50-78-202
Nevada	Nev. Rev. Stat. Ann. § 618.295
New Hampshire	N.H. Rev. Stat. Ann. § 277-A:4
New Jersey	N.J. Stat. Ann. §§ 34:5A-1, 34:5A-5, 34:5A-12
New Mexico	N.M. Stat. Ann. § 50-9-3
New York	N.Y. Lab. Law § 876
North Carolina	N.C. Gen. Stat. §§ 95-173, 95-191, 95-208
Oklahoma	Okla. Stat. Ann. tit. 40, §§ 401, 414
Oregon	Or. Admin. R. § 437-004-9800
Pennsylvania	35 Pa. Cons. Stat. Ann. §§ 7301, 7305
Rhode Island	R.I. Gen. Laws §§ 28-21-1, 28-21-8
South Carolina	S.C. Code Ann. § 41-15-100
Tennessee	Tenn. Code Ann. § 50-3-2001
Utah	Utah Code Ann. § 34A-6-201
Vermont	Vt. Stat. Ann. tit. 18, § 1725; Vt. Stat. Ann. tit. 21, § 223
Virginia	Va. Code Ann. § 40.1-51.1
Washington	Wash. Rev. Code Ann. §§ 49.70.100, 49.70.010
West Virginia	W.Va. Code § 21-3-18
Wisconsin	Wis. Stat. Ann. §§ 101.58, 101.595

Current as of October 17, 2002

The chemical comes from the manufacturer with an MSDS explaining its dangers and how it should be handled—for example, goggles should be used to protect the user's eyes. To comply with the right to know law, Ace keeps the MSDS and makes it available to employees. Ace makes sure that all containers are properly labeled, and that all employees are thoroughly trained in how to use and handle the chemical. To further protect its employees, Ace issues protective goggles to those who perform water tests using the chemical.

E. Workers' Compensation

The workers' compensation system provides replacement income and medical expenses to employees who suffer work-related injuries or illnesses. Benefits may also extend to the survivors of workers who are killed on the job.

Workers' compensation is a no-fault system. The employee is entitled to receive stated benefits whether or not the employer provided a safe workplace and whether or not the worker's own carelessness contributed to the injury or illness. But the employer, too, receives some protection because the employee is limited to fixed types of compensation—basically, partial wage replacement and payment of medical bills. The employee can't get paid for pain and suffering or mental anguish.

To cover the cost of workers' compensation benefits for employees, you'll usually need to pay for insurance—through either a state fund or a private insurance company. While self-insurance is a possibility in some states, the technical requirements usually make this an impractical alternative for a small business.

1. Coverage Requirements

Each state has its own workers' compensation statute. While the details differ from state to state, one thing is clear: If you have employees, you generally need to obtain workers' compensation coverage. Your state workers' compensation bureau can tell you about any legal requirements for informing employees of their rights—generally, you do this by displaying a poster.

State laws vary as to whether sole proprietors, partners and executive officers can or must be covered by workers' compensation. In some states, these owners and managers have the option of being covered or not. If you're in one of these states and you want this coverage—which will give you the same benefits as other workers who are injured—mention this when you apply for coverage through a state fund or a private insurance carrier. (For more on arranging for coverage, see Section E2.)

Similarly, in some states, sole proprietors, partners and executive officers are automatically covered but you have the option of excluding them. Ask a representative of the state fund or private insurance carrier how to do this when you apply for coverage.

A few states require workers' compensation coverage only if you have three or more employees.

You're Still Liable for Intentional Injuries

While workers' compensation is the employee's exclusive remedy for most work-related injuries or illnesses, there's a major exception: injuries or illnesses caused by the intentional actions of the employer. An employee who can prove that your intentional actions caused an injury or illness can take you to court and seek a full range of damages—including, for example, damages for pain and suffering as well as economic losses.

Obviously, if you or a supervisor were to physically assault an employee, that would qualify as an intentional action. But courts sometimes treat other workplace events as intentional, too. Suppose, for example, that to speed up production, you remove the safety devices from a dangerous machine. An employee is injured using the machine, but you continue to require workers to use the machine in its unsafe condition. You've probably set yourself up for an intentional injury claim because you know with "substantial certainty" that additional workers will be injured by that machine.

In that situation, injured employees would not be limited to their remedies under your state's workers' compensation law. They would be able to sue you and your business under traditional tort (personal injury) theories.

Rejecting Coverage Can Be a Mistake. In two states—New Jersey and Texas—workers' compensation coverage isn't mandatory for an employer. You can choose whether or not you want to secure workers' compensation insurance for your workplace. But if you opt not to and you're sued by an employee who claims to have been injured on the job by your negligence, you won't be able to use the employee's own carelessness as a defense. Therefore, most wise employers obtain workers' compensation, no matter where their businesses are located.

2. Arranging for Coverage

Some states allow an employer to self-insure —a process that typically requires the business to maintain a hefty cash reserve earmarked for workers' compensation claims. Usually, this isn't practical for small businesses. Most small businesses buy insurance through a state fund or from a private insurance carrier. If private insurance is an option in your state, discuss it with the insurance agent or broker who handles the basic insurance policy for your business. Often, you can save money on premiums by coordinating workers' compensation coverage with property damage and public liability insurance. A good agent or broker may also be able to explain the mechanics of a state fund where that's an available option or is required.

In most states that have a state-run workers' compensation fund, you have a choice of buying coverage from the state or from a private insurer. In the following states, however, you must purchase from the state fund: North

Dakota, Ohio, Washington and West Virginia. In Wyoming, you must purchase coverage from the state fund if you are engaged in an "extra-hazardous" industry.

Insurance rates are based on the industry and occupation involved, as well as the size of your payroll. Your safety record can also influence the rate; if you have more accidents than is usually anticipated, your rate is likely to be increased.

3. Controlling Costs

Premiums are based on two factors: industry classification and payroll. If your premium is above a certain amount—$5,000 in many states—your actual experience with workers' compensation claims will affect your premiums. Your rate can go up or down, depending on how your claims compare with other businesses in your industry. The number of claims filed by your employees affects your premium more than the dollar value of the claims. That's because if you have a lot of accidents, it's assumed that you have an unsafe workplace and that the insurance company eventually will have to pay out some large claims.

Here are some steps you can take to try to keep your workers' compensation costs down.

a. Preventing accidents

Emphasize safety in the workplace. Provide proper equipment, safety devices and protective clothing. Train and retrain your employees in safe procedures and how to deal with emergencies. Set up a safety committee made up of both managers and workers. Promote

employee health by offering wellness and fitness programs.

b. Buying coverage wisely

Seek out a participating plan in which the insurance company pays dividends to its insured employers. It helps to find a solid company with a long history of paying dividends—but dividends are never guaranteed.

Consider being put on a retrospective rating plan (unfortunately, this isn't usually available to many small businesses). In such plans, the insurance company agrees to adjust your premium at the end of the year based on your actual claims experience. If you have a strong safety program, this program can be better for you than a dividend-type program —which generally looks at the insurance company's claims experience, not just the history of your business.

Make sure your business and your employees are properly classified. Don't let the insurance company mistakenly place your business in a class that pays a higher premium because of job hazards. And, since workers are also classified based on the nature of their work, check to see that the insurance company has classified them correctly.

c. Following up

Use light duty or modified work assignments to help workers who have been injured on the job but are allowed back to work on a trial basis.

Monitor claims. If you learn that an employee seems to have recovered but is still accepting workers' compensation benefits, ask him or her for an explanation. If something still seems amiss, notify the insurance company or state fund.

4. Injuries and Illnesses Covered

As an employer, you needn't dig very deeply into the fine points of workers' compensation law. The state fund or private insurance company that covers your workplace will have its own lawyers resolve legal questions about whether a worker is entitled to compensation for a particular disability and, if so, how much the worker is entitled to receive. When a worker seeks to receive benefits that are questionable, these lawyers will challenge the employee on your behalf.

Still, as a well-informed employer, you may want to learn a bit more about how the system works. While workers' compensation law varies somewhat from state to state, there's enough similarity among the states to justify some general statements.

To be covered by workers' compensation, an employee's injury needn't be caused by a sudden accident such as a fall. Basically, any injury that occurs in connection with work is covered. Many workers, for example, receive compensation for repetitive motion injuries such as carpal tunnel syndrome, which primarily afflicts the wrists, hands and forearms. (See Section I.)

In theory, if a worker's injury was intentionally self-inflicted or was caused by substance abuse or by some other nonwork cause (such as a hobby), the injury won't be covered. But in a disputed case, the worker is still likely to get the benefits by showing that his or her behavior wasn't the only thing that caused the injury.

Workers may also be compensated for some illnesses and diseases. An illness is likely to be covered by workers' compensation when the nature of the job increases the workers' chances of suffering from that disease. Illnesses that are the gradual result of work conditions—for example, emotional illness, heart conditions, lung disease and stress-related digestive problems—increasingly are being covered by workers' compensation.

Finally, there are death benefits. Dependents of workers killed on the job can usually collect workers' compensation benefits.

Don't Penalize Workers Who File Claims. In most states, it's a violation of the workers' compensation statute or public policy to discriminate against an employee for filing a workers' compensation claim. This means you can't fire, demote or take any other negative action against a worker for filing a claim.

5. Benefits Paid

Workers' compensation covers the employee's medical and rehabilitation expenses. It also provides income to the employee to offset a big part of lost wages. Typically, a worker receives two-thirds of his or her average wages up to a fixed ceiling. But since these payments are tax free, a worker who receives average wages fares reasonably well.

In most states, workers become eligible for wage loss replacement benefits as soon as they've lost a few days of work because of an injury covered by workers' compensation. The number of days required to qualify varies by state. Some states allow the payments to be made retroactively to the first day of wage loss if the injury keeps the employee out of work for an extended period.

Workers may receive lump sum benefits if they have a total disability or a permanent partial disability. In some states, there are specific amounts provided for permanent partial disability such as the loss of an eye or a foot.

6. Independent Contractors

Workers' compensation insurance is required only for employees—not for independent contractors who work for you. (Independent contractors are covered in greater detail in Chapter 11.) Small businesses sometimes buy services from independent contractors to save money on workers' compensation insurance, as well as taxes and other expenses normally associated with employees. That's fine as long as you correctly label people as independent contractors rather than employees. But if you make a mistake and a person improperly labeled as an independent contractor is injured while doing work for your business, you may have to pay large sums to cover medical bills and lost wages which should have been covered by workers' compensation insurance.

In addition, you can sometimes have a problem with a properly classified independent contractor who hires employees to perform some work for you. If the independent contractor doesn't carry workers' compensa-

tion insurance and doesn't have the money to compensate an employee who's injured on the job, the injured worker—in a search for deeper pockets—may sue your business for failing to keep a safe workplace.

 Require Proof of Insurance. When hiring an independent contractor, ask to see an insurance certificate establishing that the independent contractor's employees are covered by workers' compensation insurance. For good measure, make sure that the independent contractor also has general liability insurance.

 To learn more about hiring independent contractors, including the tests for distinguishing independent contractors from employees and information on taxes and workers' compensation insurance premiums, see *Hiring Independent Contractors*, by attorney Stephen Fishman (Nolo).

F. Disease Prevention

Under OSHA, your business may need to take precautions to protect employees from infection in the workplace. The OSHA rules apply to employees who may be exposed to blood or other potentially infectious material—and so primarily affect employees who work in hospitals, clinics, medical offices and nursing homes.

If it's reasonably likely that your employees will come into contact with blood and other infectious materials, check with OSHA to learn the requirements for protective practices and equipment.

Employees With HIV or AIDS

Under the Americans with Disabilities Act (ADA) and similar state laws, a person who is HIV positive or has AIDS is considered to have a disability. You can't discriminate against that person—or use the disability as a reason for rejecting a person if he or she is otherwise qualified for a particular job. You may also need to reasonably accommodate that person so that he or she can perform the work required. Normally, your duty to reasonably accommodate a person with a disability—including AIDS—is triggered by that person requesting an accommodation. In the case of someone who has AIDS, the accommodation may consist of a flexible work schedule, reduced hours, work at home arrangements or a reduction in travel.

You don't have to permit an HIV-infected person to continue in a position if the infection poses a health threat to others. This generally comes up only in the healthcare field.

The ADA also prohibits discrimination against people who associate with those who have AIDS. So it's unlawful, for example, to reject a job applicant because he or she lives with someone who has AIDS.

If you learn that an employee has AIDS or is HIV positive, keep the information confidential. Use it only to accommodate the person in performing his or her job.

G. Tobacco Smoke

A state law or municipal ordinance may limit or prohibit smoking on your business premises. Some laws and ordinances are designed primarily to protect nonsmoking employees from secondhand tobacco smoke. Others seek to protect nonsmoking customers and other visitors as well.

Here are a few examples of state laws.

- In Alaska, if your business has a designated smoking area, you must ventilate it to ensure that nonsmokers aren't subjected to tobacco smoke.
- In California, you can't permit smoking in an enclosed place of employment. There are some exceptions, such as employee break rooms; if you do allow smoking in permitted areas, you must separately ventilate these areas.
- In Florida, you can create a designated smoking area as long as all employees working in that area agree. If even one worker objects, however, you can't designate that area for smoking.
- In Minnesota, you can't allow smoking in an enclosed workplace, except for private enclosed offices occupied exclusively by smokers.
- In Vermont, you must adopt a smoking policy that either prohibits smoking throughout the workplace or restricts it to enclosed designated areas—although in certain circumstances, with employee approval, you can allow smoking in designated areas even if they are not enclosed.

For up-to-date information on your responsibilities and options concerning smoking in the workplace, check with your state and local health departments.

In addition to meeting the requirements of laws and ordinances that limit or prohibit smoking in the workplace, be aware that you may be liable to nonsmoking employees if you don't take appropriate action on their complaints. For example, an employee who develops bronchial asthma from exposure to tobacco smoke may be entitled to workers' compensation benefits. And an employee who has a severe respiratory ailment that's aggravated by tobacco smoke may be entitled under the ADA to a smoke-free workplace.

While you can prohibit smoking on the job, avoid a policy that prohibits an employee from smoking off the job as well. Such a broad prohibition can invade a worker's privacy and is specifically barred by some state laws.

 Smokers Can Use Some Help. Recognize that giving up smoking can be difficult. Some experts equate nicotine addiction with a cocaine or heroin habit. To demonstrate your concern, you might offer to pay the cost of an employee's tuition in a stop smoking program if the smoker successfully kicks the habit.

H. Drug and Alcohol Abuse

There is no law that prevents you from combating the use of drugs and alcohol in the workplace. There are, however, some limits on your ability to test employees for drug usage.

Legally, you're free to:
- prohibit the use of drugs and alcohol in the workplace
- require that employees not come to work or return from meals or breaks under the influence of alcohol or drugs, and
- require that employees who use alcohol or illegally use drugs meet the same performance standards you impose on other employees.

You needn't tolerate absenteeism, tardiness, poor job performance or accidents caused by alcohol or illegal drug use.

Helping Those in Need. One enlightened approach—especially if an employee with a drug or alcohol problem has valuable skills—is to offer an assistance program to help the employee deal with the problem. Or you might consider a modified work schedule to permit the person to attend a self-help program.

1. Illegal Drug Use

There's nothing wrong with firing an employee or rejecting an applicant who uses, possesses or distributes drugs illegally. This includes the use of illegal drugs and the illegal use of prescription drugs that are deemed controlled substances under federal drug laws.

> **EXAMPLE:** Starbright Corporation fires Lucy after determining that she takes amphetamines without a doctor's prescription. Amphetamines can be legally prescribed, but are classified as "controlled substances" because of their potential for abuse. If a doctor didn't prescribe amphetamines for Lucy, Starbright would be justified in firing her for illegal use of drugs.

The most reliable way to establish that an employee is using drugs illegally is through a drug test. Testing is left to your discretion. If you choose to test, however, you must observe legal guidelines.

a. Federal laws

There are a few situations in which a private employer is required to test employees for drug usage. The U.S. Department of Transportation, for example, requires drug testing of airline pilots and other transportation employees who hold jobs in which drug abuse can affect public safety. And the U.S. Department of Defense requires similar testing by companies that contract with it.

The Drug-Free Workplace Act of 1988 (41 U.S.C. § 701) requires all contractors with the federal government to certify that they will provide a drug-free workplace. To comply, you must:

- inform workers that illegal drug use is prohibited in the workplace
- create and maintain a drug awareness program
- require employees to notify you of any conviction for drug usage in the workplace—in which case you must notify the government, and
- impose remedial measures on employees convicted for using drugs in the workplace.

However, the Drug-Free Workplace Act doesn't require you to test employees.

b. Discretionary testing

Pre-employment testing is the safest type of testing from a legal standpoint. (Drug testing of job applicants is covered in Chapter 1, Section F.) After an employee is hired, testing is controlled by federal and state laws, as well as court decisions. Because these laws are rapidly changing, be sure to doublecheck your state law at a nearby library or on the Internet. (See Chapter 13, Section D, for guidance on how to do legal research.)

If you do decide to test, your primary motive should be to ensure the safety of workers, customers and members of the general public. You're most likely to withstand a legal challenge if you limit testing of employees to three situations.

Safety and security. You can require periodic testing of employees whose jobs carry a high risk of injury to people and property—for example, heavy equipment operators and workers who handle explosives. Similarly, periodic testing is generally permitted for security workers—for example, those who transport large sums of cash or guards who carry guns.

Accidents. You can require testing of an employee who's been involved in an accident —for example, a food server who's dumped a carafe of scalding coffee on a customer or a maintenance worker who's drilled through a water pipe.

Retesting. You can require periodic retesting of an employee who is currently in or has completed a drug rehabilitation program, or an employee to whom you've given a second chance—for example, one who tested positive for drugs after a personal injury accident, but was kept on the job anyway.

Even though you have a right in these situations to require a drug test as a condition of continued employment, you can't force an employee to submit to a test against his or her will. You can, however, fire an employee who refuses to be tested.

In general, avoid a policy of testing all employees—not all of them will be in a position to cause harm through drug usage. Similarly,

avoid a program of random drug testing. If you test all employees, test them randomly or test without a good reason, you may get sued for invasion of privacy or infliction of emotional harm.

To keep your drug testing program on a solid legal footing:

- use a test lab that's certified by the U.S. Department of Health and Human Services or accredited by the College of American Pathologists
- keep the results of drug tests confidential, and
- be consistent in dealing with those who test positive.

Documentation Is Essential. Because drug testing is always subject to a legal challenge, it's important to keep good records documenting why and how tests are administered. Request a receipt from each employee acknowledging that he or she has been given a copy of your drug and alcohol policy—or include the policy in your employee handbook and get a receipt for the handbook. (See Chapter 2, Section B.) Don't give a drug test without having the employee sign a consent form. Keep a record of what tests were performed, what drugs were found and in what amounts. Finally, document the chain of custody of the tested sample (that is, who had possession of it) so you can show who handled it at all pertinent times.

2. Alcoholism

The law treats alcoholism differently than drug abuse. A person disabled by alcoholism is entitled to the same protection from job discrimination as any other person with a disability.

On the other hand, you're not required to overlook the effects that this disability can have on job performance. Under the Americans with Disabilities Act (ADA), you can discipline, discharge or deny employment to an alcoholic if the person's job performance or conduct is so badly affected by alcohol usage that he or she isn't qualified to do the job.

EXAMPLE: Don, an alcoholic, often is late for work and sometimes is unable to perform his job. His employer disciplines him because of his tardiness and poor performance. The company holds Don to the same standards as its other employees —and disciplines him in a like way. This doesn't violate the ADA.

Neither the ADA nor its regulations define alcoholic or alcoholism. The lack of definitions may have little practical effect, however, since the ADA allows you to judge the employee by his or her ability to do the job. People who have an alcohol problem aren't legally entitled to any special consideration. (For more on the ADA, see Chapter 9.)

I. Repetitive Stress Disorder

The number of workers suffering from repetitive stress disorder (RSD) is rapidly growing —due in large part to the increased use of computers in workplaces. A familiar form of RSD is carpal tunnel syndrome, which causes swelling inside the tunnel created by bone and ligament in the wrist. This swelling can put pressure on nerves passing through the tunnel—leading, in turn, to pain, tingling and numbness. Other types of RSD include:

- tendinitis—tears in tissue connecting bones to muscles
- myofascial damage—tenderness and swelling from overworking muscles
- tenosynovitis—irritation of the boundary between the tendon and surrounding sheath, and
- cervical radiculopathy—compression of disks in the neck.

The last disorder often develops in workers who hold a phone on their shoulders while using computers. All of these disorders are painful and can be disabling.

It isn't clear what role (if any) OSHA will eventually play in establishing and enforcing ergonomics standards to help stem the rising tide of RSD cases. In 2001, a pending ergonomics rule was repealed. This area of governmental regulation is apparently a sensitive political matter. As this book goes to press in late 2002, the OSHA approach is to offer guidance and information to employers while a new ergonomics rule is developed. So for the time being, making sure your workplace reduces the chance or RSD problems is mostly voluntary.

Still, as an enlightened employer (and in anticipation of future regulation by OSHA), you may want to take steps to protect employees from carpal tunnel syndrome and other repetitive strain disorders. You may, for example, change the equipment employees use, train them in improving work techniques and modify the layout of work stations. Larger employers might consider hiring an ergonomics consultant to help them figure out what changes to make.

What the Future May Bring

Several states are considering regulations for businesses that use video display terminals—better known as computer workstations. Rules adopted in New Mexico for state employees who use computers can serve as a model for your business.

- Maintain room lighting at a level that reduces eyestrain and glare.
- Control glare by indirect lighting and nonreflecting furnishings.
- Use acoustic pads to control noise levels.
- Locate workstations at a reasonable distance from heating and cooling vents.
- Provide chairs that are flexible and easily adjusted.
- Allow frequent work breaks.

Chapter 8

Illegal Discrimination

A. Title VII of the Civil Rights Act 8/3

   1. Businesses Covered 8/3

   2. Discrimination Prohibited 8/3

   3. EEOC Enforcement of Title VII 8/4

   4. Retaliation 8/7

B. Sexual Harassment 8/8

   1. Prohibited Conduct 8/9

   2. Complying With the Law 8/9

   3. Preventing Sexual Harassment 8/10

C. Age 8/14

   1. The Age Discrimination in Employment Act 8/14

   2. Older Workers Benefit Protection Act 8/15

D. Pregnancy 8/16

E. Citizenship 8/16

F. Gay and Lesbian Workers 8/18

G. State and Local Laws 8/18

   1. State Laws Prohibiting Discrimination in Private Employment 8/18

7o give workers a fair opportunity to get and keep jobs, Congress and state legislatures have passed laws prohibiting discrimination in the workplace. It's illegal to discriminate against workers because of race, color, religion, gender, national origin, disability, citizenship status or age (if an employee is at least 40 years old). Depending on the state you are in, it might also be illegal to discriminate against workers based on other factors such as testing positive for HIV, being single, married or divorced, obesity or sexual orientation.

The main law prohibiting discrimination in the workplace is Title VII of the federal Civil Rights Act of 1964. It outlaws discrimination based on race, color, religion, gender and national origin. (See Section A2.) Sexual harassment in the workplace is also prohibited as a variety of illegal gender discrimination. (See Section B.)

Federal laws also bar several other kinds of workplace discrimination.

- **Age.** The Age Discrimination in Employment Act prohibits discrimination against older workers. The Older Workers Benefit Protection Act outlaws discrimination in employee benefit programs based on an employee's age. The protections in both laws apply only to workers who are at least 40 years old. (See Section C.)
- **Pregnancy.** The Pregnancy Discrimination Act makes it illegal to discriminate against a woman in any aspect of employment because of pregnancy, childbirth or related medical conditions. (See Section D.)
- **Citizenship.** The Immigration Reform and Control Act prohibits discrimination

based on whether a person is or is not a U.S. citizen. (See Section E.)
- **Gender.** The Equal Pay Act outlaws discrimination in wages on the basis of gender. (See Chapter 3, Section B.)
- **Disability.** The Americans with Disabilities Act makes it illegal to discriminate against people because of a disability. (See Chapter 9.)
- **Union membership.** The National Labor Relations Act prohibits discriminating against workers because they do or do not belong to a labor union. (See Chapter 12.)

You can find lots of helpful information by visiting the website of the Equal Employment Opportunity Commission or EEOC, the federal government agency that administers and enforces anti-discrimination laws, at www.eeoc.gov. The website offers numerous fact sheets, frequently asked questions, guidance on how the EEOC interprets and enforces these laws and much more.

For more information on laws prohibiting discrimination in the workplace, see *Primer on Equal Employment Opportunity,* by Nancy J. Sedmak and Michael D. Levin-Epstein (The Bureau of National Affairs, Inc.).

Jobs That Require Discrimination

Under Title VII and other anti-discrimination laws, you have a very limited right to hire on the basis of gender, religion or national origin if a job has special requirements that make such discrimination necessary. Such a special circumstance is called a bona fide occupational qualification (BFOQ).

EXAMPLE: A religious organization employs counselors who answer telephone inquiries from those interested in becoming members of that religion. The organization can require that the counselors it hires are people who believe in that religion. Being a member of that denomination is a BFOQ.

EXAMPLE: A department store hires young women to model clothing for teenage girls. Being a woman under the age of 20 is a BFOQ for this job.

(For more on BFOQs, see Chapter 1, Section B2.)

A. Title VII of the Civil Rights Act

Title VII (42 U.S.C. § 2000 and following), enforced by the U.S. Equal Employment Opportunity Commission (EEOC), is a federal law that addresses many types of workplace discrimination.

1. Businesses Covered

Title VII applies to your business if you employ 15 or more people—either full time or part time. Most state laws impose similar prohibitions against discrimination—and some cover employers with fewer employees. (See Section G.)

2. Discrimination Prohibited

Under Title VII, you can't use race, color, religion, gender or national origin as the basis for decisions on hirings, promotions, dismissals, pay raises, benefits, work assignments, leaves of absence—or just about any other aspect of the employment relationship. Title VII applies to everything from Help Wanted ads to working conditions, performance reviews and post-employment references.

Obviously, a business that flatly refused to hire female, black or Hispanic applicants would be ripe for legal action under Title VII or its state equivalents. Of course, few businesses today would attempt such a flagrant violation of the law. But the mere absence of a discriminatory policy isn't enough to avoid enforcement action.

A business violates Title VII if it treats people differently because of their race, gender or religion. If a company with 50 employees always passes over its African-American employees for managerial positions, there's a good chance the company is discriminating— even though the company hasn't explicitly stated a policy of no African-Americans in management. Call it corporate culture. Call it coincidence. But if the end result is that African-Americans don't get management jobs, it looks like discrimination in the workplace.

If challenged by an employee or the EEOC, the business should be prepared to show that its promotion decisions have been based on objective criteria and that the more qualified applicant has always gotten the promotion. Without a convincing business reason for the failure to promote any African-American managers, the company may be found to have violated Title VII.

Title VII also prohibits employer practices that seem neutral, but have a disproportionate impact on a group of people. Such a policy is legal only if there's a valid business reason for its existence. For example, refusing to hire people who don't meet a minimum height and weight is permissible if it's clearly related to the physical demands of the particular job —felling and hauling huge trees, for instance. But applying such a requirement to exclude applicants for a job as a cook or receptionist wouldn't pass legal muster. The height and weight standard seems neutral on its face, but would have a disproportionate impact on women and people of Asian descent, for example. There is no legitimate business reason to require a cook or receptionist to meet

this requirement, so it would violate Title VII if it ruled out disproportionate numbers of applicants of a particular race or gender. (For more about indirect discrimination, see Chapter 1, Section A1.)

Stay Alert for Indirect Discrimination. To head off allegations of indirect discrimination, review your employment practices at least once a year to make sure you have a solid business reason for everything you do. And don't brush aside complaints you get about practices that seem neutral to you but may unfairly affect some employees. Take such complaints seriously. The workers who complain may be doing you a big favor by alerting you to a potential discrimination problem.

3. EEOC Enforcement of Title VII

If an employee files a complaint with the EEOC, a staff lawyer or investigator will interview the employee. The interviewer will probably then interview you and possibly some other employees.

The EEOC will likely try to work out a settlement of the complaint through conciliation—an informal process that resolves any legal violation for the employee who filed the complaint (and any employees who are in a similar situation). Terms of the agreement will be set out in a written statement. The agreement will require the complaining employee to give up the right to sue your business, in exchange for your agreement to take the steps outlined in the document.

If the agreement requires you to take some action such as restoring a demoted employee to an earlier job or holding training sessions to make managers more sensitive to subtle discrimination in the workplace, the EEOC will follow up periodically to make sure you're complying.

If you and the employee who filed the complaint can't reach an agreement, the EEOC will likely give the employee a right to sue letter, allowing him or her to sue your business in federal court for violating Title VII. In rare cases that it finds especially egregious or groundbreaking, the EEOC may file a lawsuit against your business on behalf of the employee.

If an employee files a complaint with a state fair employment agency for violation of state anti-discrimination laws (see Section G), the investigation procedure will be much the same.

 Confidentiality Is the Best Policy. Never pass up the chance to resolve a complaint through conciliation. You have everything to gain and nothing to lose. A key advantage of conciliation is its confidentiality. Information in EEOC files concerning settlement attempts generally isn't available to the public. Neither the EEOC nor the complaining employee is allowed to make public anything that occurs during conciliation, and they can't use information disclosed there as evidence in a later proceeding without your consent.

Because the stakes can be high in a confrontation over alleged job discrimination, it may be prudent to consult a lawyer. (See Chapter 13, Section A.) If you choose to attend the conciliation conference without legal counsel, you should at least ask a lawyer to review any

written agreement before signing it. And because the anti-discrimination laws are somewhat technical, you'll undoubtedly need assistance from a lawyer in defending a lawsuit in which your business has been accused of employment discrimination.

Affirmative Action Plans May Correct Past Abuses

An affirmative action plan is one means of trying to undo the effects of past illegal discrimination. Under such a plan, an employer makes employment decisions based on race or sex—factors that ordinarily can't be considered—in order to restore equal opportunity for groups that have faced discrimination.

When a court finds that a business has discriminated and there are no other effective means to remedy the discrimination, the court may require the business to take affirmative action. For example, a court may order a company to hire one black employee for every two new white employees hired, until the company's workforce resembles the racial mix of the community.

A business may also have to set up an affirmative action plan as part of voluntarily settling a court case or EEOC proceeding. Any voluntary program must meet the EEOC's Guidelines on Affirmative Action Plans.

There are a number of remedies that a court can order if it finds workplace discrimination. You may be ordered to:

Consider Arbitrating Discrimination Claims

The Civil Rights Act of 1991 encourages employers to resolve job discrimination disputes through settlement negotiations, mediation and arbitration. In mediation, a neutral expert —the mediator—helps the employer and employee reach a voluntary resolution of the dispute. In arbitration, a neutral expert, the arbitrator, makes a binding decision that can be enforced in court.

Arbitration is often an excellent way to bring a dispute to a swift conclusion. It's quicker and cheaper than judicial proceedings—and arbitration hearings are conducted in private.

But in an employment discrimination case, an arbitration agreement isn't always binding on the employee. If the employee has a change of heart and decides to pursue a discrimination claim in court, a judge will have to decide whether the arbitration agreement must be honored. Although these agreements are generally enforced, judges have been more willing to reject or limit contracts that force employees to arbitrate discrimination disputes, since such contracts may allow employers to avoid the full impact of civil rights laws.

Judges are especially reluctant to enforce arbitration agreements that:

- the employee didn't enter into voluntarily
- limit the damages an employee can collect if the arbitrator finds that the employer violated the law
- limit the employee's right to obtain information (in legal jargon, pre-arbitration discovery)
- shorten the period for filing a claim
- make the employee pay the costs of arbitration, or
- allow the employer to choose the arbitrator.

If a judge finds that one or more provisions in an arbitration clause are unfair, the judge may refuse to enforce those provisions or may rule that the entire arbitration agreement is invalid.

And even a valid arbitration agreement won't prevent a governmental agency from suing an employer to enforce an anti-discrimination law. For example, in a 2002 case (*EEOC v. Waffle House Inc.*, 534 U.S. 279), the U.S. Supreme Court said that even though Eric Baker—a Waffle House employee—had signed a valid arbitration agreement and was therefore unable to sue his former employer in court, the EEOC could sue on his behalf for an alleged violation of his rights under the Americans with Disabilities Act.

- rehire, promote or reassign the employee to whatever job he or she lost because of the discrimination.
- compensate the employee for salary and benefits lost because of the discrimination. This can include wages, pension contributions, medical benefits, overtime pay, bonuses, vacation pay and participation in your profit-sharing plan.
- pay damages to compensate the employee for emotional suffering, inconvenience and mental anguish—and punitive damages to punish your business if you've acted maliciously or recklessly. The total amount of these damages is limited to between $50,000 and $300,000, depending on the number of people you employ.
- change your policies so that similar discrimination won't take place in the future.
- pay the employee's legal fees.

An Employee May Have Additional Recourse. If the EEOC doesn't issue a right to sue letter or file a lawsuit on the employee's behalf, the employee may take other legal action against your business, such as suing in state court for breach of contract or wrongful discharge. (See Chapter 10.) The employee may also be able to sue you for violating state anti-discrimination laws. (See Section G.)

4. Retaliation

It's illegal for you to retaliate against an employee for opposing illegal discrimination, for filing a complaint under Title VII or for coop-

erating in the investigation of such a complaint. This means you can't use these activities as a basis for firing, disciplining or refusing to promote an employee.

The best antidote to a claim that you've retaliated is to show that you had valid reasons for your actions, completely unrelated to the employee's assertions that you discriminated. Those reasons should be supported, if possible, by properly documented warnings to the employee.

EXAMPLE: George works for Cool Sweats —a company that sells sportswear by mail order. He files a complaint with the EEOC, complaining that he was passed over for a supervisor's position because he is black. A month later, Cool Sweats suspends George without pay for three days for a violation of company rules. George asserts that the suspension was in retaliation for filing the Title VII complaint.

Cool Sweats is able to refute this allegation by showing that George violated the company rules against charging personal expenses on the company's credit card and using the company van for personal business—rules stated in Cool Sweats' employee handbook. Cool Sweats is also able to show that six weeks earlier it warned George about similar infractions, and that a three-day suspension is consistent with the discipline meted out to other employees for such rule violations.

(For more on documenting worker misconduct, see Chapter 2, Section C.)

A New Defense in Discrimination Cases

Some employers are fighting back in cases of alleged discrimination by arguing that the employee shouldn't have been hired in the first place. If an employer wins this argument, the employee's lawsuit may be thrown out or the damages the employee could win may be severely limited.

EXAMPLE: Local Transit, Inc., hires Lorna to drive a delivery van. In the first few months, Local Transit cites Lorna for infractions for which male drivers were not cited. Then the firm fires Lorna. She sues, claiming sex discrimination. In defending the lawsuit, Local Transit argues that Lorna lied on her job application by claiming she had a perfect driving record, when in fact, she had two drunk driving convictions. Local Transit claims that had Lorna disclosed the truth about her driving record, the company never would have hired her. Since she isn't entitled to the job, says the company, she can't complain about discrimination. The court rules that Local Transit had a valid reason to fire Lorna.

But employers don't always win based on this defense. One skeptical judge wrote: "A false statement on an employment application is not an insurance policy covering bigotry."

To help lay the groundwork for this type of defense in a discrimination or wrongful discharge case, consider adding the following language to your job application forms in prominent type above the applicant's signature:

"I acknowledge that any misrepresentations or omissions in this application will be grounds for termination."

And make sure to enforce this policy even-handedly against everyone—not just those employees who have complained or filed lawsuits against you.

B. Sexual Harassment

Title VII of the Civil Rights Act of 1964 doesn't specifically mention sexual harassment. But in 1980, the U.S. Equal Employment Opportunity Commission (EEOC) issued guidelines stating that sexual harassment in the workplace is a form of sex discrimination prohibited by Title VII.

In 1986, the U.S. Supreme Court agreed that sexual harassment on the job is, indeed, a form of sex discrimination—and is therefore illegal (*Meritor Savings Bank v. Vinson*, 477 U.S. 57). The Court held that illegal sexual harassment occurs when unwelcome sexual advances, requests for sexual favors and other verbal or physical conduct of a sexual nature creates a hostile or abusive work environment. In 1993, the Supreme Court made it clear that a harassed employee is entitled to legal relief even without proof that the offending behavior has injured the employee psychologically (*Harris v. Forklift Systems Inc.,* 114 S.Ct. 367).

All states except Alabama have additional laws prohibiting sexual discrimination in the workplace. Although the specifics may differ from federal law, these state laws are generally interpreted to include sexual harassment as a type of prohibited discrimination.

1. Prohibited Conduct

If an employer or manager makes unwelcome sexual advances or demands sexual favors in return for job benefits, promotions or continued employment, that's sexual harassment. But sexual harassment in the workplace can consist of a wide variety of other behaviors, including:

- posting sexually explicit photos that offend employees
- telling sex-related jokes or jokes that demean people because of their gender
- commenting inappropriately on an employee's appearance
- requiring employees to dress in scanty attire
- repeatedly requesting dates from a person who clearly isn't interested
- having strippers perform at a company gathering, and
- stating that people of one gender are inferior to people of the other gender or can't perform their jobs as well.

In short, any hostile or offensive behavior in the workplace that has a sexual component can constitute sexual harassment—and violate the law.

Although sexual harassment is most often behavior committed by men against women, that's not always the case. There are instances in which women sexually harass men and where people harass others of their own gender. Laws prohibiting sexual harassment offer protection in all of these situations.

2. Complying With the Law

Your business can be held responsible for sexual harassment if executives or supervisors knew, or should have known, that it was being committed. You're also under a legal duty to take all necessary steps to prevent sexual harassment. Your first step in meeting these obligations is to promptly investigate every complaint. If you determine that there's merit to a complaint, discipline any employee who sexually harassed another on the job. Depending on the seriousness of the offense, consider reprimanding or suspending the offending employee, or placing him or her on probation. Where the harassment is especially serious, the only reasonable solution may be to fire the offending employee.

If you learn of workplace conditions that might create an uncomfortable work environment for some workers—such as the presence of pornographic magazines—take decisive steps to eliminate the offending conditions. An employee may challenge you by asking: "Who's offended by this?" The simple answer: "Me."

You're also required to take corrective action if an employee is being sexually harassed by other people who come into the workplace—

clients, patients, customers, suppliers—who are not employees of your business.

> **EXAMPLE:** Stella waits on tables at the lounge at Take Ten Bowling Lanes. One night after winning the league championship, a boisterous team of male bowlers comes into the lounge and begins to harass Stella. The lounge manager quickly sizes up the situation, switches Stella to another table and compensates her for the tip she missed from the boisterous bowlers. The manager also threatens to expel the rowdies if they continue their behavior. Through this prompt action, Take Ten met its legal duty to Stella.

By adopting an anti-harassment policy and a sound procedure for investigating and dealing with complaints, your business may be able to fend off a costly verdict if an employee sues. In a pair of cases known as *Faragher/Ellerth,* the U.S. Supreme Court ruled that an employee who suffers sexual harassment in the workplace should let the employer know so steps can be taken to stop it. If the employer has a policy in place and handles complaints in good faith, the employee has to take advantage by making an internal complaint; if the employee doesn't, she may lose the right to sue the company for damages.

Look Beyond Legal Liability. Avoiding legal liability is just one reason for a business to crack down on sexual harassment. Sexual harassment has a negative impact on employees, causing anxiety and unhappiness.

You can't expect high morale and productivity in a workplace in which sexual harassment is tolerated.

3. Preventing Sexual Harassment

Your attitude toward sexual harassment—and the steps you take to prevent it—can help assure that you won't become the object of a formal complaint. Most potential charges can be handled effectively within the workplace.

Start by adopting a formal policy stating clearly that sexual harassment won't be tolerated. Let employees know who within your business they can complain to if they've been sexually harassed. And provide a backup person to handle the complaint just in case the main person handling complaints is the accused harasser. Distribute a copy of the policy to each employee or put the policy statement in your company's employee handbook. (See Chapter 2, Section B.)

When you receive complaints, promptly investigate them and take action. Since employees may not always recognize the difference between permitted and unpermitted behavior, consider hiring outside experts to provide training workshops. These experts can be remarkably effective in making employees and managers aware of their rights and responsibilities—and they send a signal that your business is taking strong steps to squelch sexual harassment.

The following sample sexual harassment policy can be modified to fit the needs of most workplaces.

Sample Sexual Harassment Policy

SEXUAL HARASSMENT POLICY

Our company is committed to providing a work environment where women and men can work together comfortably and productively, free from sexual harassment. Such behavior is illegal under both state and federal law—and will not be tolerated here.

This policy applies to all phases of employment—including recruiting, testing, hiring, upgrading, promotion or demotion, transfer, layoff, termination, rates of pay, benefits and selection for training, travel or company social events.

This policy applies to the conduct of owners, supervisors, managers, co-workers and customers.

Prohibited Behavior

Prohibited sexual harassment includes any offensive or unwelcome conduct—verbal or physical—that is based on a person's gender. It also includes discrimination or discriminatory comments based on a person's gender.

Prohibited sexual harassment also includes unsolicited and unwelcome contact that has sexual overtones. This includes:

- written contact, such as sexually suggestive or obscene letters, notes, invitations
- verbal contact, such as sexually suggestive or obscene comments, threats, slurs, epithets, jokes about gender-specific traits, sexual propositions
- physical contact, such as intentional touching, pinching, brushing against another's body, impeding or blocking movement, assault, coercing sexual intercourse, and
- visual contact, such as leering or staring at another's body, gesturing, displaying sexually suggestive objects or pictures, cartoons, posters or magazines.

Sexual harassment also includes continuing to express sexual or social interest after being informed directly that the interest is unwelcome—and using sexual behavior to control, influence or affect the career, salary or work environment of another employee.

Sample Sexual Harassment Policy (continued)

It is impermissible to suggest, threaten or imply that failure to accept a request for a date or sexual intimacy will affect an employee's job prospects. For example, it is forbidden either to imply or actually withhold support for an appointment, promotion, or change of assignment, or suggest that a poor performance report will be given because an employee has declined a personal proposition.

Also, offering benefits, such as promotions, favorable performance evaluations, favorable assigned duties or shifts, recommendations or reclassifications in exchange for sexual favors is forbidden.

Harassment by Nonemployees

In addition, Company will take all reasonable steps to prevent or eliminate sexual harassment by nonemployees—such as customers, clients and suppliers—who are likely to have workplace contact with our employees.

Monitoring

Company shall take all reasonable steps to see that this policy prohibiting sexual harassment is followed by all employees, supervisors and others who have contact with our employees. This prevention plan will include training sessions, ongoing monitoring of the worksite and a confidential employee survey to be conducted and evaluated every six months.

Discipline

Any employee found to have violated this policy shall be subject to appropriate disciplinary action, including warnings, reprimand, suspension or discharge, according to the findings of the complaint investigation.

If an investigation reveals that sexual harassment has occurred, the harasser may also be held legally liable for his or her actions under state or federal anti-discrimination laws or in separate legal actions.

Retaliation

Any employee bringing a sexual harassment complaint or assisting in investigating such a complaint will not be adversely affected in terms and conditions of employment, or discriminated against or discharged because of the complaint. Complaints of such retaliation will be promptly investigated and punished.

Sample Sexual Harassment Policy (continued)

Complaint Procedure and Investigation

Joe Shmoe is designated as the Sexual Harassment Counselor. All complaints of sexual harassment and retaliation for reporting or participating in an investigation shall be directed to the Sexual Harassment Counselor or to a supervisor of your choice, either in writing or by requesting an individual interview. All complaints shall be handled as confidentially as possible. The Sexual Harassment Counselor will promptly investigate and resolve complaints involving violations of this policy and recommend to management the appropriate sanctions to be imposed against violators.

Training

Company will establish yearly training sessions for all employees concerning their rights to be free from sexual harassment and the legal options available if they are harassed. In addition, training sessions will be held for supervisors and managers, educating them in how to keep the workplace as free from harassment as possible and in how to handle sexual harassment complaints.

A copy of the policy will be distributed to all employees and posted in areas where all employees will have the opportunity to freely review it. Company welcomes your suggestions for improvements to this policy.

C. Age

As the baby boomers age, there are increasing numbers of older people in the workforce. And there are laws protecting them discrimination on the job.

1. The Age Discrimination in Employment Act

The Age Discrimination in Employment Act (ADEA) prohibits discrimination against those 40 years old or older. It applies to private businesses with 20 or more employees as well as the federal government. Although the ADEA also protects state government workers, these workers cannot file a lawsuit against the state for age discrimination—only the EEOC can take action to protect state employees from age discrimination. As with the rest of Title VII, the ADEA prohibits discrimination in all aspects of employment—hiring, firing, compensation and all other terms of employment.

The ADEA prohibits you from discriminating against older workers in favor of those under 40 years old. But it also prohibits discrimination among older workers themselves.

> **EXAMPLE:** Mary is 53 years old and Wilbur is 43 years old. Both apply for the same job. The employer can't choose Wilbur simply because he's younger, even though both applicants are protected by the ADEA. But the employer is on safe ground if Wilbur is chosen because of his superior skills.

Some employers believe that it costs more to hire older workers than younger workers. They overlook the possibility that younger workers may be less competent and need more training, making them more expensive. At any rate, a desire to save costs isn't a legitimate reason to discriminate against older workers.

Avoiding Age Discrimination Claims

A few sensible precautions can help you avoid discrimination claims by older workers.

Become aware of remarks that betray a subtle—or not-so-subtle—age bias. A thoughtless comment such as "You can't teach an old dog new tricks" may be used against you if an older employee sues your company. Emphasize to supervisors that your business won't tolerate such dangerous and unfair comments.

Apply your performance standards even-handedly to all employees, regardless of their age. Because older people are disproportionately represented on many juries, you want to be able to show that your business deals equally with all employees.

Offer equal training opportunities for employees of all ages. If you're inclined to put more money into training younger workers on the assumption that they'll be with your company longer, forget it. That kind of strategy is a great way to invite an age discrimination lawsuit.

2. Older Workers Benefit Protection Act

Another law, the Older Workers Benefit Protection Act (29 U.S.C. § 623 and following), makes it illegal for your business to use an employee's age as the basis for discrimination in benefits. Like the ADEA, this Act covers employees who are at least 40 years old. Under this law, you cannot, for example, reduce health or life insurance benefits for older employees, nor can you stop their pensions from accruing if they work past their normal retirement ages. The Act also discourages your business from targeting older workers when you cut staff. Most of the provisions of this law are very difficult for anyone but an experienced benefits administrator to understand. You'll probably have to consult with such an expert if you plan to take action involving a cutback of older workers' benefits.

One relatively clear provision of the law regulates the legal waivers that some employers ask employees to sign in connection with early retirement programs. You might, for example, offer a handsome retirement package to induce an older employee to leave your company voluntarily. As part of the process, you'd ask the employee to sign a waiver—often called a release or covenant not to sue—in which the employee would agree not to take any legal action against your business.

The law sets limits on your use of such waivers as they relate to age discrimination claims under the ADEA.

- You must write the waiver in plain English.
- The waiver can't cover rights or claims that may arise after the worker signs the waiver.
- The waiver must specifically state that the worker is waiving any rights or claims he or she may have under the federal Age Discrimination in Employment Act.
- You must offer the worker something of value—something over and above what you already owe to the worker—in exchange for the waiver.
- You must advise the worker, in writing, to consult with a lawyer before signing the waiver. Of course, you can't require the worker to hire a lawyer.
- You must give the employee a fixed period of time in which to decide whether to sign the waiver. That period must be at least 21 days if the waiver has been presented to the employee alone. If you've presented the waiver to a group or class of employees, you must give each worker at least 45 days to decide whether or not to sign. In either case, a worker has seven days after agreeing to such a waiver to revoke his or her decision.

(See Chapter 10, Section F2, for a sample release contained in a severance agreement.)

In addition, if you're making the offer to a group or class of employees as part of an incentive program to encourage early retirement, you must tell each employee in writing and in plain English what class or group of employees is covered by the program; the eligibility requirements for the program; any time limits for accepting the offer; the job titles and ages of all the individuals to whom the offer is being made; and the ages of all the employees in the same job classification or unit who are not eligible for the program.

Because the statute doesn't specify how many employees it takes to constitute a class or group, the most prudent course of action is to provide the information any time you seek a waiver from an employee who's at least 40 years old if you're also offering a retirement incentive package to one or more other employees.

D. Pregnancy

The Pregnancy Discrimination Act or PDA (92 U.S.C. § 2076) is an amendment to Title VII. Under the PDA, it's a form of gender discrimination to treat an employee differently because of pregnancy, childbirth or related medical conditions. If a woman is affected by such a condition, you must treat her in the same way that you treat other people in the workforce who are either able or unable to work. You violate the PDA, for example, if you fire a woman whose pregnancy keeps her from working, but you don't fire other workers who are temporarily unable to do the job because of other physical problems. Similarly, if a pregnant worker is able to do the job, you can't lay her off because you think it's in her best interests to stay home.

On the other hand, you don't violate the PDA if you apply medically based job restrictions to a pregnant woman—as long as you apply those same policies to employees who are not pregnant but who are under medical restrictions.

Note also that the Family and Medical Leave Act allows unpaid leave for childbirth, adoptions and foster care placements—and for an employee's serious health condition, which can include some complications or conditions relating to pregnancy and childbirth. (See Chapter 6.)

E. Citizenship

The Immigration Reform and Control Act of 1986 (IRCA), which applies to businesses with four or more employees, makes it illegal to discriminate against a person because he or she isn't a U.S. citizen or national. The law forbids you from discriminating against aliens who have been lawfully admitted to the U.S. for permanent or temporary residence—and aliens who have applied for temporary residence status.

This can be tricky because, as an employer, you must meet specific legal requirements to avoid hiring illegal aliens, including asking new employees to show you documents verifying their citizenship and their legal ability to be employed in the United States. (See Chapter 1, Section A.) In meeting these verification duties, you can't ask to see more or different documents than those required for completion of INS Form I-9—and it's illegal to refuse to honor documents offered by the employee, as long as they appear to be genuine.

English-Only Rules

The law remains unclear on whether and when you can require employees to speak only English on the job. The EEOC views English-only rules as a form of national origin discrimination—and takes a very dim view of such rules. The EEOC says you can require that workers speak only in English at certain times, but only if you can show there's a business necessity for the rule. Similarly, California law prohibits employers from adopting English-only rules unless it's a business necessity.

The courts, however, may take a more lenient position toward employers than the EEOC does. In a leading case, Spun Steak Company received complaints that two employees were making derogatory, racist comments in Spanish about two co-workers—one of whom was African-American and the other Chinese-American. For this and other reasons, Spun Steak adopted this rule:

"It is hereafter the policy of this Company that only English will be spoken in connection with work. During lunch, breaks and employees' own time, they are obviously free to speak Spanish if they wish. However, we urge all of you not to use your fluency in Spanish in a fashion which may lead other workers to suffer humiliation."

Spanish-speaking workers sued. The court of appeals held that to show that the English-only rule was discriminatory, the workers would have to show that the rule had a significant, adverse impact on them. Nearly all of the workers were bilingual; as to those workers, the court held that the rule didn't have a significant, adverse impact and, therefore, wasn't discriminatory. As to workers who weren't bilingual, the court sent the case back to the trial judge to determine whether there was an adverse impact. (*Garcia v. Spun Steak Co.*, 998 F.2d 1480 (1993).)

Even though that employer won, if you're thinking of implementing an English-only rule, it's best to proceed cautiously and to be quite sure you can show there's a business necessity for the rule. If language is a problem in your workplace, one alternative is to offer instruction in English as a second language so that workers can become more proficient in its use and not feel under attack because they're more comfortable speaking in another language.

F. Gay and Lesbian Workers

Although there is no federal law that specifi-
cally prohibits private employers from dis-
criminating on the basis of sexual orientation,
such discrimination is illegal in the District of
Columbia and 12 states: California, Connecticut,
Hawaii, Maryland, Massachusetts, Minnesota,
Nevada, New Hampshire, New Jersey, Rhode
Island, Vermont and Wisconsin.

If your state does not have a law that prohibits workplace discrimination on the basis
of sexual orientation, your city or county might.
There are hundreds of cities and counties
throughout the country that prohibit sexual
orientation discrimination in public or private
employment—or both—from Albany, New
York, to Ypsilanti, Michigan.

If you are a private employer and you
operate your business in a state, county or
city that has a law or ordinance prohibiting
sexual orientation discrimination, you must
follow that law, despite the fact that there is
no federal law in place.

Furthermore, even if there is no law in
your state, city or county prohibiting sexual
orientation discrimination, you must still tread
lightly in this area. If you have an employee
who feels that he or she has been treated
unfairly and/or injured because of his or her
sexual orientation, that employee can still sue
you under a number of legal theories that apply
to everyone, including gays and lesbians.
Those theories include:

- intentional or negligent infliction of
  emotional distress
- harassment
- assault

- battery
- invasion of privacy
- defamation
- interference with an employment contract,
  and
- wrongful termination.

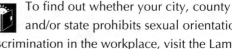 To find out whether your city, county
and/or state prohibits sexual orientation
discrimination in the workplace, visit the Lambda
Legal Defense and Education Fund website at
www.lambdalegal.org, where Lambda maintains
an updated list of state and local anti-discrimination laws.

G. State and Local Laws

Nearly all state and local laws prohibiting
discrimination in employment are echoes of
federal anti-discrimination law in that they
outlaw discrimination based on race, color,
religion, gender, age and national origin. But
the state and local laws also tend to go into
more detail and may create categories of
protection against discrimination—such as
discrimination based on marital status or
sexual orientation—that aren't covered by
federal law.

1. State Laws Prohibiting Discrimination in Private Employment

This is a state-by-state synopsis of factors that
private employers may not use as the basis for
any employment decisions. In legal parlance,

Religion in the Workplace

An increasing number of employees are claiming religious discrimination. In the past, the typical complaint would have been that a person was fired or disciplined or denied a promotion because he or she practiced a certain faith. But today, claims of religious discrimination tend to be much more subtle—and challenging. An employee might claim, for example, that a supervisor is seeking to impose his or her own religious beliefs on the employee by pressuring the employee to attend prayer sessions or Bible study meetings at work. Or an employee may claim that he or she is being unfairly deprived of the right to pray at work or to use a company meeting room to discuss the Koran with other employees. Still another employee may claim that wearing a "Stop Abortion" badge with a color photo of a fetus is an exercise of religious rights—while other employees may find the badge disturbing and offensive and a violation of their own rights.

Unfortunately, the law in this delicate area is unclear. As always, tolerance and common sense are your best guides. It also helps to be blessed with the wisdom of Solomon, so to speak.

The law protects your right to discuss your own religious beliefs with an employee, if you're so inclined, but you can't persist to the point that the employee feels you're being hostile, intimidating or offensive. So if an employee objects to your discussion of religious subjects or you even get an inkling that your religious advances are unwelcome, back off. Otherwise, you may find yourself embroiled in a lawsuit or administrative proceeding.

If employees complain to you that a co-worker is badgering them with religious hectoring, you have a right—if not a duty—to intervene, although you must, of course, use the utmost tact and sensitivity.

While you may feel that the best way to resolve these knotty problems is to simply banish religion from the workplace, that's generally not a viable alternative. You're legally required to make a reasonable accommodation to the religious needs of employees. You don't, however, need to do anything that would cost more than a minimum amount or that would cause more than minimal inconvenience. Allowing workers to use an empty office for voluntary group prayer at lunchtime might be a reasonable accommodation. Letting workers take a limited amount of time off work to attend religious observances might also be a reasonable accommodation—although it might be better to simply give all employees a few days of personal leave time each year so that religious workers aren't viewed as receiving special privileges.

people who have these characteristics fall into what are called "protected classes."

Keep in mind that this is only a synopsis. Each state has its own way of interpreting who is or is not a member of a protected class. For example, one state may have a different way of determining who is disabled under its laws than other states do. In addition, many of the laws in this chart apply only to employers with a minimum number of employees, often five or more.

For details about your state laws, contact the agency listed in the Appendix. Where no special agency has been designated to enforce anti-discrimination laws, your state's labor department or the closest office of the federal Equal Employment Opportunity Office should direct you to the agency or person who can give you information about fair employment laws in your state. (See Appendix for contact details.)

You can also learn details about your state laws by reading the laws themselves. To do so, use the citation listed in the chart. You can find the statute at your local law library or by using Nolo's online research center at www.nolo.com.

This list only describes state laws. Your city or county may have its own set of fair employment ordinances. To learn more about those, contact someone within your local government, such as your county clerk's office. Also, local offices of the Small Business Administration or the Chamber of Commerce can be good sources for information about local laws.

Laws Prohibiting Discrimination in Employment

Private employers may not make employment decisions based on

State	Law applies to employers with	Age	Ancestry or national origin	Disability	AIDS/HIV	Gender	Marital status	Pregnancy, childbirth and related medical conditions	Race or color	Religion or creed	Sexual orientation	Genetic testing information	Additional protected categories
Alabama Ala. Code §§ 21-7-1; 25-1-20	20 or more employees	40 and older											
Alaska Alaska Stat. §§ 18.80.220; 47.30.865	One or more employees	40 and older	✓	Physical and mental	✓	✓	✓ (Includes changes in status)	✓ (Includes parenthood)	✓	✓			Mental illness
Arizona Ariz. Rev. Stat. § 41-1461	15 or more employees	40 and older	✓	Physical	✓	✓			✓	✓		✓	
Arkansas Ark. Code Ann. §§ 16-123-101; 11-4-601; 11-5-403	9 or more employees		✓	Physical and mental		✓		✓	✓	✓		✓[1]	
California Cal. Gov't. Code §§ 12920,12941; Cal. Lab. Code § 1101	5 or more employees	40 and older	✓	Physical and mental	✓	✓		✓	✓	✓	✓		• Medical condition • Political activities or affiliations
Colorado Colo. Rev. Stat. §§ 24-34-301, 24-34-401; 27-10-115	Law applies to all employers.	40 to 70	✓	Physical, mental and learning	✓	✓		✓	✓	✓			• Lawful conduct outside of work • Mental illness
Connecticut Conn. Gen. Stat. Ann. §§ 46a-51, 46a-60	3 or more employees	40 and older	✓	Present or past physical, mental or learning	✓	✓	✓	✓	✓	✓		✓	Mental retardation
Delaware Del. Code Ann. tit. 19, § 710	4 or more employees	40 to 70	✓	Physical or mental	✓	✓	✓	✓	✓	✓		✓	
District of Columbia D.C. Code Ann. §§ 2-1401.01; 7-1703.03	Law applies to all employers.	18 and older	✓	Physical or mental	✓	✓	✓	✓ (Includes parenthood)	✓	✓	✓		• Enrollment in vocational or professional or college education • Family duties • Personal appearance • Political affiliation • Smoker

[1] Employers covered by FLSA

Laws Prohibiting Discrimination in Employment (continued)

State	Law applies to employers with	Age	Ancestry or national origin	Disability	AIDS/HIV	Gender	Marital status	Pregnancy, childbirth and related medical conditions	Race or color	Religion or creed	Sexual orientation	Genetic testing information	Additional protected categories
Florida Fla. Stat. Ann. §§ 760.01, 760.50; 448.075	15 or more employees	No age limit	✓	"Handicap"	✓	✓	✓		✓	✓			Sickle cell trait
Georgia Ga. Code Ann. §§ 34-6A-1; 34-1-23; 34-5-1	15 or more employees (disability) 10 or more employees (gender)	40 to 70		Physical or mental		✓[2]							
Hawaii Haw. Rev. Stat. § 378-1	One or more employees	No age limit	✓	Physical or mental	✓	✓	✓	✓ (Includes breast-feeding)	✓	✓	✓		Arrest and court record (unless there is a conviction directly related to job)
Idaho Idaho Code § 67-5909	5 or more employees	40 and older	✓	Physical or mental		✓		✓	✓	✓			
Illinois 775 Ill. Comp. Stat. §§ 5/1-101, 5/2-101; Ill. Admin. Code tit. 56, § 5210.110	15 or more employees	40 and older	✓	Physical or mental	✓	✓	✓	✓	✓	✓			• Arrest record • Citizen status • Military status • Unfavorable military discharge
Indiana Ind. Code Ann. §§ 22-9-1-1, 22-9-2-1	6 or more employees	40 to 70	✓	Physical or mental		✓			✓	✓			
Iowa Iowa Code § 216.1	4 or more employees	18 or older	✓	Physical or mental	✓	✓		✓	✓	✓			
Kansas Kan. Stat. Ann. §§ 44-1001, 44-1111, 44-1125; 65-6002(e)	4 or more employees	18 or older	✓	Physical or mental	✓	✓			✓	✓		✓	Military status
Kentucky Ky. Rev. Stat. Ann. §§ 344.040; 207.130; 342.197	8 or more employees	40 or older	✓	Physical (Includes black lung disease)	✓	✓			✓	✓			Smoker or nonsmoker

[2] Wage discrimination only

Laws Prohibiting Discrimination in Employment (continued)

State	Law applies to employers with	Age	Ancestry or national origin	Disability	AIDS/HIV	Gender	Marital status	Pregnancy, childbirth and related medical conditions	Race or color	Religion or creed	Sexual orientation	Genetic testing information	Additional protected categories
Louisiana La. Rev. Stat. Ann. §§ 23:301 to 23:352	20 or more employees		✓	Physical or mental		✓		✓ (Applies to employers with 25 or more employees)	✓	✓		✓	Sickle cell trait
Maine Me. Rev. Stat. Ann. tit. 5, §§ 4551, 4571	Law applies to all employers.	No age limit	✓	Physical or mental		✓		✓	✓	✓	✓	✓	
Maryland Md. Code 1957 Art. 49B, § 15	15 or more employees	No age limit	✓	Physical or mental		✓	✓	✓	✓	✓	✓	✓	
Massachusetts Mass. Gen. Laws ch. 151B, § 1	6 or more employees	40 or older	✓	Physical or mental	✓	✓			✓	✓	✓	✓	
Michigan Mich. Comp. Laws §§ 37.1201, 37.2201, 37.1103	One or more employees	No age limit	✓	Physical or mental	✓	✓	✓	✓	✓	✓		✓	• Height or weight • Arrest record
Minnesota Minn. Stat. Ann. §§ 363.01; 181.974	One or more employees	18 or older	✓	Physical or mental	✓	✓	✓	✓	✓	✓	✓	✓	• Member of local commission • Receiving public assistance
Missouri Mo. Rev. Stat. §§ 213.010; 191.665; 375.1306	6 or more employees	40 to 70	✓	Physical or mental	✓	✓		✓	✓	✓		✓	
Montana Mont. Code Ann. §§ 49-2-101, 49-2-303	One or more employees	No age limit	✓	Physical or mental		✓		✓	✓	✓			
Nebraska Neb. Rev. Stat. §§ 48-1101; 48-1001; 20-168	15 or more employees	40 to 70 [3]	✓	Physical or mental	✓	✓	✓	✓	✓	✓		✓	
Nevada Nev. Rev. Stat. Ann. § 613.310 and following	15 or more employees	40 or older	✓	Physical or mental		✓		✓	✓	✓	✓	✓	Lawful use of any product when not at work

[3] Employers with 25 or more employees

Laws Prohibiting Discrimination in Employment (continued)

State	Law applies to employers with	Age	Ancestry or national origin	Disability	AIDS/HIV	Gender	Marital status	Pregnancy, childbirth and related medical conditions	Race or color	Religion or creed	Sexual orientation	Genetic testing information	Additional protected categories
New Hampshire N.H. Rev. Stat. Ann. §§ 354-A: 2 and following; 141-H:3	6 or more employees	No age limit	✓	Physical or mental		✓	✓	✓	✓	✓	✓	✓	
New Jersey N.J. Stat. Ann. §§ 10:5-1; 34:6B-1	Law applies to all employers.	18 to 70	✓	Past or present physical or mental	✓	✓	✓	✓	✓	✓	✓	✓	• Hereditary cellular or blood trait • Military service or status • Smoker or nonsmoker
New Mexico N.M. Stat. Ann. § 28-1-1	4 or more employees	40 or older	✓	Physical or mental		✓	✓ (Applies to employers with 50 or more employees)	✓	✓	✓			Serious medical condition
New York N.Y. Exec. Law § 292; N.Y. Lab. Law § 201-d	4 or more employees	18 and over	✓	Physical or mental	✓	✓	✓	✓	✓	✓		✓	• Lawful use of any product when not at work • Political activities
North Carolina N.C. Gen. Stat. §§ 143-422.2; 168A-1; 95-28.1; 130A-148	15 or more employees	No age limit	✓	Physical or mental	✓	✓			✓	✓		✓	• Lawful use of any product when not at work • Sickle cell trait
North Dakota N.D. Cent. Code §§ 14-02.4-01; 34-01-17	One or more employees	40 or older	✓	Physical or mental	✓	✓	✓	✓	✓	✓			• Lawful conduct outside of work • Receiving public assistance
Ohio Ohio Rev. Code Ann. §§ 4111.17; 4112.01	4 or more employees	40 or older	✓	Physical, mental or learning		✓		✓	✓	✓			

Laws Prohibiting Discrimination in Employment (continued)

State	Law applies to employers with	Age	Ancestry or national origin	Disability	AIDS/HIV	Gender	Marital status	Pregnancy, childbirth and related medical conditions	Race or color	Religion or creed	Sexual orientation	Genetic testing information	Additional protected categories
				Private employers may not make employment decisions based on									
Oklahoma Okla. Stat. Ann. tit. 25, § 1301; tit. 36, § 3614.2; tit. 40, § 500; tit. 44, § 208	15 or more employees	40 or older	✓	Physical or mental		✓			✓	✓		✓	• Military service • Smoker or nonsmoker
Oregon Or. Rev. Stat. §§ 659A.100 and foll.; 659A.303	One or more employees	18 or older	✓	Physical or mental[4]		✓		✓	✓	✓		✓	
Pennsylvania 43 Pa. Cons. Stat. Ann. § 953, 336.3	4 or more employees	40 to 70	✓	Physical or mental		✓		✓ (Pregnancy not treated as a disability in terms of benefits)	✓	✓			• Familial status • GED rather than high school diploma
Rhode Island R.I. Gen. Laws §§ 28-6-17; 28-5-11; 2-28-10; 23-6-22; 23-20.7.1-1	4 or more employees	40 or older	✓	Physical or mental	✓	✓		✓	✓	✓	✓	✓	• Domestic abuse victim • Gender identity or expression • Smoker or nonsmoker
South Carolina S.C. Code Ann. § 1-13-20 and following	15 or more employees	40 or older	✓	Physical or mental		✓		✓	✓	✓			
South Dakota S.D. Codified Laws Ann. §§ 20-13-1; 60-12-15; 60-2-20; 62-1-17	Law applies to all employers.		✓	Physical, mental and learning		✓			✓	✓		✓	Preexisting injury
Tennessee Tenn. Code Ann. §§ 4-21-102; 4-21-401 and following; 8-50-103; 50-2-202	8 or more employees	40 or older	✓	Physical or mental		✓		✓ (Full-time employee who worked the previous 12 months is entitled to 4 months maternity leave. Pay at discretion of employer.)[5]	✓	✓			

4 Employers with 6 or more employees
5 Employers with 100 or more employees

Laws Prohibiting Discrimination in Employment (continued)

State	Law applies to employers with	Age	Ancestry or national origin	Disability	AIDS/HIV	Gender	Marital status	Pregnancy, childbirth and related medical conditions	Race or color	Religion or creed	Sexual orientation	Genetic testing information	Additional protected categories
Private employers may not make employment decisions based on												
Texas Tex. Lab. Code Ann. §§ 21.002, 21.101, 21.401	15 or more employees	40 or older	✓	Physical or mental		✓		✓	✓	✓		✓	
Utah Utah Code Ann. § 34A-5-102	15 or more employees	40 or older	✓	Follows federal law	✓[6]	✓		✓	✓	✓			
Vermont Vt. Stat. Ann. tit. 21, § 495; tit. 18, § 9333	One or more employees	18 or older	✓	Physical, mental or learning	✓	✓			✓	✓	✓	✓	Place of birth
Virginia Va. Code Ann. §§ 2.2-3900; 40.1-28.6; 51.5-3	Law applies to all employers.	No age limit	✓	Physical or mental		✓	✓	✓	✓	✓			
Washington Wash. Rev. Code Ann. §§ 49.60.040, 49.60.172 and foll.; 49.12.175; 49.44.090; Wash. Admin. Code § 162-30-020	8 or more employees	40 or older	✓	Physical, mental or sensory	✓	✓	✓	✓	✓	✓			Member of state militia
West Virginia W.Va. Code §§ 5-11-3, 5-11-9; 21-5B-1	12 or more employees	40 or older	✓	Physical or mental	✓	✓[7]			✓	✓			Smoker or non-smoker
Wisconsin Wis. Stat. Ann. § 111.32	One or more employees	40 or older	✓	Physical or mental	✓	✓	✓	✓	✓	✓	✓	✓	• Arrest or conviction • Lawful use of any product when not at work • Military service or status
Wyoming Wyo. Stat. §§ 27-9-105; 19-11-104	2 or more employees	40 to 69	✓			✓			✓	✓			• Military service or status • Smoker or nonsmoker

[6] Follows federal ADA statutes

[7] Employers with one or more employees

Chapter 9

Workers With Disabilities

A. The Americans with Disabilities Act 9/3

B. Businesses That Are Covered 9/5

C. Who Is Protected 9/5

    1. People With Disabilities 9/5

    2. People Who Are Qualified for the Job 9/9

D. Exceptions to Coverage 9/10

    1. Illegal Drug Use 9/10

    2. Gay and Lesbian Workers 9/10

    3. Sexual and Behavioral Disorders 9/10

    4. Physical and Psychological Characteristics 9/10

E. Providing Reasonable Accommodations 9/11

    1. When Accommodations Are Required 9/11

    2. Undue Hardship 9/12

    3. Deciding What Accommodations Are Needed 9/13

    4. Improving Accessibility 9/14

    5. Other Types of Accommodation 9/15

F. Workers With Emotional or Mental Impairments 9/18

    1. Covered Disorders 9/18

    2. Conditions Specifically Not Covered 9/18

    3. Handling Psychiatric Information 9/18

    4. Special Accommodations 9/19

    5. Threats and Other Unacceptable Conduct 9/19

    6. Dress Codes and Courtesy Rules 9/20

G. Financial Assistance 9/21

    1. Tax Credit for Small Businesses 9/21

    2. Tax Deduction for Removing Barriers 9/21

    3. Targeted Jobs Tax Credit 9/23

H. Health and Safety Standards 9/23

I. Medical Exams 9/25

J. Enforcement 9/25

*M*any employers are reluctant to hire people who have disabilities. They assume that an applicant with a disability won't be able to handle a particular job. This assumption may be correct for some applicants, but way off the mark for many others. Not only is it bad business sense to pre-judge people with disabilities—it's illegal. The federal government and many state governments have laws prohibiting discrimination based on disability. In this chapter, we take a close look at the main federal law. To find out if your state has a disability discrimination law, refer to the chart in Chapter 8, Section G.

A. The Americans with Disabilities Act

To help eliminate discrimination against people with disabilities, Congress passed the Americans with Disabilities Act or ADA (29 U.S.C. § 706 and following). One part of the ADA sets out rules for how businesses must deal with job applicants and employees. That part of the law, known as Title I, is explained in this chapter.

The idea behind the employment provisions of the ADA is that it's unfair to write off every applicant who has a disability. Many people who have a disability are able to perform many specific jobs. Some may need an accommodation—special equipment, perhaps, or a simple adjustment in their working conditions—to help them get the job done.

Basically, the ADA states that in making hiring and employment decisions, it's illegal to discriminate against anyone because of a disability. If a person is qualified to do the work, or to do it once a reasonable accommodation is made, you must treat that person the same as all other applicants and employees.

Numbers Tell the Story

- Only 32% of disabled people who are aged 18 to 64 work full time or part time, compared to 81% of the non-disabled population, a gap of 49 percentage points.
- Fully 57% of disabled people aged 18 to 64 feel that they are capable of working despite their disability or health condition. More than half of those people (56% of that group) do work—shrinking the gap between them and people without disabilities who work to 25%.

- More than three out of ten people (36%) of people with disabilities who are employed say they've run into some form of discrimination due to their disabilities—typically, not being offered a job for which they're qualified.
- **Of those people who have disabilities and do not work, two out of three (67%) would prefer to be working.**

Source: Poll by Louis Harris and Associates, commissioned by the National Organization on Disability, 2000

Although the concept is simple, the ADA requirements can get fairly complicated.

For employers, the ADA has perhaps its heaviest impact on the hiring process. You must, for example:

- write job descriptions that focus on the core tasks so that a person with a disability isn't eliminated from consideration because he or she can't perform a marginal job duty
- avoid questions in job applications and interviews that focus on possible disabilities, and
- defer pre-employment medical exams and inquiries until after you've made a conditional offer of employment.

(These hiring requirements are discussed in Chapter 1.)

In addition to laying down rules for employment, the ADA spells out what a business must do to make its services and facilities accessible to customers and other visitors with disabilities. That part of the law, known as Title III, applies to a wide range of businesses that serve the public, including:

- places that serve food or drink—such as restaurants and bars
- businesses that sell or rent goods—such as bakeries, grocery stores and hardware stores
- service businesses—such as laundromats, drycleaners, barber shops, travel agencies, shoe repair services and doctors and lawyers offices, and
- recreational facilities—such as gyms, health spas and bowling alleys.

ADA Coverage Is Broad

Under the ADA, you can't discriminate against a person with a disability in any aspect of employment, including:

- applications
- interviews
- testing
- hiring
- job assignments
- evaluations
- disciplinary actions
- training
- promotion
- medical exams
- layoffs
- firing
- compensation
- leave, and
- benefits.

In addition, you can't deny a job to someone or discriminate against an employee because that person is related to or associates with a person who has a disability. For example, you can't:

- refuse to hire someone because that person's spouse, child or other dependent has a disability
- refuse to hire someone because that person's spouse, child or other dependent has a disability that's not covered by your current health insurance plan or that may cause increased healthcare costs, or
- fire an employee because that employee has a roommate or close friend who has AIDS, or because the employee does volunteer work for people who have AIDS.

Businesses covered by Title III must take reasonable steps to remove barriers in existing buildings that can limit access by disabled people. Stricter rules apply to new buildings and those undergoing major renovation.

 The U.S. Equal Employment Opportunity Commission (EEOC) maintains a website at www.eeoc.gov. There you'll find extensive information about your responsibilities under the ADA, and a list of helpful publications you can order. The *Technical Assistance Manual* is quite comprehensive.

B. Businesses That Are Covered

You're covered by the ADA if you have 15 or more employees working for you for 20 or more weeks during the current calendar year —or if you had that many for 20 or more weeks last year. Part-time employees are counted.

C. Who Is Protected

The ADA protects "qualified individuals with disabilities." To be protected from job discrimination, a person must not only have a disability, but must also be qualified for a particular job.

1. People With Disabilities

The ADA's protections extend to the disabled —defined as a person who:

- has a physical or mental impairment that substantially limits one or more major life activities
- has a record of being substantially limited, or
- is regarded as being substantially limited.

Because this definition can take on unexpected twists, it's useful to look at each part of it.

a. Impairments limiting a life activity

When deciding whether an applicant or employee is protected by the ADA, you must first determine whether that person has a physical or mental impairment. The ADA broadly defines physical and mental impairments. A physical impairment can be any disorder, condition, cosmetic disfigurement or anatomical loss affecting any of the body systems. A mental impairment is any mental or psychological disorder.

Just having a physical or mental impairment is not enough to trigger the ADA, however. That impairment must also substantially limit one or more major life activities. Under the ADA, major life activities include:

- walking
- speaking
- breathing
- performing manual tasks
- seeing
- hearing
- learning
- taking care of oneself
- working
- sitting

- standing
- lifting, and
- reading.

It's not enough, for purposes of the ADA, that the impairment affects or touches on one of these major life activities; it must substantially limit the activity. For example, a person with mild asthma who occasionally becomes short of breath, but remains able to perform other daily tasks, will not be considered impaired under the ADA. However, a person with a more serious respiratory problem may be considered to have a disability—in which case it may be necessary for you to provide a smoke-free workplace under the ADA. (For more on smoking restrictions, see Chapter 7, Section G.)

A condition may only mildly affect some workers but severely limit others. The degree of limitation may determine whether the worker is a person with a disability under the ADA.

> **EXAMPLE:** Erwin has cerebral palsy. Cerebral palsy is a disorder that often restricts major life activities such as speaking, walking and performing manual tasks. In Erwin's case, however, the cerebral palsy is very mild and only slightly interferes with his ability to speak; it doesn't affect his other major life activities. Erwin isn't a person with a disability under the ADA definition. Joselyn, on the other hand, has a severe form of cerebral palsy that severely restricts her ability to walk and perform manual tasks; she is a person with a disability under the ADA.

In determining whether an impairment substantially limits a person, you must look at the effect of the impairment on that person's activities.

> **EXAMPLE:** Millie, a receptionist, injures her back. The resulting pain permanently restricts her ability to walk, sit, stand, drive, care for her home and engage in sports. Because her problems are permanent and substantially limit her life activities, Millie has a disability.

> **EXAMPLE:** Reginald, a general laborer, injures his back and recovers well. After a short period of rehabilitation, he is able to continue an active life, including recreational sports. He finds a new job as a security guard. Reginald doesn't have a disability under the ADA definition.

In *Toyota v. Williams* (534 U.S. 184 (2002)), the U.S. Supreme Court helped clarify how impairments are to be evaluated. The Court said that in deciding whether a person is protected by the ADA, you need to look beyond how a disability affects the person's ability to perform job duties. The key question is whether the person is unable to perform the variety of tasks central to most peoples' daily lives—such as doing household chores, bathing and brushing one's teeth. In that case, the Court found that the fact that a worker's carpal tunnel condition may affect her ability to perform certain work in a car plant doesn't automatically mean she's protected by the ADA.

What If the Impairment Is Correctable?

In deciding whether a worker is "disabled" such that he or she is entitled to ADA protection, you can consider whether the worker's asserted problem is easily correctable. If it is, then the worker generally doesn't qualify for ADA protections.

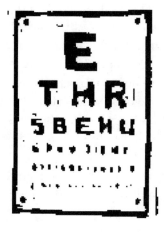

EXAMPLE: Chuck is nearsighted. Without glasses, his vision is 20/200, but with glasses, he has normal 20/20 vision. Because his eyesight is easy to correct, he's not a person with a disability under the ADA.

You must consider disabilities on a case-by-case basis. A worker may be partly helped by a corrective measure, but still be substantially impaired such that he or she is entitled to ADA protection.

EXAMPLE: Melanie walks with the aid of an artificial leg, but she must walk carefully and slowly. Because she is significantly limited even when using her prosthesis, she's entitled to the ADA's protections.

Obesity: No Verdict Yet

It's not yet clear whether extreme obesity is a disability under the ADA. The issue is still being debated in the courts.

The EEOC takes the position that someone who is 100% over normal weight—morbidly obese, in medical terms—has a disability, regardless of what caused the overweight condition. For less obese people (such as someone who is 50 pounds overweight), the EEOC maintains that the person may have a disability if the obesity was caused by disease.

At least one court has held that extreme obesity can be a disability if the overweight person is perceived as being disabled—and so is within the protections of the ADA. (For more on perceived disabilities, see subsection c below.)

In interpreting state laws granting rights to disabled workers, most state courts have held that excess poundage doesn't by itself constitute a disability—but it may in conjunction with a physical disorder such as diabetes, high blood pressure or heart disease.

EXAMPLE: Toni, a five-foot-four inch tall woman who weighs 305 pounds, applies for a job at Community Foods, a health food store. Despite her food store experience, Toni doesn't get the job. She sues Community Foods, claiming she was discriminated against because of a disability—too much weight. The court dismisses the case because Toni can't prove her weight is caused by a physical condition. (*Cassista v. Community Foods, Inc.*, 5 Cal. 4th 1050 (1993).)

b. Record of impairment

The ADA also protects people who have a history of a disability—cancer or heart disease, for example—whose illnesses are either cured, controlled or in remission. And it protects people with a history of mental illness.

If a person has a record of disability and you rely on that record to reject that person for a job, that's a violation of the ADA if the person is currently qualified to do the work.

> **EXAMPLE:** Beatrice, who has a learning disability, applies for a job as a secretary-receptionist. Records from a previous employer state that she is mentally retarded. Still, her resume shows that she meets all requirements for the secretary-receptionist job. The new employer doesn't interview her because he doesn't want to hire a mentally retarded person. Relying on the records from the prior employer violates the ADA.
>
> In this situation, it's best to determine the applicant's ability through practical tests that measure the skills needed for the job—for example, handling phone calls, taking messages, greeting customers, sorting mail and doing light typing.

c. Regarded as impaired

Some job applicants are not severely limited by a disability—yet, employers perceive them to have such a limitation. And, acting on these false perceptions, employers discriminate against these people.

There are several circumstances in which false assumptions violate the protections of the ADA.

A person may have an impairment which is at most a minor inconvenience, but the employer treats the impairment as if it's highly limiting.

> **EXAMPLE:** Ed has high blood pressure which is controlled by pills. His condition doesn't affect his work activities. Just the same, Ed's employer reassigns him to a less strenuous job with a lower salary because of a baseless fear that Ed may suffer a heart attack if he stays in his present job.

A person may have an impairment that's a problem mostly because of other people's attitudes.

> **EXAMPLE:** Vern, an experienced assistant manager of a convenience store, has a prominent facial scar. Vern's employer passes him over for promotion to store manager, instead promoting a less experienced part-time clerk in the belief that customers and vendors won't want to look at Vern.

A person may have no impairment at all, but the employer regards the person as being substantially limited.

> **EXAMPLE:** Jill is fired because of a false rumor that she has HIV. She has no impairment, but is being treated by her

employer as if she does. Therefore, her firing falls within the Act.

In considering whether to hire an applicant or to demote or fire an employee who has a disability, you may be concerned about productivity, safety, insurance, liability or attendance. Or you may worry that your business will have to spend money to accommodate a supposed disability or that co-workers and customers won't accept the applicant or employee. The best way to avoid problems under the ADA is to get the facts before you act; you must base all employment decisions on legitimate, nondiscriminatory reasons.

2. People Who Are Qualified for the Job

To be protected by the ADA, a person must not only have a disability; he or she must also be qualified to do a particular job. This emphasizes a key point about the ADA: You don't have to hire or retain anyone who can't do the work.

To figure out if a disabled person is qualified for a job in your business, go through these two steps.

Step 1: Qualified to work. Determine whether the person is qualified for the job by education, work experience, training, skills, licenses, certificates and other job-related requirements—good judgment, for example, or the ability to work with other people.

> **EXAMPLE:** Trudy, a bookkeeper who has cerebral palsy, applies for a job as a bookkeeping manager. If the company's

policy is that all managers must have at least three years of experience working with the company and Trudy has worked there only two years, she's not qualified for a management position. Therefore, she's not protected by the ADA.

Requirements used to screen out candidates must be job-related and based on business needs.

Step 2: Essential job functions. Determine if the person can perform what the ADA deems the essential functions of the job.

The ADA puts a lot of weight on two words: essential functions. The reason is that historically, many disabled people who were able to perform the basic tasks necessary for a job were denied employment because they couldn't meet requirements that were marginal at best.

> **EXAMPLE:** The job description for a file clerk at Stony Creek Corporation states that the job includes answering the phone. In fact, most time on the job is spent filing and retrieving written materials; other employees usually answer the phone. A hearing-impaired person may have trouble handling phone calls, but may be perfectly qualified to file and retrieve papers. Under the ADA, Stony Creek shouldn't disqualify a hearing-impaired applicant for the file clerk job because answering the phone isn't an essential job function.

If you can write an accurate job description that identifies the essential functions of a job, you'll have an easier time deciding whether a person with a disability is qualified for the job. (See Chapter 1, Section B, for more on essential functions.) This emphasizes the importance of periodically reviewing your job descriptions to make sure they are current.

D. Exceptions to Coverage

Certain people and conditions aren't protected under the ADA.

1. Illegal Drug Use

People can't claim they're disabled and entitled to ADA protection because they illegally use drugs. This includes people who use prescription drugs illegally as well as those who use illegal drugs. Applying this part of the ADA becomes tricky, since the law may protect people who have been rehabilitated after drug use or who are in a drug or alcohol rehab program. (See Chapter 1, Section F5.)

2. Gay and Lesbian Workers

Homosexuality and bisexuality are not considered disabilities under the ADA, although many state laws prohibit discrimination based on sexual orientation. (See Chapter 8, Section F.)

3. Sexual and Behavioral Disorders

The term "disability" doesn't include the following sexual and behavioral disorders:

- transvestitism, transsexualism, pedophilia, exhibitionism, voyeurism, gender identity disorders not resulting from physical impairments, or other sexual behavior disorders
- compulsive gambling, kleptomania or pyromania, or
- psychoactive substance use disorders resulting from current illegal use of drugs.

4. Physical and Psychological Characteristics

Under the ADA, simple physical characteristics—eye or hair color, left-handedness, or height or weight within a normal range—are not treated as disabilities. Nor are personality traits such as poor judgment or quick temper. Also, environmental, cultural or economic disadvantages—such as lack of education or a prison record—are not disabilities.

> **EXAMPLE:** Rita can't read because she has dyslexia, a learning disability; Rita has an impairment under the ADA. Sonny can't read because he dropped out of school; his lack of education isn't a legal disability.

You don't have to hire or retain an employee who would pose a direct threat to his or her health or safety—or that of other employees. But be careful. You can't deny employment to a person with a disability because of a slightly increased risk. If you turn down an applicant or fire someone you've already employed, you must be prepared to show there is or would be a significant risk and a high probability of substantial harm if that person remained part of the workforce.

EXAMPLE: Carlita has Parkinson's disease, which restricts her manual dexterity. An employer can't assume that Carlita can't work in a lab because she'd pose a risk of breaking bottles that contain dangerous chemicals. The employer must evaluate Carlita's specific abilities and limitations.

Sometimes, you can get rid of or reduce the health or safety risk through a reasonable accommodation—a legal concept discussed at greater length in Section E. If an employee were to contract tuberculosis, for example, a reasonable accommodation might be to grant the employee a two-week leave of absence. With proper medication, the employee would no longer be contagious at the end of the two-week period.

Psychological behavior is more difficult to evaluate. However, if an employee is violent, aggressive or destructive, or makes threats, this can be good evidence that he or she may pose a direct threat to the safety of others. Still, before you make an employment decision based on such behavior, you may want to protect your legal position by asking a psychologist or other mental health professional to evaluate the behavior and the potential for harm.

E. Providing Reasonable Accommodations

The ADA requires you to accommodate the physical or mental limitations of a qualified applicant or employee who has a disability. However, you're excused from this require-ment if making an accommodation would place an undue hardship on your business. (For more on what constitutes undue hard-ship, see Section 2, below.)

The idea of a reasonable accommodation is quite simple: You may have to make some changes to help a disabled person do a job. This can take a number of forms, such as changing the job, an employment practice or the work environment. But you need not be psychic. Generally, the person with the disability needs to ask you for a reasonable accommodation. (See Section 3, below.)

1. When Accommodations Are Required

You may have to make a reasonable accom-modation for any part of the employment process—from completing the application, conducting the interview and testing the applicant, through changing workplace con-ditions and promoting the worker.

Job applications. Someone using a wheel-chair may need an accommodation if the hiring office or interview site isn't wheelchair accessible; you may need to move the inter-view to a place that the applicant can get to. A person with bad eyesight may need help in filling out an application; you may need to provide the needed assistance at company expense. (See Chapter 1, Section D.)

Job performance. Someone with poor hearing may need a special telephone that amplifies voices to perform a job. You may need to provide such a telephone at company expense. (See Section 4, below.)

Access to benefits. Employees with disabilities must have unrestricted access to lunchrooms, lounges, rest rooms, meeting rooms, and other services such as health programs, transportation and social events. You may need to modify existing facilities or schedules.

2. Undue Hardship

The ADA doesn't require you to accommodate a disabled applicant or employee if it would place an undue hardship on the business—that is, if it would require significant difficulty or expense. Many legal battles have been waged over this imprecise language.

Whether something is an undue hardship is decided on a case-by-case basis. What's easily managed by a large company may be very difficult for a small or mid-sized business. The law takes this into account by focusing on your business, not businesses in general. Under EEOC guidelines, several factors are considered in determining whether an accommodation would place an undue hardship on your business.

The net cost of the accommodation. The cost of accommodating an employee may be less than it first appears. You may qualify for a tax credit or deduction, and there are sources of funding to help pay for some accommodations. (See Section G.)

The size of the business and its financial resources. Obviously, larger and wealthier businesses are better able to put money into accommodations.

The structure of the business. A small facility that's part of a larger company may have access to funds from the home office. If so, the company's total resources become part of the equation.

The impact of the accommodation on business operations. Even an affordable accommodation might be an undue hardship if it changes the nature of your business.

> **EXAMPLE:** Flo, who has an eyesight problem, applies for a waitress job at Rendezvous Night Club. The club keeps its lights dim to create an intimate setting. Flo requests bright lighting so that she can see to take orders. Rendezvous doesn't have to accommodate her; to do so would seriously affect the nature of the business. If Flo were applying for a bookkeeping position at the same nightclub, and would work in a poorly lit office away from customer areas, the employer could be required to provide brighter lighting as a reasonable accommodation.

Similarly, you wouldn't be required to raise the workplace temperature to accommodate a disabled employee if doing so would make it uncomfortably hot for other employees or customers. That solution would be unduly disruptive—but you could be required to provide a small space heater.

Sometimes, the right of one employee to a reasonable accommodation can conflict with the seniority rights of another employee. The U.S. Supreme Court, in *US Airways v. Barnett* (535 U.S. 391 (2002)), ruled that the ADA doesn't usually require you to accommodate a disabled employee by offering a job that normally would go to a more senior employee. However, the Court did leave the door open for a disabled employee show some "special circumstance" that might require you to override your seniority rules. For example, if you make frequent exceptions to the seniority system for other reasons, a disabled employee can reasonably argue that you should make a similar exception as a reasonable accommodation.

3. Deciding What Accommodations Are Needed

Figuring out viable accommodations usually requires cooperation between the employer and the applicant or employee with a disability. If a disabled person asks for an accommodation, chances are excellent that he or she will be able to explain his or her functional limitations to you. But if the person isn't articulate or is medically unsophisticated, it may take a letter from a doctor or psychologist to clarify the nature of the problem.

You may have your own creative ideas about an appropriate accommodation, but don't overlook the disabled person as a good source of ideas. In fact, the EEOC recommends that you consult with the employee or applicant to identify potential accommodations and assess how effective each would be in enabling the person to do the job. Such consultation gets the relationship started on a positive note, since you and the disabled person are working together to solve a problem. Moreover, this cooperative approach can yield dollar-and-cents benefits to your business; a person with

a disability is often able to suggest a cost-effective accommodation that you wouldn't have considered.

> **EXAMPLE:** Tandex Company, a small manufacturer, believes that hiring Chester, a prospective employee who uses a wheelchair, will require it to install a special lower drinking fountain. Chester, however, points out that he can use the existing fountain if Tandex simply provides paper cups next to the fountain.

Sometimes, there are several accommodations that would enable a person with a disability to handle a job. The EEOC recommends that you consider the preference of the disabled person. Still, under the ADA, you're free to make the final choice—for example, selecting an accommodation that's cheaper or easier to provide.

Refusing an accommodation can be costly. So think twice before you decide to save a few dollars by denying a reasonable accommodation to a worker with a disability.

> **EXAMPLE:** Carol, a computer operator with multiple sclerosis, asked her employer for a covered parking space. Carol's doctor confirmed to the employer that the heat of an uncovered space would worsen her condition. Nevertheless, the employer refused, claiming it had already made a number of accommodations for Carol's illness. When Carol's condition worsened and she became bedridden, she sued. She was awarded $225,000—

considerably more than what it would have cost the employer to grant the request for a covered space.

Help Identifying Reasonable Accommodations. The Job Accommodation Network (JAN) is a federally funded service that provides free information and advice on making reasonable accommodations for employees with disabilities. For a telephone consultation, call 800-526-7234. Visit the agency's website at www.jan.wvu.edu for more information.

You can also seek assistance from the U.S. Equal Employment Opportunity Commission, from state or local vocational rehabilitation agencies, or state or local organizations representing or providing services to individuals with disabilities.

4. Improving Accessibility

Under the ADA, you may be required to make your facilities accessible to a variety of people. This is a confusing area of the law for businesses—in part because the ADA covers more than equal employment opportunities for people with disabilities. As mentioned, it also requires businesses to make their facilities accessible to members of the general public. To further complicate matters, the accessibility requirements for existing facilities differ from the requirements for facilities that are being renovated or are under construction.

As an employer, you must make it possible for an individual applicant to apply for a job, which may include moving the interview site

for him or her. You must also provide access to the job for an individual employee with a disability. This includes access to a building, to a worksite, to needed equipment and to all facilities used by the employee. You must provide such access unless it would cause an undue hardship.

a. Existing facilities

The ADA doesn't require you to change existing facilities unless and until a particular applicant or employee with a particular disability needs an accommodation. Then the modifications should meet that individual's work needs. You don't have to make changes to provide access in places or facilities that won't be used by that person.

Here are some workplace alterations you might consider:

- Install a ramp at the entrance to your building.
- Remove raised thresholds.
- Reserve wide parking spaces close to the worksite for people in wheelchairs.
- Provide accessible toilet stalls, sinks, soap and towels in rest rooms.
- Rearrange office furniture and equipment.
- Make drinking fountains accessible.
- Provide clear paths to copying machines, meeting and training rooms, lunchrooms and lounges.
- Remove potential hazards from the path of blind people.
- Add flashing lights to alarm bells to alert hearing-impaired people in an emergency.

b. Renovation or new construction

As an employer, you must meet more extensive requirements for accessibility if you renovate your facilities or start new construction. The EEOC claims that remodeled buildings can usually be made to meet accessibility requirements at minimal additional cost.

 Renovation and new construction requirements are described in the ADA Accessibility Guidelines which are part of the Department of Justice Title III regulations. For technical assistance and publications, call the Architectural and Transportation Barriers Compliance Board at 800-USA-ABLE. You can also visit its website at www.access-board.gov.

c. Access to goods and services

If your business is a place of public accommodation—for example, a retail store, theater, hotel or restaurant—Title III of the ADA requires you to make your goods and services accessible to everyone. You're required to remove architectural barriers if this is structurally possible and can be done at reasonable expense. Be aware, too, that state and local building codes may require that existing commercial buildings be modified so they are accessible to people with disabilities.

 To learn what is practical and affordable for existing facilities, you'll need the advice of an architect or other expert who knows the ins and out of the ADA requirements.

5. Other Types of Accommodation

Not all accommodations involve physical changes to the workplace. There are other things you can do to help qualified people with disabilities work effectively. You might, for example, restructure a job by transferring marginal or nonessential functions to another employee. Or you might modify work schedules. You could permit a worker with a mental disability to take off time for twice-a-week visits to a psychiatrist. Or you could assign a fixed shift to a diabetic employee who needs to eat on a regular schedule and take insulin at set times each day—departing from your usual practice of requiring employees to rotate their shifts.

Similarly, a reasonable accommodation might consist of having a flexible leave policy. You don't have to give additional paid leave, but consider allowing employees to use accrued leave or leave without pay to get needed rest or medical treatment. Or you may decide that it's better to reassign an employee to a different job. But be careful in choosing this option. To avoid discriminating against other employees on the job, you must reassign the disabled worker to a position that is vacant, and for which he or she is qualified.

Often you can buy equipment—or modify existing equipment—to accommodate an employee. Some examples of equipment and devices that may be used include:

- TDDs (Telecommunication Devices for the Deaf) that enable people with hearing or speech impairments to communicate over the phone
- telephone amplifiers, useful for people with hearing impairments
- software to enlarge print or convert print documents to spoken words for people with vision or reading disabilities
- telephone headsets and adaptive lights for people with cerebral palsy or other manual difficulties, and
- speaker phones, effective for people who are amputees or have other mobility impairments.

Be Alert for Harassment of Workers With Disabilities

Just as you need to spot and crack down on sexual harassment and racial harassment in the workplace, you need to nip in the bud any harassment of disabled workers—whether by supervisors or co-workers. Otherwise, you may get sued for tolerating the bad behavior. Cases against employers have been brought by:

- A hair salon manager with AIDS who claimed that his co-workers had threatened a walkout.
- A saleswoman with multiple sclerosis who claimed that her supervisor mimicked and ridiculed her speech and gait.
- A store manager with a back injury who claimed that his supervisor told him he had to work every minute of his shift and threatened to "ride him until he quit."

Of course, it's out of line to make light of someone else's disability. But as an employer, you can't depend on people honoring that understanding. You need to make sure that employees know they'll be disciplined or even discharged if they engage in this type of behavior. Make a clear statement to that effect in your employee handbook—and be prepared to take prompt disciplinary action if this objectionable behavior surfaces.

Solutions That Don't Cost a Bundle

As noted earlier, the Job Accommodation Network (JAN) is a free service funded by the federal government. Its consultants can offer practical suggestions for accommodating disabled workers. You can reach JAN by calling 800-526-7234 or on the Internet at www.jan.wvu.edu.

Many examples from JAN and other sources for accommodating people with disabilities are contained in *A Technical Assistance Manual on the Employment Provisions (Title I) of the Americans with Disabilities Act.* (See Section A for ordering information.)

Here are some examples of low-cost accommodations.

- A timer with an indicator light allowed a medical technician who was deaf to perform laboratory tests.
  Cost: $27
- A clerk with limited use of her hands was provided a rotating file holder that enabled her to reach all materials needed for her job.
  Cost: $85
- A groundskeeper who had limited use of one arm was provided a detachable extension arm for a rake. This enabled him to grasp the handle on the extension with the impaired hand and control the rake with the functional arm.
  Cost: $20
- A desk layout was changed from the right to the left side to enable a data entry operator who is visually impaired to perform her job.
  Cost: $0
- A telephone amplifier designed to work with a hearing aid allowed a plant worker to retain his job and avoid being transferred to a lower paying job.
  Cost: $24

F. Workers With Emotional or Mental Impairments

According to the U.S. Equal Employment Opportunity Commission (EEOC)—the federal office that enforces the ADA—about 13% of ADA cases involve workers claiming emotional or psychiatric impairment. This includes workers with anxiety disorders, depression, bipolar disorder (manic depression) and schizophrenia.

The EEOC has issued guidelines to help you meet your responsibilities to workers and job applicants with these and other mental difficulties.

1. Covered Disorders

The ADA protects a worker if his or her mental impairment limits "a major life activity" or if the worker has a record of such an impairment. The impairment may be one that restricts the worker's ability to learn, think, concentrate, interact with others, care for himself or herself or perform manual tasks.

The impairment must be more than just a short-term problem. The EEOC offers these examples:

- Jane has had major depressions for almost a year. She has been intensely sad and withdrawn, has had problems sleeping and difficulty concentrating. The depth and duration of her problems qualify her for ADA protection.
- Joe, on the other hand, was distressed by his breakup with his girlfriend and, for about a month, sometimes became agitated at work. He sought counseling

and his mood improved. He doesn't have a disability under the ADA.

2. Conditions Specifically Not Covered

People can't claim they're disabled and entitled to ADA protection because they illegally use drugs. This includes people who use prescription drugs illegally as well as those who use illegal drugs.

Also, homosexuality and bisexuality aren't considered disabilities under the ADA, although many state laws prohibit discrimination based on sexual orientation.

Finally, the term disability doesn't include sexual behavior disorders, compulsive gambling, kleptomania or pyromania.

3. Handling Psychiatric Information

Your job application form must not ask about mental or emotional illness or psychiatric disability, treatment or hospitalization. In addition, don't ask disability-related questions before you offer someone a job—although you can inquire further if an applicant asks for a reasonable accommodation for the hiring process itself.

For example, suppose an applicant for a secretarial job asks to take a typing test in a quiet location instead of a busy reception area "because of a medical condition." You can ask for additional information to verify that the applicant needs a quiet location for the test.

After you offer someone a job, you can require a medical or psychiatric exam—as long as you do the same for all entering employees in that job category.

Be sure to keep medical information confidential. This includes psychiatric information. You can only share this information with supervisors on a need-to-know basis and with first aid and safety workers who may need to deal with emergencies.

Probably the knottiest confidentiality problem is what to tell other employees when you provide time off or other accommodations to a worker with psychiatric problems. In response to co-workers' questions, you can only say that you're "acting for legitimate business reasons" or "acting in compliance with federal law." That's it.

4. Special Accommodations

Reasonable accommodations vary from case to case. Examples of some accommodations that may reasonably be required for a person with a mental disability include:

- giving the employee time off from work or a modified work schedule
- installing room dividers, partitions or other soundproofing or visual barriers between workspaces for an employee who has trouble concentrating, for instance
- moving an employee away from noisy machinery or lowering the volume or pitch of telephones
- providing a job coach
- modifying a workplace policy, and
- adjusting supervisory methods.

The last two points—workplace policies and supervision—provide the most common

glitches for employers. A couple of illustrations may help.

a. Workplace policies

- A store doesn't let its cashiers drink beverages at checkout stations. Cashiers are limited to two 15-minute breaks during an eight-hour shift, in addition to a meal break. Lillian, a cashier, needs to drink water every hour to combat dry mouth, a side effect of psychiatric medicine she takes. To accommodate Lillian, the store should consider changing its policy against drinking beverages at checkout stations or changing its policy limiting cashiers to two 15-minute breaks.

b. Supervision

- Ted asks for more guidance and feedback because of limitations associated with his psychiatric disability. It's reasonable for Ted's employer to consult with him, his doctor and his supervisor to work out a plan for adding structure to his job, such as weekly meetings with the supervisor to review long-term projects.

On a related point, you're not expected to make sure that an employee takes his or her medication as prescribed.

5. Threats and Other Unacceptable Conduct

You remain free to discipline an employee for violating standards of conduct—even if the misconduct resulted from a mental disability. Nothing in the ADA prevents you from maintaining a workplace free of violence or threats of violence, or from disciplining a worker who steals or destroys property.

For example, you needn't put up with an employee who threatens a supervisor with physical harm.

And you can discipline a worker who steals money from you—even though the worker claims the misconduct was caused by a disability. The EEOC views a policy against employee theft as being related to a worker's job and consistent with business necessity.

6. Dress Codes and Courtesy Rules

In some cases, strict enforcement of an employer's dress code and courtesy rules can violate the ADA rules—especially if the enforcement isn't necessary from a business standpoint.

> **EXAMPLE:** Arthur, an employee with a psychiatric disability, works in a warehouse loading boxes onto pallets. He has no customer contact and doesn't come into regular contact with other workers. Lately, Arthur has come to work appearing disheveled. His clothes don't fit right and are torn. When co-workers try to engage him in small talk, he turns his back and walks away. When he must talk to a co-worker, he's abrupt and rude. The employer's handbook requires employees to have a neat appearance and to be courteous to one another. Arthur claims that his appearance and behavior are the

result of a psychiatric disability and that the rules shouldn't be strictly applied to him. The EEOC agrees, based on its conclusion that these rules of conduct are not job-related for Arthur's warehouse job. Because Arthur has no customer contact and doesn't come into regular contact with other employees, the standards aren't a business necessity. Therefore, the EEOC reasons, if the employer discharges or disciplines Arthur for not complying the rules, the employer is violating the ADA.

Here are examples of some other situations in which an employer may have to yield to or provide an accommodation for an employee's disruptive conduct if the conduct results from a psychiatric condition.

- A reference librarian frequently loses her temper, disrupting the library atmosphere by shouting at patrons and co-workers. Her employer may discipline her for violating a rule prohibiting disruptive conduct, since the rule is job-related and consistent with business necessity. But the employer should grant a request for a leave of absence to seek treatment for her condition, as long as it won't cause an undue hardship.
- An employee with depression is often late because his medicine makes him groggy in the morning. He can be disciplined for his tardiness but the employer should consider adjusting the work schedule, perhaps allowing the employee to work from 10:00 to 6:30 instead of the normal 9:00 to 5:30 workday.

G. Financial Assistance

There may be financial help available to assist you in complying with the ADA.

1. Tax Credit for Small Businesses

If your business has gross receipts of $1 million or less for the tax year, or if you have 30 or fewer employees, you can take a tax credit of up to $5,000 a year for accommodations you make to comply with the ADA. You can take this credit for one-half the cost of certain access expenses, including removing physical barriers and providing interpreters or readers. The credit applies to expenses that are more than $250, but not more than $10,250.

EXAMPLE: ABC Company spends $10,250 to widen doorways to accommodate employees in wheelchairs. The company gets a tax credit of $5,000 ($10,250 minus $250, divided by 2).

To be eligible, you must meet the ADA Accessibility Guidelines. These are available for viewing and downloading at www.access-board.gov, the website maintained by the Architectural and Transportation Barriers Compliance Board. The Guidelines deal with technical details, such as how wide aisles must be to accommodate the needs of people using wheelchairs.

2. Tax Deduction for Removing Barriers

Any business can deduct up to $15,000 a year for the cost of removing specified architectural and transportation barriers—including steps, narrow doors and inadequate parking spaces, toilet facilities and vehicles. If your business meets the size and income requirements for the tax credit described in Section 1, it can take both the tax credit and the tax deduction. Contact a local IRS office for more details.

EXAMPLE: CompuWay Corporation, a company with gross receipts of $950,000, spends $24,000 to widen its parking spaces and to add wide bathroom stalls that are more accessible to workers with disabilities. CompuWay can take the $5,000 tax credit for the first $10,250 and may deduct the remaining $13,750 from its taxable income.

Ten Tips on Communicating With People Who Have Disabilities

1. When talking with a person who has a disability, speak directly to that person rather than through a companion or sign language interpreter who may be present.

2. When introduced to a person with a disability, it is appropriate to offer to shake hands. People with limited hand use or who wear an artificial limb can usually shake hands. It's perfectly acceptable to greet people by shaking hands with the left hand.

3. When meeting a person who is blind or has partial sight, always identify yourself and others who may be with you. When conversing in a group, remember to identify the person to whom you are speaking.

4. If you offer assistance, wait until the offer is accepted. Then listen to or ask for instructions.

5. Treat adults as adults. Address people who have disabilities by their first names only when extending that same familiarity to all others present. Never patronize people who use wheelchairs by patting them on the head or shoulder.

6. Leaning or hanging on a person's wheelchair is similar to leaning or hanging on a person and is generally considered annoying. The chair is part of the personal body space of the person who uses it.

7. Listen attentively when you're talking with a person who has difficulty speaking. Be patient and wait for the person to finish, rather than correcting or speaking for the person. If necessary, ask short questions that require short answers, a nod or a shake of the head. Never pretend to understand if you are having difficulty doing so. Instead, repeat what you have understood and allow the person to respond. The response will clue you in and guide your understanding.

8. When speaking with a person who uses a wheelchair or crutches, position yourself at eye level in front of the person.

9. To get the attention of a person who is deaf or hard of hearing, tap the person on the shoulder or wave your hand. Look directly at the person and speak clearly, slowly and expressively to establish if the person can read your lips. Not all people with a hearing impairment can lip-read. For those who do lip-read, be sensitive to their needs by facing the light source and keeping hands, cigarettes and food away from your mouth when speaking.

10. Relax. Don't be embarrassed if you happen to use accepted, common expressions, such as "See you later" or "Did you hear about this," that seem to relate to the person's disability.

Source: Adapted by Karen Meyer for United Cerebral Palsy Associations, Inc.

3. Targeted Jobs Tax Credit

Your business may also be eligible for a tax credit if you hire specific people with disabilities who were referred to you by a qualifying governmental agency, such as a state or local vocational rehabilitation agency, state commission on the blind or the U.S. Department of Veteran Affairs. These workers must be certified by a state employment service.

If you hire such an employee, you can take a tax credit of up to 40% of the first $6,000 of his or her first-year salary. Congress authorizes this program on a year-to-year basis. For more information, or to check the current status of this credit, check with the office in your state that helps place employees.

Additional sources of funding are described in the *Technical Assistance Manual* described earlier in this chapter. The manual includes an ADA Resource Directory that's quite extensive.

H. Health and Safety Standards

The ADA doesn't stop you from establishing standards to ensure that your workplace is safe and that your workers are qualified and competent. You're free to set minimum requirements based on education, skills and work experience—and to specify physical and mental standards needed for job performance, health and safety. And you're able to hire the best qualified person for a job. However, so that you don't exclude people with disabilities from jobs they can perform, the ADA requires that your standards and selection criteria for workers be job-related and consistent with real business needs.

Don't Forget the Reasonable Accommodation Rule. If your job standards are job-related and consistent with your business needs, you must also consider whether a disabled person could meet the standards through a reasonable accommodation—such as a modified workstation or special equipment. (See Section E.)

You can require, as a job standard, that a person not pose a direct threat to his or her own health and safety, or to the health and safety of others in the workplace.

EXAMPLE: Alex applies for a position at Truck Parts Unlimited. The job requires employees to use a forklift truck to move heavy loads through a parts storage facility. Alex is disabled by narcolepsy; he frequently and unexpectedly loses consciousness. The job poses a risk to Alex and other employees working in the building since they could be seriously injured if Alex were to lose consciousness while operating the forklift truck. Because the risk to others can't be reduced by reasonable accommodation, Truck Parts Unlimited may drop Alex from its list of prospects without violating the ADA.

Employers Can Refuse to Let Employees Endanger Themselves

The U.S. Supreme Court recently confirmed, in *Chevron v. Echazabal* (No. 00-1406, June 11, 2002), that employers can refuse to hire applicants for positions that would pose a direct threat to their own health or safety. In this case, the Court found that Chevron was within its rights when it refused to hire Mario Echazabal to work in an oil refinery. Echazabal had been diagnosed with Hepatitis C. Chevron refused to hire him after its doctors found that his condition could be aggravated by exposure to toxins at the refinery.

Before this case was decided, there was some dispute over whether the ADA allowed an employer to refuse to hire a worker who posed a direct threat only to him- or herself. Although the language of the ADA itself mentions only direct threats to others, the EEOC's regulations interpreting the ADA say that an employer can refuse to hire someone if doing the job in question would pose a direct threat to the applicant's own health or safety. The *Chevron* case resolves this issue once and for all—employers may legally refuse to hire an applicant for a position that would create a direct threat to the applicant's safety or health.

The ADA requirements for exempting job candidates on health or safety grounds are intentionally tough—designed to prevent employers from acting on a stereotype or patronizing assumptions about people with disabilities. If you plan to exclude someone from consideration for a particular job on health or safety grounds, be sure you have specific evidence that the employee would create a risk.

Special Rules for Food Handlers

The ADA recognizes that people with certain infectious or communicable diseases may be a direct threat to the health or safety of others if they're handling food. Each year, the U.S. Department of Health and Human Services and its Centers for Disease Control update a list of contagious diseases that may be transmitted through food handling—diseases such as hepatitis and salmonella poisoning. The list also describes the methods by which these diseases are transmitted.

The list is short—and, in conformance with medical opinion, doesn't include AIDS or the HIV virus.

The list emphasizes that the greatest danger of food-transmitted disease comes from infected animals and contamination in food processing. If someone with a listed disease applies for a food handling job, the usual rules apply: Consider whether there's a reasonable accommodation that would eliminate risks to the health of others. In the case of an employee who becomes infected with one of the diseases on the list, see if you can reassign the person to a job that doesn't require food handling. Be sure that the person is qualified, the job is vacant and the reassignment wouldn't pose an undue hardship.

I. Medical Exams

The strict ADA rules that govern medical inquiries and exams during the hiring process are described in Chapter 1. After you hire someone, the rules are even tougher. Any medical exam or medical inquiry about the employee must be job-related and justified by business necessity. You may order an exam if you learn of a problem related to job performance or safety, but again, the exam must be related to job performance. In the case of a physically demanding job, you may order an exam to find out if employees continue to be fit to perform the work.

EXAMPLE: Nelson is a warehouse laborer. He has a back impairment that affects his ability to lift objects. Nelson's employer can require that he be examined by an orthopedic surgeon—but can't require Nelson to submit to an HIV test. Such a test isn't related to either the job or to Nelson's impairment.

You can, however, order a medical exam or make medical inquiries if:

- an employee is having difficulty performing his or her job effectively
- an employee becomes disabled
- the exam is needed for you make a reasonable accommodation to an employee's disability, or
- exams, screening or monitoring are required by other laws.

You can also conduct medical exams and tests as part of wellness and health screening programs—but only if they are voluntary.

J. Enforcement

The U.S. Equal Employment Opportunity Commission (EEOC) enforces the employment provisions of the ADA. The Commission investigates charges of discrimination and attempts to resolve any discrimination it finds. If those attempts don't succeed, the EEOC may sue on its own or—more likely—may issue a right to sue letter to the person who filed the charge.

The EEOC has acknowledged that disputes about ADA requirements are often the result of misunderstandings between employers and disabled people. It emphasizes that those who have a conflict should try to resolve these disputes through informal negotiation or mediation if possible. (See Chapter 8, Section A3, for more on enforcement procedures.)

If an ADA case goes through the formal enforcement procedures and your business is found to have discriminated against a disabled person, you may be ordered to take a number of steps, including: hiring, reinstating or promoting the disabled person; giving back pay or front pay; making reasonable accommodation; or taking other actions. Your company may also have to pay lawyers' fees, expert witness fees and court costs. What's more, if you're found to have discriminated intentionally, your company may have to pay compensatory and punitive damages.

 The following sources can provide additional information about the ADA.

Information about Employment Provisions:

Equal Employment Opportunity Commission
1801 L Street, NW
Washington, DC 20507
202-663-4900
800-669-4000
www.eeoc.gov

Information about Public Accommodation Provisions:

Office on the ADA
U.S. Department of Justice
Civil Rights Division Disability Rights
  Section—NYAVE
950 Pennsylvania Ave., NW
Washington, DC 20530
800-514-0301
www.usdoj.gov/crt/crt-home.html

Architectural and Transportation Barriers
Compliance Board
(the "Access Board")
1331 F Street, NW
Suite 1000
Washington, DC 20004-1111
800-872-2253
www.access-board.gov ■

Chapter 10

Termination

A. Wrongful Discharge Cases 10/3
   1. Statutes 10/3
   2. Court Decisions 10/5

B. Guarding Against Legal Claims 10/7
   1. Having a Valid Reason 10/7
   2. Safely Handling Layoffs 10/7

C. Guidelines for Firing Employees 10/9
   1. Contractual Commitments 10/9
   2. Lawful Reasons for Firing 10/10
   3. Independent Review 10/11

D. Investigating Complaints Against Workers 10/11
   1. The Investigation 10/12
   2. Hiring Investigators 10/12

E. Alternatives to Firing 10/14

F. The Firing Process 10/14
   1. Severance Packages 10/14
   2. Preparing the Paperwork 10/16
   3. Return of Property 10/17
   4. The Termination Meeting 10/18

G. Heading Off Trouble 10/18
   1. Offering a Chance to Resign 10/18

2. Offering a Favorable Reference 10/20

3. Help With Finding a New Job 10/20

H. Final Paychecks 10/20

I. Continuing Health Insurance 10/26

J. Unemployment Compensation 10/26

1. The Claims Process 10/26

2. Saving Money 10/28

K. Protecting Your Business Information 10/29

1. Enforcing Noncompete Agreements 10/29

2. Protecting Trade Secrets 10/30

L. Handling Postemployment Inquiries 10/31

1. Legal Requirements 10/31

2. Deciding What to Say 10/32

*F*iring an employee has always been an uncomfortable task, but it used to be clearcut—and relatively free of legal complications. You simply paid the former employee for accrued wages plus any earned but unused vacation time to which the employee was entitled.

Things are more complicated now. Firing someone—even a person who is demonstrably incompetent—can be a risky endeavor. Do it for the wrong reason or in the wrong way and you can be obligated either to pay substantial money in damages or to rehire the worker.

When firing employees, you must beware of potential legal sticking points. For example, a former employee who believes that he or she was fired in retaliation for reporting a workplace hazard to OSHA may have legal grounds for filing a claim against you. And, in some situations, an employee who asserts that your employee handbook amounted to a contractual guarantee of job security may be found to have a valid claim.

As a result of these and other exceptions to the at-will employment principle, lawsuits by former employees against their former employers have increased. And despite the fact that many employees have been fired for valid reasons, some of them have won cases based on illegal firing simply because the employer was sloppy in terminating the employment relationship.

For a more in-depth discussion of how to fire employees without running afoul of the law or harming your business, see *Dealing With Problem Employees: A Legal Guide,* by attorneys Amy DelPo and Lisa Guerin (Nolo).

A. Wrongful Discharge Cases

Cases in which former employees claim that they were terminated for an improper reason or that an employer bungled the process are known as wrongful discharge cases—and they're based on a number of legal theories. You can better avoid being sued for wrongful discharge if you grasp these legal principles.

Because state laws and court decisions vary in this area, not all of the legal theories for wrongful discharge will be available to all former employees. Also, since the law can change—and many recent changes favor workers, not employers—you need to keep up to date on the specific rules in your state.

Many state trade associations publish newsletters or magazines to help keep their members informed of changes in employment law. Your state chamber of commerce may also have helpful publications on this subject. (For more suggestions on doing your own legal research, see Chapter 13, Section D.)

1. Statutes

If you discriminate illegally in firing an employee, a statute may give him or her the right to sue you for wrongful discharge on that basis. Other statutes prohibit firing an employee for specified reasons, unrelated to discrimination. The main statutes that employees rely upon in asserting wrongful discharge claims are described here.

a. Race, color, religion and national origin discrimination

Under federal law and the laws of many states, it's illegal to discriminate against workers based on race, color, religion or national origin. Don't forget that your state statute may prohibit discrimination based on other characteristics not protected by the federal statute, such as marital status or sexual orientation. (To find out what characteristics your state anti-discrimination laws protect, see Chapter 8, Section G.) These same statutes make it illegal to retaliate against a worker who complains about discrimination or who otherwise asserts his or her rights under the statute. (See Chapter 8.)

b. Age, gender, pregnancy and sexual orientation discrimination

Federal law and the laws of many states bar discrimination based on age, gender and pregnancy. These same statutes make it illegal to retaliate against a worker who complains about discrimination or who otherwise asserts his or her rights under the statute. (See Chapter 8.) And discrimination based on sexual orientation is also prohibited in a growing number of states, cities and counties.

c. Sexual harassment

Sexual harassment is a form of illegal discrimination covered primarily by statutes prohibiting sex discrimination. (See Chapter 8.) If you fire a worker for complaining about sexual harassment, or decide to resolve a harassment problem by getting rid of the harassed employee rather than taking action against the harasser, you will run afoul of these laws.

d. Disability discrimination

Federal law and the laws of many states bar discrimination against people with physical or mental disabilities. They also bar retaliation against people who complain about discrimination or who otherwise assert their rights under these statutes. (See Chapter 9.)

e. Refusal to submit to lie detector test

A federal law, the Employee Polygraph Protection Act, makes it illegal to fire an employee for refusing to take a lie detector test. Many state laws also set out strong prohibitions against using lie detector tests in employment decisions. (See Chapter 1, Section F.)

f. Alien status

The federal Immigration Reform and Control Act prohibits you from using alien status as a reason to fire a worker who is legally eligible to work here. (See Chapter 1, Section K.)

g. Complaining about safety or health conditions

Under the Occupational Safety and Health Act and many state health and safety laws, you can't fire (or otherwise retaliate against) someone for complaining that working conditions don't comply with state or federal safety and health rules. (See Chapter 7.)

2. Court Decisions

Wrongful discharge lawsuits are not always based on statutes. Many courts have awarded wrongful discharge damages to former employees for nonstatutory or common law reasons—that is, legal theories that courts have developed when deciding individual cases. The main ones are discussed here.

a. Breach of contract

Employers sometimes make promises to job applicants to entice them to become employees. And some employers may also dangle inducements in front of current employees to discourage them from leaving. A number of judges have ruled that if a person relies on such promises, an enforceable contract of employment has been created. An employer may be held liable for wrongful discharge if the employee is fired in violation of that contract.

> **EXAMPLE:** Betty, a diligent worker at AutoTec, is offered a job by a rival employer. She declines the job after AutoTec's president tells her she'll have a job for life at AutoTec if she continues to effectively manage her workload. Three years later, AutoTec fires Betty even though she has kept up with her work. Betty sues for wrongful discharge, claiming AutoTec violated its employment contract with her by firing her.

Specific promises of job security—either written or oral—are not always necessary for a judge to rule that an employee can't be fired arbitrarily. Some judges have allowed fired employees to collect damages or be reinstated to jobs because the employer created a legitimate expectation that employees wouldn't be fired without good cause. The typical focus in these cases is on inferences of job security made by the employer in a written document such as an employee handbook. It, too, may be enforced as a contract. (See Chapter 2, Section B, for tips on how to avoid this pitfall.)

EXAMPLE: After six months on the job, Tom is fired from his job at Syspro, a small software house. He sues for wrongful discharge, claiming that Syspro's employee handbook led him to believe that he'd only be fired for good cause—and that, in fact, Syspro fired him without a good reason. The judge agrees that it was reasonable for Tom to conclude, after reading the employee handbook, that his job was secure. The court rules that the employer's wording of the handbook constituted an implied contract.

b. Breach of good faith and fair dealing

Some wrongful discharge cases are based on the premise that every employment relationship includes an automatic commitment by the employer to deal fairly and in good faith with the employee. Applying this doctrine, judges have held that a discharge was wrongful when an employer has dealt arbitrarily with an employee. Many of these cases have involved longtime employees who were fired as they neared retirement age.

EXAMPLE: Rita has worked for Jones Enterprises for nearly 25 years. The company fires her just three months before her retirement benefits are to become permanent. In a wrongful discharge case against Jones, the judge finds that the company fired Rita to save itself the expense of paying her the full benefit of her retirement program. The judge rules in Rita's favor because the firing breached the implied covenant of good faith and fair dealing.

c. Violation of public policy

Judges sometimes rule that a firing was wrongful because it was against the best interests of the public. Most courts do not allow an employer to fire an employee, for instance, because he or she was trying to correct a potentially harmful business practice.

EXAMPLE: Clinical Lab Center, a small company that processes blood tests for doctors, fires Joe, a medical technician, because he has twice complained to management that the inadequate testing of blood samples by other technicians has led to many inaccurate test results. A judge rules that Joe's firing was wrongful because it violated public policy. Workers, the judge notes, should be free to speak up about sloppy practices they find on the job—especially those affecting public health or safety.

Courts have held that it's against public policy to fire a worker for refusing to file phony reports with a state environmental agency, bribe public officials, commit perjury or engage in industrial espionage. Courts have also held that it is against public policy to fire an employee for refusing to commit an illegal act or for threatening to report an employer's illegal conduct. And it generally violates public policy to fire a worker for exercising a legal right—to vote or serve on a jury, for example.

B. Guarding Against Legal Claims

Given the many legal weapons that a disgruntled fired worker can aim at you under the rubric of a wrongful discharge lawsuit, you can understand the danger in blithely carrying on as The Boss, believing in your unfettered right to fire any employee. Consider, too, that juries are often sympathetic to fired workers, regarding them as underdogs—sometimes in the face of considerable evidence to the contrary.

1. Having a Valid Reason

The safest approach any time you fire someone is to be sure you have a legitimate business reason—a reason that you have thought out and documented. If challenged on a particular firing, you should be able to show, for example, that the employee did not adequately perform specific job duties or that the employee violated a clearly stated company policy.

> **EXAMPLE:** The Mail Shoppe employs two men and one woman, Virginia, in its packaging department. One Friday afternoon, the owner fires Virginia. She then files a lawsuit claiming she's been discriminated against because of gender. In court, The Mail Shoppe's owner is able to show that Virginia frequently put too little postage on packages and often neglected to insert the bubble wrap as instructed, causing breakage and numerous customer complaints. The owner also shows that

three written warnings were given to Virginia over a six-week period. The judge dismisses the gender discrimination complaint.

In addition to bolstering your legal position, using an open and consistent policy for disciplining and firing employees will usually help improve worker morale. It's reassuring to hard-working, competent employees to know that they won't be fired on a whim. They'll also respect you for knowing who's getting the job done and who isn't—and they'll likely feel relieved when sloths and incompetent workers are let go.

2. Safely Handling Layoffs

Generally, you're free to lay off or terminate employees because business conditions require a reduction in the workforce. But if you do cut back, don't leave your business open to claims that the layoffs were really a pretext for getting rid of employees for illegal reasons. If your layoff primarily affects black workers, or women or older employees, for example, someone may well question your motives. So if you need to drop employees, be sensitive to how your actions may be perceived. Spread the pain around; don't let the burden of a reduction in force fall on just one group of employees.

If you're a larger employer, you must comply with the Worker Adjustment and Retraining Act, or WARN, (29 U.S.C. § 2101 and following). The law covers your business if:

- you have 100 or more full-time employees, or

• you have 100 or more employees whose total work amounts to 4,000 or more hours a week, not counting overtime hours.

To comply with WARN, you must notify employees if you plan to:

• close an employment site, causing 50 or more full-time employees at the site to lose their jobs, or

• lay off at least one-third—but not fewer than 50—of the full-time employees at a site.

In those situations, you must notify each employee—or the employee's union representative—in writing 60 days before you close the site or lay off the employees. You must also send written notice to the state's dislocated worker unit and the chief elected officer of the municipality where the closing or layoff will take place. There are a number of exceptions to WARN. For example, you needn't give a full 60 days' notice if a closing or layoff is caused by unforeseen business circumstances or a natural disaster.

If you fail to give the required notice, your employees can sue you for back pay and benefits. You may also have to pay penalties if you don't give timely notice to the local government.

For more information, get the pamphlet, "A Guide to Advance Notice of Closings and Layoffs," prepared by the U.S. Department of Labor. It's available at www.doleta.gov/programs/factsh/warn.htm. For detailed information on WARN's requirements and prohibitions—and a complete list of the exceptions to WARN—see *Federal Employment Laws: A Desk Reference,* by Amy DelPo & Lisa Guerin (Nolo).

A Firing Is Sometimes Implied

Usually, it's clear when an employee has been fired. That's because the employer typically informs the employee of that fact in no uncertain terms. Sometimes, however, the termination is much more subtle; if an employer's conduct is so extreme that it makes it virtually impossible for the employee to continue on the job, the employer's conduct may be treated as being equal to a formal firing. In legal jargon, the employer's conduct can add up to a "constructive discharge."

This can occur, for example, where an employer has:

• created an abusive or hostile environment
• insisted that an employee put in excessive overtime
• subjected the employee to intolerable working conditions
• demoted an employee
• offered the employee a "quit or be fired" ultimatum
• substantially changed the employee's job duties, or
• harassed the employee.

The legal consequences of a constructive discharge are exactly the same as an actual discharge: If the employee can show that working conditions really were intolerable, the employee will be able to seek damages for being wrongfully discharged under any of the legal theories discussed in Section A.

C. Guidelines for Firing Employees

Even though your motives for firing someone may be completely honorable and legitimate, you still run a legal risk—the employee may decide to take his or her chances in court, regardless of your actions. But there are several steps you can take to greatly reduce the chances of a former employee suing your business and being awarded a judgment against you.

1. Contractual Commitments

Before you fire an employee, check into whether you've made an oral or written contractual commitment that may limit your right to fire. Consider the following:

- Is there a written or oral contract or document (including a hiring letter) that promises the employee a job for a fixed period of time?
- When you hired the employee, did you make any statements about job security?
- Have you assured the employee that you'd only fire him or her for good cause?
- Have you listed causes for termination—in a contract, employee handbook or elsewhere—in a way that limits you to those specified causes?
- Does your employee handbook or other written policy or memo make any promises about job security?
- Does your company follow written or customary procedures before firing an employee?

Your answers to these questions will help you identify whether you've limited your ability to fire the individual. Even if you are positive that you have never given the employee any assurances of job security—either oral or written—you should still proceed with caution, especially when dealing with an employee who has been with your business for a number of years. Some courts have held that a long employment relationship can imply assurances of job security, which in turn can imply an employment contract that limits your ability to fire the employee. If an employee has only been working for you for a few months—or even for a year—you probably don't have to worry about this issue. If the employee has been with your business for, say, ten years, however, you should be careful. If you don't have a really good reason for firing the employee, consider consulting an attorney before taking action.

Employment contracts can be a two-way street. While they may limit your right to fire an employee, the flipside is that they usually spell out the employee's obligations to your business. If the employee isn't performing well, chances are that he or she is in breach of the contract, giving you the legal right to terminate the relationship. Because the interpretation of contract terms can involve legal subtleties, consider having a brief conference with a lawyer before firing an employee who has a written contract.

Say What You Mean and Mean What You Say

The words you use in hiring someone and in writing an employee handbook can create a contractual commitment that you didn't anticipate. Your employee handbook and similar documents should reserve your right to terminate employees at your discretion. (See Chapter 2, Section B.) While you may also wish to list some specific types of conduct that will result in termination, such as dishonesty or excessive absenteeism, those shouldn't be stated in a way that implies they are the only reasons to end the relationship. Also, your handbook and other communications with employees should not make any promises about long-term job security. If they do, it's time for a rewrite.

---

2. Lawful Reasons for Firing

To head off the possibility that an employee may try to base a wrongful termination action on alleged illegal conduct or motives in your workplace, be prepared to show the real—legitimate—reason for the firing.

Reasons that may support a firing include:

- performing poorly on the job
- refusing to follow instructions
- abusing sick leave
- being absent excessively
- being tardy habitually
- possessing a weapon at work
- violating company rules
- being dishonest
- endangering health and safety
- engaging in criminal activity
- using alcohol or drugs at work
- behaving violently at work
- gambling at work, and
- disclosing company trade secrets to outsiders.

Depending on the nature of your business, you may have other legitimate reasons to fire employees as well. Whatever your reasons, it's absolutely essential that you treat your employees evenhandedly. That is, if you regularly let some employees engage in prohibited conduct, you'll be on shaky legal ground if you fire others for the same reason.

> **EXAMPLE:** Andrew, a black patient attendant, is a half-hour late for work three days in a row. His employer, a medical clinic, fires him. In suing for wrongful discharge based on illegal discrimination,

Andrew shows that two white attendants had been similarly tardy in recent weeks, but received only a verbal warning to shape up. Even though excessive tardiness is a valid business reason for firing someone, the jury awards damages to Andrew because the employer applied the rules unevenly and unfairly.

Getting Help Before Firing a Violent Employee. Almost always, if an employee behaves violently or makes threats in the workplace, that will constitute a valid reason to fire him or her. After all, you need to protect other employees as well as customers and others likely to come into contact with the violent person. Yet, judges in a few cases have suggested that a violent or threatening employee may be entitled to some latitude or accommodation if the violent behavior stems from a mental or emotional disorder. On balance, it's generally best to proceed decisively and fire the violent employee—as humanely as possible, of course. You may, however, want to confer in advance with an experienced employment lawyer to reduce the likelihood of later legal entanglements.

3. Independent Review

Avoid giving an employee's direct supervisor the sole authority to hire and fire. The supervisor may be too close to the situation to make an objective decision. Since firing is such a drastic and traumatic step—and has such potentially serious legal consequences—consider conducting an independent review within your business before anyone is fired. Although this may not be practical in small

companies, you should use this procedure if it's feasible.

Any independent review should verify that:

- the firing wouldn't violate antidiscrimination or other statutes
- the firing wouldn't be a breach of contract, including oral assurances of job security or statements made in an employee handbook
- your company has given the employee adequate and documented warnings that he or she faced being fired—except where the misconduct clearly warrants immediate firing
- you have followed your stated personnel practices, and
- you have followed the same procedures in similar situations involving other employees.

D. Investigating Complaints Against Workers

You may learn of misconduct that requires you to discipline or fire an employee from a complaint by a co-worker, a manager or even a customer or other outsider. This is particularly likely in complaints for sexual harassment or dishonesty.

Investigating the facts can be tricky. The law doesn't require you to learn the truth with absolute certainty—or even beyond a reasonable doubt. But to protect yourself legally, your safest course is to investigate complaints quickly, thoroughly, fairly and as confidentially as is possible under the circumstances—before you penalize or fire an employee.

For a detailed discussion of investigating employee complaints, including step-by-step instructions and sample forms, see *Dealing With Problem Employees: A Legal Guide*, by attorneys Amy DelPo and Lisa Guerin (Nolo).

1. The Investigation

It's usually best to have private interviews with each witness and the accused employee. Listen carefully and take good notes. Don't show any bias for or against the accused. Further investigate any evidence that surfaces, such as a claim that another employee is aware of facts that will shed light on the complaint. Have good reasons for whatever conclusions you reach. If you follow reasonable procedures and reach a reasonable result, you can't be faulted legally, even if another person may have reached a different conclusion.

After an employee files a complaint, it's a good idea to keep him or her informed about the general steps you're taking to investigate. The complaining employee needs to know that you're taking the matter seriously. But that doesn't mean the employee is entitled to know all the details of what you find out. If you give out information too freely, you could easily step on the toes (and violate the privacy rights) of other employees.

2. Hiring Investigators

If you have qualms about your ability to investigate a complaint, consider hiring an experienced employment consultant or someone else who knows the ropes. Far better to lay out some cash to do it right than risk the consequences of a clumsy investigation. For example, if there's an issue of employee dishonesty or criminal conduct, look into companies that specialize in corporate security.

The Fair Credit Reporting Act (FCRA) applies to most investigations by outside investigators. In Chapter 1, Section G, you'll find the requirements for complying with the FCRA when you screen job applicants. That same law also applies when you hire an investigator to look into allegations of employee misconduct. The investigator will probably interview co-workers of the person whose conduct is being looked into, and the investigator is probably in the business of assembling reports for businesses based on such interviews. In short, the investigator likely is a *consumer reporting agency* as defined by the FCRA, and the report furnished to you likely is an *investigative consumer report*. This means that before you order the report, you need to get the written authorization of the person under investigation. After you get the report, special rules apply if you're going to fire or discipline the person based on it (see Chapter 1, Section G, for details). Complying with the FCRA can hamper your ability to investigate allegations of sexual harassment or other misconduct. Many people view this as an unintended consequence of the legislation. Unfortunately, to avoid FCRA compliance, your choices are to hire an investigator who doesn't regularly conduct investigations covered by the statute (usually not a great idea) or to limit yourself to a strictly internal investigation.

Investigations May Help Establish Good Faith

A California case illustrates the value of conducting a fair and thorough investigation. An insurance brokerage firm received complaints that Ralph, a senior vice president, had sexually harassed other employees. Ralph denied the charges, so the company interviewed 21 people who worked with Ralph—including five that he asked be interviewed. The company concluded that it was more likely than not that harassment had occurred, so it fired Ralph.

Ralph sued for wrongful discharge, claiming he had an implied contract requiring good cause for firing him and that there was no good cause because he had not engaged in the alleged misconduct. The jury agreed that the company had not proven that Ralph had sexually harassed anyone—and it returned a verdict of $1.8 million against the company. But on appeal, the California Supreme Court reversed the verdict.

The court ruled that it wasn't necessary for the company to prove that Ralph had actually committed the sexual harassment. The company had only to show that it had a good faith belief that Ralph had engaged in the misconduct. The results of the company's extensive investigation were sufficient to establish that good faith belief. *Cotran v. Rollins Hudig Hall Int'l, Inc.*, 948 P.2d 412 (1998).

Similarly, if someone charges sexual harassment because a manager has displayed offensive cartoons or photos in a work area, consider hiring a consultant experienced in sexual harassment issues to review your entire workplace and recommend a course of action. Bringing in an outsider may also help to defuse tensions between workers—especially if anyone involved in the incident doubts the company's ability to be impartial.

Locating a Good Investigator

When you suspect an employee of dishonesty or criminal conduct, a private investigator may help sort out the facts. The job of interviewing witnesses, analyzing documents, watching for misconduct and preserving evidence isn't easy. The investigator must follow procedures that respect the accused employee's legal rights. If a court later finds that you trampled an employee's due process rights during an investigation, your business may have to pay for that violation.

It's crucial to find an investigator who's experienced in conducting internal investigations for businesses. There are many people who have recently hung out their shingles as consultants, but don't really have training or experience.

This is sensitive work and the stakes are high. No matter where you find names of possible investigators—from phone book listings, management newsletters, trade associations or other businesspeople—ask for references. Look for positive feedback from at least two or three other businesses before you hire an investigator.

E. Alternatives to Firing

Sometimes, firing a troublesome employee is the best course of action. You owe it to your business—and to your diligent, conscientious employees—to get rid of a troublemaker who can't be turned around. But occasionally, there are good alternatives to firing a worker —alternatives that can help you avoid the risk of a wrongful discharge lawsuit while at the same time providing the spared employee with a chance to better use his or her skills.

One possibility is to redesign the employee's job to eliminate the problem areas. Or you may assign the employee to another job. For example, an employee who has a tendency to quarrel with customers, but is otherwise organized and efficient, might do an excellent job working alone in the warehouse. Of course, you must be careful not to unload work unfairly on other employees who are already working at peak efficiency.

If yours is a slightly larger business, and there's a personality clash between an employee and a supervisor, you may be able to assign the employee to a different supervisor. Where the conflict is between two employees, neither of whom is a supervisor, you may be able to assign them to separate work areas. If a personal problem is at the root of an otherwise good employee's difficulties, you might offer to pay for at least a limited amount of counseling—or offer the employee a leave of absence to get help with the problem.

Sometimes you and an employee can come to an understanding that the working relationship isn't a good fit for either of you

and that the employee is expected to move elsewhere in the near future. Allowing the employee to look for a new job during regular working hours may be one rational way to handle such a situation.

F. The Firing Process

Where possible, give employees ongoing feedback about job performance, conduct formal job evaluations once or twice a year and impose progressive discipline. (See Chapter 2.) Ideally, a firing shouldn't come suddenly or as a surprise.

When you've reached the point where firing an employee is the best or only option, you must mind some legal strictures as you carry out the firing.

Speedy Action Is Sometimes Appropriate. There can be situations in which moving quickly to fire someone—without a warning— may be the best course. For example, if your delivery truck driver is convicted of drunk driving, it makes sense to get rid of the driver. Similarly, you shouldn't feel it necessary to give advance warning to a bookkeeper who has embezzled money from your company. In general, use your judgment and err on the side of giving an employee a chance to correct a problem. But in extreme circumstances, don't hesitate to act quickly.

1. Severance Packages

Many employers and employees wrongly believe that every fired employee is legally entitled to severance pay. The truth is that the law only requires you to give severance in those instances where you have promised the employee that you would do so—for example, though a contract with the employee, through a written policy in your employee handbook or through a clearly established pattern of conduct in which you have given severance to other employees in similar circumstances. Even if the law does not require you to pay severance, however, you may wish to offer severance pay and other benefits to help cushion the impact of a firing—and alleviate ill will.

If you're inclined to offer a severance package, it makes sense to be more generous with longtime employees than with those who have been with you just a year or two. For a short-term employee—someone who's worked for you for two years, for example—you might offer one month's pay plus payment of health insurance premiums for 90 days. For an employee who's been on your payroll for 15 years, it would be reasonable to offer six months of salary plus one year's worth of paid health insurance premiums.

You can be creative in putting together a severance package. The benefits you may wish to consider include:

- severance pay
- continuation of employee benefits, such as payment of health insurance premiums for a limited time
- a favorable letter of reference if your normal policy is to give only a former employee's position and term of employment

- releasing the employee from special obligations (such as a covenant not to compete)
- allowing the employee to keep any advance of expense funds or commissions that otherwise would be repayable to your business
- allowing the employee to keep the desk, chair, computer, cellular phone or tools that he or she has been using
- agreeing not to contest the employee's right to unemployment compensation
- paying for outplacement services, and
- promising to pay an employee's moving expenses, up to a stated limit.

Also, consider paying the employee for unused vacation time that the employee would otherwise lose. Unless state law requires you to pay out unused vacation time, you are free to adopt a policy whereby departing employees forfeit any unused vacation days.

EXAMPLE: Alpine Ski Shop pays its employees for two weeks of vacation time each year, but states in its employee's handbook: "You must take your vacation during June, July or August and while you are on Alpine's payroll. Vacation time not used during that period will be forfeited unless you secure prior approval." Employee Kurt takes one week of his vacation in July and doesn't ask for permission to take the second week later. In October, Alpine fires Kurt because of an attitude problem. As part of a severance package, Alpine pays Kurt for the unused week of vacation time.

Paying for Vacation Time May Be Mandatory. In some states, the law doesn't allow an employer to set a policy forcing employees to forfeit unused vacation or sick time once it has accrued. In such states, the accrued vacation or sick time is treated as wages and must be included in an employee's final paycheck. The key legal issue is whether the vacation time has already been earned. Check with the state department of labor to learn how much latitude you have regarding payment for vacation and sick time. (See the Appendix for contact details.)

2. Preparing the Paperwork

Before you fire an employee, prepare a letter describing the severance package you intend to offer. And if you want the employee to waive possible legal claims against your business to qualify for the severance benefits, consider preparing a severance agreement as well.

a. Termination letter

To soften the shock of a firing, you may wish to present the employee with a letter such as the following during the termination meeting.

Sample Termination Letter— No Release Required

Dear Joe Shmoe

Your employment with XYZ Company is being terminated at 5 p.m. on July 1, 20XX.

You will receive a paycheck covering the wages you have earned and for your accrued vacation time. In addition, you will receive the following severance benefits:

1. Four weeks of additional pay.

2. Payment of your health insurance premiums for six months (or until you begin work at a new job, if that occurs sooner).

3. You will be allowed to keep the $500 advanced to you for job-related expenses.

4. The Company will not contest your right to receive unemployment compensation.

I wish you well in your further endeavors.

June 10, 20XX

Lars Ingram
President, XYZ Company

Use such a letter if you're not requiring the employee to sign a release waiving possible legal claims against your business to qualify for the severance package.

b. Release of claims

You may wish to provide a severance package to a terminating employee only if the employee agrees to waive all potential legal claims—a reasonable condition in many situations.

For a release to be enforceable, you must offer the employee something of value—for example, the severance package—in exchange for giving up his or her possible claims against your business.

If the law already requires you to pay severance (for example, because you have already promised it to the employee through a written contract), then you must give something to the employee beyond what the severance package requires in exchange for the employee signing the release. (See Section F1, above, for an explanation of when you are required to give severance to your employees.)

Also, give the employee a reasonable time—two or three weeks, for example—to decide whether to accept your severance package and sign the severance agreement containing a release of claims. A coerced release is legally worthless.

Special rules apply if the employee is releasing claims under the Age Discrimination in Employment Act. If you present a release to an individual employee who's 40 years old or older, you must give the employee a fixed period of time in which to decide on signing the waiver. That period must be at least 21 days if the waiver has been presented to the employee alone. If you've presented the waiver to a group or class of employees, you must give each worker at least 45 days to decide whether or not to sign. In either case, a worker has seven days after agreeing to such a waiver to revoke his or her decision. (See Chapter 8, Section C2, for details.)

 For more information on severance agreements, see "Using Releases in Employment Termination Cases," by Nancy E. Sasamoto and Stephen M. Proctor, *The Practical Lawyer,* June 1994. A single issue of *The Practical Lawyer* costs $9. An annual subscription, consisting of eight issues, costs $40. Call 800-253-6397 or write 4025 Chestnut Street, Philadelphia, PA 19104-3099. You can also email the publisher at www.publications@ali-aba.org.

3. Return of Property

In planning for the termination meeting, make a list of all company property that has been given to the employee. Be prepared to get these items back from the employee either at the meeting or within a reasonable time afterward. Items to think about include:

- automobiles
- computers, cellular phones and beepers
- confidential manuals and other documents
- keys, credit cards, uniforms, ID badges, and
- parking permits.

Don't overlook any expense account funds you advanced to the employee. You may be entitled to deduct such advances from the employee's final paycheck. (See Section H for more legal rules on final paychecks.)

4. The Termination Meeting

Call the employee into a private office or meeting room and inform him or her of your decision. Be honest and direct in stating your reasons for ending the employment. If you've given the employee ongoing feedback, the firing shouldn't come as a complete shock. Make it clear that this is a final decision and that you're not going to change your mind. Unless the employee is likely to be a menace in the workplace, allow a day or so—but no longer—to clear out his or her desk and say goodbye to co-workers.

Go over any severance package the employee will receive—and explain the severance agreement if you require one to be signed. (See Section 2, above.)

Then give the employee a reasonable chance to vent his or her feelings about the discharge. Just listen and don't argue. Don't insult or abuse the employee no matter how angry, bitter or insulting he or she is to you. Typically, the employee's anger and disappointment will fade with time.

The Right to Have a Co-Worker Present. All employees have the right to have a co-worker present with them at investigatory interviews or meetings that the employee believes will result in disciplinary action from their employer. Disciplinary action could include termination.

This right is called a Weingarten right after a U.S. Supreme Court decision. (To read that decision—*NLRB v. J. Weingarten,* 420 U.S. 251 (1975)—go to Nolo's Legal Research Center at www.nolo.com.) That decision only gave the right to employees who were members of a union. In 2000, however, that right was expanded to nonunion employees as well.

Although no court has held that employers have an affirmative duty to inform employees of this right, it's prudent to do so—and to allow the employee to have a witness by his or her side.

G. Heading Off Trouble

As noted, there are many ways to fortify your legal position so that an employee will be less likely to succeed in a claim against you for wrongful discharge. Some additional practical steps can help you keep the goodwill of an employee who's being terminated, making it less likely that you'll be sued in the first place.

1. Offering a Chance to Resign

Permitting the employee to resign gives him or her the opportunity to save face—which, in turn, may make the employee less bitter about the termination and less hostile to your business. Be aware, however, that if you give the employee a stark choice between resigning and being fired, it's probably not legally considered a voluntary termination. The

Common Sense Can Help Avert Violence

You may have zeroed in on scary newspaper headlines about disgruntled former employees who open fire on former employers. Although the actual incidence of such violence is quite low, it pays to be prudent.

Violence following a firing is most apt to occur in a workplace where there are high levels of stress, autocratic and unpredictable managers, poor communication and employees who feel powerless.

Be especially careful if you're firing an employee for performing poorly—a charge that may be emotionally loaded. Some workers who are fired without warning can go over the edge because they feel there was nothing they could do to control the situation. In giving feedback before a firing, let workers know if their performances are below par—and focus on the specific ways in which job performance falls short of the mark. Warn workers that they may lose their jobs if they don't improve.

At a termination meeting with a potentially volatile employee, confine your discussion to the specific behavior about which the employee was warned. Never attack the worker personally. Remind the worker that he or she was given fair warning and an ample opportunity to change work habits.

Let the fired employee know that you won't be discussing the reasons for the firing with his or her former co-workers. This will help preserve the employee's self-esteem, making violence less likely.

Troubled employees often exhibit behavioral clues that you shouldn't ignore: high absenteeism, known substance abuse, chronic tardiness, fascination with weapons and harassing and threatening others. If you're about to fire someone who appears to have a potential for violence, consider consulting first with a psychologist who specializes in workplace issues.

employee likely will be eligible for unemployment compensation benefits. (See Section J.) And a forced resignation may be treated the same as a firing if the employee does decide to sue for wrongful discharge.

2. Offering a Favorable Reference

If you would be willing to give a former employee a positive reference, tell him or her as soon as possible. Knowing that he or she will get a favorable recommendation can help temper a worker's ire over a termination. Obviously, such a reference isn't always possible. But quite often, an employee who wasn't a good fit at your business could do well elsewhere and you won't have a difficult time emphasizing the employee's good qualities.

When other employers call, follow through and accentuate the positive. Keep in touch with the former employee by phone and by sending copies of any letters in which you state positive things (for more on references, see Section L).

3. Help With Finding a New Job

You may be able to inform an employee of openings elsewhere that would be better suited to his or her skills and personality. Or, if it's a longtime employee to whom you feel a lot of loyalty, you may even consider footing the bill to have a personnel agency assist the employee in finding another job. Another possibility is to give an employee paid time off to find a new job—using your phone, if necessary, to call prospects.

H. Final Paychecks

Most states have a law specifying when you must give a final paycheck to a terminated employee. Most of these laws set different deadlines for employees who have quit and those who have been fired. (See the following chart.) If you don't give a final paycheck on time, you may have to pay damages to the employee and perhaps a penalty to the state as well.

Note that in many states, the law requires that the final paycheck include accrued vacation pay and anything else owed to an employee who's covered by the law. If you have additional questions about final paychecks, contact the wage and hour division of your state's labor department to double-check your state law. (See the Appendix for contact details.)

State Laws That Control Final Paychecks

State	Paycheck due when employee is fired	Paycheck due when employee quits voluntarily	Unused vacation pay included	Contract employees or certain industries
Alaska Alaska Stat. § 23.05.140	Within 3 days.	Next regular payday at least 3 days after employee gave notice.	Yes	
Arizona Ariz. Rev. Stat. § 23-353	Next payday or within 3 days, whichever is sooner.	Next payday.	Yes	
Arkansas Ark. Code Ann. § 11-4-405	Within 7 days from discharge date.	No provision.		Railroad or railroad construction employees: pay due on day of discharge.
California Cal. Lab. Code §§ 201, 202, 227.3	Immediately.	Immediately if employee has given 72 hours notice; otherwise, within 72 hours.	Yes	Seasonal agricultural workers: within 72 hours of termination. Motion picture business: if fired, within 24 hours (excluding weekends & holidays); if laid off, next payday. Oil drilling industry: within 24 hours (excluding weekends & holidays) of layoff or discharge.
Colorado Colo. Rev. Stat. § 8-4-104	Immediately.	Next payday.	Yes	
Connecticut Conn. Gen. Stat. Ann. § 31-71c	Next business day after discharge.	Next payday.		
Delaware Del. Code Ann. tit. 19, § 1103	Next payday.	Next payday.		
District of Columbia D.C. Code Ann. § 32-1303	Next business day.	Next payday or 7 days from date of quitting, whichever is sooner.	Yes	
Hawaii Haw. Rev. Stat. § 388-3	Immediately.	Next payday.		

State Laws That Control Final Paychecks (continued)

State	Paycheck due when employee is fired	Paycheck due when employee quits voluntarily	Unused vacation pay included	Contract employees or certain industries
Idaho Idaho Code § 45-606	Next payday or within 10 days (excluding weekends & holidays), whichever is sooner. If employee makes written request for earlier payment, within 48 hours of receipt of request (excluding weekends & holidays).	Next payday or within 10 days (excluding weekends & holidays), whichever is sooner. If employee makes written request for earlier payment, within 48 hours of receipt of request (excluding weekends & holidays).	Yes	
Illinois 820 Ill. Comp. Stat. § 115/5	At time of separation if possible, but no later than next payday.	At time of separation if possible, but no later than next payday.	Yes	
Indiana Ind. Code Ann. §§ 22-2-5-1, 22-2-9-2	Next payday.	Next payday.		
Iowa Iowa Code §§ 91A.4, 91A.27(b)	Next payday.	Next payday.	Yes	If employee is owed commission, employer has 30 days to pay.
Kansas Kan. Stat. Ann. § 44-315	Next payday.	Next payday.		
Kentucky Ky. Rev. Stat. Ann. §§ 337.010(c), 337.055	Next payday or 14 days, whichever is later.	Next payday or 14 days, whichever is later.	Yes	
Louisiana La. Rev. Stat. Ann. § 23:631	Next payday or within 15 days, whichever is earlier.	Next payday or within 15 days, whichever is earlier.	Yes	
Maine Me. Rev. Stat. Ann. tit. 26, § 626	Next payday or within 2 weeks of requesting final pay, whichever is sooner.	Next payday or within 2 weeks of requesting final pay, whichever is sooner.	Yes	
Maryland Md. Code Ann., [Lab. & Empl.] § 3-505	Next scheduled payday.	Next scheduled payday.		

State Laws That Control Final Paychecks (continued)

State	Paycheck due when employee is fired	Paycheck due when employee quits voluntarily	Unused vacation pay included	Contract employees or certain industries
Massachusetts Mass. Gen. Laws ch. 149, § 148	Day of discharge.	Next payday. If no scheduled payday, then following Saturday.	Yes	
Michigan Mich. Comp. Laws §§ 408.474 to 408.475	Next payday.	Next payday.	Yes	Hand-harvesters of crops: within one working day of termination.
Minnesota Minn. Stat. Ann. §§ 181.13 to 181.14	Within 24 hours.	Next payday. If payday is less than 5 days from last day of work, then following payday or 20 days from last day of work, whichever is earlier.	Yes	Migrant workers who resign: within 5 days.
Missouri Mo. Rev. Stat. § 290.110	Day of discharge.	No provision.		
Montana Mont. Code Ann. § 39-3-205	Fired for cause or laid off, immediately (unless employer has written policy that extends time to next payday or 15 days).	Next payday or within 15 days, whichever comes first.		
Nebraska Neb. Rev. Stat. §§ 48-1229 to 48-1230	Next payday or within 2 weeks, whichever is sooner.	No provision.	Yes	
Nevada Nev. Rev. Stat. Ann. §§ 608.020 to 608.030	Immediately.	Next payday or 7 days, whichever is earlier.		
New Hampshire N.H. Rev. Stat. Ann. §§ 275:43(III), 275:44	Within 72 hours. If laid off, next payday.	Next payday or within 72 hours if employee gives one pay period's notice.	Yes	
New Jersey N.J. Stat. Ann. § 34:11-4.3	Next payday.	Next payday.		

		State Laws That Control Final Paychecks (continued)		
State	Paycheck due when employee is fired	Paycheck due when employee quits voluntarily	Unused vacation pay included	Contract employees or certain industries
New Mexico N.M. Stat. Ann. §§ 50-4-4 to 50-4-5	Within 5 days.	Next payday.		If paid by task or commission, 10 days after discharge.
New York N.Y. Lab. Law §§ 191, 198-c	Next payday.	Next payday.	Yes	
North Carolina N.C. Gen. Stat. §§ 95-25.7, 95-25.12	Next payday.	Next payday.	Yes	If paid by commission or bonus, on next payday after amount calculated.
North Dakota N.D. Cent. Code § 34-14-03	Next payday. Must pay by certified mail or as agreed upon by both parties.	Next payday.		
Oklahoma Okla. Stat. Ann. tit. 40, §§ 165.1 to 165.3	Next payday.	Next payday.	Yes	
Oregon Or. Rev. Stat. §§ 652.140 to 652.145	First business day after termination.	If 48 hours notice given, immediately (excluding weekends & holidays). Otherwise, within 5 days (excluding weekends & holidays) or next payday, whichever comes first.	Yes	Seasonal farm workers: if fired or quitting with 48 hours notice, immediately; if quitting without notice, within 48 hours or next payday, whichever comes first.
Pennsylvania 43 Pa. Cons. Stat. Ann. § 260.5	Next payday.	Next payday.		
Rhode Island R.I. Gen. Laws § 28-14-4	Next payday.	Next payday.	Yes (if employee has worked for one full year)	
South Carolina S.C. Code Ann. § 41-10-50	Within 48 hours or next payday, which may not be more than 30 days.	Within 48 hours or next payday, which may not be more than 30 days.		

State Laws That Control Final Paychecks (continued)

State	Paycheck due when employee is fired	Paycheck due when employee quits voluntarily	Unused vacation pay included	Contract employees or certain industries
South Dakota S.D. Codified Laws Ann. §§ 60-11-10 to 60-11-11	Next payday (extended if employee has not returned employer's property).	Next payday (extended if employee has not returned employer's property).		
Tennessee Tenn. Code Ann. § 50-2-103	Next payday or 21 days, whichever is later.	Next payday or 21 days, whichever is later.	Yes	
Texas Tex. Lab. Code Ann. § 61.014	Within 6 days.	Next payday.		
Utah Utah Code Ann. § 34-28-5	Within 24 hours.	Next payday.		
Vermont Vt. Stat. Ann. tit. 21, § 342(c)(1)	Within 72 hours.	Next payday.		
Virginia Va. Code Ann. § 40.1-29	Next payday.	Next payday.		
Washington Wash. Rev. Code Ann. § 49.48.010	Next payday.	Next payday.		
West Virginia W.Va. Code §§ 21-5-1, 21-5-4	Within 72 hours.	If employee has given one pay period's notice, immediately; otherwise, next payday.	Yes	
Wisconsin Wis. Stat. Ann. §§ 109.01(3), 109.03	Next payday. If termination is due to merger, relocation or liquidation of business, within 24 hours.	Next payday.	Yes	Does not apply to sales agents working on commission basis.
Wyoming Wyo. Stat. Ann. § 27-4-104	Within 5 working days.	Within 5 working days.		

Current as of June 2002

I. Continuing Health Insurance

If you have 20 or more employees and you offer a group health insurance plan, a federal law called the Consolidated Omnibus Budget Reconciliation Act or COBRA requires you to offer former employees the option of continuing their coverage for some time after their employment ends. Your state may also have a health insurance continuation law. (For more, see Chapter 4, Section A.)

J. Unemployment Compensation

Employees who are terminated because of cutbacks or because they are not a good fit for a job are generally entitled to unemployment benefits under state unemployment insurance programs. Employees who are fired for serious misconduct—stealing or selling drugs in the workplace, for example —or who voluntarily leave a job without good cause, are not entitled to unemployment payments.

Applying these categories to a particular termination isn't always easy. For example, suppose you and an employee get into an argument and she leaves shortly afterward. If she has quit, benefits are not legally due. If she was fired, however, she's entitled to unemployment benefits absent truly bad conduct. It's sometimes difficult to discern whether a termination is a quitting or a firing.

1. The Claims Process

Although the details of unemployment compensation vary in each state, some general principles apply in most cases. As a private employer, you contribute a relatively small amount to an unemployment insurance fund in your state. Your rate is normally based on the size of your payroll and the amount of unemployment benefits paid from your account. Employers with smaller payrolls and low levels of unemployment claims will, over time, pay lower taxes.

An unemployment claim typically proceeds through a number of steps.

a. Filing the claim

The former employee files a claim with the state unemployment program. You receive written notice of the claim and can file a written objection—usually within seven to ten days. If you want to file an objection, don't miss this deadline. If you do, you may not be allowed to object.

b. Eligibility determined

The state agency makes an initial determination of whether the former employee is eligible to get unemployment benefits. Usually there's no hearing at this stage.

c. Referee's hearing

You or the former employee can appeal the initial eligibility decision and request a hearing before a referee—a hearing officer who is on the staff of the state agency. Normally conducted in a private room at the unemployment office, this airing of the situation is the most important step in the process. At the hearing, you and the former employee each have your say. In addition, you're entitled to have a lawyer there and to present witnesses and any relevant written records, such as employee evaluations or warning letters.

Before the hearing, ask to see the agency's complete file on the claim. This will give you a chance to be prepared to refute inaccurate statements. Bring all pertinent employment records to the hearing. Also, line up witnesses who can give firsthand testimony about why the former employee was guilty of misconduct, quit voluntarily or is otherwise ineligible for benefits.

It may be too expensive to hire a lawyer to handle an unemployment compensation hearing. In some states, you have the alternative of hiring an experienced nonlawyer specialist to oppose claims at a fraction of what lawyers charge. A clerk in the referee's office may know of someone who performs these services in your area. But since the procedures in the hearing are designed to be simple and nontechnical, you probably won't need any hired help.

⚠ Serious Charges May Be Raised. The referee's decision sometimes influences what happens in a related civil lawsuit. For example, if the referee rules that the employee quit because he or she was being sexually harassed, that ruling may be decisive in a later harassment lawsuit that the employee brings

against your business. Consult a lawyer if you anticipate that complicated legal issues—such as sexual harassment, illegal discrimination or retaliation for complaining about a workplace hazard—may surface at the hearing.

d. Administrative appeal

Either side can appeal the referee's decision to an administrative agency, sometimes called a board of review. This appeal usually is based solely on the testimony and documents recorded at the referee's hearing, although some states allow the review board to hear additional evidence. While the review board is free to draw its own conclusions from the evidence and overrule the referee, it usually goes along with the referee's ruling.

e. Judicial appeal

Either side can appeal to the state court system, but this is rare. Typically, a court will overturn the agency's decision only if the decision is contrary to law or isn't supported by substantial evidence.

 For more information, see *Employer's Unemployment Cost Control Handbook,* published by the National Foundation for Unemployment Compensation and Workers' Compensation, 1201 New York Avenue, NW, Suite 750, Washington, DC 20005; 202-682-1515. The cost is $20. You can also email the organization at info@uwcstrategy.org. While the book recommends taking a more aggressive stance in fighting claims than may be prudent, it also contains lots of useful information.

Doing Your Own Research

Many states keep records of decisions by the review board. By looking at these records, you can see how cases similar to yours were decided. This can be a helpful resource if you represent your business in an administrative appeal. Your state's unemployment agency can tell you if and where such decisions are kept for public inspection.

Similarly, when an unemployment case is reviewed by a state appeals court, the written decision becomes a public record and is placed in bound books alongside other court decisions. To locate court decisions dealing with unemployment law, start with the annotated version of your state's statutes—often called an annotated code. It should be available at larger public libraries.

Look up the unemployment compensation law and you'll find short summaries of each case in which an appeals court interpreted the law. If there are cases that sound similar to yours, look up the full decision in the case reports—the books that collect all appeals court decisions in your state. (For more on how to do your own legal research, see Chapter 13, Section D.)

2. Saving Money

In theory, at least, you'll save money if you recognize and successfully oppose questionable claims. But this isn't always true, for several reasons. First, lots of claims you think are questionable probably will be allowed under unemployment compensation laws, which are deliberately lenient to give unemployed workers a transitional source of income. Unless there's strong evidence that the employee pilfered from the company or engaged in other fairly extreme conduct, he or she will usually win in a claims contest.

Second, fighting a claim can be time consuming, emotionally draining and costly for you—especially when balanced against the fact that a few unemployment claims spread over several years are unlikely to greatly increase your insurance rate. Third, fighting an unemployment claim will guarantee an angry former employee—a person far more likely to file a lawsuit or harm you or your business in some other way. Of course, this might happen anyway. But your challenge to the employee's right to receive unemployment benefits may be the irritant that prompts the former employee to strike back.

Balance the benefits of saving on unemployment taxes against the trouble it takes to fight the claim and the risk of inviting a lawsuit against your business.

In addition to challenging questionable claims, there are other ways you may be able to reduce the costs of unemployment benefits.

Doublecheck the information your state unemployment agency uses to compute your tax rates and to compute benefits paid to former employees. Make sure the agency's records don't indicate that your business has had more claims filed against it than it really did have. Clerical errors can be costly.

Also, keep in mind that a former employee may be eligible for benefits at first, but later become ineligible. For example, three weeks after being fired, a claimant may decide to return to school full time, meaning that he or she is unavailable to take a new job. Or a former employee may receive retirement or vacation pay that means he or she is no longer eligible for unemployment benefits or that the amounts should be reduced. Or you may hear that the employee is working for another business, but being paid under the table so as to keep getting unemployment benefits. If you learn any such information, notify the state agency promptly.

K. Protecting Your Business Information

Some employees have access to sensitive business information or trade secrets. When these employees leave—either because they quit or because you've fired them—you may be concerned that they'll use this information to their personal advantages. For example, a former employee may open a business that competes with yours or go to work for a competitor.

Chapter 1, Section A5, discusses how you can protect yourself by asking certain employees to sign covenants not to compete and agreements not to divulge or use trade secrets. This section explains what to do if a former employee begins to compete unfairly with your business in violation of such a covenant or agreement.

1. Enforcing Noncompete Agreements

You might assume it would be difficult to learn whether a former employee is competing with you. However, many businesses are fairly public, which makes it difficult for a former employee to hide. Also, there's a good chance that you'll be contacted by your loyal customers if they are approached by the former employee. The lure of a lower price offered by the former employee often isn't enough to win over a customer who suspects the former employee of cheating you.

If the former employee's conduct violates a valid noncompete agreement and your business will suffer immediate damage, you can seek a court order (called an injunction) to put a legal stop to the unfair activities. You'll probably need to hire a lawyer to help. (See Chapter 13, Section A.)

Fortunately, the procedures for getting a ruling from a judge in this situation are fairly fast and efficient. A lawyer will likely ask the judge assigned to your case to set an early hearing to decide whether to issue a preliminary injunction—an order that prohibits the former employee from unfairly competing with you while the case is pending. A judge who's convinced that the threat of damage to your business is great may even grant a temporary restraining order forbidding the former employee from taking any action until the initial hearing can be held.

A restraining order or injunction is a powerful legal weapon. If a former employee violates such an order, he or she can be found in contempt of court. The punishment for contempt is a fine, imprisonment or both.

Weighing Your Chances of Success

Whether a judge will enforce a covenant not to compete is always an iffy question. The legal system puts a high value on a person's right to earn a living. In California, non-competes are illegal in all but the most limited circumstances. Elsewhere, covenants not to compete won't be enforced if they're found to be unreasonable. A covenant may be held unreasonable if it covers too wide a geographic area or lasts for too long a time.

EXAMPLE: Walt—a veterinarian who operates three animal hospitals in Anderson County—hires Fred, another veterinarian, to work for him. Fred signs an employment contract which states that for three years after his employment ends, he won't practice veterinary medicine within 15 miles of any veterinary practice operated by Walt. Together, the three prohibited areas embrace nearly all of Anderson County, plus parts of several adjoining counties. The contract also states that Fred will pay $30,000 in damages if he violates the covenant.

Fred quits his job and begins a mobile veterinary practice in Anderson County, bringing his work within the restricted areas. Walt sues Fred for $30,000 but the court holds the covenant can't be enforced because it's unreasonably broad. (*Stringer v. Herron*, 424 S.E.2d 547 (1992).)

A covenant may also be held unreasonable if the information revealed to the worker isn't all that sensitive.

EXAMPLE: Image Supplies Inc., a printing supply company in Chicago, hires John as a salesman. John signs a covenant stating that for one year after his job ends, he won't compete with Image Supplies within 100 miles of Image Supplies' headquarters. John resigns and goes to work for a competitor in the Chicago area.

Image Supplies seeks an injunction—a court order prohibiting John from working for the competitor—because John has the names and locations of its customers and the prices charged to each customer. The court refuses to grant an injunction. It holds that Image Supplies has no protectable business interest in the information that John has. The names of firms in the printing business are easily found in the phone book and trade publications, and anyone can learn about prices by asking the customer. (*Image Supplies Inc. v. Hilmert*, 390 N.E.2d 68 (1979).)

Judges are more likely to enforce restrictive covenants against high-level managers who truly are given inside information. Such former employees are in a position to do real harm.

2. Protecting Trade Secrets

A trade secret is information that gives you a competitive advantage because it isn't generally known and can't be readily learned by other people who could benefit from it. It can be a formula, pattern, compilation, program, device, method, technique or other process that you've made reasonable efforts to keep secret.

A judge may order the employee not to use information even if he or she didn't sign a secrecy agreement—but you must show that what the employee took is truly a trade secret. This usually involves establishing two things: that the information was not readily obtainable elsewhere, and that you took precautions to keep it secret. For example, if you developed a unique plant fertilizer that you manufacture and distribute, you should be able to establish that you created the fertilizer through extensive trial and error and then made sure that employees learned the formula on a strict need-to-know basis.

Similarly, if you put together a valuable customer list that includes your customers' buying history and buying habits, you should be able to show that you painstakingly built up the list over several years and that you only allowed a limited number of employees to see it. (For more on trade secret protection, see Chapter 1, Section A.)

L. Handling Postemployment Inquiries

One of your knottiest dilemmas after an employee quits or has been fired is deciding what to tell other businesses that inquire about the former employee. You may be tugged in several directions.

- You want to tell the truth—good, bad or neutral—about the former worker.
- You may want to help the former worker find another job for which he or she is better suited.
- You may fear that if you do say anything negative, you'll be sued for libel or slander.
- You may feel that the best way to head off a possible lawsuit or complaint by an angry employee is to help him or her find another job.
- You don't want to overpraise a marginal employee and risk the anger of the new employer.

The law doesn't require you to completely clam up about a former employee. If you follow some basic legal guidelines, you can disclose significant information about the former employee without risking a lawsuit.

1. Legal Requirements

The key to protecting yourself is to stick to the facts and act in good faith. When you go beyond the facts or are motivated by a desire to harm the former employee or cover up the truth, you can find yourself in deep trouble.

Former employees who feel maligned can sue for defamation—called slander if the statements were spoken or libel if they were written. To win a defamation case, a former employee must prove that you gave out false information and that the information harmed his or her reputation. If you can prove that the information you gave out was true, the defamation lawsuit will be dismissed.

And employers in most states are entitled to limited protection in defamation cases, even if the information they provide is false. This is based on a legal doctrine called "qualified privilege." To receive the benefit of this protection, you must show that:

- you made the statement in good faith
- you and the person to whom you disclosed the information shared a common interest, and
- you limited your statement to this common interest.

The law recognizes that a former employer and a prospective employer share a common interest in the attributes of an employee. To get the protection of the qualified privilege, your main task is to stick to facts that you've reasonably investigated and to lay aside your personal feelings about the former employee.

If you can establish that you're protected by the qualified privilege, the only way a former employee can succeed in a defamation lawsuit is to prove that you knew the information was false but you passed it on anyway, or that you acted recklessly in sorting out the facts.

 Speaking Candidly. In a trend designed to encourage fuller disclosure in responding to reference checks, some states have laws that allow you to be more candid about former employees. Generally, these laws expand on the common law principles that protect you if you act in good faith. In Kansas, for example, the law presumes that you're acting in good faith when you respond to a reference check.

Under that law, to collect damages for a bad reference, the former employee must prove by "clear and convincing evidence" that you acted in bad faith. If your state has a similar law, you can rest a bit easier when discussing former employees.

2. Deciding What to Say

A practical policy—and one that gives you a high degree of legal protection—is simply not to discuss an employee with prospective employers if you can't say something positive. Just tell the person inquiring that it's not your policy to comment on former workers.

Where an employee's record is truly mixed, it's usually possible to accent the positive while you try to put negative information into a halfway favorable, or at least less negative, perspective.

> **EXAMPLE:** Madeline, a copywriter for your ad agency, started working for you right out of college. She was a creative writer with lots of clever ideas, but never really figured out how to manage the production details for the mail order catalogs that are the bread and butter of your business. After a year, you concluded that this was just not a good fit and you reluctantly gave Madeline 60 days to find a slot elsewhere—hopefully with an agency looking for the dazzling, witty prose that was Madeline's forte.
>
> Possible approach to inquiries: Emphasize that Madeline is so full of creative energy and enthusiasm that she gets bored when it comes to tracking mundane details. Suggest that Madeline would do best in a spot where creative writing and

initiative are required and where new and clever ideas are needed.

Stick to known, provable facts and scrupulously avoid passing along speculation or rumor.

EXAMPLE: Joan worked for your company for a year as your bookkeeper and manager of your checking accounts. After suspecting some shortages of funds, you hired a CPA to review the books and bank records. The CPA reported in writing that there were indeed some serious irregularities. You confronted Joan with the CPA's report and she quit her job in a huff, denying any involvement. Because Joan always seemed to be sniffling, you suspected that she had been taking money to support a cocaine habit.

Possible approach to inquiries: Describe the CPA's written report and the fact that Joan left just after it was issued, but avoid voicing your unconfirmed suspicions about Joan's drug addiction. A safer course is to say nothing at all, since no dishonesty or drug usage was actually proven.

EXAMPLE: Norm drove a delivery van for your business. In a six-month period, he had two accidents with the van as a result of speeding. You're convinced that on one occasion he'd been drinking, although he wasn't charged with drunk driving. In the second accident, a pedestrian was seriously injured. You fired Norm.

Possible approach to inquiries: Give the facts about the two accidents, but don't speculate about Norm's suspected drunk driving.

EXAMPLE: Oscar, a salesman for your company, has an explosive temper. You received reports from several customers that Oscar had lost his cool and shouted obscenities at them. In one instance, he was nose-to-nose with the customer. In another case, he grabbed the customer's shoulder. You were about to discuss these incidents with Oscar when he quit to move to another city. The scuttlebutt around the office was that Oscar would often drink three martinis at lunch.

Possible approach to inquiries: Describe Oscar's strong selling skills and then tell of documented customer complaints, but refrain from repeating gossip you overheard about Oscar's drinking.

It also pays to watch your tongue in informal settings. Don't let down your guard at trade meetings or other places where you're chatting socially with others. If a fired employee was with your business for a while, a supplier or customer may ask, "Where's John these days?" If you reply in a vindictive way, describing all your grievances that led you to fire John, word will likely spread. And John may wind up being blackballed in your field or town. This can lead to legal complications for you and your business.

Be Careful Within Your Business

Usually, when a former employee sues for defamation, it's because the old employer has gone overboard in giving information to a prospective employer. But you can also get in trouble if you're not discreet in what you say about the former employee within your own company.

To help avoid liability, follow a few commonsense policies.

- Disclose the reasons for a firing strictly on a need-to-know basis—for example, to an employee who handles unemployment compensation claims for your business.

- Avoid discussing firings at meetings and employee gatherings—and never post the details on a bulletin board. Limit announcements to something noncommittal: "Bob has left the company as of last Friday. His position is being filled by Rita."

- Be sure your personnel files reflect fairness, objectivity and good faith. A former employee who sues you will certainly subpoena his or her employment records. These must be free of unprovable gossip or your whole case may be jeopardized.

Chapter 11

Independent Contractors

A. Comparing Employees and Independent Contractors 11/2

   1. Tax Obligations 11/2

   2. Workers' Compensation 11/3

   3. Unemployment Compensation 11/3

   4. Job Benefits 11/3

   5. Workspace 11/4

   6. Firing the Worker 11/4

   7. Cost 11/4

   8. Governmental Regulations 11/4

   9. Liability for Worker's Actions 11/4

   10. Liability for Injury to Worker 11/5

   11. Worker's Preferences 11/5

   12. Employer's Preferences 11/6

B. The IRS Rules 11/6

   1. Behavioral Control 11/7

   2. Financial Control 11/9

   3. The Relationship 11/11

   4. Facts of Less Importance 11/13

C. Workers Automatically Classified As Employees 11/14

D. State Laws 11/15

E. The Risks of Misclassification 11/15

F. Hiring Independent Contractors 11/17

*M*any businesses hire independent contractors rather than employees to perform at least some of their work. There are often advantages to such an arrangement—but there can be a downside, too. If you mistakenly classify a worker as an independent contractor rather than an employee, you face potentially serious legal problems—particularly when it comes to taxes. The IRS prefers to have a worker classified as an employee rather than an independent contractor if there's any doubt about the worker's status.

The main difference between independent contractors and employees is that independent contractors have the right to control not only the outcome of a project, but also the means of accomplishing it. Problems arise because some workers fall into a gray area, creating the danger of misclassification. To avoid such problems, it pays to become familiar with the analytic tools that IRS examiners use to sort out complicated cases. (See Section B.)

A small or midsized business may hire several types of workers as independent contractors. Common examples are a lawyer or accountant, a painter who spruces up your office or a computer consultant who installs specialized software at your store and teaches your employees how to use it. Typically—but not always—independent contractors have special skills that you need to call upon only sporadically.

Hiring Independent Contractors, by Stephen Fishman (Nolo), provides clear and comprehensive guidance that will help you avoid a collision with the IRS over how you classify a worker.

A. Comparing Employees and Independent Contractors

Sometimes, your company has needs that can be filled equally well by an employee or an independent contractor.

In choosing which route to take, there are several factors worth considering.

1. Tax Obligations

Employee. You must make an employer's contribution for the worker's Social Security and Medicare taxes. You're also responsible for withholding federal and state income taxes and the worker's share of Social Security and Medicare taxes, and for keeping records and reporting on these items to the federal and state governments. Each year, you must send the employee a Form W-2 showing how much he or she earned and how much was withheld. (See Chapter 5, Sections B and C, for details on tax responsibilities.)

Independent Contractor. When you hire an independent contractor, you're not required to withhold taxes from the amount you pay the worker, and you don't have to pay any portion of the worker's Social Security and Medicare taxes. Your only tax responsibility is to complete a Form 1099-MISC at the end of the year if you paid the independent contractor $600 or more during the year. You must send copies of this form to both the IRS and the employee.

2. Workers' Compensation

Employee. You must carry workers' compensation insurance for an employee. The workers' compensation system provides replacement income and pays medical expenses to employees who are injured or become ill as a result of their jobs. (See Chapter 7, Section E.)

Independent Contractor. Generally, an employer does not pay for workers' compensation for an independent contractor.

3. Unemployment Compensation

Employee. You must contribute to an unemployment insurance fund in your state and pay a federal unemployment tax. An employee who is laid off or is fired for a reason other than serious misconduct is entitled to unemployment benefits from the state fund. (See Chapter 10, Section J, for more on unemployment compensation.)

Independent Contractor. Generally, an employer does not make contributions to a state unemployment fund or pay the federal unemployment tax for an independent contractor.

4. Job Benefits

Employee. An employer usually provides job benefits for an employee, such as paid vaca-

tions, sick leave and holidays, health insurance and a retirement plan. (See Chapter 4.)

Independent Contractor. An independent contractor is paid only for time spent working— and is responsible for paying for his or her own health insurance and retirement savings plan.

Penalties Lurk If You Misclassify a Worker

If you weigh both possibilities and conclude it's in your company's best interests to hire and classify a worker as an independent contractor rather than an employee, fine. But make sure he or she really qualifies for this status under the IRS rules. If you classify a worker as an independent contractor when the worker should have been treated as an employee, you can be required to pay:

- the employer's and employee's share of Social Security and Medicare contributions
- income tax that should have been withheld from the employee's wages, and
- federal unemployment tax.

You may also be liable for the employee's state income taxes that should have been withheld, as well as unemployment compensation taxes. And if the worker is injured on the job, you may have to pay workers' compensation benefits because you didn't cover the employee under your company's workers' compensation policy.

5. Workspace

Employee. An employer provides workspace and equipment for an employee—meaning the employer pays for rent, maintenance, property insurance and utilities, as well as for tools, computers, furniture and vehicles, depending on the type of business.

Independent Contractor. An independent contractor usually—but not always—pays for his or her own workspace and equipment.

6. Firing the Worker

Employee. If you become unhappy with an employee's work and he or she doesn't improve, you will likely have to fire the worker —often a traumatic and legally hazardous course of action. (See Chapter 10.)

Independent Contractor. The emotional and legal bonds with an independent contractor are typically looser. An independent contractor is usually hired for a set assignment to be completed by a fixed deadline. If the independent contractor isn't satisfactory, you can simply turn to another independent contractor for future work. And if the independent contractor will be doing a series of projects over a long period, a written contract allowing you or the worker to cancel on two weeks notice can simplify termination.

7. Cost

Employee. The hourly rate you pay an employee may be relatively low—but the true cost also includes the money you pay for taxes, insurance, job benefits, workspace and equipment.

Independent Contractor. The hourly rate of an independent contractor may be relatively high because the worker must earn enough to cover business expenses and taxes.

8. Governmental Regulations

Employee. An employer is subject to a wide range of governmental regulations intended to protect employees—there are, for example, laws dealing with wages and hours (see Chapter 3), employee benefits (see Chapter 4), family and medical leave (see Chapter 6), workplace health and safety (see Chapter 7) and illegal discrimination (see Chapters 8 and 9).

Independent Contractor. A company's relationship with an independent contractor—if the worker has been properly classified as such— is subject to fewer legal restrictions. For example, you needn't pay an independent contractor time-and-a-half for overtime hours, and you're not responsible for monitoring health and safety conditions at an independent contractor's own home, shop or office.

9. Liability for Worker's Actions

Employee. An employer generally is legally liable for injuries or property damage caused by an employee's negligence. If, for example, an employee carelessly injures a customer while at work or damages someone's property, the employer can be held responsible.

Independent Contractor. If you hire an independent contractor, your company generally won't be liable for the negligence of that person. Be aware, however, that in some situations, your company may be liable for the actions of an independent contractor—especially if he or she was acting as your agent.

10. Liability for Injury to Worker

Employee. An employer is responsible for medical treatment for an employee hurt on the job and for paying money to partially cover the employee's lost wages. This is generally handled through workers' compensation insurance. These payments are required whether or not your company was at fault for the employee's injuries. (See Chapter 7, Section E.)

Independent Contractor. If an independent contractor is injured because of some dangerous situation at your business premises, he or she can recover medical bills and lost income from your business, as well as money for pain and suffering. But first, the independent contractor must show that you were negligent. You're not liable for injuries the independent contractor receives elsewhere while working for you—unless you truly had control over those premises.

Consider Leasing Workers. If you need extra workers for peak periods, a leasing service may be the answer. Leasing services hire workers as their employees, taking care of all the normal employer responsibilities—payroll, taxes and insurance. You pay the leasing service to provide qualified workers to you for short-term assignments. Obviously, the leasing service must make a profit, so the cost to you is higher than if you hired the workers directly. The advantage to you is the convenience—and the fact that you're not going to be hassled by the IRS for possibly misclassifying a worker.

11. Worker's Preferences

Employee. A worker may prefer to be an employee because that status promises a steady, predictable salary, paid vacations, medical care and other job benefits at the employer's expense—and freedom from worry about the paperwork and recordkeeping required of people who are in business for themselves. What's more, an employee usually doesn't have to invest in tools and equipment. If an employee incurs business expenses, he or she will usually be reimbursed by the employer. If not, the employee can take a tax deduction to the extent such expenses exceed 2% of his or her adjusted gross income.

Independent Contractor. A worker may prefer to be an independent contractor to have greater control over working hours and conditions, and to maintain the freedom to work for several businesses. Some like the fact that there's no withholding of taxes; they feel that they have a better cash flow, even though they're ultimately responsible for paying their taxes. Workers may also see benefits in being treated as independent contractors because they're able to deduct their business expenses from their gross incomes, including money spent on cars, home offices and even some travel and entertainment.

12. Employer's Preferences

Employee. An employer may prefer to hire a worker as an employee because the business has that worker's undivided loyalty and can better control the worker's hours and methods of doing the job.

Independent Contractor. An employer may prefer to hire a worker as an independent contractor because it allows more flexibility to adjust to fluctuating needs. For example, if an employer anticipates a two-month crunch on a project, farming out the extra work to an independent contractor may involve less workplace disruption than hiring an employee, providing workspace and then laying off the employee once the project is complete.

B. The IRS Rules

To determine whether someone is an employee or an independent contractor, the IRS looks at the degree of control you have over the worker. If you control—or can control—not only what is to be done but also how it's done, the worker is an employee.

⚠ Other Tests May Apply. The IRS tests for independent contractor status are emphasized here because the IRS is the agency with which you're most likely to have a problem. Be aware, however, that in dealing with other agencies and laws, slightly different tests may be used. For example, a different test is used to determine if a person is an independent contractor under the Fair Labor Standards Act. (See Chapter 3, Section A1.) And other tests may apply under state laws dealing with workers' compensation insurance and unemployment compensation. (See Section D, below.)

The IRS doesn't care what label you apply to a worker. You can designate someone as a partner, co-venturer, agent or independent contractor. But if the person legally qualifies as an employee, the IRS insists that you withhold income taxes and the employee's share of Social Security and Medicare contributions —and pay the employer's share of those contributions.

In deciding whether a person is an employee or an independent contractor, the IRS used to rely on a list of 20 factors cobbled together from various court decisions. The IRS, however, didn't spell out what weight it accorded to any one factor, which led to inconsistent rulings and considerable confusion.

Because a worker's status often remained unclear after applying the traditional test, it was easy for the IRS to classify the worker as an employee—an IRS preference grounded in the assumption that the government stands to collect more tax revenue if a worker is classified as an employee rather than as an independent contractor.

Although the IRS hasn't formally repealed the 20-factor test, it decidedly moved away from that test in 1996, when it published the worker classification training materials it now uses for indoctrinating IRS examiners. For employers trying to figure out where they stand on independent contractor issues, the training materials are a vast improvement over the old 20-factor test. The training materials provide welcome guidance on the weight given to various factors.

For a free copy of the worker classification training materials, call 202-622-5164, or write to: IRS Freedom of Information Office, Freedom of Information Reading Room, P.O. Box 795, Ben Franklin Station, Washington, DC 20044. You can also get the training materials on the Internet at www.irs.gov.

To determine whether a worker should be classified as an employee rather than as an independent contractor, IRS examiners are instructed to look primarily at three categories:

- **Behavioral control.** Do you have the right to direct or control how the worker performs the specific task for which he or she is hired?
- **Financial control.** Do you have the right to direct or control how the business aspects of the worker's activities are conducted?
- **The relationship.** How do you and the worker perceive your relationship?

The following sections discuss these categories in more detail.

1. Behavioral Control

The type of instruction or training you give a worker helps show the extent to which you retain the right to control the worker's method of getting the job done. IRS examiners may check on other types of behavioral control as well.

a. Instruction

The IRS recognizes that you'll probably impose some form of instruction on all workers—whether they're independent contractors or employees. For example, you might require that the job be performed within a specified time period. The big question is how far you go in telling the worker how the job should be done rather than just indicating the end result. Giving a worker autonomy in making decisions is evidence that you're not controlling the worker's behavior.

> **EXAMPLE:** Star Brite Manufacturing Company hires Lou Ann as a management consultant for its sales department. She is to ensure that the department is fully staffed and that sales brochures are stocked and available. She is also to review all sales contracts. Star Brite requires Lou Ann to get prior approval before she hires or fires anyone in the sales department, purchases additional sales materials or accepts any sales contract.
>
> The IRS views the requirement of prior approval as evidence that Star Brite controls Lou Ann's behavior in the performance of her services. If Star Brite were not to require these prior approvals but were to leave matters to Lou Ann's discretion, this would be evidence of her autonomy in doing the work and therefore, consistent with independent contractor status.

The IRS distinguishes between telling a worker what is to be done and how it is to be done. A worker can be an independent contractor even though you indicate what the job entails.

EXAMPLE: Jim is an independent truck driver. Young Industries, Inc., calls him to make a delivery run from the Gulf Coast to the Texas Panhandle. Jim accepts the job and agrees to pick up the cargo the next morning. Upon arriving at the ware-house, Jim is given an address to which to deliver the cargo and is advised that the delivery must be completed within two days. The IRS treats this as a direction of what is be done—not how it is to be done—and therefore consistent with independent contractor status. Jim is still free to choose his route, plan his driving time and perhaps perform other work along the way.

On the other hand, if you give too much instruction on how the work is to be done, you may have to classify the worker as an employee.

EXAMPLE: Tess, a truck driver, does local deliveries for Zancor. She reports to Zancor's warehouse each morning. The warehouse manager tells Tess what deliveries have to be made, how to load the cargo in the truck, what route to take and the order in which the cargo is to be delivered. This is instruction on how the work is to be performed—consistent with employee status, in the eyes of the IRS.

b. Training

If you provide periodic or ongoing training to a worker, it's usually strong evidence of an employer-employee relationship. That's not true, however, of training that merely informs a worker about your policies, a new product line or applicable governmental regulations. Similarly, the IRS won't imply an employer-employee relationship from programs a worker attends voluntarily and without compensation.

c. Suggestions

Mere suggestions to a worker don't constitute control over the worker's behavior. So suggesting that a worker avoid Main Street because of traffic congestion is consistent with the worker's status as an independent contractor.

d. Business identification

In the past, requiring a worker to identify himself or herself with your business was evidence of employment status. For example, if you required a worker to wear a uniform bearing your company's name or to paint your logo on his or her truck, that would have been an indication that the worker was an employee.

Today, the IRS recognizes that safety concerns play into these types or rules; people often want reassurance about who's coming to their homes or workplaces. The result: If there's a valid security reason for requiring a uniform or logo, the requirement is now a neutral fact in analyzing whether an employment relationship exists.

2. Financial Control

The IRS looks at whether your business has the right to direct or control the economic aspects of the worker's activities.

a. Significant investment

Although it's not necessary for a worker to buy or rent costly equipment to be considered an independent contractor, evidence of such an investment does help to establish indepen-dent contractor status. There are no precise dollar guidelines on what constitutes a significant investment.

There can be a significant investment even if you're selling or leasing the equipment to the worker—but the worker must pay the full market value or full rental value. Otherwise, the evidence may be insufficient to establish a significant investment.

> **EXAMPLE:** Cal operates a backhoe for Yorba Distributing Company. He leases the backhoe from Yorba at less than its fair rental value and can turn it in at any time without liability for further payments. Yorba pays for liability insurance and regular maintenance on the backhoe. Although Cal is paying something to rent the backhoe, the facts here don't establish that he's made a significant investment.

b. Business expenses

The extent to which a worker chooses to incur expenses and be responsible for them can affect the worker's potential to make a profit or sustain a loss. A worker's unreimbursed business expenses can be evidence that the worker has the right to control the financial side of his or her business operations—helping to show independent contractor status.

But there are limits to this principle. If the unreimbursed expenses are minor, this isn't evidence of an independent contractor relationship. The same is true of heavier expenses that are customarily borne by an employee in a particular line of business, such as an auto mechanic's tools.

c. Advertising and visibility

An independent contractor is generally free to seek out other business opportunities. The fact that a worker advertises or maintains a visible business location to attract new clients is evidence that the worker is an independent contractor. On the other hand, neither advertising nor having a visible business location is a requirement for independent contractor status. A worker with special skills who gets jobs through word of mouth can qualify as an independent contractor.

In addition, the IRS recognizes that a person who has negotiated a long-term contract may find advertising unnecessary and may even be unavailable to work for others for the duration of the contract—and that will not affect the person's status as an independent contractor. Other independent contractors may find that a visible business location doesn't produce enough business to justify the expense.

In short, the IRS treats the absence of advertising or a visible business location as well as the temporary inability to work for others as neutral factors.

EXAMPLE: Unicorn Ventures engages Cindy to mow the lawn weekly and trim the hedges yearly at Unicorn's headquarters. Cindy advertises in the Yellow Pages that she does landscaping. The advertising indicates that Cindy is available to perform services to the relevant market. This is evidence that she is an independent contractor.

EXAMPLE: Cindy negotiates a long-term contract with Unicorn to maintain all of Unicorn's business locations. Cindy decides to drop her Yellow Pages advertising, although she continues to be available to other businesses. The lack of advertising doesn't automatically change her independent contractor status.

d. Method of payment

A worker who's paid hourly, weekly or by another unit of time is guaranteed a return for labor. This is generally evidence of an employer-employee relationship, even when a commission is also paid. However, in some fields, such as law, it's typical to pay independent contractors on an hourly basis, so the hourly payment can be a neutral factor.

Paying a worker a flat fee for a particular project is generally evidence of an independent contractor relationship, especially if the worker incurs expenses in performing the job. When you pay the worker—daily, weekly or monthly—isn't relevant.

A person who's paid solely on a commission basis can be either an independent contractor or an employee. The worker's status may depend on his or her ability to realize a profit or incur a loss in performing services.

e. Profit or loss

A worker's ability to earn a profit or incur a loss is probably the strongest evidence that the worker controls the business aspects of the work. The four economic factors discussed above all relate to the worker's potential for profit or loss. A key question is whether the worker can make decisions that affect his or her bottom line. These might, for example, be decisions involving ordering inventory, investing money or purchasing or leasing equipment.

A worker's ability to decide whether to work longer hours to earn more money or to work fewer hours and take less money is a neutral factor.

3. The Relationship

The IRS considers how you and the worker view your relationship. Your perceptions and those of the worker may suggest what the two of you intend regarding the all-important issue of control.

a. Written contract

If you have a written contact with a worker, the IRS will focus on its substance—not on labels. Calling the worker an independent contractor isn't enough. The more important clauses are those dealing with the method of compensation, payment of expenses and, most crucial, the rights and obligations of you and the worker regarding how work is to be performed.

b. Form W-2

Filing a Form W-2 usually indicates that the worker is an employee—but the IRS may find independent contractor status anyway, depending on the economic realities of the relationship.

c. Incorporation

If a worker has formed a corporation and you hire the corporation to do the work, the IRS will almost always treat the worker as an employee of his or her own corporation—not as an employee of your business.

Sidestep IRS Problems by Contracting With Corporations

If you want to hire someone as an independent contractor but you're not convinced that the worker will pass IRS muster as an independent contractor, the easiest solution is to require the worker to form a corporation.

One-person corporations are simple to create. After the worker incorporates, your business signs a contract with the corporation in which the worker's corporation agrees to provide the needed services. You pay the corporation as specified in the contract. The worker receives a paycheck—and possibly bonuses as well—from his or her corporation, which is the employer.

The IRS will recognize this arrangement except in cases of clear abuse—and independent contractor status will no longer be an issue. Presumably, you can reach the same result if a worker forms a limited liability company instead of a corporation, although the IRS hasn't addressed this issue yet.

d. Employee benefits

Providing a worker with benefits traditionally associated with employee status can be evidence that the worker is an employee. If you give the worker paid vacation days, paid sick days, health insurance, life or disability insurance or a pension, that's some evidence of employee status. The evidence of employee status is strongest if you provide benefits under a tax-qualified retirement plan, a 403(b) annuity or a cafeteria plan.

If you exclude a worker from a benefit plan because you don't consider the worker to be an employee, that's relevant but not conclusive evidence that the worker is an independent contractor.

e. Discharge or termination

The IRS may look at the conditions under which you or the worker can terminate the working relationship. It's clear, however, that the IRS regards this as a complicated legal question and doesn't usually treat it as a decisive factor in deciding whether a worker has been properly classified.

f. Permanency

If you and the worker arranged for work to be done with the expectation that the relationship would continue indefinitely rather than for a specific project or period, that's generally evidence that the two of you intended to create an employment relationship. However, this requires more than simply setting up a long-term relationship, which is consistent with either employee or independent contractor status. The IRS recognizes that your relationship with an independent contractor may be long-term because that's what your work agreement requires or because you renew the agreement regularly due to superior service, competitive prices or lack of competition.

For these reasons, if a relationship is long-term but the worker has a clearly defined role (for example, cleaning your windows regularly or providing specialized computer training as needed), the IRS disregards this as a factor in looking at the worker's status. The IRS also treats the temporary nature of a relationship as a neutral factor.

g. Regular business activity

The IRS may look at whether the services performed by a worker are a key aspect of your company's regular business. This can be a bit subtle.

The mere fact that a service is desirable, necessary or even essential to your business doesn't mean that the service provider is an employee. If you have an appliance store, for example, you need workers to install electricity and plumbing in your building. This work can be done equally well by employees or independent contractors. The IRS examiner focuses on the fact that the work of the electricians and plumbers isn't part of your regular business.

By contrast, the work of an attorney or legal assistant is part of the regular business of a law firm. It's likely that a law firm will direct or control the work of a lawyer or legal assistant it hires since the firm's name will go on documents the worker produces. In this situation, the IRS will probe for further facts showing the firm's right to direct and control the worker.

4. Facts of Less Importance

In addition to the three primary categories of evidence listed above, the IRS looks at other facts—but gives them less weight.

a. Part-time or full-time work

Whether a worker performs services on a full-time or part-time basis is a neutral fact. The same is true whether a worker performs services for one business or several.

b. Place of work

Whether work is performed on your premises or somewhere you select often has no bearing on worker status. Usually it's only relevant as part of the IRS inquiry into your right to control how the work is to be done.

In many cases, services can only be performed at one location. To repair a leaky pipe, for example, a plumber must go to the site where the pipe is located. Similarly, a camera operator must shoot a commercial where the director and actors are located. These requirements aren't evidence of the right to direct and control how the work is to be performed.

Sometimes, work can be performed at many different locations. Off-site work can be consistent with either independent contractor or employee status. If a worker has his or her own office or business location, this can be evidence of an independent contractor relationship—but the IRS gets into this as part of its examination of the worker's investment, unreimbursed expenses or opportunity for profit or loss.

c. Hours of work

The IRS generally considers hours of work when it looks at the extent of the instructions you give the worker. As with work location, some work, by its nature, must be performed at a specific time; the photographer must shoot the commercial at the time scheduled for the director and actors to be present.

Flexible workhours are not given much importance by the IRS, as they can be consistent with either employee or independent contractor status.

Seeking a Safe Harbor

Despite the strict IRS rules, a business that wrongly classifies a worker as an independent contractor may escape the usual harsh consequences in some circumstances.

In theory at least, you're protected by the safe harbor language of the tax law if you had a reasonable basis for classifying a worker as an independent contractor—for example:

- You relied on court rulings, IRS rulings or advice given to you by the IRS.
- You were audited by the IRS and weren't assessed for employment taxes for workers holding jobs similar to the one held by the misclassified worker.
- You followed a long-standing and recognized practice of your industry.

But theory is one thing—and the real world experience of challenging the IRS is another. If you seek the protection of the safe harbor provisions, the IRS won't give up without a fight. Be prepared for a pitched legal battle.

C. Workers Automatically Classified As Employees

In most situations, the status of a worker is determined by the factors already explained. (See Sections B1 and B2.) Certain workers, however, fall into special categories, and the usual IRS criteria don't apply to them. For example, the federal tax law says that certain workers are automatically employees—in legal lingo, statutory employees—including:

Delivery drivers. Drivers who deliver meat, vegetables, fruit, bakery products or beverages other than milk, or who pick up and deliver laundry or dry cleaning. These drivers are employees if they're legally agents of a company and are paid on a commission. (An agent is someone who's authorized by another to act on his or her behalf.)

> **EXAMPLE:** Rachel, a bread truck driver, sells on commission to a customer route for Barry's Bakery and no other bakeries; under the federal law, she's a statutory employee of the bakery. But Allen, a restaurant supply distributor who buys bread from Barry's Bakery at wholesale prices and resells it at a profit, is neither an agent nor a statutory employee of Barry's Bakery.

Insurance agents. Insurance sales agents whose main job is selling life insurance, annuity contracts or both, primarily for one life insurance company.

Home workers. People who work at home according to a company's specifications on materials or goods that are supplied by a company and must be returned to that company or to someone the company designates.

Business-to-business salespeople. People whose main job is to sell for a company and turn in orders to that company from wholesalers, retailers, contractors, hotels, restaurants or other business establishments. The goods sold must be merchandise for resale or supplies for use in the buyer's business, rather than goods bought for home consumption.

Federal tax law also provides that licensed real estate agents and door-to-door salespeople are generally treated as "nonemployees" or "exempt employees," but they may be treated as employees for the purpose of liability and workers' compensation.

D. State Laws

The IRS list of factors for differentiating between employees and independent contractors is similar to the standards followed in most states for state taxes and unemployment compensation, but there can be some differences. For example, in deciding whether a worker is an employee for purposes of workers' com-

pensation coverage or unemployment compensation benefits, a state may use a simple economic reality test.

If you plan to hire independent contractors, check first with the labor department in your state to see what rules are in effect. (See the Appendix for contact details.)

E. The Risks of Misclassification

There are at least three ways that the IRS can learn about your hiring and classification practices. First, the IRS may look into the affairs of an independent contractor who hasn't been paying his or her income taxes. Second, disgruntled employees may complain to the IRS if they think independent contractors are getting favored treatment. Third, during tax audits, the IRS routinely checks to see if workers have been misclassified as independent contractors.

The presumption is that the worker is an employee unless proven otherwise. If the IRS questions the status of a worker, it's up to you to prove that the worker is an independent contractor rather than an employee.

If the IRS determines that an employee was misclassified, the cost to your business will be heavy. You'll be responsible for paying the employee's Social Security tax, federal income tax and federal unemployment insurance for up to three years. In addition, the IRS can add penalties and interest to the tally you must pay.

State government officials are also interested in businesses that misclassify employees as independent contractors. A state employment

The IRS Can Be Tough

The IRS has been aggressively cracking down on employers that have misclassified workers as independent contractors. Underlying this crackdown is a belief that tax revenue is slipping through the cracks because independent contractors aren't reporting all of their income.

Also, IRS officials know that potential tax revenue is lost because even independent contractors who do report their full income can deduct a wide range of business expenses—deductions that employees have difficulty taking.

Fighting the IRS can be expensive. Raleigh Air Cargo Express learned that the hard way. For years, the company hired college students and retirees to make occasional freight runs using rented trucks. Because of the sporadic nature of the work, the small North Carolina company paid these workers as independent contractors.

Eventually, Raleigh shifted these workers to employee status—a move that ironically triggered an IRS audit and a demand that Raleigh pay some $47,000 in back taxes, plus interest and penalties. It took Raleigh nearly three years and $27,000 in legal and accounting fees, but the tenacious company eventually got a fair hearing from a sympathetic IRS appeals officer who canceled the IRS claim. And not a moment too soon. Fighting the IRS nearly put Raleigh out of business.

Moral of the story: The fate of your business can hang on something as tenuous as getting the right IRS person to listen to you on the right day.

office may audit your business to see if there's been any misclassification. The audit can be the result of a spot check by the state employment office or a request by an independent contractor for unemployment or workers' compensation benefits. You may wind up owing money to a state unemployment insurance fund.

F. Hiring Independent Contractors

There are several things you can do to help establish that a worker is properly classified as an independent contractor right from the start of the relationship. (See Chapter 1 for a detailed discussion of hiring employees.)

Sign a contract with the independent contractor clearly spelling out his or her responsibilities and how payment is to be determined for each job. (See sample contract below.) The contract should allow the independent contractor to hire his or her own assistants—and should specifically state that the contractor will carry his or her own insurance, including workers' compensation. In addition to helping satisfy the federal or state government that a worker is truly an independent contractor, a good written contract will reduce disputes with the independent contractor about the details of the relationship.

Require the independent contractor to supply all or most of the tools, equipment and material needed to complete the job and to pay for his or her own liability insurance.

Give the independent contractor the maximum possible freedom to decide how to perform the work.

Avoid a commitment to reimburse the independent contractor for his or her business expenses; have the independent contractor assume that responsibility.

Arrange to pay a flat fee for the work rather than an hourly or weekly rate, if that's feasible to do.

Don't provide employee-type benefits such as paid vacation days, health insurance or retirement plans.

Make it clear that the independent contractor is free to offer services to other businesses.

Keep a file containing the independent contractor's business card, stationery samples, ads and employer identification number. These items can help show that the contractor has an established business.

Finally, consider asking the independent contractor to incorporate. Then, sign a contract with the corporation instead of the individual. As explained in Section B3 above, this is probably your most effective means of avoiding a shoot-out with the IRS over the proper classification of a worker.

Trade Secrets Need Special Protection. In some situations, you may disclose trade secrets of your business to an independent contractor. If so, include a clause in the agreement prohibiting the independent contractor from disclosing or making any other unauthorized use of the trade secrets. (See Chapter 1, Section A5.)

Sample Contract With an Independent Contractor

AGREEMENT

This agreement made on _____ June 1, _____, 20 **XX** , beween

_____ Joe Nolo _____, Client,

of _____ 555 Parker Street _____

and _____ Lou Moses _____, Contractor,

of _____ 41 Willow Lane _____ .

1. **Services to Be Performed.** Contractor agrees to perform the following services for Client:

    [Description of Services] _____

    _____

2. **Time for Performance.** Contractor agrees to complete the performance of these services on or before __July 1 _____, 20 **XX** .

3. **Payment.** In consideration of Contractor's performance of these services, Client agrees to pay Contractor as follows:

    [Description of how payment will be computed] _____

    _____

4. **Invoices.** Contractor will submit invoices for all services performed.

5. **Independent Contractor.** The parties intend Contractor to be an independent contractor in the performance of these services. Contractor shall have the right to control and determine the method and means of performing the above services; Client shall not have the right to control or determine such method or means.

6. **Other Clients.** Contractor retains the right to perform services for other clients.

7. **Assistants.** Contractor, at Contractor's expense, may employ such assistants as Contractor deems appropriate to carry out this agreement. Contractor will be responsible for paying such assistants, as well as any expense attributable

to such assistants, including income taxes, unemployment insurance and Social Security taxes, and will maintain workers' compensation insurance for such employees.

8. **Equipment and Supplies.** Contractor, at Contractor's own expense, will provide all equipment, tools and supplies necessary to perform the above services, and will be responsible for all other expenses required for the performance of those services.

_____

Contractor

_____

Client

Source: _The Legal Guide for Starting & Running a Small Business,_ by Fred S. Steingold (Nolo).

Chapter 12

Unions

A. The National Labor Relations Act 12/2

B. Unionizing a Workplace 12/2

    1. The Bargaining Unit 12/3

    2. Authorization Cards 12/3

    3. NLRB Elections 12/3

    4. Negotiating a Contract 12/4

C. Employer Rights and Limitations 12/4

    1. What Is Permitted 12/4

    2. What Is Not Permitted 12/5

D. Employee Rights and Limitations 12/5

E. Making Unions Unnecessary 12/6

Only 9% of U.S. workers in the private sector belonged to unions in the year 2000—and most of them work in larger businesses. Why membership is declining is open to debate. Perhaps unions are less necessary today because of the growing array of laws that protect workers. Perhaps the changing nature of work plays a role.

The effect on small and midsized businesses is clear: If your business isn't unionized now, it's unlikely that it ever will be. Still, workers do have the legal right to form unions and, despite the odds, a union could be formed in your workplace. So you need a basic understanding of workers' rights as well as your own.

This chapter discusses the legal highlights of the relationship between employers and workers who choose to unionize. If your workplace is already unionized or if workers decide to form a union, it's wise to consult a lawyer experienced in labor law. (See Chapter 13, Section A, for more on finding and working with a lawyer.)

A. The National Labor Relations Act

The National Labor Relations Act or NLRA (29 U.S.C. § 151 and following) is the most sweeping law regulating the formation of unions. It establishes the right of most—but not all—workers to organize into unions and, through union representatives, to negotiate an employment contract covering all members of the union.

Private sector employees who are not covered by the NLRA include:

- managers and supervisors
- confidential employees—such as company accountants
- farm workers
- members of an employer's family
- most domestic workers, and
- workers in certain industries—such as the railroad industry—that are covered by other labor laws.

The National Labor Relations Board (NLRB) administers the law and interprets its provisions. The role of the NLRB in overseeing the unionizing of a workplace is discussed in Section B3.

B. Unionizing a Workplace

Workers who choose to form or join a union usually believe that they'll have more bargaining clout than they would if they dealt with their employer one-on-one. They feel that the union can get them better pay, benefits and working conditions than they could obtain on their own—and that, through structured grievance procedures, the union can get them a fairer shake in resolving workplace disputes.

And just as business trade associations may offer attractive services and products to employers, larger unions may provide valuable enticements to workers—for example, low-interest credit cards, home mortgage programs, free or reduced rate legal services, low-cost prescription plans and competitive car insurance.

1. The Bargaining Unit

Employees can form their own union or can choose to affiliate with a national union. Either way, the employees must be part of a proper bargaining unit—a group of employees who perform similar work and logically have similar concerns about issues such as pay rates, work-hours and working conditions.

A workplace may have several bargaining units—each represented by a different union—and some workers in such a workplace may not be represented by any union.

> **EXAMPLE:** Offices Unlimited sells office equipment and supplies. The checkout clerks have formed one bargaining unit and the warehouse workers another. Other workers, such as the sales assistants, are not represented by a union.

If a majority of workers in a bargaining unit authorize a union to represent them, the union becomes the sole representative of all the employees in that unit to bargain over wages, hours and other working conditions. This is known as collective bargaining.

2. Authorization Cards

Workers express their wishes to be represented by a union by signing authorization cards. If you receive authorization cards signed by a majority of the workers in a bargaining unit, you can voluntarily recognize the union as the sole representative of the unit—but you don't have to do so.

If you don't voluntarily recognize the union, the workers can ask for an election to be conducted by the NLRB.

3. NLRB Elections

If 30% or more of the workers in a proposed bargaining unit have signed authorization cards, the union can petition the NLRB to hold a secret election to determine whether a majority of the workers support the union. The union's petition will include a description of the group of workers the union would like to have included in the bargaining unit.

Then the NLRB will conduct an election to determine whether or not the workers in the bargaining unit want to be represented by the union. If a majority of the workers who vote cast their ballots for the union, it's officially certified as the sole bargaining agent for the unit.

Voicing Your Opposition

You may have good reasons to refuse to recognize a union. For example, you may object that it includes workers who have managerial duties. Or you may suspect that some signatures indicating a wish to unionize were not truly voluntary, but were the result of intimidation.

Employers' most common challenge is to question the union's description of the bargaining unit. One basis for a challenge is that the workers included by the union don't do similar work. You may also be able to exclude from the bargaining unit any employee who has authority to:

- assign work or direct employees
- evaluate work
- grant time off
- schedule work hours
- discipline employees
- hire or fire
- keep time records, or
- adjust grievances.

An employee can be excluded, too, if he or she can effectively recommend action on any of these tasks.

4. Negotiating a Contract

After a union is voluntarily recognized as the official representative of the bargaining unit or is certified by the NLRB, the representatives of the union and the employer negotiate a contract—a collective bargaining agreement. A contract typically covers wages, benefits, work breaks, overtime, holidays, vacation and sick time, seniority for promotions and safety rules. Often, there's a grievance procedure under which workers can bring their complaints to the union, which then takes the problems to the employer. Employees represented by the union pay monthly dues—often through a payroll deduction called a checkoff.

 Since negotiating a labor contract is governed by special rules that don't apply to ordinary business contracts, it's wise to consult a labor lawyer who's experienced in labor negotiations. (See Chapter 13, Section A.)

C. Employer Rights and Limitations

If you are an employer facing unionization efforts in your workplace, the law shapes how you may and may not voice any objections.

1. What Is Permitted

You can try to dissuade employees from forming or joining a union. You can, for example, use letters, posters, brochures and speeches to tell employees that they currently enjoy many job benefits and that their wages and benefits compare favorably to those of other workers in your industry. Make sure you can document your claims.

You're legally allowed to state that your door is open to hear complaints and that you will attempt to take appropriate action. You can explain that you prefer to settle complaints with employees personally rather than through union agents.

Pointing out potentially negative features of union representation is also permitted. For example, you might emphasize that workers will be paying dues and fees if they unionize, and will be subject to union rules and regimentation.

You can explain, too, that those signing authorization cards aren't bound to vote for the union in the secret balloting conducted by the NLRB and that they don't have to stand for undue pressure by the union. Depending on the composition of your workforce, you might mention that the union's emphasis on seniority may put newer workers at a disadvantage.

2. What Is Not Permitted

Some actions in opposing a union are off limits. Most courts have ruled that under the NLRA you may not:

- ask employees for their thoughts on union matters or how they plan to vote
- attend union meetings or spy on employees
- grant or promise employees a promotion, pay raise, desirable work assignment or

other special favors if they oppose unionizing efforts
- close down a worksite or transfer work or reduce benefits to pressure workers not to support unionization
- dismiss, harass, reassign or otherwise punish or discipline workers—or threaten to—if they support unionization, or
- refuse to bargain collectively with the employees' union representative.

 Sometimes the distinctions between what you can and can't do are subtle. Before acting to oppose a union, consult a lawyer who knows the ropes. (See Chapter 13, Section A.)

D. Employee Rights and Limitations

Generally, courts have ruled that the NLRA gives workers the right to:

- discuss union membership and distribute union literature during nonwork time in nonwork areas, such as an employee lounge or locker room
- use your bulletin board to post union notices
- sign a card asking you to recognize the union and bargain with it
- sign petitions and grievances concerning employment terms and conditions
- ask co-workers to sign petitions and grievances, and
- display pro-union sentiments by wearing message-bearing items such as hats, pins and T-shirts on the job.

But workers have no right to threaten or intimidate other workers to gain support for a union. And union organizers who are not employed by your business have no right to be on your premises. But don't rush to call the police to have outside organizers ejected as trespassers—especially if their activities are not disrupting your business. Such an approach may alienate employees. It's better to emphasize to workers the advantages of staying union-free. (See Section E.)

E. Making Unions Unnecessary

Unions usually gain a foothold because employees are dissatisfied with some aspects of their work life. Contented workers don't generally seek to unionize, as it entails some degree of bureaucracy and workplace politics.

Be sensitive to what's going on in the workplace and make reasonable changes if required. Encourage employees to come to you with their workplace complaints—and listen carefully to what they're saying. If there's a health or safety problem, fix it. If a workplace procedure is annoying or seems unfair to workers, look into changing it.

Be fair and consistent in enforcing work rules and disciplining employees. They need to know what to expect—and they can become frustrated and angry if you act arbitrarily.

To the extent possible, give employees some control over how they perform their jobs. In almost any job position, it's possible to allow some degree of worker autonomy. Employees who have some freedom to put their imprints on their work tend to be most content on the job. Periodically survey what similar businesses are paying their workers—and make sure that the wages and benefits you provide are competitive. Offer incentives for excellent performance.

Try to keep your workforce steadily employed. Hiring employees for seasonal overloads and laying them off when the work levels off creates feelings of insecurity. Consider hiring temporary workers for seasonal increases in the workflow. ■

Chapter 13

Lawyers and Legal Research

A. Getting Help From a Lawyer 13/2

    1. Getting Leads 13/2

    2. Shopping Around 13/4

B. Paying a Lawyer 13/6

    1. Types of Fee Arrangements 13/6

    2. Saving on Legal Fees 13/7

C. Resolving Problems With Your Lawyer 13/8

D. Legal Research 13/9

    1. Finding a Law Library 13/9

    2. Federal and State Laws 13/9

    3. Sources of Legal Research 13/9

    4. How to Begin 13/10

    5. Online Research 13/12

*W*hen you own or run a business, you need lots of legal information on employment issues. For example, you may need to learn how an anti-discrimination law is being interpreted by the EEOC or whether an agreement with a departing employee will be enforced by a court. Lawyers, of course, are prime sources of this information. But if you bought all the needed information at the rates they charge—$150 to $250 or more an hour—you'd quickly empty your bank account. Fortunately, for an intelligent employer, there are a number of other ways to acquire a good working knowledge of the legal principles and procedures necessary to handle employment and other issues.

How frequently you'll need a lawyer's help will depend on the nature of your business, the number of employees you hire, how many locations you have and the kinds of problems you run into with employees and governmental agencies. Your challenge isn't to avoid lawyers altogether, but to use them cost-effectively.

Lawyers aren't the only source for legal help. The U.S. Department of Labor, the Internal Revenue Service, the U.S. Equal Employment Opportunity Commission, the U.S. Department of Justice and other federal agencies offer publications at little or no cost explaining federal laws and regulations that affect employers. Many are referred to in this book. Similarly, many state agencies have helpful printed materials available. And representatives of federal and state agencies can help explain how the laws they administer are interpreted.

And keep in mind that professionals who charge less than lawyers—for example, accountants and workplace consultants—can also help you within their areas of expertise.

A. Getting Help From a Lawyer

Ideally, you should find a lawyer who's willing to help you educate yourself. Then you can do the preliminary work on your own, turning to your lawyer from time to time for advice and fine-tuning.

In working with a lawyer, remember that you're the boss. A lawyer, of course, has specialized training, knowledge, skill and experience in dealing with legal matters. But that's no reason for you to abdicate control over legal decision-making and how much time and money should be spent on a particular legal problem. You have an intimate knowledge of your business and are in the best position to call the shots—even though a lawyer may be willing or even eager to do it all for you.

Since you almost surely can't afford all the services a lawyer might offer, you need to set priorities. When thinking about a legal problem, ask yourself: "Can I do this myself?" "Can I do this myself with some help from a lawyer?" "Should I simply put this in my lawyer's hands?"

1. Getting Leads

Of the almost 900,000 lawyers in America today, probably fewer than 50,000 have sufficient training and experience in small business law to be of real help to you. And even fewer have significant experience in employment law.

Don't expect to locate a good employment lawyer by simply looking in the phone book, consulting a law directory or reading an advertisement. There's not enough information in those sources to help you make a valid judgment. Almost as useless are lawyer referral services operated by bar associations. Generally, these services make little attempt to evaluate a lawyer's skill and experience. They simply supply the names of lawyers who have listed with the service, often accepting the lawyer's own word for what types of skills he or she has.

A better approach is to talk with people in your community who own or operate excellent businesses. These people are likely to have ferreted out the best lawyers. Ask them who their lawyers are and a little about their experiences. Ask them about other lawyers they've worked with and what led them to make a change. If you talk to half a dozen employers, chances are you'll come away with several leads on good, experienced business lawyers.

Other people who provide services to the business community may also help you identify lawyers you might consider hiring. For example, speak with your banker, accountant, insurance agent and real estate broker. These people come into frequent contact with lawyers who represent employers and are in a position to make informed judgments. Friends, relatives and business associates within your own company can also provide names of lawyers. But ask them specifically about lawyers who have had experience working for employers; a good divorce lawyer would likely make a poor employment advisor, for example.

There are several other sources to which you can turn for possible candidates in your search for a lawyer.

- The director of your state or local chamber of commerce may know of several employment lawyers who have the kind of experience that you seek.

- Articles about employment law in trade magazines and newspapers are often written by lawyers. Track down these authors and call them. Most will be flattered to help or provide other referrals.

- The director of your state's continuing legal education (CLE) program—usually run by a bar association, a law school or both—can identify lawyers who have

lectured or written on employment law for other lawyers. Someone who's a "lawyer's lawyer" presumably has the extra depth of knowledge and experience to do a superior job for you—but may charge more, unfortunately.

- The chairperson of a state or county bar committee for business lawyers may be able to point out some well-qualified practitioners in your vicinity.

Once you have the names of several lawyers, a good source for more information about them is the *Martindale-Hubbell Law Directory,* available at most law libraries, some local public libraries and on the Internet. This resource contains biographical sketches of most practicing lawyers and information about their experience, specialties, education and the professional organizations to which they belong. Many firms also list their major clients in the directory—an excellent indication of the types of industries and problems with which they've had experience. Be aware, however, that lawyers purchase the space for their biographical sketches, so don't be overly impressed by long entries.

In addition, almost every lawyer listed in the directory, whether or not he or she has purchased space for a biographical sketch, is rated AV, BV or CV. These ratings come from confidential opinions that Martindale-Hubbell solicits from lawyers and judges.

The first letter is for Legal Ability, which is rated as follows:

A—Very High to Preeminent
B—High to Very High
C—Fair to High.

The V part of the rating stands for Very High General Recommendation—meaning that the rated lawyer adheres to professional standards of conduct and ethics. But the V part is practically meaningless, because lawyers who don't qualify for it aren't rated at all. *Martindale-Hubbell* prudently cautions that such absence shouldn't be construed as a reflection on the lawyer, since there could be many reasons for the absence of a rating. Some lawyers, for example, ask that their rating not be published and others are too new to a community to be known among the local lawyers and judges who are the sources for the information on which the ratings are based.

Don't make the rating system your sole criterion for deciding on a potential lawyer for your business. But you can be reasonably confident that a lawyer who gets high marks from other business clients and an "AV" rating from *Martindale-Hubbell* will have experience and expertise.

Computer buffs can reach Martindale-Hubbell online at www.martindale.com. The online listings contain everything except the ratings. Another excellent source of information about lawyers is *West's Legal Directory,* which you'll find at www.wld.com.

2. Shopping Around

After you get the names of several good prospects, shop around. Most lawyers will be willing to speak with you for a half hour or so at no charge so that you can size them up and make an informed decision about whether to hire them. Look for experience and for the ability to listen and communicate. These characteristics may be apparent almost immediately, but in some cases may take longer to evaluate. So even after you've hired a lawyer who seems right for you, stay open to the possibility that you may have to make a change later.

Pay particular attention to the rapport between you and your lawyer. No matter how experienced and well recommended a lawyer is, if you feel uncomfortable with that person during your first meeting or two, you may never achieve an ideal lawyer-client relationship. Trust your instincts and seek a lawyer whose personality is compatible with your own.

Your lawyer should be accessible when you need legal services. Unfortunately, the complaint logs of all legal regulatory groups indicate that many lawyers are not. If you consistently face delays of several days before you can talk to your lawyer on the phone or get an appointment, you'll lose precious time, not to mention sleep. And almost nothing is more aggravating to a client than to leave a legal project in a lawyer's hands, then wait weeks or even months while nothing happens.

You want a lawyer who will work hard on your behalf and follow through promptly on all assignments. Unfortunately, it's usually difficult to tell at the outset how attentive the lawyer will be later on. But it can be helpful to ask how the lawyer intends to keep in touch with you. Perhaps you can exact a promise that you'll receive a status report at least monthly.

Costs Can Mount Up

In addition to the fees they charge for their time, lawyers often bill for some costs as well—and these costs can add up quickly. When you receive a lawyer's bill, you may be surprised at both the amount of the costs and the variety of the services for which the lawyer expects reimbursement. These can include charges for:

- long distance phone calls
- photocopying
- faxes
- overnight mail
- messenger service
- witness fees
- court filing fees
- process servers
- work by investigators
- work by legal assistants or paralegals
- deposition transcripts
- online legal research, and
- travel.

You'd think that a lawyer would absorb the cost of many of these items as normal office overhead—part of the cost of doing business—but that's not always the case. So in working out the fee arrangements, discuss the costs you'll be expected to pay. Try to avoid being charged for long distance calls, photocopies and faxes—and negotiate an overall cap on costs, if possible.

B. Paying a Lawyer

When you hire a lawyer, have a clear understanding about how fees will be computed. And as new jobs are brought to the lawyer, ask specifically about charges for each. Many lawyers initiate fee discussions, but others forget or are shy about doing so. Bring up the subject yourself. Insist upon a written explanation of how the fees and costs will be paid.

1. Types of Fee Arrangements

There are four basic ways that lawyers charge, usually depending on the type of legal help you require.

a. Hourly fees

In most parts of the United States, you can get competent services for your business for $150 to $250 an hour. You will probably have to pay more in large metropolitan areas.

b. Flat fees

Sometimes, a lawyer quotes you a flat fee for a specific job. For example, a lawyer may offer to draw up an employment agreement for $300, or to represent you in a labor department dispute for $3,000. You pay the same amount regardless of how much time the lawyer spends.

c. Contingent fees

A contingency fee is a percentage (such as 33⅓%) of the amount the lawyer obtains for you in a negotiated settlement or through a trial. If the lawyer recovers nothing for you, there's no fee. However, the lawyer does generally expect reimbursement for out-of-pocket expenses such as filing fees, long distance phone calls and transcripts of testimony. Contingent fees are common in personal injury cases, but relatively unusual in employer's-side employment cases (they are common in plaintiff's-side employment cases). The only time you might expect a contingency fee arrangement is if you are suing an employee for a substantial amount of money—for stealing and using your trade secrets, for example—and the employee has the financial wherewithal to pay up.

d. Retainer fees

You may be able to hire a lawyer for a flat annual fee, called a retainer, to handle all of your routine legal business. You'll usually pay in equal monthly installments and, normally, the lawyer will bill you an additional amount for extraordinary services—such as representing you in a wrongful discharge lawsuit filed by a former employee. Obviously, the key to making this arrangement work is to have a written agreement clearly defining what's routine and what's extraordinary.

Comparison shopping among lawyers will help you avoid overpaying. But the cheapest hourly rate isn't necessarily the best. A novice who charges only $80 an hour may take three hours to review a consultant's work-for-hire contract. A more experienced lawyer who charges $200 an hour may do the same job in half an hour and make better suggestions. If a lawyer will be delegating some of the work on your case to a less experienced associate, paralegal or secretary, that work should be billed at a lower hourly rate. Be sure to get this information recorded in your initial written fee agreement.

2. Saving on Legal Fees

There are many ways to hold down the cost of legal services.

Be organized. It's important to gather important documents, write a short chronology of events and concisely explain a problem to your lawyer. Since papers can get lost in a lawyer's office, keep a copy of everything that's important.

Ask the lawyer to be your coach. Make it clear that you're eager to do as much work as possible yourself, with the lawyer coaching you from the sidelines. For example, you can write your own employee handbook, giving your lawyer the relatively inexpensive task of reviewing and polishing the document. In defending a wrongful discharge case, you can assemble needed documents and line up witnesses. But get a clear understanding about who's going to do what. You don't want to do the work and get billed for it because the lawyer duplicated your efforts. And you certainly don't want any crucial elements to fall through cracks because you each thought the other was attending to the work.

Read trade journals in your field. They'll help you keep up with specific legal developments that your lawyer may have missed. Send pertinent clippings to your lawyer—and encourage your lawyer to do the same for you. This can dramatically reduce legal research time.

Show that you're an important client. The single most important thing you can do to tell your lawyer how much you value the relationship is to pay your bills on time. Beyond that, let your lawyer know about plans for expansion and your company's possible future legal needs. And drop your lawyer a line when you've recommended him or her to your business colleagues.

Group your legal matters together. You'll save money if you consult with your lawyer on several matters at one time. For example, in a one-hour conference, you may be able to review with your lawyer the annual updating of your corporate record book, renew your lease and get final approval of a noncompetition agreement you've drafted for new employees to sign.

For detailed information on finding and working with a lawyer, and an explanation of every step in a lawsuit, from start to finish, see *The Lawsuit Survival Guide: A Client's Companion to Litigation*, by Joseph Matthews (Nolo).

A Tax Tip

If you visit your lawyer on a personal legal matter (such as reviewing a contract for the purchase of a house) and you also discuss a business problem (such as a pending OSHA inspection), ask your lawyer to allocate the time spent and send you separate bills. At tax time, you can easily list the business portion as a tax-deductible business expense.

C. Resolving Problems With Your Lawyer

If you see a problem emerging with your lawyer, nip it in the bud. Don't just sit back and fume; call, visit or write your lawyer. The problem won't get resolved if your lawyer doesn't even know there's a problem. An open exchange is essential for a healthy lawyer-client relationship.

Whatever it is that rankles, have an honest discussion about your feelings. Maybe you're upset because your lawyer hasn't kept you informed about what's going on in your case or has missed a promised deadline. Or maybe last month's bill was shockingly high or lacked any breakdown of how your lawyer's time was spent.

One good test of whether a lawyer-client relationship is a good one is to ask yourself if you feel able to talk freely with your lawyer about your degree of participation in any legal matter and your control over how the lawyer carries out a legal assignment. If you can't frankly discuss these sometimes sensitive matters with your lawyer, its time to hire another one. Otherwise, you'll surely waste money on unnecessary legal fees and risk having legal matters turn out badly. Remember that you're always free to change lawyers and to get all important legal documents back from a lawyer you no longer employ.

Out With the Old—Then, In With the New. Be sure to fire your old lawyer before you hire a new one. Otherwise, you could find yourself being billed by both lawyers at the same time.

If you have a dispute over fees, the local bar association may be able to mediate it for you. And if a lawyer has violated legal ethics, the bar association can take action to discipline or even disbar the lawyer. Where a major mistake has been made—for example, a lawyer has missed the deadline for filing a case—you can sue for malpractice. Virtually all lawyers carry malpractice insurance.

Your Rights As a Client

As a client, it's reasonable to expect:

- to be treated courteously by your lawyer and the members of his or her staff
- to receive an itemized statement of services rendered and a full explanation of billing practices
- to be charged reasonable fees
- to receive a prompt response to phone calls and letters
- to have confidential legal conferences, free from unwarranted interruptions
- to be kept informed of the status of your case
- to have your legal matters handled diligently and competently, and
- to receive clear answers to all questions.

If your lawyer consistently fails to meet these basic expectations, consider taking your business elsewhere.

D. Legal Research

Law libraries are chock-full of valuable information—information that you can easily find on your own. All you need is a rudimentary knowledge of how that information is organized.

1. Finding a Law Library

Your first step is to find a law library that's open to the public. You may find such a library in your county courthouse or at your state capitol. Public law schools generally permit the public to use their libraries, and some private law schools grant access to their libraries—sometimes for a modest fee. The reference department of a major public library may have a fairly decent legal research collection. Finally, don't overlook the law library in your own lawyer's office. Most lawyers, on request, will gladly share their books with their clients.

 There are a number of sources that provide good guidance in how to do your own legal research.

Legal Research: How to Find & Understand the Law, by Stephen Elias and Susan Levinkind (Nolo). This nontechnical book explains how to use all major legal research tools and helps you frame your research questions.

The Plain-Language Law Dictionary for Home and Office, edited by Robert S. Rothenberg (Penguin Books). This paperback book defines over 6,500 technical words and phrases in easily understood language—a valuable resource if you don't speak legalese.

2. Federal and State Laws

Employment is governed by both federal law and state law. Federal statutes, for example, deal with wages and hours, continuation of health insurance coverage when an employee is terminated, withholding employee taxes and Social Security contributions, unpaid family and medical leave, illegal discrimination and workplace safety. State statutes often touch on many of these same topics, as well as unemployment compensation and workers' compensation. The law of wrongful discharge —except where it involves claims of illegal discrimination—is primarily a matter of state law, most of which comes from judges' decisions rather than from statutes.

3. Sources of Legal Research

In doing legal research, there are several sources you may find useful, broadly categorized as primary and secondary sources. You use primary sources to find out the current status of the law. They include:

- constitutions (federal and state)
- legislation (laws—also called statutes or ordinances—passed by congress, your state legislature and local governments)
- administrative rules and regulations (issued by the federal and state administrative agencies charged with implementing statutes)
- case law (decisions of federal and state courts interpreting statutes—and sometimes making law, known as common law, if the subject isn't covered by a statute).

A small or midsized employer rarely gets involved in questions of constitutional law. You're far more likely to be concerned with law created by a federal or state statute, or by an administrative rule or regulation. At the federal level, that includes the Internal Revenue Code and regulations adopted by the Internal Revenue Service; regulations dealing with wages and hours adopted by the U.S. Department of Labor; and anti-discrimination statutes such as Title VII of the Civil Rights Act administered by the Justice Department and Equal Employment Opportunity Commission.

At the state level, you'll likely be interested in state statutes dealing with unemployment compensation and workers' compensation. You may also need to look into county and city ordinances addressing workplace issues such as tobacco smoke and discrimination.

4. How to Begin

Obviously, primary sources—statements of the "raw law"—are important. But most legal research begins with secondary sources— books that comment on, summarize, organize or describe the law.

It often makes sense to start with one of the two national encyclopedias, *American Jurisprudence 2d* (cited as Am. Jur. 2d) or *Corpus Juris Secundum* (cited as C.J.S.). If your state has its own encyclopedia, check that, too. These encyclopedias organize the case law and some statutes into narrative statements organized alphabetically by subject. Through citation footnotes, you can locate the full text of the cases and statutes on which the entries are based.

It's also helpful if you can find a treatise on the subject you're researching. A treatise is simply a book or series of books that covers a specific area of law. You may want to look at:

- *Labor Law in a Nutshell*, by Douglas L. Leslie
- *Workers' Compensation and Employee Protection Law in a Nutshell,* by Jack B. Hood, Benjamin A. Hardy, Jr., and Harold S. Lewis, Jr., or
- *Sex Discrimination in a Nutshell,* by Claire Sherman Thomas.

The entire "Nutshell" series is published by West Publishing Company.

Nolo publishes a comprehensive guide to employment law, *Federal Employment Laws: A Desk Reference*, by Amy DelPo & Lisa Guerin. This book gives detailed information on the most important federal employment statutes, including who they cover, what they require and prohibit, recordkeeping and posting rules and tips for compliance. It also includes the text of the laws themselves.

Law reviews (collections of articles on legal topics published by law schools) and other legal periodicals may also contain useful summaries of the law. The *American Bar Association Journal* as well as the journal published by your state bar association should be available in the law library that you use. In these journals, you'll often find timely articles on legal issues that affect small businesses. You can locate law review and bar journal articles through *The Index to Legal Periodicals*. Be forewarned, however, that law school reviews contain articles by law professors and students, and are usually of more academic than practical interest.

How to Read a Case Citation

There are several places where a case may be reported. If the case was decided by the U.S. Supreme Court, you can find it in either the United States Reports (U.S.) or the Supreme Court Reporter (S.Ct.). If it is a federal case decided by a court other than the U.S. Supreme Court, it will be in either the Federal Reporter, Second Series (F.2d) or the Federal Supplement (F. Supp.).

Most states publish their own official state reports. All published state court decisions are also included in the West Reporter System. West has divided the country into seven regions— and publishes all the decisions of the supreme and appellate state courts in the region together. These reporters are:

A. and A.2d. Atlantic Reporter (First and Second Series), which includes decisions from Connecticut, Delaware, the District of Columbia, Maine, Maryland, New Hampshire, New Jersey, Pennsylvania, Rhode Island and Vermont.

N.E. and N.E.2d. Northeastern Reporter (First and Second Series), which includes decisions from New York,* Illinois, Indiana, Massachusetts and Ohio.

N.W. and N.W.2d. Northwestern Reporter (First and Second Series), which includes decisions from Iowa, Michigan, Minnesota, Nebraska, North Dakota, South Dakota and Wisconsin.

P. and P.2d. Pacific Reporter (First and Second Series), which includes decisions from Alaska, Arizona, California,* Colorado, Hawaii, Idaho, Kansas, Montana, Nevada, New Mexico, Oklahoma, Oregon, Utah, Washington and Wyoming.

S.E. and S.E.2d. Southeastern Reporter (First and Second Series), which includes decisions from Georgia, North Carolina, South Carolina, Virginia and West Virginia.

So. and So.2d. Southern Reporter (First and Second Series), which includes decisions from Alabama, Florida, Louisiana and Mississippi.

S.W. and S.W.2d. Southwestern Reporter (First and Second Series), which includes decisions from Arkansas, Kentucky, Missouri, Tennessee and Texas.

A case citation will give you the names of the people or companies on each side of a case, the volume of the reporter in which the case can be found, the page number on which it begins and the year in which the case was decided. For example:

Smith v. Jones Int'l, 123 N.Y.S.2d 456 (1994)

Smith and Jones are the names of the parties having the legal dispute. The case is reported in volume 123 of the New York Supplement, Second Series, beginning on page 456; the court issued the decision in 1994.

*All California appellate decisions are published in a separate volume, the California Reporter (Cal. Rptr.) and all decisions from New York appellate courts are published in a separate volume, New York Supplement (N.Y.S.).

One good periodical for background information is *The Practical Lawyer,* published by the Joint Committee on Continuing Legal Education of the American Law Institute and American Bar Association (ALI-ABA). Each edition contains half a dozen clear and practical articles—many of which address topics of interest to employers. The checklists and forms are superb. This resource is virtually unknown outside the legal profession. An annual subscription, consisting of eight issues, costs $49. Call 800-253-6397 or write to: 4025 Chestnut Street, Philadelphia, PA 19104-3099. You can also email the publisher at publications@ali-aba.org.

Finally, practically every state has an organization that provides continuing legal education to practicing lawyers. Some of these organizations publish excellent books on business law subjects which focus on the law in your state and contain state-specific forms and checklists. You can also find a wealth of relevant information in the course materials prepared for continuing legal education seminars. To locate the organization that provides continuing legal education in your state, call your local or state bar association.

5. Online Research

For the computer savvy, online research is not only avant-garde but, more to the point, can be speedy and inexpensive. The logical starting point is Nolo's own website, www.nolo.com, where you'll discover valuable online information, including material on employment law and links to statutes and cases. In addition, Nolo's *Legal Research: How to Find & Under-*

stand the Law, by Steve Elias and Susan Levinkind, contains an entire chapter on online research.

Virtually all of the federal agencies that enforce employment laws and regulations have websites that contain an enormous amount of information—much of it geared specifically to the owners of small businesses—about the rights and responsibilities of employers and employees in the workplace. These websites also contain information about resources that can help you both understand the law and abide by it. These websites can be very valuable tools for you:

- U.S. Department of Labor: www.dol.gov
- U.S. Equal Employment Opportunity Commission: www.eeoc.gov
- U.S. Department of Justice: www.usdoj.gov
- The Internal Revenue Service: www.irs.gov.

State agencies that enforce state employment and labor laws often have websites as well. Contact your state department of labor for details. (See the Appendix for contact information.)

Lawyers who do computer research rely primarily on two systems: Westlaw and Lexis. A small but growing number of public law libraries offer these services. Those that do offer them usually require a sizable advance or a credit card; you pay as you go. Ask a law librarian for details, but be prepared for sticker shock. You can end up paying as much as $300 an hour.

It's more practical to use other online sources that cost you nothing more than the usual charge for online access time.

For an introduction to the vast amount of information that's out there, sample these sites:

- Lawyers Weekly at www.lweekly.com. Here you'll find up-to-date news on a wide range of legal topics. Check out the aptly named Treasure Chest of Important Documents for items you might want to download.
- The Thomas Legislative Information site at http://thomas.loc.gov. Named for Thomas Jefferson, this site contains a wealth of information on bills pending in Congress and laws recently adopted.
- The Court TV Small Business Law Center at www.courttv.com/legalhelp/business. Look for articles and forms on small business law in general and employment law in particular.
- Lectric Law Library at www.lectlaw.com. This is a good place to explore a wide range of business law issues. Many employment law topics are covered in reasonable depth.
- The Commerce Clearinghouse Business Owner's Toolkit, at www.toolkit.cch.com. This handy site includes a wealth of information, news and tools for employers, including sample policies and forms and extensive human resource materials.

Tips for Researching Employment Law

When looking up statutes, use the annotated versions. They typically come in multi-volume sets and contain the text of the laws, references to court and administrative decisions interpreting the statutes and citations to treatises and articles that discuss the law. Statutes are frequently amended. Always check the supplement at the back of statute books to make sure you have the latest edition.

Most federal statutes and many state statutes are interpreted in regulations which have the force of law. For example, the U.S. Department of Labor has enacted many regulations concerning the Fair Labor Standards Act. (See Chapter 3.) Where regulations exist, they're an essential part of your research.

Using the Shepard Citation system, you can look up a case that interests you and find a list of every other case that refers to it. This can expand your research—and also let you know if the law has changed recently. *Legal Research: How to Find & Understand the Law,* by Stephen Elias and Susan Levinkind (Nolo), has a good, easy-to-follow explanation of how to use the Shepard's system.

A relatively unknown resource for quickly locating business laws in your state is the United States Law Digest volume of the *Martindale-Hubbell Law Directory*. It contains a handy summary of laws, including statutory citations, for each state. But you may need a magnifying glass: The print is minuscule.

Appendix

Resources

U.S. Department of Labor A/2

State Labor Departments A/2

State Agencies That Enforce Laws Prohibiting Discrimination in Employment A/7

U.S. Department of Labor

200 Constitution Avenue, NW
Washington, DC 20210
202-693-4650
www.dol.gov

You can find a list of regional offices of the Wage and Hour Division at the Department of Labor's website at www.dol.gov/dol/esa/public/contacts/whd/america2.htm.

State Labor Departments

Alabama

Department of Labor
100 North Union Street
Montgomery, AL 36130-3500
334-242-3460
www.alalabor.state.al.us

Alaska

Department of Labor
1111 West Eighth Street
Post Office Box 21149
Juneau, AK 99801-1149
907-465-5980
www.labor.state.ak.us

Arizona

Industrial Commission
800 West Washington Street
Phoenix, AZ 85007
602-542-4411
www.ica.state.az.us

Arkansas

Department of Labor
10421 West Markham Street
Little Rock, AR 72205
501-682-4500
www.state.ar.us/labor

California

Division of Labor Standards Enforcement
  Department of Industrial Relations
455 Golden Gate Avenue, 8th Floor East
San Francisco, CA 94102
415-557-7878

320 West Fourth Street, Suite 450
Los Angeles, CA 90013
213-620-6330
www.dir.ca.gov/DLSE/dlse.html

Colorado

Department of Labor and Employment
1515 Arapahoe Street, Tower 2, Suite 400
Denver, CO 80202
303-318-8000
www.coworkforce.com

Connecticut

Department of Labor
200 Folly Brook Boulevard
Wethersfield, CT 06109
860-263-6000
www.ctdol.state.ct.us

Delaware

Department of Labor
4425 North Market Street
Wilmington, DE 19802
302-761-8085
www.delawareworks.com

District of Columbia

Office of Labor Relations and Collective
  Bargaining
441 4th Street, NW, Suite 200S
Washington, DC 20001
202-724-4953
http://dc.gov/agencies

Florida

Department of Labor and Employment Security
303 Hartman Building
2012 Capitol Circle, SE
Tallahassee, FL 32399-2152
850-922-7021
www2.myflorida.com/les

Georgia

Department of Labor
148 International Boulevard NE, Suite 600
Atlanta, GA 30303-1751
404-656-3017
www.dol.state.ga.us

Hawaii

Department of Labor and Industrial Relations
830 Punchbowl Street
Honolulu, HI 96813
808-586-8865
http://dlir.state.hi.us

Idaho

Department of Labor
317 Main Street
Boise, ID 83735-0600
208-332-3570
www.labor.state.id.us

Illinois

Department of Labor
160 North LaSalle St., 13th Floor, Suite C
Chicago, IL 60601
312-793-2800
FAX: 312-793-5257
www.state.il.us/agency/idol

Indiana

Department of Labor
402 West Washington, Room W-195
Indianapolis, IN 46204
317-232-2655
www.in.gov/labor

Iowa

Iowa Workforce Development
1000 East Grand Avenue
Des Moines, IA 50319-0209
515-281-5387
www.state.ia.us/iwd

Kansas

Office of Employment Standards, Department
  of Human Resources
1430 SW Topeka Blvd., 3rd Floor
Topeka, KS 66612
785-296-4062
www.hr.state.ks.us/home-html/empstand.htm

Kentucky

Labor Cabinet
U.S. Highway 127 South, Suite 4
Frankfort, KY 40601
502-564-3070
www.kylabor.net

Louisiana
Department of Labor
Post Office Box 94094
Baton Rouge, LA 70804
504 342-3202
www.ldol.state.la.us

Maine
Department of Labor
45 State House Station
Augusta, ME 04333-0045
207-624-6400
www.state.me.us/labor

Maryland
Department of Labor, Licensing and Regulation
1100 North Eutaw Street
Baltimore, MD 21201
410-767-2236
www.dllr.state.md.us

Massachusetts
Division of Employment and Training
19 Staniford Street
Boston, MA 02114
617-626-5400
www.detma.org

Michigan
Consumer and Industry Services
525 W. Ottawa, Post Office Box 30004
Lansing, MI 48909
517-373-1820
www.cis.state.mi.us

Minnesota
Department of Labor and Industry
443 Lafayette Road North
St. Paul, MN 55155
651-284-5000
www.doli.state.mn.us

Mississippi
Employment Security Commission
1520 West Capitol
Post Office Box 1699
Jackson, MS 39215
601-354-8711
www.mesc.state.ms.us

Missouri
Department of Labor and Industrial Relations
3315 West Truman Boulevard, Room 213
Post Office Box 504
Jefferson City, MO 65102-0504
573-751-4091
www.dolir.state.mo.us

Montana
Department of Labor and Industry
1327 Lockey Avenue
Helena, MT 59624
406-444-9091
http://dli.state.mt.us

Nebraska
Department of Labor and Safety Standards
301 Centennial Mall South
Lincoln, NE 68509
402-471-2239
www.dol.state.ne.us

Nevada

Office of the Labor Commissioner, Department
of Business & Industry
555 E. Washington Ave., Ste. 4100
Las Vegas, NV 89101-1050
702-486-2650
http://labor.state.nv.us

New Hampshire

Department of Labor
95 Pleasant Street
Concord, NH 03301
603-271-3176
www.labor.state.nh.us

New Jersey

Department of Labor
Post Office Box 110
John Fitch Plaza
Trenton, NJ 08625
609-292-2323
www.state.nj.us/labor

New Mexico

Department of Labor
501 Mountain Rd.
Albuquerque, NM 87102
505-841-8983
www3.state.nm.us/dol

New York

Department of Labor
State Office Building Campus, Room 500
Albany, NY 12240-0003
518-457-9000
www.labor.state.ny.us

North Carolina

Department of Labor
4 West Edenton Street
Raleigh, NC 27601
919-733-7166
www.dol.state.nc.us

North Dakota

Department of Labor
600 East Boulevard, Dept. 406
Bismarck, ND 58505-0340
701-328-2660
www.state.nd.us/labor

Ohio

Industrial Commission
30 W. Spring Street
Columbus, OH 43215-2233
614-466-6136
www.ic.state.oh.us/index.jsp

Oklahoma

Department of Labor
4001 N. Lincoln Boulevard
Oklahoma City, OK 73105
405-528-1500
www.state.ok.us/~okdol

Oregon

Bureau of Labor & Industries
800 NE Oregon, #32, Suite 1070
Portland, OR 97232
503-731-4200
www.boli.state.or.us

Pennsylvania

Department of Labor & Industry
Room 1700, 7th and Forster Streets
Harrisburg, PA 17120
717-787-5279
www.dli.state.pa.us

Rhode Island

Department of Labor
Pastore Government Center
1511 Pontiac Ave.
Cranston, RI 02920
401-462-8870
www.dlt.state.ri.us

South Carolina

Department of Labor, Licensing and Regulation
110 Centerview Drive
Columbia, SC 29210
803-896-4300
www.llr.state.sc.us

South Dakota

Department of Labor
700 Governors Drive
Pierre, SD 57501-2291
605-773-3101
www.state.sd.us/dol/dol.asp

Tennessee

Department of Labor and Workforce
  Development
710 James Robertson Parkway
Nashville, TN 37243
615-741-2257
www.state.tn.us/labor-wfd

Texas

Texas Workforce Commission
101 E. 15th Street
Austin, TX 78778
512-463-2222
www.twc.state.tx.us

Utah

Labor Commission
160 East 300 South, 3rd Floor
Post Office Box 146600
Salt Lake City, UT 84111
801-530-6800
http://laborcommission.utah.gov

Vermont

Department of Labor and Industry
National Life Building, Drawer 20
Montpelier, VT 05620-3401
802-828-2288
www.state.vt.us/labind

Virginia

Department of Labor and Industry
13 South 13th Street
Richmond, VA 23219
804-371-2327
www.dli.state.va.us

Washington

Department of Labor and Industries
Post Office Box 44851
Olympia, WA 98504-4851
360-902-4200
www.lni.wa.gov

West Virginia

Division of Labor
State Capitol Complex, Bldg. 6, Room B749
Charleston, WV 25305
304-558-7890
www.state.wv.us/labor

Wisconsin

Department of Workforce Development
201 E. Washington Avenue, GEF-1
Madison, WI 53702
608-266-7552
www.dwd.state.wi.us

Wyoming

Labor Standards Office, Department of
  Employment
Herschler Building, 2nd Floor East
122 West 25th Street
Cheyenne, WY 82002
307-777-7672
http://wydoe.state.wy.us

State Agencies That Enforce Laws Prohibiting Discrimination in Employment

Alaska

Commission for Human Rights
800 A Street, #204
Anchorage, AK 99501
907-274-4692
800-478-4692
www.gov.state.ak.us/aschr/aschr.htm

Arizona

Civil Rights Division
1275 W. Washington Street
Phoenix, AZ 85007
602-542-5263
877-491-5742
www.attorneygeneral.state.az.us/civil_rights/
  index.html

Arkansas

Equal Employment Opportunity Commission
425 West Capitol, #625
Little Rock, AR 72207
501-324-5060
www.eeoc.gov/index.html

California

Department of Fair Employment and Housing
Sacramento District Office
2000 O Street, #120
Sacramento, CA 95814
916-227-0551
800-884-1684
www.dfeh.ca.gov

Colorado

Civil Rights Division
1560 Broadway, #1050
Denver, CO 80202
303-894-2997
800-262-4845
www.dora.state.co.us/Civil-Rights

Connecticut

Commission on Human Rights & Opportunities
21 Grand Street
Hartford, CT 06106
860-541-3400
800-477-5737
www.state.ct.us/chro

Delaware

Office of Labor Law Enforcement
Division of Industrial Affairs
4225 N. Market Street
Wilmington, DE 19802
302-761-8200
www.delawareworks.com/divisions/
   industaffairs/law.enforcement.htm

District of Columbia

Office of Human Rights
441 4th Street NW, # 570
Washington, DC 20001
202-727-4559
www.ohr.dc.gov/main.shtm

Florida

Commission on Human Relations
325 John Knox Road
Building F, Suite 240
Tallahassee, FL 32303
850-488-7082
800-342-8170
http://fchr.state.fl.us

Georgia

Atlanta District Office
U.S. Equal Employment Opportunity
   Commission

100 Alabama Street, #4R30
Atlanta, GA 30303
404-562-6800
www.eeoc.gov

Hawaii

Hawai'i Civil Rights Commission
830 Punchbowl St., Room 411
Honolulu, HI 96813
808-586-8640 (Oahu only)
800-468-4644 x68640 (other islands)
www.state.hi.us/hcrc

Idaho

Idaho Human Rights Commission
1109 Main St., 4th Floor
Boise, ID 83720
208-334-2873
888-249-7025
www2.state.id.us/ihrc

Illinois

Department of Human Rights
100 West Randolph St.
James R. Thompson Center, Suite 10-100
Chicago, IL 60601
312-814-6200
www.state.il.us/dhr

Indiana

Civil Rights Commission
100 N. Senate Ave., Room N-103
Indianapolis, IN 46204
317-232-2600
800-628-2909
www.in.gov/icrc

Iowa

Iowa Civil Rights Commission
211 East Maple Street
Des Moines, IA 50309
515-281-4121
800-457-4416
www.state.ia.us/government/crc

Kansas

Human Rights Commission
900 SW Jackson, #851 South
Landon State Office Bldg.
Topeka, KS 66612
785-296-3206
www.ink.org/public/khrc

Kentucky

Human Rights Commission
332 W. Broadway, 7th Floor
Louisville, KY 40202
502-595-4024
800-292-5566
www.state.ky.us/agencies2/kchr

Louisiana

Commission on Human Rights
1001 N. 23rd St., #262
Baton Rouge, LA 70802
225-342-6969
www.gov.state.la.us/depts/lchr.htm

Maine

Human Rights Commission
51 Statehouse Station
Augusta, ME 04333
207-624-6050
www.state.me.us/mhrc/index.shtml

Maryland

Commission on Human Relations
William Donald Schaefer Towers
6 Saint Paul St., # 900
Baltimore, MD 21202
410-767-8600
800-637-6247
www.mchr.state.md.us

Massachusetts

Commission Against Discrimination
One Ashburton Place, Room 601
Boston, MA 02108
617-727-3990
www.state.ma.us/mcad

Michigan

Department of Civil Rights
State Plaza Building, 6th Floor
1200 Sixth Avenue
Detroit, MI 48226
313-256-2663
800-482-3604
www.mdcr.state.mi.us

Minnesota

Department of Human Rights
Army Corps of Engineers Centre
190 East 5th Street, #700
St. Paul, MN 55101
651-296-5663
800-657-3704
www.humanrights.state.mn.us

Missouri

Commission on Human Rights
3315 West Truman Blvd.
Jefferson City, MO 65102
573-751-3325
www.dolir.state.mo.us/hr

Montana

Human Rights Bureau
Employment Relations Division
Department of Labor & Industry
1625 11th Avenue
Helena, MT 59624
406-444-2884
http://erd.dli.state.mt.us/HumanRights/
    HRhome.htm

Nebraska

Equal Opportunity Commission
301 Centennial Mall South, 5th Fl.
Lincoln, NE 68509
402-471-2024
800-642-6112
www.nol.org/home/NEOC

Nevada

Equal Rights Commission
2450 Wrondel Way, #C
Reno, NV 89509
775-688-1288
http://detr.state.nv.us/nerc

New Hampshire

Commission for Human Rights
2 Chenell Drive
Concord, NH 03301
603-271-2767
http://webster.state.nh.us/hrc

New Jersey

Division of Civil Rights
31 Clinton Street
Newark, NJ 07102
973-648-2700
www.state.nj.us/lps/dcr

New Mexico

Human Rights Division
1596 Pacheco Street
Santa Fe, NM 87505
505-827-6838
800-566-9471
www.dol.state.nm.us/dol_hrd.html

New York

Division of Human Rights
One Fordham Plaza, 4th Floor
Bronx, NY 10458
718-741-8400
www.nysdhr.com

North Carolina

Employment Discrimination Bureau
Department of Labor
4 West Edenton Street
Raleigh, NC 27601
919-807-2827
www.dol.state.nc.us/edb/edb.htm

North Dakota

Human Rights Division
Department of Labor
600 E. Boulevard Avenue, Dept. 406
Bismarck ND 58505
701-328-2660
800-582-8032
www.state.nd.us/labor/services/human-rights

Ohio

Civil Rights Commission
1111 E. Broad Street, 3rd Floor
Columbus, OH 43205
614-466-2785
888-278-7101
www.state.oh.us/crc

Oklahoma

Human Rights Commission
Jim Thorpe Building, #480
2101 North Lincoln Blvd.
Oklahoma City, OK 73105
405-521-2360
www.onenet.net/~ohrc2

Oregon

Civil Rights Division
Bureau of Labor and Industries
800 NE Oregon Street
Portland, OR 97232
503-731-4200
www.boli.state.or.us/civil/index.html

Pennsylvania

Human Relations Commission
711 State Office Building
1400 Spring Garden Street
Philadelphia, PA 19130
215-560-2496
www.phrc.state.pa.us

Rhode Island

Commission for Human Rights
10 Abbott Park Place
Providence, RI 02903
401-277-2661
www.state.ri.us/manual/data/queries/
    stdept_.idc?id=16

South Carolina

Human Affairs Commission
2611 Forest Drive, #200
Columbia, SC 29204
803-737-7800
800-521-0725
www.state.sc.us/schac

South Dakota

Division of Human Rights
118 West Capitol Avenue
Pierre, SD 57501
605-773-4493
www.state.sd.us/dcr/hr/HR_HOM.htm

Tennessee

Human Rights Commission
531 Henley Street, #701
Knoxville, TN 37902
865-594-6500
800-251-3589
www.state.tn.us/humanrights

Texas

Commission on Human Rights
6330 Highway 290 East, #250
Austin, TX 78711
512-437-3450
888-452-4778
http://tchr.state.tx.us

Utah

Anti-Discrimination & Labor Division
Labor Commission
160 East 300 South, 3rd Floor
Salt Lake City, UT 84111
801-530-6801
800-222-1238
http://laborcommission.utah.gov//
    utah_antidiscrimination___labo.htm

Vermont

Attorney General's Office
Civil Rights Division
109 State Street
Montpelier, VT 05609
802-828-3657
888-745-9195
www.state.vt.us/atg/civil%20rights.htm

Virginia

Council on Human Rights
Washington Building #1202
1100 Bank Street
Richmond, VA 23219
804-225-2292
www.chr.state.va.us

Washington

Human Rights Commission
Melbourne Tower, #921
1511 Third Avenue
Seattle, WA 98101
206-464-6500
800-605-7324
www.wa.gov/hrc

West Virginia

Human Rights Commission
1321 Plaza East, Room 108A
Charleston, WV 25301
304-558-2616
888-676-5546
www.state.wv.us/wvhrc

Wisconsin

Department of Workforce Development
Equal Rights Division
1 South Pinckney Street, #320
Madison, WI 53708
608-266-6860
www.dwd.state.wi.us/er

Wyoming

Department of Employment
Labor Standards Office
1510 East Pershing Blvd., #2015
Cheyenne, WY 82002
307-777-7261
http://wydoe.state.wy.us/doe.asp?ID=3

Current as of March 8, 2002

Index

A

"Access Board," 9/15, 9/26

Accessibility improvements, ADA and, 9/14–15

Accounting methods, 5/11

Accrued paid leave and FMLA leave substitution, 6/6

ADA. *See* Americans with Disabilities Act (ADA)

ADEA (Age Discrimination in Employment Act), 8/14

Administrative employees and FLSA exemption, 3/5–6

Adoption
  assistance programs, 4/26
  FMLA leave and, 6/3

Advertisements
  independent contractor status and, 11/10
  for jobs, 1/14–15

Affirmative action plans, 8/5

Age discrimination, 8/14–16
  wrongful discharge and, 10/4

Age Discrimination in Employment Act (ADEA), 8/14

Agricultural jobs, child labor rules, 3/30

AIDS. *See* HIV/AIDS, employees with

Alcoholism, 7/31–32
  See also Drug and alcohol testing

Americans with Disabilities Act (ADA), 9/3–5
  Accessibility Guidelines, 9/15
  alcoholism, 7/32
  broad coverage of, 9/4
  businesses covered by, 9/5
  communicating with disabled workers, 9/22
  EEOC resources about hiring and the ADA, 1/19, 9/5, 9/26
  enforcement by EEOC, 9/25–26
  essential job functions in job description, 1/13, 9/9–10
  exceptions to coverage, 9/10–11
  financial assistance, 9/21, 9/23
  FMLA and, 6/18–19
  harassment of workers, 9/16
  health and safety standards, 9/23–24
  healthcare coverage and, 4/4–5
  HIV/AIDS, employees with, 7/28
  medical exam rules, 9/25
  medical information disclosure, 2/4
  medical tests and job applicants, 1/25–26
  mental or emotional impairments, 9/18–20
  obesity and, 9/7

people covered by, 9/5–10

pre-employment inquiries and, 1/16–19

psychological and aptitude tests, 1/23–24

qualified to work, 9/9

reasonable accommodations, 9/11–17

recovering addicts are protected, 1/27

skills tests and, 1/23

smoke-free workplace, 7/29

Apprentices and FLSA exemption, 3/9

Aptitude tests, 1/23–24

Arbitration, for discrimination claims, 8/6

Architectural and Transportation Barriers Compliance Board, 9/15, 9/26

Arrest records. *See* Criminal history

At-will employment, applicant acknowledges, 1/7

Authorization cards, unions and, 12/3

B

Background checks

employee's consent to, 1/19

FCRA regulations and, 1/36

privacy and, 1/9

See also Investigations and job applicants

Back taxes, deducting from paycheck, 3/33

Bargaining unit, unions and, 12/3

Behavioral control, independent contractor status and, 11/7–9

Benefits. *See* Employee benefits

BFOQ. *See* Bona fide occupational qualification

Birth of a child, FMLA leave and, 6/3

Bona fide occupational qualification (BFOQ), 8/3

guidelines, 1/13–14

See also Illegal discrimination

Bonuses and gifts, business expense deduction, 5/10–11

Breach of contract, wrongful discharge and, 10/5–6

Breach of good faith and fair dealing, wrongful discharge and, 10/6

Business expenses

independent contractor status and, 11/9

tax deductions for employer, 5/10–13

Business-to-business salespeople, 11/14

C

Cafeteria plans, 4/27

Cash accounting method, 5/11

"Catch-up" retirement plan contributions, 4/21–22

Center for Substance Abuse Prevention, 1/27

Certification of need for FMLA leave, 6/7–9

Certification of Physician or Practitioner, 6/8

Checklists, hiring of employee, 1/55

Child labor rules, 3/29–31

Children of employees, and healthcare coverage, 4/4

Child support, deducting from paycheck, 3/33

Citizenship and discrimination, 8/16–17

Civil Rights Act. *See* Title VII of the Civil Rights Act

Classification of workers

automatic classification as employees, 11/14–15

IRS tests for independent contractor status, 11/6–14

Clothing and grooming rules, in employee handbook, 2/15

COBRA coverage, 4/5–7

Commissions, 3/21–22

Compensatory time, 3/19–20

Complaint handling, in employee handbook, 2/15

Compliance Guide to the Family and Medical Leave Act, 6/2

Computers and RSD, 7/32–33

Computer specialists and FLSA exemption, 3/8

Conciliation, for settlement of discrimination complaints, 8/4–5

Confidentiality
employee files, 2/3
See also Privacy rights of job applicants; Trade secret protection

Consolidated Omnibus Budget Reconciliation Act, 4/5–7

Constructive discharge, 10/8

Consumer Credit Protection Act, 3/32–33

Consumer reporting agency (CRA), 1/36–37, 10/12

Contingency fees for lawyers, 13/6

Contracts
and firing employees, 10/9–10
truth in hiring and, 1/8
with unions, 12/4
written contracts and independent contractors, 11/11
wrongful discharge and breach of, 10/5–6

Conviction records. *See* Criminal history

Courtesy rules and the ADA, 9/20

Covenants not to compete. *See* Noncompete agreement

CRA (consumer reporting agency), 1/36–37, 10/12

Credit history, job applicants and, 1/39

Criminal history
expunging the record, 1/50
job applicants and, 1/39, 1/50
state laws on employee arrest & conviction records, 1/40–49

D

Debts and wage garnishments, 3/32–33

Debts owed to employer, deducting from paycheck, 3/32

Defamation suits and terminated employees, 10/31–34

Defined benefit plans, 4/20

Defined contribution plans, 4/20–21

Delivery people, statutory employee status, 5/14–15, 11/14

Dependent care assistance programs, 4/26

Disability and workers. *See* Americans with Disabilities Act (ADA)

Disability discrimination, wrongful discharge and, 10/4

Disability insurance, 4/25

Discipline
ADA and, 9/19–20
in employee handbook, 2/14
progressive discipline policy, 2/23–24

Disclaimers in employee handbooks, 2/12

Discretionary drug testing, 7/30–31

Discrimination, illegal. *See* Illegal discrimination

Discrimination, permitted. *See* Bona fide occupational qualification (BFOQ)

Discrimination policy, in employee handbook, 2/14

Disease prevention, 7/27–28

Docking pay of salaried employee, 3/7

Doctors, certification of health problem, 6/7–9

Dress codes and the ADA, 9/20

Driving records, 1/50

Drug and alcohol abuse policy, in employee handbook, 2/14

Drug and alcohol testing
employee drug testing plan, 7/30–31
job applicants and, 1/26–27
state laws, 1/28–35

Drug-Free Workplace Act, 1/26, 7/30

E

Educational assistance programs, 4/25–26

EEOC
   enforcement of the ADA, 9/25–26
   enforcement of Title VII by, 8/4–7
   and English-only rules, 8/17
   manual on hiring and the ADA, 1/19, 9/5
   on obesity as a disability, 9/7
   website resources, 8/2–3, 13/12
EIN (Employer Identification Number), 1/52,
   5/3–5
Email policy, 2/13
Emotional or mental impairments, 9/18–20
Employee benefits, 4/2–27
   adoption assistance programs, 4/26
   as business expense deduction, 5/13
   cafeteria plans, 4/27
   dependent care assistance programs, 4/26
   disability insurance, 4/25
   educational assistance programs, 4/25–26
   in employee handbook, 2/14
   healthcare coverage, 4/3–20
   independent contractors and, 11/3
   life insurance, 4/24–25
   retirement plans, 4/20–24
Employee files, 2/2–5
   access by employees, 2/4–5
   confidentiality of, 2/3
   correcting mistakes in, 2/3
   I-9 forms in separate file, 2/3
   informing employees about contents of, 2/5
   medical information, 2/4
   state laws on employee access, 2/6–11
Employee handbooks, 2/5, 2/12–16
   contents of, 2/13–16
   disclaimers in, 2/12
   email policy, 2/13
   Employee Handbook Acknowledgment,
      2/16, 2/17
   legal exposure and, 2/12

Employee health problems, FMLA leave and,
   6/4
Employee Polygraph Protection Act, 1/24–25,
   10/4
Employee Retirement Income Security Act
   (ERISA), requirements, 4/23–24
Employer Identification Number (EIN), 1/52,
   5/3–5
Employment law research, 13/13
Employment letter sample, 1/51
English-only rules, 8/17
Equal Employment Opportunities Commission.
   See EEOC
Equal Pay Act, 3/15–16
Ergonomics and RSD prevention, 7/32–33
ERISA administration requirements for retire-
   ment plans, 4/23–24
Essential job functions in job description, 1/13,
   9/9–10
Estimated taxes, 5/9
Evaluations. *See* Performance reviews
Executive employees and FLSA exemption, 3/6
Expunging criminal records, 1/50

F

Fair Credit Reporting Act
   investigating complaints against workers,
      10/12
   job applicants and, 1/36–37
Fair Labor Standards Act, 3/3–9
   booklet about exemptions, 3/6–7
   businesses covered by, 3/3–4
   child labor rules, 3/29–31
   cost of clothing deducted from wages and,
      2/15
   enforcement of, 3/8
   Equal Pay Act, 3/15–16
   exempt employees, 3/5–9

mislabeling of jobs, 3/7
overtime pay, 3/16–19
penalties for violations, 3/8
recordkeeping duties, 3/29
Family and medical leave, 6/2–19
    ADA and, 6/18–19
    advance notice requirement, 6/6–7
    certification of need, 6/7–9
    Compliance Guide to the Family and Medical Leave Act, 6/2
    eligibility, 6/2
    enforcement, 6/19
    Family and Medical Leave Act (FMLA), 6/2
    family relationships defined by FMLA, 6/4
    health benefits during leave, 6/9–10
    paid leave substituted for, 6/6
    reasons for leave, 6/2–4
    recertification of medical condition, 6/9
    returning to work, 6/10–11
    scheduling leave, 6/4
    state laws and, 6/11–17
    temporary job transfers, 6/5
Family and Medical Leave Act (FMLA), 6/2
Family health problems, FMLA leave and, 6/3
Family Support Act, 3/33
FCRA. *See* Fair Credit Reporting Act
Federal taxes, 5/2–15
    credits for ADA compliance, 9/21, 9/23
    deductions for ADA compliance, 9/21
    deductions for expenses, 5/10–13
    deposit requirements, 5/7–8
    Employer Identification Number (EIN), 1/52, 5/3–5
    federal income tax withholding (FIT), 5/6
    federal unemployment taxes (FUTA), 5/7
    independent contractors, 5/13–14, 11/2–3
    payroll services, 5/8
    self-employment taxes, 5/8–9

Social Security taxes (FICA), 5/6–7
    statutory employees, 5/14–15
Federal Trade Commission. *See* FTC
Fee arrangements for lawyers, 13/6–7
FICA withholding, 5/6–7
Financial assistance, for ADA compliance, 9/21, 9/23
Financial control, independent contractor status and, 11/9–11
Firing process, 10/14–18
    guidelines for, 10/9–11
    independent contractors and, 11/4
    paperwork, 10/16–17
    return of property, 10/17–18
    severance packages, 10/14–16
    termination meeting, 10/18
    See also Termination
Fitness to work, FMLA leave and return to work, 6/11
FLSA. *See* Fair Labor Standards Act
FMLA. *See* Family and Medical Leave Act
Food handlers and the ADA, 9/24
Former employers, information provided by, 1/38
Foster care, FMLA leave and, 6/3
401(k) plans, 4/21–22
Fringe benefits. *See* Employee benefits
FTC, FCRA rights publication, 1/37
FUTA payments, 5/7

G

Garnishments, 3/32–33
Gay workers
    and the ADA, 9/10
    and discrimination, 8/18
Gender
    as BFOQ, 1/14
    and discrimination, 8/3–4

wrongful discharge and, 10/4
Government regulations and independent
  contractors, 11/4
Grooming and clothing rules, in employee
  handbook, 2/15

H
Hazardous jobs, child labor rules, 3/30
Hazardous substances. See Occupational Safety
  and Health Act (OSHA)
Health and safety, 7/3–33
  ADA compliance and, 9/23–24
  complaints about and wrongful discharge,
    10/4
  disease prevention, 7/27–28
  drug and alcohol abuse, 7/29–32
  in employee handbook, 2/15
  food handlers and the ADA, 9/24
  Occupational Safety and Health Act, 7/3–8
  repetitive stress disorder, 7/32–33
  state OSHA laws, 7/18–20, 7/22
  tobacco smoke, 7/28–29
  workers' compensation, 7/23–27
Healthcare coverage, 4/3–20
  choosing between options, 4/3–4
  continuing coverage for former employees
    (COBRA), 4/5–7
  cost reduction tips, 4/19
  FMLA leave and, 6/9–10
  limitations on, 4/4–5
  medical savings accounts, 4/19
  older workers, 4/20
  pregnant women, 4/20
  state laws, 4/8–18
  termination and, 10/26
  types of, 4/3
Healthcare providers, certification of health
  problem, 6/7–9

Health insurance. See Healthcare coverage
Health Insurance Portability and Accountability
  Act, 4/5
Health maintenance organization (HMO), 4/3
Health problems, FMLA leave and, 6/3, 6/4
Highly paid employees, FMLA leave and return
  to work, 6/10–11
Hiring guidelines, 1/3–55
  advertisements, 1/14–15
  applications for jobs, 1/15–20
  false promises about job security, 1/6–7
  illegal discrimination, avoiding, 1/3–5
  immigration law requirements, 1/53
  interviews, 1/20–22
  investigations, 1/36–50
  job descriptions, 1/12–14
  job offers, 1/50, 1/51
  negligent hiring claims, 1/7, 1/9
  New Hire Reporting form, 1/53–54
  privacy rights of applicants, 1/5–6
  rejecting applicants, 1/50, 1/52
  tax compliance, 1/52
  testing of applicants, 1/22–27
  truth in hiring, 1/8
  unfair competition, protections for, 1/9–12
HIV/AIDS, employees with, ADA and, 7/28
HMO (health maintenance organization), 4/3
Home workers, statutory employee status, 5/15
Honesty tests, 1/24–25
  wrongful discharge and, 10/4
Housing costs, deducting from paycheck,
  3/31–32

I
Illegal discrimination
  age discrimination, 8/14–16
  avoiding during hiring, 1/3–5
  citizenship, 8/16–17

healthcare coverage and, 4/5

pregnancy, 8/16

religion in the workplace, 8/19

resources, 8/2–3

sexual harassment, 8/8–13

sexual orientation, 8/18

state agencies that enforce laws against, A/7–12

state and local laws, 8/18–26

Title VII of the Civil Rights Act, 8/3–8

workers' compensation claim filing, 7/26

and wrongful discharge, 10/4

See also Bona fide occupational qualification (BFOQ)

Illegal drug use, 7/30–31

as exception to ADA coverage, 9/10

Immigration and Naturalization Service. *See* INS

Immigration law requirements, 1/53

Immigration Reform and Control Act (IRCA), prohibition against discrimination, 8/16

Impairment

limiting a life activity, 9/5–7

mental or emotional impairments, 9/18–20

record of, 9/8

regarded as impaired, 9/8–9

Income tax withholding, 5/6

Incorporation, independent contractor status and, 11/11

Independent contractors, 11/2–19

automatic classification as employees, 11/14–15

compared to employees, 11/2–6

contract sample, 11/18–19

exempt from FLSA, 3/4

hiring of, 11/17

IRS rules, 11/6–14

misclassification of, 11/3, 11/15–17

safe harbour provisions and the IRS, 11/14

state laws, 11/15

and taxes, 5/13–14

and workers' compensation, 7/27

Indirect discrimination, 8/4

Initiatives Inc., 6/5

Injury and illness log, 7/5

INS Form I-9 (Employment Eligibility Verification), 1/53

separate file for, 2/3

INS *Handbook for Employers,* 1/53

Instruction, independent contractor status and, 11/7–8

Insurance salespeople, statutory employee status, 5/15, 11/14

Internal Revenue Service. *See* IRS

Interstate commerce

FLSA and, 3/3

OSHA and, 7/4

Interviewing job applications, 1/20–22

Investigating complaints against workers, 10/11–13

Fair Credit Reporting Act and, 10/12

locating an investigator, 10/13

right to have co-worker present during interview, 2/23, 10/18

Investigations and job applicants, 1/36–50

credit history, 1/39

criminal history, 1/39–50

driving records, 1/50

Fair Credit Reporting Act and, 1/36–37

former employers, 1/38

school transcripts, 1/38–39

See also Background checks

IRCA. *See* Immigration Reform and Control Act

IRS

tax requirements for retirement plans, 4/22–23

tests for independent contractor status, 11/6–14

See also Resources

IRS Form 1099-MISC, 11/2–3

IRS Form SS-4 (EIN application), 1/52, 5/3–5

IRS Form W-2, 11/11

IRS Form W-4, 1/52

IRS Form W-9, 5/14

IRS wage levy notice, 3/33

J

JAN (Job Accommodation Network), 9/14, 9/17

Job Accommodation Network, 9/14, 9/17

Job advertisements, 1/14–15

Job applications, 1/15–20

Job attendance in employee handbook, 2/14

Job descriptions, 1/12–14, 9/9–10

Job offers, 1/50, 1/51

Job protection, returning after FMLA leave, 6/10

Job security, false promises about, 1/6–7

L

Labor contracts, 12/4

Lambda Legal Defense and Education Fund, 8/18

Law libraries, 13/9

Lawyers

   costs for services, 13/5

   locating, 13/2–5

   paying for, 13/6–7

   problems with, 13/8

   saving on legal fees, 13/7

Layoffs, handling safely, 10/7–8

Lectures, meetings and training seminars, and pay, 3/24

Legal research, 13/9–13

   case law citations, how to read, 13/11

   employment law, 13/13

federal and state laws, 13/9

law libraries, 13/9

sources of, 13/9–12

Lesbian workers

   and the ADA, 9/10

   and discrimination, 8/18

Liability and independent contractors, 11/4–5

Lie detector tests. *See* Honesty tests

Life activity, impairments limiting, 9/5–7

Life insurance, 4/24–25

Local taxes, 5/2

Lodging, business expense deduction, 5/12–13

Long test for FLSA exemptions, 3/5–7

Lying on job application, 1/19–20

M

Martindale-Hubbell Law Directory, 13/4

Material Safety Data Sheets (MSDS), 7/21

"Maximum Tip Credit," 3/10

Meal and rest breaks

   and pay, 3/24

   state laws, 3/25–29

Meals

   business expense deduction, 5/11–12

   deducting from paycheck, 3/31–32

Medical healthcare providers, certification of health problem, 6/7–9

Medical leave. *See* Family and medical leave

Medical records

   OSHA recordkeeping, 7/5

   psychiatric information, 9/18–19

Medical savings account (MSA), 4/19

Medical tests

   ADA and, 9/25

   and job applicants, 1/25–26

   See also Testing guidelines

Medication information in employee files, 2/4

Meetings and training seminars, and pay, 3/24

Mental or emotional impairments, 9/18–20

"Minimum Cash Wage," 3/10

Minimum wage, 3/9

   state laws, 3/10–14

MSA (medical savings account), 4/19

MSDS (Material Safety Data Sheets), 7/21

N

National Directory of New Hires, 1/54

National Labor Relations Act (NLRA), 12/2

National Labor Relations Board (NLRB)

   certification of union by, 12/4

   elections conducted by, 12/3–4

National origin

   as BFOQ, 1/14

   and discrimination, 8/3–4

   wrongful discharge and, 10/4

Negligent hiring claims, preventing, 1/7, 1/9

New Hire Reporting form, 1/53–54

NLRA. *See* National Labor Relations Act

NLRB. *See* National Labor Relations Board

Noncompete agreement

   enforcing after termination, 10/29–30

   unfair competition and, 1/11–12

Notice of contest, OSHA citation, 7/8

Notice posting. *See* Posting requirements

O

Obesity and the ADA, 9/7

Occupational Safety and Health Act (OSHA), 7/3–8

   employees' rights under, 7/8

   exemption from recordkeeping, 7/5

   Material Safety Data Sheets (MSDS), 7/21

   penalties for violations, 7/7–8

   posting requirements, 7/4

   recordkeeping requirements, 7/4–5

   reporting requirements, 7/4–5

   resources for rules and regulations, 7/16

   right to know law, 7/21

   safety codes, 7/16–17

   safety standards, 7/4

   safety training, 7/5–6

   state OSHA laws, 7/18–20, 7/22

   who is covered, 7/4

Occupational Safety and Health Administration (OSHA), 7/4

   inspections, 7/6–7

   search warrants, 7/7

   state sources for consultations, 7/8–15

Older workers

   age discrimination, 8/14–16

   "catch-up" retirement plan contributions, 4/21–22

   healthcare coverage, 4/20

   Older Workers Benefits Protection Act, 4/22, 8/15–16

On-call periods and pay, 3/23

Online resources. *See* Resources

OSHA. *See* Occupational Safety and Health Act; Occupational Safety and Health Administration

OSHA Form 200 (injury and illness log), 7/5

Outside salespeople and FLSA exemption, 3/8

Overtime pay, 3/16–19

   attitudes about, 3/19

   computing overtime pay rate, 3/17–18

   exempt employees, 3/17

   federal rules publication, 3/17

   partially exempt employees, 3/17

P

Paid leave substituted for unpaid FMLA leave, 6/6

Paid time off, 3/22

Paperwork checklists, hiring of employee, 1/55

Part-time employees, and healthcare coverage, 4/4

Pay and salaries
   in employee handbook, 2/13–14
   See also Wages and hours

Pay requirements, 3/9–20
   minimum wage, 3/9–15

Payroll services, 5/8

Payroll withholding, 3/31–33
   See also Federal taxes

Performance reviews, 2/16, 2/18–22
   benefits of, 2/16, 2/18
   evaluation process, 2/18–19
   sample evaluation form, 2/20–22

Personnel practices, 2/2–24
   disciplining employees, 2/23–24
   employee files, 2/2–5
   employee handbooks, 2/5, 2/12–16
   performance reviews, 2/16, 2/18–22
   state laws on employee access to personal files, 2/6–11

Physical characteristics and the ADA, 9/10

Polygraph tests, 1/24–25, 10/4

Portal-to-Portal Pay Act, 3/22

Postemployment inquiry handling, 10/31–34

Posting requirements
   Employee Polygraph Protection Act poster, 1/24–25
   Family and Medical Leave Act poster, 6/2
   Federal Minimum Wage poster, 3/15
   Job Safety and Health Protection poster, 7/4

PPO (preferred provider organization), 4/3

Practical Lawyer, 13/12

Pre-adverse action disclosure, 1/37

Pre-employment inquiries, 1/16–19

Pre-employment testing, 1/22–27

Preexisting conditions, healthcare coverage and, 4/5

Preferred provider organization (PPO), 4/3

Pregnancy Discrimination Act, 8/16

Pregnant women, healthcare coverage, 4/20

Privacy rights of job applicants, 1/5–6
   background checks and, 1/9

Professional employees and FLSA exemption, 3/6–7

Progressive discipline policy, 2/23–24

Psychological and aptitude tests, 1/23–24

Psychological characteristics and the ADA, 9/10, 9/11

Psychological disorders and the ADA, 9/18–20

Public policy violations, wrongful discharge and, 10/6

Q

QDRO, retirement benefits and, 4/24

Qualified domestic relations order (QDRO), retirement benefits and, 4/24

Qualified privilege, references for terminated employees, 10/32

Qualified to work, and the ADA, 9/9

R

Racial discrimination. *See* Title VII of the Civil Rights Act

Reasonable accommodations, 9/11–17
   accessibility improvements, 9/14–15
   deciding on, 9/13–14
   mental disabilities and, 9/19
   other types of, 9/15–17
   requirements for, 9/11–12
   resources, 9/14
   undue hardship on business, 9/12–13

Recertification of medical condition, 6/9

Recordkeeping duties
   under FLSA, 3/29
   under OSHA, 7/5

Recovering addicts, ADA protection for, 1/27

References for terminated employees, 10/31–33

Regarded as impaired, 9/8–9

Rejecting job applicant, 1/50, 1/52

Release of claims, in severance agreements, 10/17

Religion
  as BFOQ, 1/14
  and discrimination, 8/4–5
  in the workplace, 8/19
  wrongful discharge and, 10/4

Repetitive stress disorder (RSD), 7/32–33

Resignation instead of termination, 10/18, 10/20

Resources
  ADA, 9/26
  ADA Accessibility Guidelines, 9/15
  ADA and FMLA relationship, 6/19
  Architectural and Transportation Barriers Compliance Board, 9/15, 9/26
  Center for Substance Abuse Prevention, 1/27
  Certification of Physician or Practitioner, 6/8
  discrimination in the workplace, 8/2–3
  EEOC and discrimination, 8/2–3
  EEOC manual on hiring and the ADA, 1/19, 9/5
  firing employees, 10/3
  FLSA exemptions booklet, 3/6–7
  FMLA requirements, 6/19
  FTC publication of FCRA rights, 1/37
  government websites, 13/12
  healthcare portability law, 4/5
  independent contractor hiring, 11/2
  Initiatives Inc., 6/5
  INS *Handbook for Employers,* 1/53
  investigating complaints against workers, 10/12
  IRS publications
    on business tax year, 5/3
    for employers, 1/52
    on employment taxes, 5/6, 5/8
    on statutory employees, 5/15
    on tax withholding and estimated tax, 5/9
  Job Accommodation Network, 9/14, 9/17
  lawyers, locating and working with, 13/4, 13/7
  layoffs and WARN requirements, 10/8
  legal research, 13/9
    books, 13/10
    online sources, 13/12–13
  Martindale-Hubbell Law Directory, 13/4
  OSHA rules and regulations, 7/16
  overtime pay publication, 3/17
  periodicals, 13/12
  Practical Lawyer, 13/12
  reasonable accommodation, 9/14
  recordkeeping duties under FLSA, 3/29
  severance agreements, 10/17
  sexual orientation discrimination, 8/18
  state labor departments, A/2–7
  taxes, 5/6
  unemployment cost controls, 10/27
  U.S. Dept. of Labor, A/2
  websites, 13/12, 13/13
  West's Legal Directory, 13/4
  worker classification, 11/7

Rest breaks. *See* Meal and rest breaks

Resume fraud, 1/19–20

Retainer fees for lawyers, 13/6–7

Retention period for OSHA records, 7/5

Retirement plans, 4/20–24
  defined benefit plans, 4/20
  defined contribution plans, 4/20–21
  divorce and ERISA, 4/24

ERISA administration requirements, 4/23–24
401(k) plans, 4/21–22
IRS tax law requirements, 4/22–23
termination of, 4/24
Return of property, termination and, 10/17–18
Right to know laws (hazardous chemicals),
7/21–22
RSD (repetitive stress disorder), 7/32–33

S

Safety. *See* Health and safety
Salaries
business expense deduction, 5/10
See also Wages and hours
School transcripts, 1/38–39
Sealing criminal records, 1/50
Search warrants, OSHA inspectors and, 7/7
Self-employment taxes, 5/8–9
Severance packages, 10/14–16
release of claims, 10/17
Sexual and behavioral disorders and the ADA,
9/10
Sexual harassment, 8/8–13
compliance, 8/9–10
policy in employee handbook, 2/14
policy sample, 8/11–13
prevention, 8/10
prohibited conduct, 8/9
wrongful discharge and, 10/4
Sexual orientation
and discrimination, 8/18
wrongful discharge and, 10/4
Short test for FLSA exemptions, 3/5–7
Skills tests, 1/22–23
Sleep time and pay, 3/23
Small necessities state laws, 6/12
Smoking, in employee handbook, 2/15
Social Security taxes (FICA), 5/6–7

Spouses, FMLA leave and, 6/3
State agencies that enforce laws against
employment discrimination, A/7–12
State labor departments, A/2–7
State laws
discrimination in employment, 8/21–26
drug and alcohol testing, 1/28–35
employee access to personal records, 2/6–11
employee arrest & conviction records,
1/40–49
employee health insurance, 4/8–18
family and medical leave, 6/11–17
final paychecks, 10/21–25
former employers disclosure about
employee, 1/38
meal and rest breaks, 3/25–29
minimum wage, 3/10–14
OSHA, 7/18–20
pay interval, 3/20
small necessities laws, 6/12
State taxes, 5/2
Statutory employees and taxes, 5/14–15

T

Targeted job tax credit, 9/23
Tax compliance, of employer, 1/52
Tax credits, for ADA compliance, 9/21, 9/23
Taxes. *See* Federal taxes; Local taxes; State
taxes
Temporary job transfers, FMLA leave and, 6/5
Termination, 10/3–34
alternatives to, 10/14
business information protection, 10/29–31
constructive discharge, 10/8
favorable references, 10/20
final paychecks and state laws, 10/20–25
firing guidelines, 10/9–11
firing process, 10/14–18

health insurance continuation, 10/26

investigating complaints against workers, 10/11–13

letter sample, 10/16

noncompete agreement enforcement, 10/29–30

outplacement help, 10/20

postemployment inquiry handling, 10/31–34

protecting against legal claims, 10/7–8

resignation instead of, 10/18, 10/20

trade secret protection, 10/30–31

unemployment compensation, 10/26–29

violence after, 10/19

wrongful discharge, 10/3–6

Testing guidelines

drug tests, 1/26–27, 7/30–31

honesty tests, 1/24–25

medical tests, 1/25–26, 9/25

pre-employment testing, 1/22–27

psychological and aptitude tests, 1/23–24

skills tests, 1/22–23

state drug and alcohol testing laws, 1/28–35

See also Drug and alcohol testing

Tests for FLSA exemptions, 3/5–7

Threats, ADA and, 9/19–20

Time off and pay, 3/22

Tips, 3/21

and state minimum wage laws, 3/10–14

Title VII of the Civil Rights Act, 8/3–8

affirmative action plans, 8/5

arbitration for claims, 8/6

discrimination prohibited, 8/3–4

enforcement by EEOC, 8/4–7

indirect discrimination, 8/4

remedies, 8/7

retaliation, 8/7

who is covered, 8/3

wrong discharge and, 10/4

See also Illegal discrimination

Trade secret protection

independent contractors and, 11/17

termination and, 10/30–31

unfair competition and, 1/10–11

Training

independent contractor status and, 11/8

and pay, 3/24

Training records, safety training, 7/5

Transportation costs, deducting from paycheck, 3/31–32

Traveling salespeople, statutory employee status, 5/15

Travel time and pay, 3/22–23

Treatment restrictions, healthcare coverage and, 4/5

Truth in hiring, 1/8

U

Unacceptable conduct, ADA and, 9/19–20

Undue hardship on business, reasonable accommodations and, 9/12–13

Unemployment compensation

independent contractors and, 7/27, 11/3

termination and, 10/26–29

Unemployment taxes (FUTA), 5/7

Unfair competition, protecting against, 1/9–12

Unions, 12/2–6

employee rights and limitations, 12/5–6

employer rights and limitations, 12/4–5

National Labor Relations Act, 12/2

tips for avoiding unionizing, 12/6

unionizing a workplace, 12/2–4

Unpaid leave. *See* Family and medical leave

U.S. Dept. of Labor, A/2

V

Vacation pay, 3/22

business expense deduction, 5/10
  as part of severance package, 10/15–16
Video display terminals, rules for, 7/33
Violence and termination, 10/19

W

Wage and Hour Division, enforcement of
  FLSA, 3/8
Wage garnishments, 3/32–33
Wages and hours, 3/3–33
  business expense deduction for wages, 5/10
  calculating pay, 3/20–22
  calculating workhours, 3/22–29
  child labor rules, 3/29–31
  compensatory time, 3/19–20
  equal pay for equal work, 3/15–16
  Fair Labor Standards Act, 3/3–9
  independent contractors and, 11/4, 11/10
  overtime pay, 3/16–19
  pay requirements, 3/9–20
  payroll withholding, 3/31–33
  recordkeeping duties, 3/29
WARN (Worker Adjustment and Retraining
  Act), 10/7–8

Website resources. *See* Resources
Weingarten right, 2/23, 10/18
West's Legal Directory, 13/4
Worker Adjustment and Retraining Act
  (WARN), 10/7–8
Workers' compensation, 7/23–27
  benefits paid, 7/26–27
  cost control, 7/25–26
  coverage requirements, 7/23–24
  independent contractors and, 7/27, 11/3
  injuries and illnesses covered, 7/26
  obtaining coverage, 7/24–25
  penalizing workers who file claims, 7/26
  rejecting coverage, 7/24
Workhour calculations, 3/22–29
Workplace civility, in employee handbooks,
  2/15
Written contracts and independent contractors,
  11/11
Wrongful discharge, 10/3–6
  court decisions, 10/5–6
  statutes and, 10/3–4

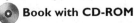

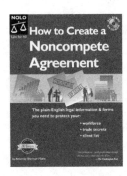

CATALOG

...more from nolo

	PRICE	CODE

BUSINESS

Avoid Employee Lawsuits	$24.95	AVEL
The CA Nonprofit Corporation Kit (Binder w/CD-ROM)	$59.95	CNP
Consultant & Independent Contractor Agreements (Book w/CD-ROM)	$29.95	CICA
The Corporate Minutes Book (Book w/CD-ROM)	$69.99	CORMI
The Employer's Legal Handbook	$39.99	EMPL
Everyday Employment Law	$29.99	ELBA
Drive a Modest Car & 16 Other Keys to Small Business Success	$24.99	DRIV
Firing Without Fear	$29.95	FEAR
Form Your Own Limited Liability Company (Book w/CD-ROM)	$44.99	LIAB
Hiring Independent Contractors: The Employer's Legal Guide (Book w/CD-ROM)	$34.95	HICI
How to Create a Buy-Sell Agreement & Control the Destiny of your Small Business (Book w/Disk-PC)	$49.95	BSAG
How to Create a Noncompete Agreement	$44.95	NOCMP
How to Form a California Professional Corporation (Book w/CD-ROM)	$59.95	PROF
How to Form a Nonprofit Corporation (Book w/CD-ROM)—National Edition	$44.99	NNP
How to Form a Nonprofit Corporation in California (Book w/CD-ROM)	$44.99	NON
How to Form Your Own California Corporation (Binder w/CD-ROM)	$59.99	CACI
How to Form Your Own California Corporation (Book w/CD-ROM)	$34.99	CCOR
How to Get Your Business on the Web	$29.99	WEBS
How to Write a Business Plan	$29.99	SBS
The Independent Paralegal's Handbook	$29.95	PARA
Leasing Space for Your Small Business	$34.95	LESP
Legal Guide for Starting & Running a Small Business	$34.99	RUNS
Legal Forms for Starting & Running a Small Business (Book w/CD-ROM)	$29.95	RUNS2
Marketing Without Advertising	$22.00	MWAD
Music Law (Book w/CD-ROM)	$34.99	ML
Nolo's California Quick Corp	$19.95	QINC
Nolo's Guide to Social Security Disability	$29.99	QSS
Nolo's Quick LLC	$24.95	LLCQ
Nondisclosure Agreements	$39.95	NAG
The Small Business Start-up Kit (Book w/CD-ROM)	$29.99	SMBU
The Small Business Start-up Kit for California (Book w/CD-ROM)	$34.99	OPEN
The Partnership Book: How to Write a Partnership Agreement (Book w/CD-ROM)	$39.99	PART
Sexual Harassment on the Job	$24.95	HARS
Starting & Running a Successful Newsletter or Magazine	$29.99	MAG
Tax Savvy for Small Business	$34.99	SAVVY
Working for Yourself: Law & Taxes for the Self-Employed	$39.99	WAGE
Your Limited Liability Company: An Operating Manual (Book w/CD-ROM)	$49.99	LOP
Your Rights in the Workplace	$29.99	YRW

CONSUMER

Fed Up with the Legal System: What's Wrong & How to Fix It	$9.95	LEG
How to Win Your Personal Injury Claim	$29.99	PICL
Nolo's Encyclopedia of Everyday Law	$29.99	EVL
Nolo's Pocket Guide to California Law	$24.95	CLAW
Trouble-Free Travel...And What to Do When Things Go Wrong	$14.95	TRAV

Prices subject to change.

	PRICE	CODE

ESTATE PLANNING & PROBATE

	PRICE	CODE
8 Ways to Avoid Probate	$19.95	PRO8
9 Ways to Avoid Estate Taxes	$29.95	ESTX
Estate Planning Basics	$21.99	ESPN
How to Probate an Estate in California	$49.99	PAE
Make Your Own Living Trust (Book w/CD-ROM)	$39.99	LITR
Nolo's Law Form Kit: Wills	$24.95	KWL
Nolo's Simple Will Book (Book w/CD-ROM)	$34.99	SWIL
Plan Your Estate	$44.99	NEST
Quick & Legal Will Book	$15.99	QUIC

FAMILY MATTERS

	PRICE	CODE
Child Custody: Building Parenting Agreements That Work	$29.95	CUST
The Complete IEP Guide	$24.99	IEP
Divorce & Money: How to Make the Best Financial Decisions During Divorce	$34.99	DIMO
Do Your Own Divorce in Oregon	$29.95	ODIV
Get a Life: You Don't Need a Million to Retire Well	$24.95	LIFE
The Guardianship Book for California	$39.99	GB
How to Adopt Your Stepchild in California (Book w/CD-ROM)	$34.95	ADOP
A Legal Guide for Lesbian and Gay Couples	$29.99	LG
Living Together: A Legal Guide (Book w/CD-ROM)	$34.99	LTK
Using Divorce Mediation: Save Your Money & Your Sanity	$29.95	UDMD

GOING TO COURT

	PRICE	CODE
Beat Your Ticket: Go To Court and Win! (National Edition)	$19.99	BEYT
The Criminal Law Handbook: Know Your Rights, Survive the System	$34.99	KYR
Everybody's Guide to Small Claims Court (National Edition)	$24.95	NSCC
Everybody's Guide to Small Claims Court in California	$26.99	CSCC
Fight Your Ticket ... and Win! (California Edition)	$29.99	FYT
How to Change Your Name in California	$34.95	NAME
How to Collect When You Win a Lawsuit (California Edition)	$29.99	JUDG
How to Mediate Your Dispute	$18.95	MEDI
How to Seal Your Juvenile & Criminal Records (California Edition)	$34.95	CRIM
Nolo's Deposition Handbook	$29.99	DEP
Represent Yourself in Court: How to Prepare & Try a Winning Case	$34.99	RYC

HOMEOWNERS, LANDLORDS & TENANTS

	PRICE	CODE
California Tenants' Rights	$27.99	CTEN
Deeds for California Real Estate	$24.99	DEED
Dog Law	$21.95	DOG
Every Landlord's Legal Guide (National Edition, Book w/CD-ROM)	$44.99	ELLI
Every Tenant's Legal Guide	$26.95	EVTEN
For Sale by Owner in California	$29.99	FSBO
How to Buy a House in California	$34.99	BHCA
The California Landlord's Law Book: Rights & Responsibilities (Book w/CD-ROM)	$44.99	LBRT
The California Landlord's Law Book: Evictions (Book w/CD-ROM)	$44.99	LBEV
Leases & Rental Agreements	$29.99	LEAR
Neighbor Law: Fences, Trees, Boundaries & Noise	$26.99	NEI
The New York Landlord's Law Book (Book w/CD-ROM)	$39.95	NYLL
Renters' Rights (National Edition)	$24.99	RENT
Stop Foreclosure Now in California	$29.95	CLOS

HUMOR

	PRICE	CODE
29 Reasons Not to Go to Law School	$12.95	29R
Poetic Justice	$9.95	PJ

IMMIGRATION

	PRICE	CODE
Fiancé & Marriage Visas	$44.95	IMAR

	PRICE	CODE
How to Get a Green Card	$29.95	GRN
Student & Tourist Visas	$29.99	ISTU
U.S. Immigration Made Easy	$44.99	IMEZ

MONEY MATTERS

	PRICE	CODE
101 Law Forms for Personal Use (Book w/CD-ROM)	$29.99	SPOT
Bankruptcy: Is It the Right Solution to Your Debt Problems?	$19.99	BRS
Chapter 13 Bankruptcy: Repay Your Debts	$34.99	CH13
Creating Your Own Retirement Plan	$29.99	YROP
Credit Repair (Book w/CD-ROM)	$24.99	CREP
How to File for Chapter 7 Bankruptcy	$34.99	HFB
IRAs, 401(k)s & Other Retirement Plans: Taking Your Money Out	$29.99	RET
Money Troubles: Legal Strategies to Cope With Your Debts	$29.99	MT
Nolo's Law Form Kit: Personal Bankruptcy	$24.99	KBNK
Stand Up to the IRS	$24.99	SIRS
Surviving an IRS Tax Audit	$24.95	SAUD
Take Control of Your Student Loan Debt	$26.95	SLOAN

PATENTS AND COPYRIGHTS

	PRICE	CODE
The Copyright Handbook: How to Protect and Use Written Works (Book w/CD-ROM)	$39.99	COHA
Copyright Your Software	$34.95	CYS
Domain Names	$26.95	DOM
Getting Permission: How to License and Clear Copyrighted Materials Online and Off (Book w/CD-ROM)	$34.99	RIPER
How to Make Patent Drawings Yourself	$29.99	DRAW
The Inventor's Notebook	$24.99	INOT
Nolo's Patents for Beginners	$29.99	QPAT
License Your Invention (Book w/CD-ROM)	$39.99	LICE
Patent, Copyright & Trademark	$34.95	PCTM
Patent It Yourself	$49.99	PAT
Patent Searching Made Easy	$29.95	PATSE
The Public Domain	$34.95	PUBL
Web and Software Development: A Legal Guide (Book w/ CD-ROM)	$44.95	SFT
Trademark: Legal Care for Your Business and Product Name	$39.95	TRD

RESEARCH & REFERENCE

	PRICE	CODE
Legal Research: How to Find & Understand the Law	$34.99	LRES

SENIORS

	PRICE	CODE
Choose the right long-Term Care: Home Care, Assisted Living & Nursing Homes	$21.99	ELD
The Conservatorship Book for California	$44.99	CNSV
Social Security, Medicare & Goverment Pensions	$29.99	SOA

SOFTWARE

Call or check our website at www.nolo.com for special discounts on Software!

	PRICE	CODE
LeaseWriter CD—Windows	$129.95	LWD1
LLC Maker—Windows	$89.95	LLP1
PatentPro Plus—Windows	$399.99	PAPL
Personal RecordKeeper 5.0 CD—Windows	$59.95	RKD5
Quicken Lawyer 2003 Business Deluxe—Windows	$79.95	SBQB3
Quicken Lawyer 2003 Personal—Windows	$79.95	WQP3

Order Form

Name _____

Address _____

City _____

State, Zip _____

Daytime Phone _____

E-mail _____

Our "No-Hassle" Guarantee

Return anything you buy directly from Nolo for any reason and we'll cheerfully refund your purchase price. No ifs, ands or buts.

☐ Check here if you do not wish to receive mailings from other companies

Item Code	Quantity	Item	Unit Price	Total Price

Method of payment

☐ Check   ☐ VISA   ☐ MasterCard
☐ Discover Card   ☐ American Express

Subtotal	
Add your local sales tax (California only)	
Shipping: RUSH $9, Basic $5 (See below)	
"I bought 3, ship it to me FREE!"(Ground shipping only)	
TOTAL	

Account Number _____

Expiration Date _____

Signature _____

Shipping and Handling

Rush Delivery—Only $9

We'll ship any order to any street address in the U.S. by UPS 2nd Day Air* for only $9!

* Order by noon Pacific Time and get your order in 2 business days. Orders placed after noon Pacific Time will arrive in 3 business days. P.O. boxes and S.F. Bay Area use basic shipping. Alaska and Hawaii use 2nd Day Air or Priority Mail.

Basic Shipping—$5

Use for P.O. Boxes, Northern California and Ground Service.

Allow 1-2 weeks for delivery. U.S. addresses only.

For faster service, use your credit card and our toll-free numbers

**Call our customer service group
Monday thru Friday 7am to 7pm PST**

Phone	1-800-728-3555
Fax	1-800-645-0895
Mail	Nolo
950 Parker St.
Berkeley, CA 94710

Order 24 hours a day @ **www.nolo.com**

Remember:

Little publishers have big ears.
We really listen to you.

Take 2 Minutes & Give Us Your 2 cents

Your comments make a big difference in the development and revision of Nolo books and software. Please take a few minutes and register your Nolo product—and your comments—with us. Not only will your input make a difference, you'll receive special offers available only to registered owners of Nolo products on our newest books and software. Register now by:

PHONE
1-800-728-3555

FAX
1-800-645-0895

EMAIL
cs@nolo.com

or **MAIL** us
this registration card

fold here

Registration Card

NAME _____ DATE _____

ADDRESS _____

_____

CITY _____ STATE _____ ZIP _____

PHONE _____ EMAIL _____

WHERE DID YOU HEAR ABOUT THIS PRODUCT? _____

WHERE DID YOU PURCHASE THIS PRODUCT? _____

DID YOU CONSULT A LAWYER? (PLEASE CIRCLE ONE)   YES   NO   NOT APPLICABLE

DID YOU FIND THIS BOOK HELPFUL?   (VERY)   5   4   3   2   1   (NOT AT ALL)

COMMENTS _____

_____

_____

WAS IT EASY TO USE?   (VERY EASY)   5   4   3   2   1   (VERY DIFFICULT)

We occasionally make our mailing list available to carefully selected companies whose products may be of interest to you.
☐ If you do not wish to receive mailings from these companies, please check this box.
☐ You can quote me in future Nolo promotional materials.
Daytime phone number _____.

EMPL 5.0

Nolo
in the
NEWS

"Nolo helps lay people perform legal tasks without the aid—or fees—of lawyers."

—USA TODAY

Nolo books are ..."written in plain language, free of legal mumbo jumbo, and spiced with witty personal observations."

—ASSOCIATED PRESS

"...Nolo publications...guide people simply through the how, when, where and why of law."

—WASHINGTON POST

"Increasingly, people who are not lawyers are performing tasks usually regarded as legal work... And consumers, using books like Nolo's, do routine legal work themselves."

—NEW YORK TIMES

"...All of [Nolo's] books are easy-to-understand, are updated regularly, provide pull-out forms...and are often quite moving in their sense of compassion for the struggles of the lay reader."

—SAN FRANCISCO CHRONICLE

fold here

- -

Nolo
950 Parker Street
Berkeley, CA 94710-9867

Attn: EMPL 5.0